Glimpses

Selections from th

Claire Russell

GLIMPSES
of the
Church Fathers

Selections from the writings
of the Fathers of the Church

SCEPTER
London   New York

This edition of *Glimpses of the Church Fathers* is published:
in England by Scepter (U.K.) Ltd., 21 Hinton Avenue,
 Hounslow TW4 6AP; e-mail: scepter@pobox.com;
in the United States by Scepter Publishers Inc., P. O. Box 211,
 New York, NY 10018; e-mail: info@scepterpublishers.org

With ecclesiastical approval

© Scepter, London, 1994
© This edition – Scepter, London, 2008

All rights reserved. No part of this book may be reproduced,
stored in a retrieval system or transmitted, in any form or by
any means, electronic, mechanical, photocopying or otherwise,
without the prior permission of Scepter, London.

ISBN 978 0 906138 70 0

Cover design & typeset in England by KIP Intermedia, and
printed in Thailand.

Contents

Introduction — xiii

POPE SAINT CLEMENT OF ROME — 1
Holiness: Faith and Deeds — 3

SAINT IGNATIUS OF ANTIOCH — 7
Traits of the Good Shepherd — 9
Apostolic Spirit and the Birth of our Lord — 12

ANONYMOUS WRITER — 15
An Apologia for the Faith — 16

EPISTLE OF BARNABAS — 23
The Way of Light — 25

ANON: LETTER TO DIOGNETUS — 29
The Christian Vocation — 30

SAINT JUSTIN THE MARTYR — 35
True Wisdom — 37

ANON WRITER OF THE 2ND CENTURY — 43
The Fruits of the Passion — 44

SAINT IRENAEUS OF LYONS — 49
With one voice — 51
The life-giving Spirit — 56

SAINT CLEMENT OF ALEXANDRIA — 61
The value of riches — 62

TERTULLIAN — 67
The effectiveness of Prayer — 69
Confessing one's sins — 72

ORIGEN — 77
When it's time to pray — 79
Mary's Magnificat — 83
Priest and Victim — 86

SAINT CYPRIAN OF CARTHAGE — 91
Just one Church — 93
The Good of Patience — 96

SAINT EPHRAEM THE SYRIAN — 103
Glory to the Virgin Mary — 104
Mary's cradle song — 107
Mother most admirable — 110
Pray always and everywhere — 112
A hymn to Mary — 118

SAINT ZENO OF VERONA — 121
Faith, Hope and Charity — 122
Job, a type of Christ — 127

SAINT CYRIL OF JERUSALEM — 129
The Holy Chrism — 131
The dignity of man — 135
The Holy Spirit — 139
True to the Faith — 143

SAINT HILARY OF POITIERS	**145**
Workers for the harvest	**147**
SAINT GREGORY NAZIANZEN	**151**
The Christian virtues	**153**
True God and True Man	**157**
Preparing for death	**160**
Time and eternity	**161**
SAINT BASIL THE GREAT	**163**
In the presence of God	**164**
The action of the Holy Spirit	**169**
Configured to Christ	**171**
SAINT GREGORY OF NYSSA	**175**
The dignity of man	**177**
The Christian is another Christ	**181**
SAINT AMBROSE	**183**
The Body of Christ	**185**
On friendship	**189**
Interior martyrdom	**194**
Divine mercy	**197**
The riches of the Psalms	**201**
The mercy of Christ	**205**
The Visitation of our Lady	**207**
The untimely friend	**209**
SAINT CROMACIOUS OF AQUILEYA	**213**
The beatitudes	**214**
A life-giving catch	**221**

SAINT JEROME — 227
- The figure of the priest — 229
- To Give Fruit — 234

SAINT JOHN CHRYSOSTOM — 239
- The relics of the saints — 241
- The presence of the Holy Spirit — 247
- The Natural Law — 252
- Like salt and light — 257
- A Christian's battle — 261
- The dignity of the priesthood — 265
- Beginning again — 269
- Praise of Mary, Mother of God — 273
- On friendship and the education of children — 275
- *We have found the Messiah!* — 281
- Learning temperance — 283
- Joseph, a just man — 288

SAINT AUGUSTINE OF HIPPO — 291
- Episcopal service — 293
- The wedding at Cana — 297
- Tribute to Mary — 301
- The moral virtues — 305
- On prayer — 311
- Invocation to the Lord — 315
- Christ died for all — 321
- Love for our separated brethren — 323
- The boat in a tempest — 325
- With Christian Purity — 328
- Eternal life — 333
- In praise of Charity — 338
- When Christ passes by — 341
- The miraculous catch — 346

SAINT PETER CHRYSOLOGUS	355
The symbolic meaning of two miracles	357
The Lord's Prayer	363
The living sacrifice of one's daily life	368
The triumph of Faith	373
SAINT VINCENT OF LERINS	379
Progress in Church doctrine	381
The rule of Faith	387
SAINT MAXIMUS OF TURIN	391
Always giving thanks to God	393
The good thief	397
SAINT LEO THE GREAT	401
As Lent begins	403
An assault for holiness	407
The Birth of our Lord	411
The Virgin Mother	415
Spiritual childhood	419
In the likeness of God	423
SAINT CYRIL OF ALEXANDRIA	427
The Mother of God	429
Faith in God's Word	433
SALVIANUS THE PRESBYTER	437
The Lord's Precepts	438
JOHN MANDAKUNI	441
How to approach the Blessed Sacrament	442

JAMES OF SARUGH — 447
Seat of all Graces — 448

SAINT FULGENTIUS OF RUSPE — 453
The Sacrifice of Christ — 455

SAINT CAESARIUS OF ARLES — 459
Temples of God — 461
On mercy — 467

ROMAN THE CANTOR — 471
The wedding at Cana — 473

SAINT GREGORY THE GREAT — 477
The holy angels — 479
True and false Justice — 483
In praise of John the Baptist — 487

SAINT SOPHRONIUS — 491
Hail Mary — 492
The festival of light — 494

SAINT MAXIMUS THE CONFESSOR — 497
Consoler of the Church — 498

SAINT ILDEPHONSUS OF TOLEDO — 501
To honour Mary — 502

SAINT ANDREW OF CRETE — 505
Mother most pure — 506

SAINT GERMANUS OF CONSTANTINOPLE — 509
Mother of Grace — 511
Worthy of veneration twice over — 515

ST ANASTASIUS SINAITA — 519
Receiving Holy Communion with dignity — 520

SAINT BEDE THE VENERABLE — 523
Mary's Magnificat — 524

SAINT JOHN DAMASCENE — 527
Mother of glory — 529
The power of the Cross — 534
Mary's Assumption — 537

SAINT THEODORUS THE ESTUDITE — 541
The saving Cross — 543

Subject Index — 547

Introduction

In recent years there has a been a growing awareness among lay people of the importance of Tradition within the Catholic Church. A primary source of this Tradition is the collection of what the Fathers of the Church had to say in Her early history. Although a number of works have been translated into English, many are out of print or not easily available. A number of busy working men and women have drawn to the publisher's attention the need for a selection of writings which covers a wide range of topics, and presented in easily 'digestible' units. It is to this kind of reader that this volume is addressed.

A definition

The word *Father* is used in the New Testament to mean a teacher of spiritual things. Through these the soul of man is born again into the likeness of Christ. The first teachers of Christianity are also called *the Fathers*. Thus the term 'the Fathers of the Church' refers to the earliest teachers who in the period of the Church's infancy and first growth instructed her members in the teachings of Christ and his Apostles.

There is no clear cut-off date after which someone may not be call a Father of the Church. It is usual to include people until the fifth century (the Council of Chalcedon was held in 451). But it is clear that among the Fathers must be included St Gregory the Great (d. 604), St Isidore of Seville (d. 636), the Venerable Bede (d. 735) and St John Damascene (d. 749).

Sources

The earliest histories of patristic literature are those contained in the works of Eusebius of Caesarea and St Jerome (d. 420). The great editions of the Fathers began when printing became common. But it was Abbe Migne (1800-75) who has provided the most comprehensive set of documents. The works of the Latin Fathers are collected in a 222-volume set entitled *Patrologia Latina*, while the Greek Fathers are in 161 volumes under the title *Patrologia Graeca*. Thus PL and PG are often the quoted references in patristic studies.

Who is a Father of the Church?

St Vincent of Lerins writing in a famous document, *Commonitorium*, in 434, offers an accurate description. The Fathers of the Church are *those alone who, though in diverse times and places yet persevering in the communion and faith of the one Catholic Church, have been approved teachers*. Modern theologians reach the same conclusion by requiring a Father of the Church to be of orthodox doctrine and learning, living a saintly life and being of certain antiquity.

The criteria by which one can judge whether an ecclesiastical writer is a Father or not, are: citation by a general council, reference in the public Acts of the Popes addressed to the Church, inclusion in the Roman martyrology as *sanctitate et doctrina insignis*, public reading in the Churches in the early centuries, and citation with praise (as an authority as to the Faith) by one of the more celebrated Fathers.

The Lerinese *Commonitorium* offers a triple test as to matters of faith. The ordinary rule is the living magisterium of the Church. But in those matters where no decision is forthcoming, the three tests to be applied in

INTRODUCTION

succession are *quod ubique, quod semper, quod ab omnibus* – otherwise *universitas, antiquitas, consensio*.

Thus if an error is found in one corner of the Church, then the first test, *universitas, quod ubique* – what is held everywhere, universally – is an unanswerable refutation. But if an error attacks the whole Church, then *antiquitas, quod semper* – what has always been believed – is to be appealed to i.e. a consensus before the novelty arose. If, further, one or two teachers of great fame have erred in the previous period, then *consensio, quod ab omnibus* – what is held by all people i.e. to the many against the few. Thus even Tertullian and Origen (whose works while they were faithful sons of the Church are of great value), when they erred in later life are reminders that if something new or unheard of is introduced beyond or against the saints, then it pertains not to religion but to temptation, and *you shall not listen to the words of that prophet or to that dreamer of dreams, for the Lord your God is testing you to know whether you love the Lord your God with all your heart and with all your soul* (Deut 13:4). A consensus of the Fathers is not, however, to be expected in very small matters.

The authority of the Fathers

Does one have to agree with everything that a Father of the Church says? The witness of any one Father is occasionally of great weight for doctrine when taken singly, if he is teaching a subject on which he is recognised by the Church as an especial authority. Examples are St Augustine on the Blessed Trinity and St Athanasius on the divinity of the Son. But the authority of single Fathers in itself is not infallible. However piety and sound reason agree that the theological opinions of such individuals should not be treated lightly, and should not without great caution be interpreted in a sense which clashes with the common doctrine of other Fathers. For they were holy men, who are not to be presumed to have intended to swerve from the doctrine of the Church, and their doubtful utterances are to be taken in the best sense of which they are capable.

Classifying the Fathers

There are several ways of dividing the writings of the Fathers.

☐ A) Chronologically, by periods:

i) the Fathers prior to the Council of Nicaea (325);

ii) the Golden Age of the fourth and fifth centuries (325-451);

iii) the later Fathers.

☐ B) Geographically: the Eastern and Western Fathers, the former including Syriac, Armenian and Coptic writers. In the Roman Empire either Greek or Latin was used. Although the ecclesiastical provinces did not follow the division exactly, these are roughly how they are classified: Eastern as Greek and Western as Latin.

☐ C) Methods of commentaries: The literal school of exegesis had its home at Antioch, while the allegorical school was Alexandrian. On the whole the West followed the allegorical method, introducing literalism in different degrees.

A brief overview

☐ In the 2nd Century we have

• the Apostolic Fathers, the chief ones being St Clement, St Ignatius of Antioch and St Polycarp.

• the Greek apologists follow, mainly philosophical in their treatment of Christianity. St Justin the Martyr and St Irenaeus are outstanding among these.

• the western apologists: although not a Father of the Church, we include the writings of Tertullian whose works

INTRODUCTION xvii

on prayer and penance are masterpieces.

☐ The third century gives us
- the Alexandrian writers of the catechetical school. One of the most prolific of these was Origen; though he lived the life of a saint, some of his works fell under the ban of the Church.
- Antioch of Palestine was the dead see, and several writers in the area are included here.
- Rome, with St Hippolytus (d. 235) works in Greek.
- the great African writers: St Cyprian was bishop of Carthage (249-259): his works give us a wonderful insight on the state of the Church. With Eusebius' history, it is one of the primary sources available to us.

☐ The fourth century is the great age of the Fathers.
In the East we have:
- the apologetic and historical works of Eusebius of Caesarea and St Cyril of Jerusalem
- the Alexandrian writers like Athanasius
- the Cappadocians: the illustrious triad of St Basil, his friend St Gregory Nazianzen and his brother St Gregory of Nyssa. The classical culture and literary form of the Cappadocians, united with their sanctity and orthodoxy, makes them a unique group in Church history.
- the School of Antioch: St John Chrysostom is the crowning glory of this school. He preached his greatest sermons at Antioch, before becoming bishop of Constantinople. He is the chief of the Greek Fathers, the first of all commentators, and the greatest orator, in the East or the West.
- the Syriac writers: St Ephraem (306-73) is the greatest writer Syria produced in this century. He was deacon of Edessa.

In the West

- St Hilary of Poitiers and St Ambrose (d. 397) are the most famous of the early opponents of Arianism. St Ambrose's sanctity and actions make him one of the imposing figures of the patristic period. St Zeno of Verona is of this period.

- St Jerome, in Rome and Bethlehem, is known as the *Doctor maximus in Sacris Scripturis*. He is, of course, very well known for his translations of the Old Testament (from Hebrew into Latin) and for the revision of the New Testament Latin.

- St Augustine was the brilliant protagonist of the African Catholics.

- In Spain and Gaul there are a number of writers, the poet Prudentius from Saragossa being the most famous.

☐ In the fifth century

- St Cyril of Alexandria opposed the writings of Nestorius, and has left voluminous writings. With him the great Alexandrian school closes, as does the Antiochene school with Theodoret.

- The school of Lerins produced a number of writers, like St Vincent and St Caesarius of Arles. Other Gallic writers are Salvianus and Gennadius.

- In Rome stands St Leo, the greatest of the early popes, whose sanctity and steadfastness saved Rome from Attila. His sermons and dogmatic letters show him to us as the most lucid of theologians.

☐ In the sixth Century closes with

- St Gregory the Great. His works are full of instruction and wisdom, and his comments on the spiritual life and on contemplation are of special interest.

- Many of the other late writers in the West belong to the medieval period, but Bede is definitely patristic.
- In the East, the second half of the fifth century and the sixth are quite barren. The importance of St Maximus the Confessor, Anastasius of Mt Sinai and Andrew of Caesarea must be mentioned.

□ Close of the Patristic Age
- St John Damascene (d. 749) closes the patristic period with his polemics against heresies, with his exegetical and ascetical writings. His *Fountain of Wisdom* is an anticipation of scholasticism.

The Pope Speaks (*Address*, Rome, 30 October 1993)

"The development of patristic studies is close to my heart, for there can be no true formation of Christian understanding without constantly drawing on the tradition of our Fathers in the faith. As I said at the beginning of my pontificate in the Apostolic Letter, *Patres Ecclesiae*, 'the Church never tires of returning to their writings, full of wisdom and incapable of ageing – and of renewing their memory continually...'

The Fathers of the Church did not cease to meditate upon the Mystery of Christ and to seek to transmit to their contemporaries what they themselves received. They were able to remain free with regard to the cultural context of their time and to give it its true dimension. I am thinking here of St Justin and his famous expression *semina Verbi*. In the best works of the pagan world there was an anticipation of the Gospel proclamation.

One of the chief merits of the Fathers, and the reason for their permanent value, lies in their having perceived and demonstrated in their time the unity of the Old and New Testaments in the person of Christ. It is known that

St Augustine summarised this basic perception of Christian exegesis in the axiom: *Novum Testamentum in Veter latebat; Vetus nunc in Novo patet*. He was inspired in this regard by the insights of the first generation of Christians, notably St Paul and his reflection on allegory.

As exegetes of the two Testaments, the Fathers are also responsible for the origin of theological reflection and the first great dogmatic formulations. They made possible a rational expression of the Christian faith which could be assimilated by minds converted from paganism. They were the first theologians, for they were able to examine the Mystery of Christ by drawing on ideas borrowed from the thought of their time, when necessary formulating them with no hesitation, to give them a universal meaning. It was largely due to them that the Second Vatican Council was able to say of theology: 'It relies on the written word of God, taken together with sacred Tradition, as on a permanent foundation' (Dei Verbum, 24).

The intellectual understanding of the mysteries of faith would not suffice for the Christian life if the former were not a spiritual experience nourished by the sacraments and the whole liturgical life. Now, on this point too, the Fathers offer us the fruit of their contemplation of the incarnate Word. When late on Christmas Eve St Leo began his homily by proclaiming, *Hodie Christus natus est*, he was reminding his contemporary listeners and his future readers that the Mystery of Christ is simultaneously for one age and for all ages. In the liturgy the *hodie* of God is identified – by his will – with the *hodie* of mankind.

May the Doctors of the Western and Eastern Churches, witnesses of a single faith, never cease to help you. May the readers delight be given you to share each day by Him who is true Wisdom, who manifests himself only so that he may be sought further."

Pope Saint Clement of Rome

Clement of Rome (to distinguish him from the Alexandrian) is the first of the successors of St Peter about whom anything definitive is known. He is the first of the Apostolic Fathers. Origen tells us that he was a disciple of the Apostles. St Irenaeus states that he was the fourth bishop of Rome. Eusebius of Caesaria, the historian, validates this testimony, establishing the chronology of the early papacies: Linus (until 80 A.D.) Anacetus (80-92) and Clement (92-101). He had been ordained by St Peter.

Irenaeus says that Clement "saw the blessed Apostles and conversed with them, and had yet ringing in his ears the preaching of the Apostles, and had their tradition before his eyes, and not he only, for many were then surviving who had been taught by the Apostles."

Neither Eusebius nor St Jerome say anything about his death, but the *Martyrium Sancti Clementis* written between the fourth and the sixth centuries, refers to his death as a martyr in exile near the Black Sea.

The Church at Corinth had been led into sedition against its rulers by some violent spirits. The *Epistle to the Corinthians* was sent in the name of the Church of Rome by St Clement to restore peace and unity. It was written between 96-98. The style of the Epistle is earnest and simple, restrained and dignified, and sometimes eloquent. Clement writes clearly as the Bishop of Rome, and it is one of the earliest examples of the authority of the Roman

Church.

The Epistle is a document of primary importance because it also gives us information on the Theology and Liturgy of Rome. The author shows a deep knowledge of the Old Testament and of Greek culture. The main body of the letter (chapters IV-XXXIX) are interwoven with exhortations from the Old Testament, which Clement wishes to use to demonstrate the ill-effects of envy and hate which have come about in the history of mankind, and of the benefits which have resulted from humility and peace.

Saint Clement of Rome

HOLINESS: FAITH AND DEEDS

Let us come before the Lord, then, in sanctity of soul, lifting pure and undefiled hands to him, loving our gentle and merciful Father who has made us His chosen portion. For it is written: *When the Most High divided the nations, when He scattered the sons of Adam, He set up the boundaries of nations according to the number of angels of God. His people, Jacob, became the portion of the Lord; Israel was the allotment of his inheritance* (Deut 32:8-9). And in another place He says: *Behold, the Lord takes to himself a nation from the midst of nations, as a man takes the first-fruit of his threshing floor, and from that nation shall come forth the Holy of Holies* (Deut 4:34; 14:2; Num 18:27; Ezech 48:12).

Since we are a portion of the Holy One, let us do all that belongs to holiness, fleeing from evil speech, and abominable and impure embraces, from drunkenness and from rioting, and detestable lusts, foul adultery, and detestable pride. *For God*, he says, *resists the proud but gives grace to the humble* (Prov 3:34; Jas 4:6; 1 Pet 5:5). Let us then join with those to whom grace is given from God; let us put on concord in meekness of spirit and in self-control, keeping ourselves far from all gossip and evil speaking, being justified by works and not by words. For He says: *He that speaks much shall also hear much; or does he that speaks fair think that he is just? Blessed is the man born of woman who has a short life. Be not full of words* (Job 11:2-3).

Let our praise be with God (cf Rom 2:29), and not from ourselves, for God hates those who praise themselves. Let the testimony of our good deeds be given by others, as it was given to our fathers, who were righteous. Boldness and arrogance and presumption belong to those who are cursed by God; gentleness and humility and meekness belong to those who are blessed by God.

Let us, then, cling to his blessing, and let us see what are the ways of blessedness. Let us recall the events of old (cf Gen 12:2-3; 18:18; 22:7ff; 28ff). Why was our father Abraham blessed? Was it not because he performed justice and truth through faith? Isaac was willingly led forth as a sacrifice, facing the future with confidence. Jacob left his own country with meekness because of his brother, and went to Laban and served him, and the twelve tribes of Israel were given to him.

If anyone will examine fairly each example, he will recognise the greatness of the gifts given by God. And we also, having been called through his will in Christ Jesus, are not justified by ourselves, or by our own wisdom or understanding or piety or the works we have done in holiness of heart, but through the faith, by which the Almighty God has justified all men from the beginning; to whom be glory for all ages. Amen.

Faith should produce good works

What, then, shall we do (cf Rom 6:1), brothers? Shall we slacken from doing good and abandon charity? May the Lord never allow this to happen to us, but let us be diligent to accomplish every good work (Tit 3:1) with earnestness and zeal.

For the Creator and Lord of the universe himself takes joy in his works. In his overwhelming might He has set up the heavens, and by his unsearchable wisdom He has put them in order. He has separated the earth from the surrounding water and placed it on the solid foundation of his own will; and He has called into existence the animals that move in it by his own arrangement. Having prepared the sea and the living creatures that are in it, He enclosed them by his own power. Over all, with his holy and pure hands He formed man, the most excellent and greatest in intelligence, with the stamp of his own image. Let us consider that all the saints have been adorned with good works; and the Lord himself, adorning himself with good works, rejoiced. Holding this pattern, then, let us follow out his will without hesitation; let us do the work of justice with all our strength.

The good labourer receives the bread of his labour with confidence; the lazy and careless one does not look his employer in the face. We must, therefore, be zealous in doing good; for all things are from him. He warns us: *Behold the Lord comes, and his reward is before his face, to pay each man according to his work.* He therefore urges us who believe in him with all our heart not to be lazy or careless in any good work. Let our glorying and our confidence be in him; let us be subject to his will.

How blessed and wonderful, beloved, are the gifts of God! Life in immortality, splendour in righteousness, truth in boldness, faith in confidence, continence in holiness: and all these things are submitted to our understanding.

What, then, are the things which are being prepared for those who wait for Him? The Creator and Father of the ages, the All-holy One, Himself knows their greatness and beauty. Let us then strive to be found among the number of those that wait, that we may receive a share of the promised gifts.

But how shall this be, beloved? If our understanding be fixed faithfully on God; if we seek the things which are well-pleasing and acceptable to Him; if we fulfil the things that are in harmony with His faultless will, and follow the way of truth, casting away from ourselves all iniquity and wickedness, covetousness, strife, malice and fraud, gossiping and evil speaking, hatred of God, pride and arrogance, vain-glory and inhospitality. For those who do these things are hateful to God, and not only those who do them, but also those who take pleasure in them.

Epistola ad Corinthios, 30-34

Saint Ignatius of Antioch

St Ignatius was born in Syria and died in Rome between 98 and 117. Several ecclesiastical writers give credence to the story that Ignatius was the child whom Our Lord took in his arms (cf Mark 9:38). It is also believed that his friend Polycarp was among those who received his instruction from the lips of St John the Apostle.

Ignatius was the third bishop of Antioch, and appointed by St Peter himself. St John Chrysostom lays special emphasis on the honour conferred upon the martyr in receiving the episcopal consecration at the hands of the Apostle. Associated with the writings of St Ignatius is a work called *Martyrum Ignatii*, which purports to be an eye-witness account of St Ignatius' martyrdom.

The oldest collection of St Ignatius' writings known to exist was that made use of by Eusebius the historian in the first half of the fourth century, but which is no longer extant. It was made up of seven letters written by Ignatius on his way to Rome. They were addressed to Christians in various cities. The seventh of these is to Polycarp.

There are three themes developed in St Ignatius' letters:
a) the role of the bishop;
b) the Incarnation of Christ;
c) Ignatius' desire to suffer for Christ.

It is scarcely possible to exaggerate the importance of the testimony which the Ignatian letters offer to the dogmatic character of Apostolic Christianity, for Ignatius is the most important link between the Apostles and the Fathers of the Church. He received the substance of Revelation from the Apostles themselves, and also their inspired interpretation of it. Cardinal Newman states that 'the whole system of Catholic doctrine may be discovered, at least in outline, not to say in parts filled up, in the course of his seven epistles'.

Saint Ignatius of Antioch

TRAITS OF THE GOOD SHEPHERD

I exhort you by the grace with which you are clothed to press forward in the race, and exhort all others, so that they may be saved. Live up to the demands of your office by unceasing care in your practical and spiritual duties. Be preoccupied about unity, for nothing is better than this. Help others along, as the Lord helps you. Bear with all out of love, as indeed you do. Find time for unceasing prayer. Ask for more wisdom than you have. Keep your spirit awake and on the watch. Copy the ways of God in speaking to each as an individual person. Like an athlete in perfect condition, give a hand to all who are sick. Where there is more work, there is much reward.

There is no thanks for liking good pupils. The real task is by mildness to bring to obedience the ones who plague you. Not every wound is healed by the same salve. Where the pains are sharp, give relief with embrocation. In all things be wise as the serpent and at all times be as simple as the dove (cf Matt 10:16). You are made of flesh and spirit so that you may be able to persuade what you can see to come to you; as for the invisible realities, pray that they may be revealed to you. In this way nothing will be lacking, and you will abound in every gift. The age is in need of you, if it is to reach God – as pilots need the winds and as a storm-tossed sailor needs port. Be temperate, like an athlete of God; the prize is immortality and eternal life. Of this you have no doubt. I offer up all for you, both myself and my bonds which you loved.

There are some who seem plausible enough, but who teach heretical doctrine. Do not let them disturb you. Stand firm like an anvil under the hammer. A great boxer will take a beating and yet win through. We ought to put up with anything especially for the sake of God, so that He will put up with us. Become even more zealous than you are. Understand the age in which we live (cf Luke 12:56). Look for Him who is beyond all time, the Eternal, the Invisible who became visible for our sake, the Impalpable, the Impassible who suffered for our sake, who endured every outrage for our sake.

Do not let the widows be neglected. After God, you should be their guardian. Let nothing be done without your consent; and continue, as at present, to do nothing yourself without the consent of God. Do not weaken. Let your assemblies be more frequent. Seek out all by name.

Avoid anything like magic, but do not fail to speak to the people about such things. Tell my sisters to love the Lord and to be satisfied with their husbands in flesh and spirit. In the same way tell my brothers in the name of Jesus Christ to love their wives as the Lord does the Church (cf Eph 5:25). If anyone is able to persevere in chastity to the honour of the flesh of the Lord, let him do so in all humility. If he is boastful about it, he is lost; if he should be more esteemed than the bishop, his purity is gone. When men and women marry, the union should be made with the consent of the bishop, so that the marriage may be according to the Lord and not merely out of lust. Let all be done to the glory of God.

Pay attention to the bishop, if you would have God pay attention to you. I offer myself up for those who obey the bishop, priests and deacons. May it be my lot to be with them in God. Toil and train together, run and suffer together, rest and rise at the same time, as God's stewards, assistants and servants. Please the leader under whom you serve, for from him you receive your pay. May none of you turn out a deserter. Let your baptism be ever your shield, your faith a helmet, your charity a spear, your patience a panoply. Let your works be deposits, so that you may receive the sum that is due to you. In humility be patient with one another, as God is with you.

Epistola ad Polycarpum, I-VI

Saint Ignatius of Antioch

APOSTOLIC SPIRIT AND THE BIRTH OF OUR LORD

Some among you have acquired the vice of going about with the Holy Spirit on your lips, while indulging in practices which are an insult to God. Those people you must avoid as wild beasts; they are rabid dogs that bite in secret. You must beware of them for they are hard to cure...

Apostolic spirit

Pray increasingly for the rest of men. There is still hope that they may be converted and find their way to God. By the testimony of your upright lives, offer them an opportunity of becoming your fellow disciples.

Meet their angry outbursts with your gentleness, their boasts with your humility, their contempt with your prayers, their errors with your constancy in the faith, their cruelty with your serenity. Above all, do not try to match their example. Let us prove ourselves to be their brothers by kindness.

The Birth of Our Lord

There is one Physician who is both Flesh and Spirit, born and unborn, who is God and became Man, true life in death. He sprang both from Mary and from God. He was therefore subject to suffering, and in respect of the other, incapable of it... Our God, Jesus Christ, was

The Birth of Our Lord

conceived by Mary according to God's plan; of the seed of David, it is true, but also of the Holy Spirit.

The virginity of Mary, and her giving birth were hidden from the Prince of this world, as was also the death of the Lord. Three mysteries of a cry which were wrought in the stillness of God. How then was He manifested to the world?

A star shone in heaven beyond all the stars, and its light was unspeakable, and its newness caused astonishment, and all the other stars, with the sun and moon, gathered in chorus round this star, and it far exceeded them all in its light; and there was perplexity, whence came this new thing, so unlike them. By this all magic was dissolved and every bond of wickedness vanished away, ignorance was removed, and the old kingdom was destroyed, for God was manifest as man for the 'newness' of eternal life, and that which had been prepared by God received its beginning.

Hence all things ere disturbed, because the abolition of death was being planned.

Epistle to the Ephesians

ANONYMOUS WRITER

SAINT POLYCARP OF SMYRNA

St Polycarp was born in the year 69, probably to a Christian family which was not of the Judeao-Christian tradition. St Irenaeus who knew him, says that he had received the teachings of the Apostles directly and that they had consecrated Polycarp as Bishop of Smyrna. His pastoral work was very fruitful. He was also highly effective in dealing with heresies, managing to reconvert very many followers of several Gnostic sects.

When an anti-Christian persecution arose, Polycarp hid himself, at the request of the faithful, in a house in the countryside. But through the treachery of a slave he was discovered and condemned to death by burning. He died on 22 February 155.

The *Martyrdom of Polycarp* is a letter instigated by the Christian community at Smyrna for those at Filomeltrum, a village of Phrygia, written by eye-witnesses, apparently before the first anniversary of his martyrdom.

It is the first Christian work dedicated exclusively to describing the passion of a martyr and the first to use this title to designate a Christian who has died for the faith.

Anon

AN APOLOGIA FOR THE FAITH

We write to you, brethren, the details concerning the martyrs and blessed Polycarp, who, by his martyrdom as by a seal, put an end to the persecution. For almost all the recent events occurred that the Lord might show us a martyrdom on the Gospel model. For, like the Lord, he waited to be betrayed, that we might become his imitators, *not regarding ourselves alone, but also our neighbours* (Phil 2:4). For it is a sign of real and steadfast love not to desire to save oneself alone, but to save also all the brethren. Those martyrdoms are blessed and noble, then, which take place according to the will of God, for we must be careful to ascribe to God the power over all occurrences. For everyone surely marvels at their nobility and patience and love of the Lord.

Some avoid martyrdom

There was one, Quintus by name, a Phrygian recently arrived from Phrygia, who at the sight of the beasts became a coward. He was the one who had forced himself and some others to come forward voluntarily. The Proconsul persuaded him with many pleas to take the oath and to offer sacrifice. For this reason, therefore, brethren, we do not approve those who give themselves up, because the Gospel does not teach us this.

An Apologia for the Faith

Polycarp's example

Now, when the most admirable Polycarp first heard of this, he was not disturbed, but desired to stay in the city. However, the majority persuaded him to leave quietly, so he went out secretly to a farm not a great distance from the city and, remaining with a few friends, night and day he did nothing but pray for all his people and for all the Churches throughout the world, as was his custom at all times. And, as he prayed, he fell into an ecstasy three days before his arrest, and he saw the pillow under him burning with fire, and, turning to those who were with him he said: *I must be burned alive.*

As the searchers continued after him, he went to another farm, where the searchers immediately stopped. But, not finding him, they seized two slave boys, of whom one turned informer after being tortured. For, it was not really possible for him to remain hidden, since those who betrayed him were of his own household. Then the police captain called Herod – that is the very name he had – hastened to bring him to the stadium so that, becoming a partaker of Christ, he might fulfil his special destiny, and his betrayers should suffer the punishment of Judas.

His arrest

So they brought the little boy along and on Friday, about supper time, the police and horsemen with their usual arms came out as if against a bandit (Matt 26:55). And late in the evening they converged on Polycarp and found him resting in an upper room. Though it was still in his power to get away to another locality, he did not wish to, saying: *The will of God be done* (Acts 21:14).

Accordingly, when he heard they were there, he went down and conversed with them. However, the by-standers marvelled at his age and his firmness, and wondered why there was such urgency to arrest such an old man. At once he had a table set for them to eat and drink at that hour, as much as they wished, while for himself he requested to be given an hour to pray without interference. They agreed. So he stood and prayed, so filled with the grace of God that for two hours he could not hold his peace, to the admiration of the listeners. Many even regretted that they had proceeded against such a venerable old man.

When finally he concluded his prayer, after remembering all who had at any time come his way – small folk and great folk, distinguished and undistinguished, and the whole Catholic Church throughout the world – the time for departure came. So they placed him on an ass, and brought him into the city on a great Sabbath. The captain of police, Herod, and his father Nicetas met him, and took him into their own carriage and seated at his side, tried to persuade him, saying: *But what harm is there in saying, Caesar is Lord, and in offering incense, and so forth, to be saved.*

At first Polycarp did not answer, but, when they persisted, he said: *I am not going to do what you advise me.* On failing to convince him, they spoke threateningly to him and made him descend so quickly that he bruised his shin as he got down from the carriage. Without even turning around, as though he had suffered nothing, he continued on his way eagerly and speedily, and was led into the stadium. The uproar in the stadium was such that nobody could be heard at all.

Thrown into the arena

Upon Polycarp's entrance into the arena there came a voice from heaven, *Be brave, Polycarp, and act like a man.* No one saw the speaker, but our people who were present heard the voice.

An Apologia for the Faith

Finally, when he was brought forward, the Proconsul asked him if he were Polycarp; when he admitted it, he tried to persuade him to a denial of the faith saying: *Have regard for your age,* and other suggestions such as they usually make: *Swear by the genius of Caesar; change your mind and say, Away with the atheists!*

As the Proconsul urged him and said: *Take the oath and I release you; revile Christ,* Polycarp said: *Eighty-six years have I served him, and He has done me no wrong. How can I blaspheme my King who has saved me?*

As he further insisted and said: *Swear by the genius of Caesar,* Polycarp replied: *If you vainly imagine that I will swear by the genius (fortune) of Caesar, as you say, and pretend not to know who I am, let me tell you plainly: I am a Christian. But if you desire to learn the teaching of Christianity, grant a day and a hearing.*

The Proconsul said: *Persuade the people.* But Polycarp said: *So far as you are concerned, I should have judged you to be worthy of a discussion; for we have been taught to give honour, as is proper, to rulers and authorities appointed by God, provided it does not harm us; but I do not esteem these people worthy of making a defence before them.*

The Proconsul said: *I have wild animals; to them will I throw you, unless you change your mind.* But he said: *Call them, for change of mind from better to worse is a change not allowed us; but it is good to change from wickedness to justice.*

Again he said to him: *If you scorn the wild beasts, I will have you burned by fire, unless you repent.* But Polycarp said: *You threaten the fire that burns for an hour and in a little while is quenched; for you do not know the fire of the future judgement and of eternal punishment, the fire reserved for the wicked. But why do you delay? Come, do as you wish.*

Polycarp is burned alive

Then the crowd decided to shout out unanimously to have Polycarp burned alive. This happened with indescribable speed. The crowds gathered and collected wood and faggots from the shops and baths, the Jews in particular, as is usual with them, lending zealous assistance in this. But, when the pyre was ready, he took off his upper garments, loosened his belt, and tried to take his shoes off, also, a thing he did not do in the past, because the faithful were always eager each to be the first to touch his flesh. For he had been treated with every regard on account of his holy life even before his grey hair appeared.

Immediately, the instruments prepared for the fire were laid around him; and, as they were ready also to nail him, he said: *Leave me as I am, for He who gives me power to endure the fire will grant me also to remain in the flames unmoved, even without the security which nails give you.*

Accordingly, they did not nail him, but tied him. So he put his hands behind his back and was bound like a ram marked for sacrifice out of a great flock, a holocaust prepared and acceptable to God.

As he looked up to heaven, he said: *Lord God Almighty, Father of Thy beloved and blessed Son Jesus Christ, through whom we have received knowledge of Thee, God of the angels and powers, of the whole creation and of the whole race of the righteous who live in Thy sight, I bless Thee, for having made me worthy of this day and hour; I bless Thee, because I may have a part, along with the martyrs, in the chalice of Thy Christ, unto resurrection in eternal life* (John 5:29), *resurrection both of soul and body in the incorruptibility of the Holy Spirit. May I be received today as a rich and acceptable sacrifice, among those who are in Thy presence, as Thou hast prepared and foretold and fulfilled, God who art faithful and true. For this and for all benefits I praise Thee, I bless Thee, I glorify Thee, through the eternal and heavenly High Priest, Jesus Christ, Thy beloved Son, through whom be to Thee with Him and the Holy Spirit glory, now and for all the ages to come. Amen.*

When he had uttered the 'Amen' and finished his prayer, the men in charge of the fire lighted it. As a great flame flashed out, we saw a miracle, that is, those of us to whom it was granted to see. Yes! And we were preserved to report to others what happened. For the fire took the shape of an arch, like a ship's sail filled with wind, and stood around the body of the martyr; and he was there in the midst, not like flesh burning, but like bread being baked, or gold and silver being purified in a furnace. And we also perceived a fragrant odour such as the scent of incense or the scent of some other costly spices.

Stabbed to death

Finally, the lawless men, seeing that his body could not be consumed by fire, ordered an executioner to approach and stab him with a dagger. When he had done this, there came out much blood, so that the fire was extinguished, and the whole crowd marvelled that there was such a difference between the unbelievers and the elect.

For the most glorious Polycarp certainly was one of the elect, an apostolic and prophetic teacher among our contemporaries and bishop of the Catholic Church in Smyrna; and every word which proceeded from his lips has been fulfilled and will be fulfilled.

Martyrium Polycarpi, 1, 6-11, 13-16

Epistle of Barnabas

A short letter in Greek has come to be known as the *Epistle of Barnabas* ever since the time of Clement of Alexandria. As it does not follow the rules of ancient rhetoric, it has been assumed that the author was not Greek. It is a living testament to the preaching and catechetical work of one of the evangelizers. During this period of the expansion of the recently born Church, the evangelisers laid the foundations of different Christian communities and then continued along their way in search of new territories and new peoples.

The *Epistle* is addressed to one of these recently founded communities. There is no reference to any particular one, and it cannot be identified. The community is warned about Judaizers who hanker after the practices of the Mosaic Law and attempt to make these practices a requirement of the New Law. It is for this reason that the author attempts to unravel the relationship between the old and the new alliance, underlining the supreme value of the New Law and the fathomless riches of its contents.

Ancient Christianity expresses a high esteem for this *Epistle*. This is shown by references to it in one of the oldest codices, where both the Old and the New Testaments are quoted.

In the first part, the author investigates the interpretation of passages of the Old Testament in the light of the New, thus demonstrating a deep knowledge of Scripture. The large number of quotations are of great interest as they become the vehicle for transmitting the sacred text. We also see how it is used as the foundation for dogma.

The second part, more didactic in character, contains a description of Christian life and a summary of moral norms which Christianity requires.

Epistle of Barnabas

THE WAY OF LIGHT

Let us turn now to another kind of Knowledge and Teaching. There are two ways of Teaching and of Power: that of Light and that of Darkness; and there is a great difference between the two ways. Over the one are stationed the light-bringing angels of God; over the other, the angels of Satan. And the first is Lord from eternity to eternity; the latter is the ruler of the present world of lawlessness.

The way of Light, then, is this: If anyone wish to follow the path to the appointed goal, let him be zealous in what he does. This, then, is the Knowledge given to us to walk in this path.

You shall love your Creator, you shall fear your Maker, you shall glorify Him who redeemed you from death. You shall be simple in heart and generous in spirit. You shall not join those who walk in the way of death. You shall hate everything which is not pleasing to God. You shall not abandon the command of the Lord.

You shall not exalt yourself, but shall be humble-minded in all things; you shall not take glory to yourself. You shall not take evil counsel against your neighbour; you shall not allow arrogance into your soul.

You shall not commit fornication, you shall not commit adultery; you shall not corrupt boys. The word of God shall not be spoken by you among the impure. You shall not respect persons in rebuking any for transgression. You shall be meek, you shall be quiet, you shall fear the words which you have heard. You shall not bear malice against your brother.

You shall not doubt the truths of the Faith. *Thou shalt not take the name of the Lord in vain* (Exod 20:7). You shall love your neighbour more than your own soul. You shall not murder a child by abortion, nor again kill it after birth. You shall not remove your hand from your son or from your daughter, but shall teach them the fear of God from their youth.

You shall not be found coveting your neighbour's goods, nor showing avarice. You shall not be associated in soul with the haughty, but shall associate with humble and righteous men. You shall receive the trials that befall you as benefits, knowing that nothing happens without God's permission.

You shall not be double-minded nor gossiping. In modesty and fear you shall obey your masters as a type of God; you shall not with bitterness command your servant or maid who hope in the same God, lest perhaps they cease to fear the God who is above you both. For He came not to call men with respect of persons, but those whom the Spirit prepared.

You shall not be quick to speak, for the mouth is a snare of death. So far as you can, you shall be pure for your soul's sake.

Be not one who holds out his hands to receive, but shuts them for giving. You shall love as the apple of your eye every man who speaks to you the word of the Lord.

Remember the day of judgement day and night, and seek each day the company of the saints, either labouring by speech, and going out to exhort, and striving to save souls by the word, or working with your hands for the ransom of your sins.

Do not hesitate to give and, when you give, do not

grumble; but you shall know who is the good paymaster of your reward. Keep the teachings which you have received, *adding nothing and subtracting nothing* (Deut 12:32).

Hate the Evil One thoroughly. Pass righteous judgement. Do not cause quarrels, but bring together and reconcile those who quarrel. Confess your sins. Do not go to prayer with an evil conscience.

This is the way of Light.

Epistle of Barnabas, Chapters 18-19

Anon: Letter to Diognetus

This ancient work is an apologetic exposition of the life of the early Christians, addressed to Diognetus – a purely nominal addressee, according to most informed sources – and written in Athens, in the second century. Recent research tends to identify it with the *Apologia* of Quadratus to the emperor Adrian, which was believed lost, and of which only a fragment is conserved.

The central part of this apologia presents a fundamental aspect of the life of the early Christians: the duty to sanctify themselves in the middle of the world, lighting up the things of the world with the light of Christ.

This is precisely the message which had been forgotten about for several centuries until the twentieth, when God has wished to remind men about it through the Founder of Opus Dei, Blessed Josemaría Escrivá.

ANON: LETTER TO DIOGNETUS

THE CHRISTIAN VOCATION

Christians are not different from the rest of men in nationality, speech, or customs. They do not live in states of their own, nor do they use a special language, nor adopt a peculiar way of life. Their teaching is not the kind of thing that could be discovered by the wisdom or reflection of mere active-minded men; indeed, they are not outstanding in human learning as others are. Whether fortune has given them a home in a Greek or foreign city, they follow local custom in the matter of dress, food, and way of life; yet the character of the culture they reveal is marvellous and, it must be admitted, unusual.

They live, each in his native land – but as though they were not really at home there. They share in all duties like citizens and suffer all hardships like strangers. Every foreign land is for them a fatherland and every fatherland a foreign land. They marry like the rest of men and beget children, but they do not abandon the babies that are born. They share a common board, but not a common bed. In the flesh as they are, they do not live according to the flesh. They dwell on earth, but they are citizens of heaven (cf Phil 3:20). They obey the laws that men make, but their lives are better than the laws.

They love all men, but are persecuted by all. They are unknown, and yet they are condemned. They are put to death, yet are more alive than ever (cf Cor 6:9-10, 4:12). They are paupers, but they make many rich. They lack all things, and yet in all things they abound. They are dishonoured, yet glory in their dishonour. They are maligned, and yet are vindicated. They are reviled, and yet they bless. They suffer insult, yet they pay respect. They do good, yet are punished with the wicked. When they are punished, they rejoice, as though they were getting more of life. They are attacked by the Jews as Gentiles and are persecuted by the Greeks, yet those who hate them can give no reason for their hatred.

In a word, what the soul is to the body Christians are to the world. The soul is distributed in every member of the body, and Christians are scattered in every city in the world. The soul dwells in the body, and yet it is not of the body. So, Christians live in the world, but they are not of the world. The soul which is guarded in the visible body is not itself visible. And so, Christians who are in the world are known, but their worship remains unseen.

The flesh hates the soul and acts like an unjust aggressor, because it is forbidden to indulge in pleasures. The world hates Christians – not that they have done it wrong, but because they oppose its pleasures. The soul loves the body and its members in spite of the hatred. So Christians love those who hate them. The soul is locked up in the body, yet it holds the body together. And so Christians are held in the world as in a prison, yet it is they who hold the world together. The immortal soul dwells in a mortal tabernacle. So Christians sojourn among perishable things, but their souls are set on immortality in heaven. When the soul is ill-treated in the matter of food and drink, it is improved. So, when Christians are persecuted, their numbers daily increase. Such is the assignment to which God has called them, and they have no right to shirk it.

For, as I said, it was no earthly discovery that was committed to them, nor is it mortal wisdom that they feel bound to guard so jealously, nor have they been entrusted with the dispensation of merely human mysteries. The truth is that the Almighty Creator of the Universe, the invisible God Himself, scattered from heaven among them the seed of truth and of holy thought which is higher than men's minds, and He made it take firm root in their hearts. He did not send a servant (whether angel or principality, whether of those that direct the affairs of earth or of those entrusted with arrangements in heaven), but He sent the very Artificer and Maker of the cosmos, by whom He created the heavens, Him by whom He enclosed the ocean in its proper bounds, Him whose mysterious laws all the elements faithfully observe, and by whom the measures of the length of days were given to the sun to guard, Him whom the moon obeys when it is bidden to shine by night and whom the stars obey when they follow the course of the moon, Him by whom all things are put in order and given their bounds and told to obey – the heavens and the things in heaven, the earth and the things in the earth, the sea and the things in the sea, fire and air and peace, the things in the heights and in the depths and those that are in between. To them He sent Him.

Do you really think – as someone might think – that He sent Him to impose His power with fear and terror? Certainly not. He came in gentleness and humility. He sent Him as a King would send a son and king; He sent Him as God for the sake of men. In sending Him, He acted as a Saviour, appealing to persuasion and not to power – for it is not like God to use compulsion. He acted as one inviting, not as one pursuing; as a lover, not as a judge. Later on, indeed, He will send Him as a Judge (cf John 3:17), and then who will be able to withstand His coming? (cf Mal 3:2)...

Do you not see them thrown to wild beasts to make

them deny their Lord – and yet they are not conquered? Do you not see that the more of them who are punished, the more they grow in number? Such things do not look like the works of men; they are signs of His coming.

Letter to Diognetus, 5-7

Saint Justin the Martyr

St Justin the Martyr is the most important Greek apologist of the second century, and one of the leading writers of early Christian literature.

He was born early in the second century, in Flavius Neapolis, in Palestine. Justin was a Samaritan as a consequence of his place of birth, and a Roman because of his father, Priscus, a veteran soldier settled in the new colony. Both his parents were pagans.

He was educated in various schools – with the Stoics, the Aristotelians, the Pythagoreans and the Platonists. But it was his search for the truth and the heroism of the Christian martyrs which led to his conversion to Christianity. From that moment on, as a layman, he began to use the philosophy he had learned in the service of the faith. He wore the *pallium*, a kind of shawl which was normally used by the Greek philosophers. He travelled from one place to another teaching the gospel.

Justin went to Rome during the reign of Marcus Aurellius (138-161) and founded a school there. It was the first school of Christian philosophy. According to Tacian, a disciple of his, Justin had to appear before Junius Rusticus, the Prefect of the City, for having professed his faith; it was one Crescent, a cynic philosopher, who had orchestrated a campaign against him. He was condemned to death with six other colleagues in the year 165. The *Acta S. Iustini* have preserved for us the details of his martyrdom.

Only three of the many works which Justin wrote have reached us. His style is at times difficult to follow, because of frequent digressions. But his writings have always attracted a great deal of attention. Among them is the *Dialogue with Tryphon*, the first 'apology' or defence of the faith against Judaism. Here St Justin describes his intellectual formation and his conversion, and replies to the objections to Christianity that the Jews had.

Saint Justin the Martyr

TRUE WISDOM

One morning, as I was walking along a broad avenue, a man, accompanied by some friends, came up to me and said: 'Good morning, Philosopher.' Whereupon he and his friends walked alongside me.

After returning his greeting, I asked: 'What is the matter? Is there anything special you wish of me?'

He answered: 'Corinthius the Socratic taught me in Argos never to slight or ignore those who wear your garb, but to show them every consideration and to converse with them, since from such a conversation some good might be derived by them or myself. It should be to the advantage of both if either should benefit from this meeting. Accordingly, whenever I see anyone wearing such a robe, I gladly accost him. So, for this same reason, it has been a pleasure to greet you. These friends of mine share my hope of hearing something profitable from you.'

'Who are you, indeed, most excellent sir?' I asked with a smile.

He did not hesitate to tell me his name and background. 'Trypho', he said, 'is my name. I am a Hebrew of the circumcision, a refugee from the recent war, and at present a resident of Greece, especially of Corinth.

'How,' I asked, 'can you gain as much from philosophy as from your own lawgiver and prophets?'

'Why not,' he replied, 'for do not the philosophers

speak always about God? Do they not constantly propose questions about his unity and providence? Is this not the task of philosophy, to inquire about the Divine?

'Yes, indeed,' I said, 'we, too, are of the same opinion. But the majority of the philosophers have simply neglected to inquire whether there is one or even several gods, and whether or not a divine providence takes care of us, as if this knowledge were unnecessary to our happiness. Moreover, they try to convince us that God takes care of the universe with its genera and species, but not of me and you and of each individual, for otherwise there would be no need of our praying to Him night and day. It is not difficult to see where such reasoning leads them.

It imparts a certain immunity and freedom of speech to those who hold these opinions, permitting them to do and to say whatever they please, without any fear of punishment or hope of reward from God. How could it be otherwise, when they claim that things will always be as they are now, and that you and I shall live in the next life just as we are now, neither better nor worse.

But there are others who think the soul is immortal, and therefore conclude that they will not be punished even if they are guilty of sin; for, if the soul is corporeal, it cannot suffer; if it is immortal, it needs nothing further from God.'

Then smiling politely, he said: 'Explain to us just what is your opinion of these matters, and what is your idea of God, and what is your philosophy.'

'I will explain to you my views on the subject,' I replied. Philosophy, (*Editor's Note: St Justin refers to philosophy as a participation in divine wisdom itself*), is indeed one's greatest possession, and is most precious in the sight of God, to whom it alone leads us, and they in truth are holy men who have applied themselves to philosophy. But, many have failed to discover the nature of philosophy, and the reason why it was sent down to men. Otherwise, there would not be Platonists, or Stoics, or Peripatetics, or Theoretics or Pythagoreans, since this science of philosophy is always one and the same...

(*E.N.: On reaching this point, Justin explains to his listeners that he had examined the different schools of philosophy in search of wisdom and found none satisfactory. He continues the dialogue...*)

'As I was in this frame of mind and desired absolute solitude devoid of human distractions, I used to take myself to a certain spot not far from the sea. One day, as I approached that place with the intention of being alone, a respectable old man, of meek and venerable mien, followed me at a short distance. I stopped, turned quickly, and stared sharply at him.

'Do you know me?' he asked. I replied that I did not.

'Why, therefore, do you stare at me so?' he continued.

'Because I am surprised to find you here,' I replied. 'I did not expect to see anyone here.'

'I am worried about some missing members of my household,' he said, 'and I am therefore looking around with the hope that they may show up somewhere in the vicinity. But what brings you here?'

'I take great delight in such walks,' I answered, 'where I can converse with myself without hindrance because there is nothing to distract my attention. Places like this are most suitable for philology.' (*E.N.: Justin uses this word in the sense of an exercise of the reasoning faculty.*)

'Are you a philologist then,' he asked, 'rather than a

lover of deeds and of truth? Do you not strive to be a practical man rather than a sophist?' (*E.N.: The old man uses the word philology to denote skill in the use of words.*)

'But what greater deed could one perform than to prove that reason rules all,' I replied, 'and that one who rules reason and is sustained by it can look down upon the errors and undertakings of others, and see that they do nothing reasonable or pleasing to God. Man cannot have prudence without philosophy and straight thinking.'

(*E.N.: The narrative continues with the old man asking several questions about the immortality of the soul, its capacity, the relationship between creatures and God ... Justin tries to reply, but there comes a moment when he realises that philosophers are not able with reason alone to give answers to all the questions which men ask. Justin continues telling Trypho the story...*)

'Well, then,' I asked, 'what teacher or method shall I follow, if such philosophers like Plato and Pythagoras do not know the truth?'

'A long time ago,' he replied, 'long before the time of those reputed philosophers, there lived blessed men who were just and loved by God, men who spoke through the inspiration of the Holy Spirit and predicted events that would take place in the future, which events are now taking place.

We call these men the Prophets. They alone knew the truth and communicated it to men, whom they neither deferred to nor feared. With no desire for personal glory, they reiterated only what they heard and saw when inspired by the Holy Spirit. Their writings are still extant, and whoever reads them with the proper faith will profit greatly in his knowledge of the origin and end of things, and of any other matter that a philosopher should know. In their writings they gave no proof at that time of their statements; for, as reliable witnesses of the truth, they were beyond proof; but the happenings that have taken place force you to believe their words.

They also are worthy of belief because of the miracles which they performed, for they exalted God, the Father and Creator of all things, and made known Christ, His Son, who was sent by Him. This the false prophets, who are filled with an erring and unclean spirit, have never done nor even do now, but they undertake to perform certain wonders to astound men and they glorify the demons and spirits of error.

Above all, beseech God to open to you the gates of light, for no one can perceive or understand these truths unless he has been enlightened by God and His Christ.'

When he has said these and many other things which is not now the fitting time to tell, he went on his way, after admonishing me to meditate on what he had told me, and I never saw him again. But my spirit was immediately set on fire, and an affection for the prophets, and for those who are friends of Christ, took hold of me. While pondering on his words, I discovered that his was the only sure and useful philosophy. Thus it is that I am now a philosopher.

Furthermore, it is my wish that everyone should be of the same sentiments as I, and never spurn the Saviour's words; for they have in themselves such tremendous majesty can they can instil fear into those who have wandered from the path of righteousness, whereas they ever remain a great solace to those who heed them.

Thus, Trypho, if you have any regard for your own welfare, and for the salvation of your soul, and if you believe in God, you may have the chance, since I know you are no stranger to this matter, of attaining a knowledge of the Christ of God, and, after becoming a Christian, of enjoying a happy life.

Dialogue with Trypho, 1-8

HOMILY ON EASTER

According to some studies, the homily On Easter comes from Asia Minor, and was delivered in the second half of the second century. Although we do not have sufficient information to name the author, it is beyond doubt that the source is from an environment which followed the old Hebrew system of dating the celebration of Easter as the 14th day of Nisan.

The homily, of which fragments are reproduced here, consists of an introduction, two parts and a conclusion. In the introduction the author proclaims the beauty of Easter and describes the basic themes he will deal with in the body of the homily – the law of Moses and the salvation which our Lord has achieved for us with his immolation on the Cross.

Like Mellitus of Sardes, the author of this homily attributes to Easter the sense of mystery, distinguishing three phases in its development: the events which took place in Egypt, which are a figure of the Christian Easter, the Jewish celebration with which God wanted to announce the plan of salvation, and the true and perfect Paschal mystery.

Anonymous Writer of the 2nd Century

The Fruits of the Passion

This was the Passover during which Jesus wished to suffer for us: to free us from passion with the Passion, to overcome death with his Death and to give us immortal life with invisible food.

This was the salvific desire of Jesus, this was his eminently spiritual love: to point out the figures as types and to give his disciples his sacred body: *Take, eat; this is my body... Drink from this cup all of you, for this is my blood of the covenant, which is poured out for many for the forgiveness of sins* (Matt 26:26-28). Rather than eating at the Passover, he wished to suffer it, so as to free us from that passion we had contracted as a result of eating.

It is for this reason that he substitutes one tree for another. And instead of a perverse hand which had been stretched out impiously, he allowed his immaculate hand to be nailed in a gesture of piety, showing himself to be the true Life hanging from a tree. You, O Israel were not able to eat of him; we on the other hand, with indestructible spiritual knowledge, eat him and we will not die (cf Gen 1:17; 3:4-6).

The tree of salvation

For me, this is the tree of eternal salvation: from it I am nourished and satisfied. Through its roots I deepen my roots; through its branches I expand; with its sap I am drunk; through its spirit – coming as a delightful breeze – I am made fruitful. Under its shade I have pitched my tent, and fleeing from great heat I find a refuge filled with dew. Through its flowers do I flourish, with its fruits I delight and I take them freely because from the beginning they have been allocated for me.

This tree is food to satisfy my hunger, a spring for my thirst, a dress for my nakedness; its leaves are the spirit of life and never fig-leaves (cf Gen 3:7). This tree is my protection when I fear God, my crook when I stumble, my prize when I fight and my trophy when I win. This tree is the strait path and narrow way. This tree is Jacob's ladder and the route of the angels, with its crown truly supporting the Lord.

This tree of a heavenly size, rises from the earth and reaches the heavens, squeezing itself between heaven and earth like an eternal plant, as a buttress of all things, as the hinge to the universe, as a support for the entire world and a cosmic link; which keeps together changeable human nature, nailing it with invisible nails to the Spirit, so that, as subject to the Divinity, it is not separated from her again ...

The chalice of suffering

Although he fills the universe, the Lord got rid of his clothes to fight the powers of the air, naked. And for an instant he cried out asking for this chalice to be taken away from him (cf Luke 22:42), so as to show us that He is *truly man*. But recalling his mission and wishing to fulfil the plan of salvation for which he had been sent, once again he cried out aloud: *Not my will but yours be done* (Luke 22:42). Truly, *the spirit indeed is willing, but the flesh is weak* (Matt 26:41).

As he fought a victorious battle in favour of life, his sacred head was crowned with thorns, thus blotting out the ancient curse on the earth and eradicating with his divine forehead the multitude of thorns produced by sin. After then drinking the bitter and acidic gall of the dragon, he poured out the sweet springs which flow from him.

The Lord wanted to destroy the work of the woman and to counter her who at the beginning had come from the side of Adam, as a carrier of death. He opened his sacred breast, and from it flowed blood and water, complete signs of the spiritual and mystical marriage, of adoption and regeneration. It has been written that, *He will baptise you with the Holy Spirit and fire* (Matt 3:11): here, water as baptism *in the Holy Spirit*, the blood as baptism *in fire*.

The two thieves

Two thieves were then crucified with Him. They carried within themselves signs of the two peoples: one of them was converted thorough gratitude, sincerely confessing his offences and having pity on his Sovereign; the other, on the other hand, rebelled because he was thick-skinned, showing neither gratitude nor piety towards his Lord and persisted in his old sins. They also are a sign of the two sentiments of the soul: one of them is converted from his old sins, strips himself naked before his Sovereign and thus obtains mercy and a reward, through doing penance. The other one has no excuse, because he does not want to change, and remains a thief until the end.

Fruits

When the cosmic battle ended, winning everything and for everything, the cross became implanted, without being raised like God or prostrated as man, as the end of all things, as a trophy of victory, carrying within itself a triumph over the enemy.

Then, faced with its long resistance, the universe was

filled with wonder. The heavens were moved, and the powers, the thrones and the heavenly laws, quivered, seeing the arch-enemy of the great militia being laid low. Little remained for the stars of the sky to fall, on seeing asplay He who was previous to the morning star; and for some time the flame of the sun went out, seeing the great light of the world being darkened. Then the rocks of the earth split (cf Matt 27:51) to exclaim the ingratitude of Israel: *You did not recognise the spiritual stone which you followed and from which you drank* (cf 1 Cor 14:4). The veil of the temple was rent, to take part in the Passion and to point out to the true heavenly Priest. By just a little did the entire world escape being crushed and dissolved by fright at the Passion: for the great Jesus had exhaled his divine Spirit saying, *Father, into your hands I commend my spirit* (Luke 23:46).

And while the waters were disturbed and stirred up by the apprehension of fear, when the divine spirit joined up again, immediately the universe found its stability again, almost totally enlivened, consolidated and with a new spirit.

Homily on Easter, 49-55

Saint Irenaeus of Lyons

He was born in Proconsular Asia in the first half of the second century, between 115 and 125. According to Eusebius, while Irenaeus was still young, he had seen and heard Bishop Polycarp (+155), the disciple of St John at Smyrna. We do not know why he was in Rome at the time of his master's death, but during the persecution of Marcus Aurelius, Irenaeus was a priest of the Church at Lyons. He succeeded Photinus to the bishopric there.

In the peace that followed the persecution, the new bishop divided his activities between the duties of a pastor and of a missionary, and his writings. One of his tasks as bishop was to act as mediator in the controversy over the date of Easter during the pontificate of Pope Victor I (189-198).

Nothing is known of the date of his death which is probably at the beginning of the third century. St Gregory of Tours states that he suffered martyrdom during the persecution of Septimus Severus.

Irenaeus wrote a number of works in Greek. These have secured an exceptional place for him in Christian literature because they exhibit the testimony, in controversial religious questions, of a contemporary witness of the heroic age of the Church.

None of his writings have come down to us except fragments. *Adversus haereses*, a work in five volumes, has reached us in Latin translation. It is a profound exposition not only of Gnosticism under its different guises, but also of the principal heresies which had sprung up in different Christian communities. He also aimed at confirming the faith of the baptised in true Christian doctrine. In refuting heterodox systems, St Irenaeus often proposes the true doctrine, and in this way furnishes positive and very early evidence of great importance.

Of his other works only scattered fragments exist, and many are known only through mention made by other writers.

Saint Irenaeus

WITH ONE VOICE

The Church, which is spread throughout the whole world even to the ends of the earth, has received from the Apostles and their disciples that faith in one God, the Father Almighty who made heaven, earth, the sea and all that is in them, and in one Jesus Christ the Son of God, who became incarnate for our salvation, and in the Holy Spirit. Through the prophets, the Holy Spirit preached the designs of God and the advent, the birth from a virgin, the Passion, Resurrection from the dead and bodily Ascension into heaven of our beloved Lord Jesus Christ, as well as His coming in the glory of the Father. He will come to *recapitulate all things* (Eph 1:10) and to raise up all human flesh so that, according to the pleasure of the invisible Father, every knee may bend of those in heaven, on the earth and under the earth and every tongue may confess Jesus Christ our Lord and God (cf Phil 2:10), our Saviour and King, and that He might pronounce a just judgement on all.

Unity of the Church
Since she has received this preaching and this faith, as we have said, the Church spread throughout the world carefully preserves them as though inhabiting one house, and likewise both believes them as though with one heart and one soul, and fittingly preaches, teaches and passes them on as though with one mouth.

Although there are different languages in the world,

nevertheless the strength of tradition is one and the same. Those churches which have been founded in Germany do not believe or hand on any other doctrine than those in Spain, or among the Celts, or in the East, in Egypt, in Libya or in the centre of the world.

Just as the sun, God's creature, is one and the same in the whole world, so does the preaching of the truth shine everywhere and enlighten all who desire to come to a recognition of the truth. Neither will the one who is accomplished in oratory among church leaders say anything other than these things *for no one is above his master,* nor will the one who is weak in speech diminish the tradition. Since the faith is one and the same, the one who is able to say much concerning it does not increase it, nor does the one who is able to say little diminish it.

It does not follow because men are endowed with greater and lesser degrees of intelligence, that they should therefore change the subject-matter (of the faith) itself, and should conceive of some other God besides Him who is the Framer, Maker, and Preserver of this universe, (as if He were not sufficient for them), or of another Christ, or another Only-begotten.

But the fact referred to simply implies this: that one may more accurately than another bring out the meaning of those things which have been spoken in parables, and accommodate them to the general scheme of the faith; and explain with special clearness the operation and dispensation of God connected with human salvation; and show that God manifested long-suffering in regard to the apostasy of the angels who transgressed, and also with respect to the disobedience of men; and set forth why it is that one and the same God has made some things temporal and some eternal, some heavenly and others earthly; and understand for what reason God, though invisible, manifested Himself to the prophets not under one form, but differently to different individuals; and show why it was that more covenants than one were given to mankind; and teach what was the special character of each of these covenants; and search out for what reason *God has concluded every man in unbelief, that He may have mercy upon all* (Rom 11:32); and gratefully describe on what account the Word of God became flesh and suffered; and relate why the advent of the Son of God took place in these last times, that is, in the end, rather than in the beginning (of the world); and unfold what is contained in the Scriptures concerning the end (itself), and things to come; and not be silent as to how it is that God has made the Gentiles, whose salvation was despaired of, fellow-heirs, and of the same body, and partaker with the saints; and discourse how it is that *this mortal body shall put on immortality, and this corruptible shall put on incorruption* (1 Cor 15:54); and proclaim in what sense (God) says, *That is a people who was not a people; and she is beloved who was not beloved* (Hos 2:23; Rom 9:25); and in what sense He says that *more are the children of her that was desolate, than of her who possessed a husband.*

For in reference to these points, and others of a like nature, the apostle exclaims: *Oh! the depth of the riches both of the wisdom and knowledge of God; how unsearchable are His judgements, and His ways past finding out!*

The Church and the Holy Spirit

The heretics, tossed about by every blast of doctrine, are opposed by the uniform teaching of the Church, which remains so always, and is consistent with itself.

We do faithfully preserve the doctrine which has been received from the Church, and which always, by the Spirit of God, renewing its youth, as if it were some precious deposit in an excellent vessel, causes the vessel itself containing it to renew its youth also. For this gift of God has been entrusted to the Church, as breath was to the first created man (cf Gen 2:7), for this purpose, that all the members receiving it may be vivified; and the means of communion with Christ has been distributed throughout it, that is, the Holy Spirit, the earnest of incorruption, the means of confirming our faith, and the ladder of ascent to God. *For in the Church*, it is said, *God has set apostles, prophets, teachers* (1 Cor 12:28), and all the other means through which the Spirit works, of which all those are not partakers who do not join themselves to the Church, but defraud themselves of life through their perverse opinions and infamous behaviour.

For where the Church is, there is the Spirit of God; and where the Spirit of God is, there is the Church, and every kind of grace; but the Spirit is truth. Those, therefore, who do not partake of Him, are neither nourished into life from the mother's breasts, nor do they enjoy that most limpid fountain which issues from the body of Christ (cf Rev 22:1; John 7:37); but they dig for themselves broken cisterns (Jer 2:13) out of earthly trenches, and drink putrid water out of the mire, fleeing from the faith of the Church lest they be convicted; and rejecting the Spirit, that they may not be instructed.

Alienated thus from the truth, they do deservedly wallow in all error, tossed to and fro by it, thinking differently with regard to the same things at different times, and never attaining to a well-grounded knowledge, being more anxious to be sophists of words than disciples of the truth. For they have not been founded upon the one rock, but upon sand, which has in itself a multitude of stones. Wherefore they also imagine many gods, and they always have the excuse of searching after truth (for they are blind), but never succeed in finding it. For they blaspheme the Creator, Him who is truly God, who also furnishes power to find the truth; imagining that they have discovered another God beyond God, or another Pleroma, or another dispensation.

Wherefore also the light which is from God does not illumine them, because they have dishonoured and despised God, holding Him of small account, because, through His love and infinite benignity, He has come within reach of human knowledge (knowledge, however, not with regard to His greatness, or with regard to His essence – for that no man has measured or handled – but after this sort: that we should know that He who made, and formed, and breathed in them the breath of life, and nourishes us by means of the creation, establishing all things by His Word, and binding them together by His Wisdom (cf Ps 32:6) – this is He who is the only true God).

Adversus haereses, I:10; III:24

SAINT IRENAEUS

THE LIFE-GIVING SPIRIT

What really was the case, the Apostles did record: *that the Spirit of God as a dove descended upon Him* (cf Matt 3:16); this Spirit, of whom it was declared by Isaiah, *And the Spirit of God shall rest upon Him* (Is 11:2), as I have already said. And again: *The Spirit of the Lord is upon me, because He has anointed me* (Is 61:1). That is the Spirit of whom the Lord declares, *For it is not you that speak, but the Spirit of your Father who speaks in you* (Matt 10:20). And again, giving to the disciples the power of regeneration into God, He said to them, *Go and teach all nations, baptising them in the name of the Father, and of the Son, and of the Holy Spirit* (Matt 28:19).

The Holy Spirit at work

For God promised, that in the last times He would pour the Spirit upon His servants and handmaids, that they might prophesy (cf Joel 3:1-2). He did also descend upon the Son of God, made the Son of man, becoming accustomed in fellowship with Him to dwell in the human race, to rest with human beings, and to dwell in the workmanship of God, working the will of the Father in them, and renewing them from their old habits into the newness of Christ.

This is the Spirit which David asked for the human race, saying, *And establish me with all-governing Spirit* (Ps 51:12); who also, as Luke says, descended at the day of Pentecost upon the disciples after the Lord's ascension, having power to admit all nations to the entrance of life, and to the opening of the new covenant. With one accord in all languages, they uttered praise to God, the Spirit bringing distant tribes to unity, and offering to the Father the first-fruits of all nations.

The Lord promised to send the Comforter (John 15:7), who should join us to God. For as a compacted lump of dough cannot be formed of dry wheat without fluid matter, nor can a loaf possess unity, so, in like manner, neither could we, being man, be made one in Christ Jesus without the water from heaven. And as dry earth does not bring forth unless it receive moisture, in like manner we also, being originally a dry tree (cf Luke 23:31), could never have brought forth fruit unto life without the voluntary rain from above. Our Lord was compassionate towards that erring Samaritan woman – who did not remain with one husband, but committed fornication by *contracting* many marriages – by pointing out, and promising to her living water, so that she should thirst no more, nor occupy herself in acquiring the refreshing water obtained by labour, having in herself water springing up to eternal life. The Lord, receiving this as a gift from His Father, does Himself also confer it upon those who are partakers of Himself, sending the Holy Spirit upon all the earth.

The dew of God

Gideon (cf Judg 6:37), that Israelite whom God chose that he might save the people of Israel from the power of foreigners, foreseeing this gracious gift, changed his request, and prophesied that there would be dryness upon the fleece of wool, *a type of the people*, on which alone at first there had been dew. Thus he was indicating that they should no longer have the Holy Spirit from God, as Isaiah says, *I will also command the clouds, that they rain no rain upon it* (Is 5:6), but that the dew, which is the Spirit of God, who descended upon the Lord, should be diffused throughout all the earth, *the spirit of wisdom and understanding, the spirit of counsel and might, the spirit of knowledge and piety, the spirit of the fear of God* (Is 11:2). This Spirit, He did confer upon the Church, sending throughout all the world the Comforter from heaven, from where also the Lord tells us that the devil, like lightning, was cast down (Luke 10:18).

Thus we have need of the dew of God, that we be not consumed by fire, nor rendered unfruitful, and that where we have an accuser there we may have also an Advocate (1 John 2:1), the Lord commending to the Holy Spirit His own man, who had fallen among thieves (Luke 10:35), whom He Himself had compassion on, and bound up his wounds, giving two royal *denaria*; so that we, receiving by the Spirit the image and superscription of the Father and the Son, might cause the *denarium* entrusted to us to be fruitful, counting out the increase to the Lord (Matt 25:14).

Beware of heretics

The Spirit, therefore, descended under the predestined dispensation, and the Son of God, the only-begotten, who is also the Word of the Father, came in the fullness of time, having become incarnate in man for the sake of man, and fulfilling all the conditions of human nature, our Lord Jesus Christ being one and the same, as He Himself the Lord does testify, as the apostles confess, and as the prophets announce. All the doctrines of these men who have invented subdivisions (of the Lord's person), have been proved falsehoods. These men do, in fact, set the Spirit aside altogether; they understand that Christ was one and

Jesus another; and they teach that there was not one Christ, but many.

It will therefore be incumbent upon you, and all others who give their attention to this writing, and are anxious about their own salvation, not readily to express acquiescence when they hear abroad the speeches of these men. For, speaking of things resembling the doctrine of the faithful, not only do they hold opinions which are different, but absolutely contrary, and in all points full of blasphemies. They destroy those persons who have imbibed a poison which disagrees with their constitution, just as if one, giving lime mixed with water for milk, should mislead by the similarity of the colour. As a man superior to me has said, concerning all that in any way corrupts the things of God and adulterates the truth, *Lime is wickedly mixed with the milk of God.*

Adversus Haereses, III:17

Saint Clement of Alexandria

Titus Flavius Clement was born in Athens, of pagan parents, around 150 A.D. After his conversion, he travelled the world in search of instruction from renowned Christian teachers. He attended the School of Theology of Alexandria, founded by Pantenus in 180. He settled there, and later succeeded his master as Director of that school. A few years later, during the persecution of Septimus Severus, he was forced to leave Egypt. He took refuge in Cappadocia, where he died in the year 215.

Clement of Alexandria is considered as the forerunner of systematic theology. He is the first Christian writer to recognise secular philosophy – neoplatonism, in this case – using it for a systematic expose of the faith.

Although most of his literary work has not reached us, a trilogy of prime importance has. So too has the full text of a work entitled, *Who is the rich person who will be saved?*, where he comments on a passage of St Mark's Gospel, explaining the traditional Christian doctrine on poverty, which basically consists of detachment from earthly goods.

Saint Clement of Alexandria

THE VALUE OF RICHES

A man ran up and knelt before him, and asked him, 'Good Teacher, what must I do to inherit eternal life?' ... *And Jesus, looking upon him, loved him, and said to him, 'You lack one thing; go sell what you have, and give it to the poor, and you will have treasure in heaven; and come follow me.' At that saying his countenance fell and he went away sorrowful, for he had great possessions* (Mark 10:17-22).

One misinterpretation

What is it that caused him to flee, to desert the Master, to separate himself from help, from hope and from his past good works? It is that *go, sell what you have*. And what does that mean? Not what some superficial interpretations make of it. Our Lord is not demanding that we discard our estate and get rid of our money. What he does ask is that we banish from our souls the *primacy* of riches, of unfettered greed and feverish desire for them, the thorns of this life, which suffocate the seed of true life. If this were not the case, those who did not have anything, those who were deprived of all aid, who go about begging daily, and who sleep on the streets, without knowledge of God or of his justice, by the mere fact of their extreme poverty – lacking any means for earning and living bereft of the most essential – would be the happiest and most loved by God, and the only ones to attain eternal life.

Nor is it something new to renounce riches and to distribute them among the poor and the needy. This was

THE VALUE OF RICHES

done long before Our Lord's coming: some, to be able to dedicate themselves to the arts and in search of vain knowledge; others, as in the case of Anaxagoras, Democritus and Crates, in search of fame and glory.

A true interpretation

What, then, does the Lord command as something new, as something proper to God, as the only thing which gives life, and not something which earlier failed to save? What does he point out? What pre-eminent thing does he teach, he who as the Son of God is the new creature? He does not command what the letter says and what others have already done. He is asking for something greater, more divine, more perfect than that which is stated – that we denude the soul itself of its disordered passions, that we pull out by the roots and fling away what is foreign to the spirit. Here, then, is the teaching proper to a believer, and the doctrine worthy of the Saviour. Those, who before Christ's coming despised material goods, certainly gave up their riches and lost them, but the passions of the soul increased even more. For having believed that they had done something superhuman, they came to indulge in pride, petulance, vainglory, despising others.

How then was the Saviour to recommend to those who ought to live forever something which would hurt them and destroy the life he was promising them? It could happen that someone who has got rid of the burden of his possessions including his estate, nonetheless retains and maintains a burning appetite for riches. He has certainly detached himself from his goods, but on losing them and yet wanting them, he will be doubly tormented by the absence of what is necessary and regret his actions. For it is unavoidable and impossible for a person who lacks what is necessary for life not to be worried, and thus distracted from what is more important, while he tries to obtain what he needs in whatever way he can.

How much more fruitful is the opposite! On the one hand to own what is sufficient and not to be distressed by having to obtain it; and, on the other, to be able to help those in need. For when one does not have anything, how can one share one's goods among men? How can someone not see that this doctrine of giving up everything clashes with and clearly contradicts many other very beautiful sayings of the Saviour? *Make friends for yourselves of unrighteous mammon, so that when it fails they may receive you into the eternal habitations* (Luke 16:9). How is one to give food to the hungry, drink to the thirsty, dress the naked, shelter the homeless if one starts out with none of these very things oneself? If these are not done, Our Lord threatens with eternal fire and exterior darkness.

Riches are an instrument

... Riches, then, should not be rejected if they can be of use to our neighbour. They are accurately called *possessions* because they are possessed by people, and *goods* or utilities because with them one can do good and because they have been ordained by God for the use of men. They are things which exist and are designated, as material or as instruments, to be used in the hands of those who know them to be instruments. If the instrument is used skilfully, it is beneficial; if he who uses it lacks skill, the clumsiness affects the instrument, although in itself it is not to blame.

Riches, then, are also an instrument. If they are rightly used they are at the service of justice. If they are used unjustly, they are at the service of injustice. By their nature they are destined to serve not to govern. They cannot, then, be accused of being either good or evil, something which they are not. In themselves, riches are blameless. The one to be accused is the person who has the ability, through the choice he makes, to put it to good use or to misuse it. And this is up to the mind and judgement of man, who is free and able to manage what is given to him for his use. What is to be got rid of then is not riches, but the disorderly passions of the soul which do not allow these riches to be better used. In this way, man, converted to being good and noble, can put riches to good and generous use.

The rich – who are going to find it difficult to enter the kingdom – will have to understand these words intelligently, and not in a dull and superficial way, taking it literally. For when these words were spoken they were not meant to be taken literally. Salvation is not to be found in material things, be they few or many, small or great, with or without glory, famous or not. It is to be found in virtues of the soul, in faith, hope and charity, in love for one's neighbour, in knowledge of God, in meekness, in simplicity, in truth. These are the things which are garlanded with eternal life. Just as one cannot continue to live simply because she is pretty, no one will lose her life simply through lacking this beauty. She will live who makes chaste use of the body she has been given, according to God's design; he who profanes God's temple will lose it (cf 1 Cor 3:17). And just as one who suffers from a deformity is not necessarily honest, so too can one who is pretty be chaste.

Neither strength nor size of body can give life; nor can any member take it away. No. The soul which uses the body is the one which attains eternal life or death. *If any one strikes you on the right cheek, turn to him the other also* (Matt 5:39), says the Lord. This is a precept which the strong and robust man is able to fulfil, but the weak and intemperate in spirit, on the other hand, likely to infringe. Similarly, a poor person who cannot earn a living can find himself intoxicated by concupiscence; and one who is materially rich can be sober and not looking for pleasures – he can be obedient, discreet, pure and mortified..

In conclusion, it is primarily and principally the soul which has to live. The virtues it engenders lead to salvation, while vices kill. It follows clearly that the soul will be saved if it is poor and lacking in those things which are corrupted by riches. Furthermore, if it seeks to enrich itself in those things which are initiated by riches, it dies.

Quis dives salvetur? XI-XIV, XVIII

Tertullian

Quintus Septimus Florens Tertullianus was born in Carthage around 155. He was the son of a centurion in the proconsular service. He later moved to Rome, where he became famous as an advocate. He shows close acquaintance with the procedure and terms of Roman law, and was a great orator. When he became a Christian around 193, he returned to Carthage, and there dedicated himself completely to the service of the Christian faith.

Towards the end of his life he fell into the montanist heresy, and so cannot be counted among the Fathers of the Church. In spite of this, he is doubtless one of the most original and important Latin ecclesiastical writers of the early centuries.

While he wrote some of his works in Greek, most of them were written in Latin. He was the first to use this language for theological treatises. Although some of his works have been lost, numerous writings have reached us. Among the most important of these are the ones concerning apologetics, theology and those of a moral and disciplinary nature.

The treatise *On prayer* belongs to the last group. Written in the years 198-200, it is the first to deal with this theme in Christian literature. He develops the idea that the New Testament has introduced a form of prayer which, because of its tenor and spirit, has no precedent in the Old Testament, and is quite superior as regards its closeness to, its faith and confidence in God, and its direct approach.

This work does not contain arguments of a philosophical nature. It is, on the other hand, eminently practical. It is a treatise of great value, not only because of the depth of its ideas, as for the strength with which he expresses the authentically Christian idea of life.

His treatise *On Penance* written in the year 203, is also of great importance. It was written when Tertullian was still a Christian and is witness to the practice of the Sacrament of Penance in the early Church.

TERTULLIAN

THE EFFECTIVENESS OF PRAYER

Now, this is the spiritual victim which has set aside the earlier sacrifice. *To what purpose do you offer me the multitude of your victims, saith the Lord? I am full, I desire not holocausts of rams, and fat of fatlings, and blood of calves and goats. For who required these things at your hands?* (Is 1:11-12).

The Gospel teaches what God demands. *The hour is coming,* He says, *when the true worshippers will worship the Father in spirit and in truth. For God is spirit* (John 4:23-24), and therefore He requires that His worshippers be of the same nature.

We are the true worshippers and true priests who, offering our prayer in the spirit, offer sacrifice in the spirit – that is, prayer – as a victim that is appropriate and acceptable to God; this is what He has demanded and what He has fore-ordained for Himself. This prayer, consecrated to Him with our whole heart, nurtured by faith, prepared with truth; a prayer that is without blemish because of our innocence, clean because of our chastity; a prayer that has received the victor's crown because of our love for one another: this prayer we should bring to the altar of God with a display of good works amid the singing of psalms and hymns and it will obtain for us from God all that we ask.

For what will God refuse to the prayer that comes to Him from the spirit and in truth, since this is the prayer He has exacted? What proofs of its efficacy do we read of and hear of and believe! To be sure, the prayer of old would save one from fires and wild beasts and starvation; yet, it had not received its form from Christ. But how much more is wrought by Christian prayer! It does not cause an angel of dew to appear in the midst of fire, nor does it stop the mouths of lions or take the breakfast of country folk to the hungry; it does not destroy all sense of pain by the grace that is conferred. But by patient endurance it teaches those who suffer, those who are sensitive, and those who have sorrow. By virtue it increases grace that our faith may know what comes from the Lord and understand what it suffers for the name of God.

Then, too, in the past, prayer would impose plagues, rout the armies of the enemy, and prevent the beneficial effects of rain. But now, the prayer of justice averts the wrath of God, is on the alert for enemies, and intercedes for persecutors. What wonder if it could wrest water from the heavens, when it could even ask for fire and obtain it! Prayer alone overcomes God; but Christ has willed that it work no evil; upon it He has conferred all power for good. Therefore, it has no power except to recall the souls of the dead from the very path of death, to make the weak recover, to heal the sick, to exorcise demons, to open prison doors, to loosen the chains of the innocent. It likewise remits sins, repels temptations, stamps out persecution, consoles the fainthearted, delights the courageous, brings travellers safely home, calms the waves, stuns robbers, feeds the poor, directs the rich, raises up the fallen, sustains the falling, and supports those who are on their feet.

Prayer is the wall of faith, our shield and weapons against the foe who studies us from all sides. Hence, let us never set forth unarmed. Let us be mindful of our guard-duty by day and our vigil by night. Beneath the arms of prayer let us guard the standard of our general, and let us pray as we await the bugle call of the angel.

All the angels pray, too; every creature prays; the beasts, domestic and wild, bend their knees, and as they go forth from their stables and caves they look up to heaven with no idle gaze. Even the birds, upon rising in the morning mount into the sky and stretch out their wings as a cross in place of hands and say something which might seem to be a prayer.

What need, then, is there of further discussion of the duty of prayer? Even our Lord Himself prayed, to whom be honour and power forever and ever.

De oratione, 28-29

TERTULLIAN

CONFESSING ONE'S SINS

What is the meaning for us of those themes of the Lord's parables? Is not the fact that a woman has lost a drachma, and seeks it and finds it, and invites her female friends to share her joy, an example of a restored sinner? (Luke 15:8-10). There strays one little ewe of the shepherd; but the flock was not more dear than the one: that one is earnestly sought. The one is longed for instead of all; and at length she is found, and is borne back on the shoulders of the shepherd himself; for much had she toiled in straying (Luke 15:3-7).

God awaits us

That most gentle father, I will recall, who calls his prodigal son home, and willingly receives him repentant after his indigence, slays his best fatted calf, graces his joy with a banquet (Luke 15:11-32). Why not? He had found the son whom he had lost; he had felt *him* to be all the dearer of whom he had *made a gain*. Who is that father to be understood by us to be? God, surely: no one is so truly a Father (cf Matt 23:9; Eph 3:14-15); no one so rich in paternal love. He, then, will receive you, His own son, back, even if you have squandered what you had received from Him, even if you return naked – just because you *have* returned; and will rejoice more over your return than over the sobriety of the other.

Confession

Confession of sins lightens, as much as dissimulation aggravates them; for confession is counselled by the desire of making satisfaction, dissimulation by culpable obstinacy.

The narrower, then, the sphere of action of this second repentance, the more laborious is its probation; in order that it may not be exhibited in the conscience alone, but may likewise be carried out in some external act. This act, which is more usually expressed and commonly spoken of under a Greek name, is *exomologesis*, whereby we confess our sins to the Lord, not indeed as if He were ignorant of them, but inasmuch as by confession satisfaction is settled. Of confession repentance is born; by repentance God is appeased. And thus confession is a discipline for man's prostration and humiliation, enjoining a demeanour calculated to move mercy.

With regard also to the very dress and food, it commands the penitent to lie in sackcloth and ashes, to cover his body in mourning, to lay his spirit low in sorrows, to exchange for severe treatment the sins which he has committed; moreover, to know no food and drink but such as is plain – not for the stomach's sake, but the soul's; for the most part, however, to feed prayers on fasting, to groan, to weep and roar unto the Lord your God; to roll before the feet of the presbyters, and kneel to God's dear ones; to enjoin on all the brethren to be ambassadors to bear his deprecatory supplication before God.

All this confession does that it may enhance repentance; may honour God by its fear of the incurred danger; may by itself pronouncing against the sinner, stand in the stead of God's indignation, and by temporal mortification (I will not say frustrate, but) discharge eternal punishments. Therefore, while it abases the man, it raises him; while it covers him with squalor, it renders him more clean; while it *ac*cuses, it *ex*cuses; while it condemns, it absolves. The harder you are on yourself, the more (believe me) will God forgive you your sins.

Do not delay confession

Yet most men either shun confession, as being a public exposure of themselves, or else defer it from day to day. I presume they do so as being more mindful of modesty than of salvation; just like men who, having contracted some malady in the more private parts of the body, avoid the privity of physicians, and so perish with their own bashfulness. Truly you are honourable in your modesty; bearing an open forehead for sinning, but an abashed one for deprecating! I give no place to bashfulness when I am a gainer by its loss; when itself in some sort exhorts the man, saying, *Respect not me; it is better that I perish through you than you through me.*

At all events, the time when (if ever) its danger is serious, is when it is a butt for jeering speech in the presence of insulters, where one man raises himself on his neighbour's ruin, where there is upward clambering over the prostrate. But among brethren and fellow-servants, where there is common hope, fear, joy, grief, suffering, because there is a common Spirit from a common Lord and Father, why do you think these brethren and fellow-servants to be anything other than yourself? Why flee from the partners of your own mischances, as from such as will derisively cheer them?

It is Christ who pardons

The body cannot feel gladness at the trouble of any one member; it must necessarily join with one consent in grief, and in labouring for the remedy. In a company of two is the Church; but the Church is Christ. When, then, you cast yourself at the brethren's knees, you are handling *Christ*, you are entreating *Christ*. In like manner, when they shed tears over you, it is *Christ* who suffers, *Christ* who prays the Father for mercy. What a son asks is always easily obtained.

Grand indeed is the reward of modesty, which the concealment of our fault promises us! If we do hide something from the knowledge of man, shall we equally conceal it from God? Are the judgements of men and the knowledge of God so put upon a par? Is it better to be damned in secret than absolved in public? *It is a hard thing thus to come to admit sins and confess them.* Hard, I grant; for evil does bring to misery; but where repentance is to be made, the misery ceases, because it is turned into something salutary. Miserable it is to be cut, and cauterised, and racked with the pungency of some medicinal powder. Still, the things which heal by unpleasant means do, by the benefit of the cure, excuse their own offensiveness, and make present injury bearable for the sake of the greater good we can enjoy in the future.

De Poenitencia, 7 , 4-X

ORIGEN

Origen, nicknamed *Adamancio* (man of steel), because of his extraordinary energy, was born in 185, probably in Egyptian Alexandria. His father, who died during the persecutions of Septimus Severus, had given him his first lessons in the sacred and secular writings.

His life can be divided into two phases. The first, from the year 203, when at the age of eighteen, Demetrius, bishop of Alexandria, made him Director of the Catechetical School, replacing Clement who had fled because of the persecution. The religious zeal and erudition of the young teacher very soon turned the school into a seedbed of confessors and martyrs. He went on several journeys in the early part of his life: to Rome, Arabia, Greece and Palestine. In these places he spread the gospel with ardour, and confronted the heretics.

The second stage of his life, from the year 231, took place in Caesarea of Palestine, where he spent twenty years. Here, at the request of the bishop, Origen founded a new school of theology. At the same time he made journeys to Antioch and to Arabia; he brought back to the faith the Patripassian bishop, Beryllus of Bostia.

Age did not diminish his activities. The persecution of Decius (250) prevented him from continuing the works he had begun writing. Origen was imprisoned and barbarously tortured. He died, probably as a result of these sufferings, in 253 at Tyr, a couple of years after Decius died.

Origen is not counted among the Fathers, but because of his great piety he is considered as one of the most eminent writers of early Christianity. Only a small part of his immense output – more than 6000 titles, according to St Epiphanius – have been conserved.

In his homilies, or *tractatus*, without ignoring the literal meaning of Sacred Scripture, he develops the spiritual meaning in a special way. His *Treatise on Prayer* is a gloss on the petitions of the *Our Father*, and ends with some general considerations on prayer. Written when he was mature in age, it is the first work of this kind in Christian literature.

His treatment of the following passage of the Gospel of St Luke – the *Magnificat* – interprets it with theological rigour, with Marian piety and in a refined literary sense.

Origen

WHEN IT'S TIME TO PRAY

When speaking about praying, it is very useful to keep oneself in the presence of God and to speak with him as one converses with a friend who is physically present. Just as images which are stored in the memory give rise to thoughts when those figures are thought about in the mind, so too we believe that it is useful to recall God present in the soul. He controls all our movements, even the slightest ones, when we are willing to show gratitude to the one we know to be present within us, to this God who examines the heart and scrutinises the thoughts.

Fruits of prayer

Suppose, for a moment, that we had received nothing useful from the prayer. The very fact that for the period of praying we had adopted the pious attitude described above, is no mean fruit. And if this is repeated frequently, those who dedicate a period of time to prayer conscientiously, will realise that this exercise keeps one away from sin and encourages the practice of the virtues. If simply calling to mind the figure of a sensible and prudent man encourages us to emulate him, and frequently halts impulses of our concupiscence, how much more will the recollection of God, the universal Father, throughout the prayer, help us to be convinced that we are in his presence and try to speak with He who is listening to us!

But it would be more useful if we were able to understand what a good way it would be for us to pray, and to put it into practice. The one who tries to concentrate during the prayer and puts all his effort into listening, ends up hearing: *I am here*. And before ending the prayer he will manage to lay aside every difficulty connected with providence... For the one who conforms to the Divine Will and adjusts himself to everything that occurs, finds himself free of all ties; he never raises a threatening hand against God, who ordains everything for our formation, does not mutter to himself and speaks his thoughts when men are listening.

Our advocates before God

The Son of God is the Pontiff of our offerings and our advocate before the Father. He prays for those who pray, and asks for those who ask. But he does not intercede for those who assiduously fail to make requests through Him. Nor will he defend before God, as something belonging to him, those who do not put into practice his teaching that it is necessary to pray always without ever failing... And as regards those who trust these very words of Christ, who will not be set aflame with desires to pray without discouragement when he hears the invitation: *Ask and it will be given to you... For everyone who asks, receives* (Luke 11:9-10)?

It is not only the Pontiff who unites himself to those who pray, but also the angels. They rejoice *in heaven over one sinner who repents than over ninety-nine righteous persons who need no repentance* (Luke 15:7). And the souls of the saints who already rest in peace also join them... The saints see things in this life as if in a mirror, but in the future they will see them face to face. It would be absurd not to hold the same thesis, with due regard to differences, concerning the other faculties and virtues; and even more, when one takes into account that the virtues acquired in this life will be perfected in heaven. One of the principal virtues, according to the divine mind, is charity with one's neighbour, a virtue which the saints have as regards those who are still fighting on earth... We bear in mind too that Christ has stated that he is to be found in each saint who is sick; he is also in prison, in nakedness, in guests, in one who is hungry and in one who is thirsty. Who can ignore, even though they may have handled the Gospel very little, that Christ attributes to himself and considers his own, those things which befall those who believe in him?

As regards God's angels, if they gathered around Jesus and served him, we cannot allow ourselves to think that their ministry was limited to a short space of time which covers the period when the mortal Christ was here among men. For, during the period of prayer, and having been made aware by the one who prays as to what he needs, they carry it out if they can, in virtue of the universal command which they have received. Since *even the hairs of your head are counted* (Matt 10:31), as regards the saints, he gathers them together at the time of prayer, aiming to make the one dispensing of his goodness, concentrate on those in need who ask with confidence. One has to imagine, then, that at times all the angels are gathered together, as God's observers and ministers, and they make themselves present to the person praying to try to obtain what he is looking for.

The guardian angel

The special angel of each one, which even the most insignificant member of the Church has, also contemplates the countenance of God who is in the heavens (cf Matt 17:10), watching the divinity of our Creator. He joins his prayer to ours and co-operates, in so far as it is possible for him, working in aid of our petition.

Unity of life

In addition to these considerations, I think that the very words used in prayer by the saints contain a certain divine effectiveness, above all when they pray with all their heart and soul. This destroys the spiritual viruses which the opposing powers inject into the souls of those who neglect the practice of prayer and do not heed Paul's advice, *pray without ceasing* (1 Thess 5:17) which follows Christ's exhortation.

The person who in the fulfilment of his duties unites them to his prayer, and his prayer to his deeds, prays without ceasing; for virtuous actions and the fulfilment of the precepts become part of prayer. We then come to realise that the precept *pray without ceasing*, can only be fulfilled if we are able to say that the life of a person is a great continuous prayer.

Treatise on prayer (PG 11, 415-530)

Origen

MARY'S MAGNIFICAT

Let us examine the Virgin Mary's prophecy: *My soul magnifies the Lord, and my spirit rejoices in God my Saviour* (Luke 1:46). We will ask ourselves in what way the soul can magnify the Lord, since God can neither be increased nor decreased: He is who is. Why then did Mary say: *My soul magnifies the Lord*?

If I consider that the Lord and Saviour *is the image of the invisible God* (Col 1:15), and if I recognise that my soul has been made as an image of the Creator (cf Gen 1:27) to be an image of the image (for in reality my soul is not properly speaking an image of God, but has been created as a likeness to the first image), I can then understand the words of the Virgin Mary. Those who paint images first choose what they wish to paint, for example, a portrait of a king. Then, with all their artistic ability, they make the effort to reproduce that one model. Similarly, each one of us, transforming our soul to the image of Christ, forms an image of him that is more or less large, sometimes dark and dirty, other times bright and clear, which corresponds to the original. Consequently, when the image of the image – that is to say, my soul – has been painted large, and it has been magnified by deeds, with thoughts, with the word, then the image of God is magnified, and the Lord himself, of whom my soul is an image, will be glorified in my own soul. But if we are sinners, the Lord, who previously grew in my image, now decreases and diminishes.

To be more precise, the Lord neither diminishes nor decreases, but it is we who do so. Instead of being robed with the image of the Saviour, we cover ourselves with other images. Instead of the image of the Word, of wisdom, of justice and of the other virtues, we take on the aspect of the devil, to the point when we can be called *snakes, brood of vipers* (Math 23:33).

First, the *soul* of Mary *magnifies the Lord*, and then, her *spirit rejoices in God*; that is to say, if we do not first grow, we cannot then rejoice.

And she adds *for he has looked with favour on the lowliness of his servant* (Luke 1:48). What is the humility of Mary on which he has fixed gaze? What did the Mother of the Saviour, who carried in her womb the Son of God, have which was humble and lowly? To say *he has looked with favour on the lowliness of his servant*, is as if to say that he has looked at the justice of his handmaid, he has looked at her temperance, he has looked at her fortitude and her wisdom. It is just that God adjusts his sight to the direction of the virtues. Someone could say: I understand that God looks at the justice and wisdom of his handmaid; but it is not so clear as to why he fixes his gaze on her lowliness. Whoever thinks in this way ought to recall that in Scripture itself humility is considered as one of the virtues.

The Saviour says: *learn from me; for I am gentle and humble in heart, and you will find rest for your souls* (Matt 11:29). If you want to know the name of this virtue, or rather, how the philosophers call it, realise that the humility on which God directs his gaze is the very virtue that the philosophers call *atufia* or *metriotes*. We can define it in a sentence: humility is the state of a person who far from being puffed up, debases himself. He who gets bloated, falls, as the Apostle says, *into the condemnation of the devil* – who began with being puffed up by pride. For this reason the Apostle puts us on our guard: *so as not to fall, puffed up with conceit, into the condemnation of the devil* (1 Tim 3:6).

He has looked with favour on the lowliness of his servant: God has looked upon me, says Mary, because I am humble, and because I seek the virtue of meekness and try to pass unnoticed.

From now on all generations will call me blessed (Luke 1:48). If I understand *all generations* according to common parlance, I will appreciate that a better result is obtained by adding *because the Mighty One has done great things for me* (Luke 1:49). Precisely because *those who humble themselves will be exalted* (Luke 14:11), God *has looked with favour on the lowliness of his servant, Mary. He, the Mighty One whose name is Holy*, has therefore done great things through Her.

His mercy is for those who fear him from generation to generation (Luke 1:50). The *mercy* of God does not extend to one generation, or to two, or to three, not even to five. But it is showered eternally *from generation to generation*.

He has shown strength with his arm ... and lifted up the lowly (Luke 1:51-52). You, too, if you are weak, if you seek support in the Lord, if you fear him, you can listen to the promise with which the Lord replies to your fear.

What promise are we referring to? *He has shown strength in favour of those who fear him*. His strength or his power is a real attribute. The word *kratos*, which we can translate by *strength*, is applied to the one who governs or perhaps to the one who holds all power. If you fear God, then, He will communicate to you his power and his strength, he will grant you the kingdom, in which you, subject to the *King of kings* (Rev 19:16), will possess *the strength that God supplies*, in Jesus Christ, for *to Him belongs the glory and the power forever and ever. Amen.* (1 Pet 4:11).

In Lucam homiliae, 8, 1-7

ORIGEN

PRIEST AND VICTIM

Abraham took the wood of the burnt offering, laid it on Isaac his son; and he took in his hand the fire and the knife. So they went, both of them together (Gen 22:6). In carrying the wood for the burnt offering itself, Isaac is a figure of Christ who *carried his own cross* (John 19:17). However, to carry the wood for the burnt offering belongs to the priestly office. Christ is therefore both Victim and Priest. This is what was referred to in the next sentence: *So they went, both of them together.* For while Abraham who was to offer the sacrifice carried the fire and the knife, Isaac walked not behind but alongside him, and in this way showed that he also fulfilled the priestly function equally with him.

What happened then? *Isaac said to his father Abraham, 'Father'* (Gen 22:7). Spoken in that moment by his son, this word was for Abraham the voice of temptation. Imagine for yourselves how the father's heart must have been wrung when he heard the voice of the lad who was to be sacrificed! Yet, inflexible though his faith made him, he was still able to reply tenderly: *What is it my son?* And Isaac answered: *Behold the fire and the wood; but where is the lamb for the burnt offering?* (Gen 22:7). Abraham said: *'God will provide himself the lamb for a burnt offering, my son'* (Gen 22:8).

This affectionate and careful reply is very moving to me. I do not know what Abraham saw in spirit, for he spoke not of the present but of the future when he said,

God will provide himself the lamb, and his reply to his son's query about the immediate situation was made in terms of what was to come. For it was the Lord himself who was to provide the lamb, in the person of Christ. For we also read that *Wisdom has built her house* (Prov 9:1), and that *he humbled himself and became obedient to death* (Phil 2:8). Everything you read about Christ has not happened out of necessity but freely.

Strength in faith

So they went both of them together, and came to the place of which God had told him (Gen 22:8-9). When Moses arrived at the place which the Lord had indicated to him, he was not allowed to climb. First he was told: *put off your shoes from your feet* (Exod 3:5). But Abraham and Isaac did not receive such a command; they were to go up without taking their shoes off. Perhaps the reason for this variation lies in that Moses, although great, came from Egypt, and his feet were tied down with ties of death. Abraham and Isaac, however, did not have any of this. They arrived at the appointed place, Abraham built the altar, put the firewood on top of it, tied up the boy and got ready to cut his head off.

You who find yourselves in the Church of God, listening to these words are very many. A good number of you are parents. I wish that on hearing this narrative, some of you would be filled with steadiness and strength of mind so that if, by chance you were to lose a child – even if it were the only child and a most beloved one – to a death which is common to all men, I wish you would take Abraham as an example, placing before your eyes his greatness of soul. It is true that so much is not asked of you: to tie up your own son, to force him, to prepare a sword to behead him. Such services are not asked of you. So, at least be steadfast in your resolution and in your heart: with strength in your faith, offer your son joyfully to God. Be the priest of the life of your son, for it is not fitting for the priest who offers a sacrifice to God to start weeping.

Do you want to see that this is what is asked of you? Our Lord tells us in the Gospel: *If you were Abraham's children, you would do what Abraham did* (John 8:39). This is what Abraham did. You too should go ahead and do it, but not with heavy heart, because *God loves a cheerful giver* (2 Cor 9:7). If you are prompt in God's service, he will also say to you: *Take your son whom you love, and offer him as a burnt offering upon one of the mountains which I shall tell you* (Gen 22:2). Not in the depths of the earth, not in *the vale of tears* (Ps 84:7), but offer your son on the high mountains. Show that your faith in God is stronger than the sentiments of the flesh. Abraham truly loved his son Isaac, but he put the love for God above the love of the flesh. So he found not the affections of the flesh but *the affection of Christ Jesus* (Phil 1:8), which is in the heart of the Word of God, of Truth, of Wisdom.

The ultimate sacrifice

Abraham put forth his hand, and took the knife to slay his son. But the angel of the Lord called to him from heaven, and said: "Abraham, Abraham!" And he said: "Here I am." He said: "Do not lay your hand on the lad, or do anything to him; for now I know that you fear God" (Gen 22:10-12).

Regarding this passage, one could raise an objection to the effect that God says he now knows that Abraham fears Him, as if he did not know this earlier. God did, in fact, know this; it was not hidden to him since he is the *eternal God, who does discern what is secret, and is aware of all things before they come to be* (Dan 13:42). But they have been written for you. Certainly, you too have believed in God, but if you do not carry out deeds based on faith (cf 2 Thess 1:11), if you do not obey all the commandments, even the most difficult; if you do not offer sacrifice and do not show that you do not put either father or mother or children before God (cf Matt 10:37), you will not be recognised as one who fears God, and he will not say to you: *"now I know that you fear God."*

These words were said to Abraham; they are a proclamation that he feared God. Why? Because he did not spare his son. Compare these words with those of the Apostle, when he says of God, *He did not spare his own Son but gave him up for us all* (Rom 8:32). See how magnificent is the generosity with which God deals with men! Abraham offered to God his mortal son who was not to die; God delivered his immortal Son, for all mankind. What shall we say when we come across such things? *What shall I render to the Lord for all his bounty to me?* (Ps 116:12).

God the Father did not spare his own Son for our good. Which of you might hear the voice of an angel saying to him: *now I know that you fear God because you have not withheld your son from me* (Gen 22:12), or your daughter or your wife or money, or honours or the ambitions of this life, but you have despised all of this, and you have considered all of it as dung in order to win Christ (cf Phil 3:8); because you have sold all your possessions, you have given the money to the poor and you have followed the word of God? (cf Matt 19:21). Who would be able to hear the angel saying these words to him?

Christ prefigured as a ram

Abraham listened to this voice which said to him: *because you have not withheld your son from me*. And

Abraham lifted up his eyes and looked, and behold, behind him was a ram, caught in the thicket by his horns (Gen 12:13). We have already said, I think, that Isaac was a type of Christ, but here the ram also seems equally to prefigure him. It is worthwhile making an effort to discover how Isaac, who was spared, and the ram, who was slain, could both equally represent Christ.

Christ is the Word of God; but *the Word was made flesh* (John 1:14). Christ suffers, but in the flesh. He underwent death in the flesh, prefigured here by the ram, as St John also saw: *Behold the lamb of God who takes away the sin of the world* (John 1:29). But the Word remained forever incorruptible, that is Christ according to the spirit, of whom Isaac is the image. Therefore Christ is both victim and priest according to the spirit. For he who offers the sacrifice to his Father according to the flesh is himself offered upon the altar of the Cross.

In Genesim homiliae, VIII: 7-9

Saint Cyprian of Carthage

Cyprian was born probably in Carthage around the year 205 A.D. He spent his whole life there, until 259 when he died as a victim of the Valerian persecutions.

Born into a noble pagan family, he did well at his studies in rhetoric, coming to be a brilliant teacher in this art, and known throughout Proconsular Africa. Thus, his conversion to Christianity in middle age – he was about forty at the time – caused a great stir. He was famous as an orator, and having considerable wealth held a good position in society. He was not a philosopher or a theologian, but a man of the world with vast energies. His conversion was due to an aged priest. While still a catechumen, Cyprian decided to observe celibacy, and he also gave most of his revenues to the poor. He was baptised in 246.

He was elected bishop of Carthage to popular acclaim. But the persecution led by the new emperor Decius was soon to begin (250-252). Cyprian faced this with great faith and fortitude. He moved to a safe hiding place when Pope Fabian was martyred. From there he wrote encouraging the confessors, with panegyrics on the martyrs, governing the church from outside Carthage.

In 259 he was martyred. When the Proconsul read out his condemnation, Cyprian took off his cloak, knelt down and prayed. He took off his dalmatic and gave it to the deacons; he ordered 25 gold pieces be given to his executioner. He bandaged his own eyes; the brethren cast clothes and handkerchiefs before him to catch drops of his blood. That night they carried away his body, with candles and torches, with prayer and great triumph, to the countryside.

St Cyprian was the first great Latin writer among the Christians, for Tertullian fell into heresy and his style is often harsh. Until the days of Jerome and Augustine, Cyprian's writings had no rivals in the West.

In 251 Cyprian wrote *De Ecclesiae Catholicae Unitate*. He read it to the Council which had been convened; in it Cyprian deals with the unity to be kept in each diocese by union with the bishop; the unity of the Church is maintained by the close union of the bishops 'who are glued to one another'. In 256 he wrote *De Bono Patientiae* aiming to emphasise the need for this virtue in the ascetical struggle. To restate one's struggle for the good and to resist evil requires a constant and patient effort, without discouragement or over-anxiety. He insists, above all, on bearing patiently the attacks of the devil, without giving in to his continuous attempts to persuade one to do something bad.

Cyprian's correspondence consists of some 81 letters. In addition to the treatises already mentioned, there are others like the exposition of the Lord's Prayer, on simplicity of dress proper to virgins, on mortality. Two short works *On patience* and *On rivalry and envy* were much read in ancient times.

SAINT CYPRIAN OF CARTHAGE

JUST ONE CHURCH

The Lord speaks to Peter: *I say to thee,* He says, *thou art Peter, and upon this rock I will build my church, and the gates of hell shall not prevail against it. And I will give thee the keys of the kingdom of heaven; and whatever thou shalt bind on earth shall be bound also in heaven, and whatever thou shalt loose on earth shall be loosed also in heaven* (Matt 16:18-19). Upon him, being one, He builds His Church, and although after His resurrection He bestows equal power upon all the Apostles, and says: *As the Father has sent me, I also send you. Receive ye the Holy Spirit: if you forgive the sins of anyone, they will be forgiven him; if you retain the sins of anyone, they will be retained* (John 20:21-23), yet that He might display unity, He established by His authority the origin of the same unity as beginning from one.

Surely the rest of the Apostles also were what Peter was, endowed with an equal partnership of office and of power; but the beginning proceeds from unity, that the Church of Christ may be shown to be one.

The Holy Spirit, in the Canticle of Canticles, designates this one Church in the person of the Lord and says: *One is my dove, my perfect one is but one, she is the only one of her mother, the chosen one of her that bore her* (Cant 6:8). Does he who does not hold this unity think that he holds the Faith? Does he who strives against the Church and resists her think that he is in the Church, when the blessed Apostle Paul also teaches this and sets forth the sacrament of unity saying: *One body and one Spirit, one hope of your calling, one Lord, one faith, one baptism, one God?* (cf Eph 4:4-6).

This unity we ought to hold firmly and defend, especially we bishops who watch over the Church, that we may prove that the episcopate itself is also one and undivided. Let no one deceive the brotherhood by lying. Let no one corrupt the faith by a perfidious prevarication of the truth. The episcopate is one, the parts of which are held together by the individual bishops. The Church is one. With increasing fecundity she extends far and wide into the multitude. Just as the rays of the sun are many but the light is one, and the branches of the tree are many but the strength is one founded in its tenacious root, and, when many streams flow from one source, although a multiplicity of waters seems to have been diffused from the abundance of the overflowing supply nevertheless unity is preserved in their origin.

Take away a ray of light from the body of the sun, and its unity does not allow for any division of its light. Break a branch from a tree, and the branch thus broken will not be able to bud. Cut off a stream from its source, and the stream dries up. The Church, too, bathed in the light of the Lord projects its rays over the whole world, yet there is one light which is diffused everywhere, and the unity of the body is not separated. She extends her branches over the whole earth in fruitful abundance. She extends her richly flowing streams far and wide; yet her head is one, and her source is one, and she is the one mother copious in fruit. By her womb we are born; by her milk we are nourished; by her spirit we are animated.

The spouse of Christ cannot be defiled; she is uncorrupted and chaste. She knows one home. With chaste modesty she guards the sanctity of one couch. She keeps us for God; she assigns the children whom she has created to the kingdom. Whoever is separated from the Church and is joined with an adulteress is separated from the promises of the Church. He who has abandoned the Church will not reap the rewards of Christ. He is a stranger; he is profane; he is an enemy. He cannot have God as a father who does not have the Church as a mother.

If whoever was outside the ark of Noah was able to escape, he too who is outside the Church escapes. But the Lord warns, saying: *He who is not with me is against me, and who does not gather with me, scatters* (Matt 12:30). He who breaks the peace and concord of Christ acts against Christ; he who gathers somewhere outside the Church, scatters the Church of Christ. The Lord says: *I and the Father are one* (John 10:30). And again, it is written of the Father and Son and the Holy Spirit: *And these three are one* (1 John 5:7). Does anyone believe that this unity which comes from divine power, which is closely connected with the divine sacraments, can be broken asunder in the Church and be separated by the divisions of colliding wills?

He who does not hold this unity, does not hold the law of God, does not hold the faith of the Father and the Son, does not hold life and salvation.

Chapter 4

Saint Cyprian of Carthage

THE GOOD OF PATIENCE

He who has endured even to the end will be saved (Matt 10:22). And again: *If you abide in My word, you are My disciples indeed, and you shall know the truth and the truth shall make you free* (John 8:31-32). We must endure and persevere, beloved brethren, so that, having been admitted to the hope of truth and liberty, we can finally attain that same truth and liberty, because the very fact that we are Christians is a source of faith and hope.

However, in order that hope and faith may reach their fruition, there is need for patience. For we do not strive for present glory, but for a future one, according to what Paul the Apostle teaches, saying: *For in hope we were saved. But hope that is seen is not hope. For how can a man hope for what he sees? But if we hope for what we do not see, we wait for it with patience* (Rom 8:24-25).

Perseverance

Patient waiting is necessary that we may fulfil what we have begun to be, and through God's help, that we may obtain what we hope for and believe. Accordingly, in another place, that same Apostle instructs and teaches the just and those who do works, and those who lay up for themselves heavenly treasures from the increase of divine interest, to be patient also. For he says: *Therefore while we have time, let us do good to all men, but especially to those who are of the household of faith. And in doing good let us not grow tired, for in due time we shall reap* (Gal 6:10-9).

He warns lest anyone, through lack of patience, grow tired in his good work; lest anyone, either diverted or overcome by temptations, should stop in the middle of his course of praise and glory and his past works be lost, while those things which had begun to be perfect, cease, as it is written: *The justice of the just shall not deliver him in what day soever he shall err* (Ezek 33:12). And again: *Hold fast what you have, that no other receive your crown* (Rev 3:11). And these words urge patient and resolute perseverance, so that he who strives for a crown, now with praise already near, may be crowned because his patience endures.

Patience, however, beloved brethren, not only preserves what is good, but also repels what is evil. Devoted to the Holy Spirit and cleaving to heavenly and divine things, it struggles with the bulwark of its virtues against the acts of the flesh and the body whereby the soul is stormed and captured. Accordingly, let us look at a few out of many of these acts, so that from these few, all the rest may be understood. Adultery, deceit, homicide, are mortal sins. Let patience be strong and stable in the heart, and then the sanctified body and temple of God will not be corrupted by adultery, innocence dedicated to justice will not be infected by the contagion of deceit, and the hand that has held the Eucharist will not be sullied by the blood-stained sword.

Patience and charity

Charity is the bond of brotherhood, the foundation of peace, the steadfastness and firmness of unity; it is greater than both hope and faith (cf 1 Cor 13:13); it excels both good works and suffering of the faith; and, as an eternal virtue, it will abide with us forever in the kingdom of heaven. Take patience away from it, and thus forsaken, it will not last; take away the substance of enduring and tolerating, and it attempts to last with no roots or strength. Accordingly, the Apostle when he was speaking about charity joined tolerance and patience to it, saying: *Charity is magnanimous, charity is kind, charity does not envy, is not puffed up, is not provoked, thinks no evil, loves all things, believes all things, hopes all things, endures all things* (1 Cor 13:4-5-7). By this he showed that charity can persevere steadfastly because it has learned how to endure all things. And in another place he says: *bearing with one another in love, taking every care to preserve the unity of the Spirit in the union of peace* (Eph 4:2-3). He proved that neither unity nor peace can be preserved unless brothers cherish one another with mutual forbearance and preserve the bond of unity with patience as intermediary.

How then will you be able to endure these things – not to swear or curse, not to seek again what has been taken away from you (cf Luke 6:30), on receiving a blow to offer the other cheek also to your assailant (cf Matt 5:39; Luke 6:30), to forgive your brother who offends you not only seventy times seven times, but all his offences without exception (cf Matt 18:21-22), to love your enemies, to pray for your adversaries and persecutors (cf Matt 5:44; Luke 6:27-28), if you do not have the steadfastness of patience and forbearance? We see what happened in the case of Stephen. When he was being killed by the violence and stones of the Jews, he did not ask for vengeance but forgiveness for his murderers, saying: *O Lord, do not lay this sin against them* (cf Acts 7:58-60). So it was most fitting that the first martyr for Christ who, in preceding by his glorious death the martyrs that were to come, was not only a preacher of the Lord's suffering but also an imitator of His most patient gentleness.

What shall I say of anger, of discord, of contention, evils which a Christian ought not to have? Let there be patience in the heart and these evil things can not have a place there; or if they attempt to enter, on being quickly driven out, they depart, so that the heart may continue to be a peaceful dwelling where the God of peace may delight to abide.

Accordingly, the Apostle admonishes and teaches, saying: *Do not grieve the Holy Spirit of God, in whom you were sealed for the day of redemption. Let all bitterness, and wrath, and indignation, and clamour, and reviling, be removed from you* (Eph 4:30-31). For if a Christian has withdrawn from the fury and contention of the flesh as from the storms of the sea, and has now begun to be tranquil and gentle in the harbour of Christ, he ought not to admit into his heart either anger or discord, for it is not right for him to render evil for evil or to hate.

Fruits of impatience

And, beloved brethren, that the good of patience may shine forth more brightly, let us consider, on the other hand, what evil impatience causes.

For as patience is a good of Christ, so, on the contrary, impatience is an evil of the devil; and as the man in whom Christ lives and abides is found to be a patient man, so he is always impatient whose mind is possessed by the wickedness of the devil.

Accordingly, let us consider the origins of impatience. The devil bore with impatience the fact that man was made to the image of God, and for this reason was the first to perish and cause to perish. Adam, in violation of the heavenly command, was incapable of resisting the desire of the deadly food and fell into the death of sin; he did not preserve, under the guardianship of patience, the grace received from God. Cain was impatient of his brother's sacrifice and gift and killed him (cf Gen 3:4).

Because Esau put lower things before higher, he lost his birthright through impatience for the lentils (cf Gen 25:29-34).

Why was the Jewish people faithless and ungrateful toward the divine blessings? Was it not that this crime of impatience first drew them away from God? When they could not bear the delay of Moses speaking with God they dared to demand profane gods, and to proclaim as leader of their journey the head of a calf and an earthly image (cf Exod 32). They never abandoned this very fault of impatience, but always impatient of the divine teaching and guidance, by killing all their prophets and all just men, they hastened to the cross and to the shedding of the blood of the Lord.

Impatience also produces heretics in the Church, and, after the manner of the Jews, it drives them, as rebels against the peace and charity of Christ, to hostile acts and furious hates. And so as not to be tedious by giving details; all things without exception which patience by its works builds unto glory, impatience reduces to ruin.

Exhortation to practise patience

And so, beloved brethren, after the benefits of patience and the evils of impatience have been carefully weighed, let us observe fully and maintain the patience through which we abide in Christ and with Christ are able to come to God.

That patience, rich and manifold, is not confined within a narrow compass or restrained by bounds of small extent. The virtue of patience extends widely and its wealth and abundance proceed from a source that has indeed a single name, but with its full-flowing streams it is diffused through many glorious courses, and nothing in our actions can avail towards the full realisation of merit which does not take the power for its accomplishment from that source.

It is patience that both commends us to God and saves us for God. It is that same patience which tempers anger, bridles the tongue, governs the mind, guards peace, rules discipline, breaks the onslaught of lust, suppresses the violence of pride, extinguishes the fire of dissension, restrains the power of the wealthy, renews the endurance of the poor in bearing their lot, guards the blessed integrity of virgins, the difficult chastity of widows, and the indivisible love of husbands and wives.

It makes men humble in prosperity, brave in adversity, meek in the face of injuries and insults. It teaches us to pardon our offenders quickly; if you yourself should offend, it teaches you to ask pardon often and with perseverance. It vanquishes temptations, sustains persecutions, endures sufferings and martyrdom to the end. It is this patience which strongly fortifies the foundations of our faith. It is this patience which sublimely promotes the growth of hope. It directs our action, so that we can keep to the way of Christ while we make progress because of His forbearance. It ensures our perseverance as sons of God while we imitate the patience of the Father.

De bono patientiae, 13-16, 19-20

Saint Ephraem the Syrian

St Ephraem was born into a pagan family in Nisibis, Mesopotamia, then under Roman rule, around 306 A.D. His father was a pagan and a priest of the goddess Abnil. He was instructed by the bishop of Nisibis, and at the age of eighteen when he converted to Christianity, he was forced to leave the family home. From then on he dedicated himself entirely to God's service, spending his life in study and prayer.

He was ordained a deacon and stayed beside his bishop until the year 363 when the Persians invaded his native city. The Romans ceded Nisibis to Persia, and most of the Christians abandoned it en masse. Later Ephraem went to Edessa where he spent the last years of his life as a hermit, remarkable for his severe asceticism. He died in June 373.

Twenty years after his death St Jerome mentions him as follows in his catalogue of illustrious Christians: "Ephraem, deacon of the Church at Edessa, wrote many works in Syriac, and became so famous that his writings were publicly read in some churches after the sacred scriptures. I have read in Greek a volume of his on the Holy Spirit; though this was only a translation, I recognised therein the sublime genius of the man."

Gifted with an exquisite poetical sense, he composed hundreds of hymns in honour of the Blessed Trinity, on the Incarnation, the eternal truths ... Many are included in the eastern liturgies.

SAINT EPHRAEM THE SYRIAN

GLORY TO THE VIRGIN MARY

O my zither, inventing new reasons for praising the Virgin Mary. Raise your voice and chant to the really marvellous maternity of this virgin, daughter of David, who brought life into the world.

Whoever loves her, admires her. The curious person is filled with shame and keeps silent. He is not inclined to ask how a mother gives birth to a child and still retains her virginity. And although this is more difficult to explain, the unbelievers do not dare investigate matters concerning her Son.

Her Son crushed the wicked serpent and destroyed its head. He cured Eve of the venom which the murderous dragon had deceitfully injected into her, dragging her down to death.

As on Mount Sinai, Mary has given you shelter, but you have not warmed her with your blazing flame, because you have worked in a way that your fire does not spread, nor does it set a flame alight, so that not even the Seraphims can see in its light.

He who is eternal is called the new Adam, because he dwelt in the womb of the daughter of David and in Her he became man, without seed and without pain to her. Blessed be your name forever.

The tree of life, which grew in the middle of Paradise, did not give man fruit which would give him life. The fruit of the womb of Mary gave its very self to man and gifted

GLORY TO THE VIRGIN MARY

him its life.

The Word of the Lord descended from his throne; he came to a young woman and dwelt in her. She conceived him and gave birth to him. Great is the mystery of the most pure Virgin: it goes beyond all praise.

In Eden Eve became a prisoner to sin. The evil serpent drew up, signed and sealed the sentence by which her descendants would be wounded, at birth, by death.

And because of his deceit, the old dragon saw the sin of Eve multiplied. It was a woman who believed the lie of her seducer, obeying a demon and lowered the dignity of man.

Eve came to be a prisoner to sin, but the debt passed on to Mary, so that the daughter might pay the dues of the mother and wipe off the sentence which her offspring had transmitted to all generations.

Mary carried fire in her hands and protected the flame within her arms; she brought her breasts to the pyre, and gave suck to Him who gives nourishment to all things. Who is able to speak of Her?

Worldly men multiplied the evils and the thorns which smothered the earth. They introduced death. The Son of Mary filled the orb with life and peace.

Worldly men submerged the world with illness and sorrows. They opened the gate for death to enter and move into the orb. The Son of Mary took upon his shoulders the sorrows of the world to save it.

Mary is a clear fountain, with no troubled waters. She welcomes into her womb the river of life, which with its water irrigated the world and gave life to the dead.

You are the immaculate sanctuary in whom the God king of time rested. In you by a great miracle there took place the mystery by which God was made man and man was called Son by the Father.

Mary is the vine of the blessed stock of David. Her branches gave the seed of grapes full of the blood of life. Adam drank from that wine, was resuscitated, and could return to Eden.

Two mothers raised two very different sons: one, a man whom she cursed; and Mary, through whom God filled the world with blessings.

Blessed are you, Mary, daughter of David, and blessed is the fruit you have given us. Blessed be the Father who has sent us his Son for our salvation, and Blessed be the Holy Spirit who showed us the mystery! Blessed be his name.

Carmen 18, 1

Saint Ephraem the Syrian

MARY'S CRADLE SONG

I have looked on in astonishment at Mary suckling Him who nourishes all peoples, but who has made himself a baby. He Who fills the world with himself has stayed in the womb of a girl...

A great sun has been caught and hidden in a splendid cloud. An adolescent has come to be the Mother of him who has created man and the world.

She carried a child, she caressed him, she embraced him, she whispered most beautiful words to him and adored him saying: My Master, give yourself to me for me to embrace you.

As you are my Son, I will rock you with my lullabyes. I am your Mother but I will give honour to you. My Son, I have engendered you, but You are older than I am. My Lord, I have carried you in my womb, but You sustain me on my feet.

My mind is disturbed through fear; grant me the strength to praise you. I don't know how to explain that you are silent, when I know all thunder resounds in you.

You have been born of me like a little one; but you are as strong as a giant. You are *Admirable* as Isaiah called you, when he prophesied about you.

Here, all of You is with me, and nevertheless you are totally hidden in your father. The heights of the heavens are filled with your majesty, and yet my womb has not been too small for you.

Your Home is within me and in the heavens. With the heavens I will praise you. The heavenly creatures look at me with admiration and called me Blessed.

May heaven support me with its embrace, because I have been better honoured than it. For heaven has not been your mother; but you made it your throne. How much more is the Mother of the King venerated than his throne! I will bless you, Lord, because you have wished me to be your Mother. I will celebrate with beautiful songs.

O giant who sustains the earth and has wanted her to sustain you, may you be Blessed. Glory to you, O Rich One, for you have made yourself the Son of a pauper.

May my *magnificat* be for you, who is older than everyone, and nevertheless, having been made a child, you descended to me. Sit on my knees, in spite of the whole world, the highest peaks and the deepest abyss, hanging from you...

You are with me, and all the angelic choirs adore you. While I cradle you within my arms, you are carried by the cherubims.

The heavens are full of your glory, and yet the womb of a daughter of the earth completely contains you. You live in a blaze among celestial creatures, yet you do not burn earthly creatures.

The seraphims proclaim you three times Holy. What more can I say, O Lord? The cherubims bless Thee trembling; how are you going to be honoured by my songs?

Listen to me now and come to me old Eve, our mother of old; raise your head, the head that was humiliated by the shame of an orchard.

Uncover your countenance and be happy with yourself, because you have flung away your shame. Listen to words full of peace, because a daughter of yours has paid your debt.

The serpent who seduced you has been crushed by you, a shoot which has been born in my womb. For your sake, the cherubim and his sword have been withdrawn, so that Adam can return to the paradise from which he had been expelled.

Adam and Eve will turn to you and gather from me the fruit of life; through you he will recover the sweetness of his lips, which the forbidden fruit had turned bitter.

The expelled servants will return through you, so that they may obtain those goods which they had been relieved of. For them it will be a suit of glory, to cover their nakedness.

Hymn, 18, 1-23

Saint Ephraem the Syrian

Mother Most Admirable

The Virgin Mary invites me to sing the mystery which I contemplate with admiration.

Son of God, give me your admirable gift; make me temper my lyre and may I obtain the details of the absolutely beautiful image of the truly loving Mother.

The Virgin Mary gave her Son to the world while remaining a virgin; she nurses him who feeds the nations, and in her chaste bosom she sustains him who maintains the universe. She is virgin and mother. What isn't she?

Holy in body, simply beautiful in soul, pure in spirit, sincere in intelligence, perfection in senses, pure of heart, and loyal, she possesses all the virtues.

In Mary the whole lineage of virgins rejoices, for one of them has given birth to the One who sustains creation, to the One who has freed the human race which groaned in slavery.

In Mary, old Adam rejoices, the one hurt by the serpent. For Mary gives Adam a line of descent which allows him to crush the cursed serpent, and heal his mortal wound.

Priests rejoice in the Blessed Virgin. She has given the world an eternal priest, who is at the same time a Victim. He has brought ancient sacrifices to an end, having made of himself a Victim which appeases the Father.

In Mary, all the prophets rejoice. In her their visions have been fulfilled, their prophecies have been realised, their oracles have been confirmed.

In Mary all the patriarchs rejoice. Just as she received the blessings promised to them, so She has made them perfect in her Son. Through him the prophets, the just and the priests, have found themselves purified.

In place of the bitter fruit collected by Eve from the fatal tree, Mary has given fruit, which is sweetness itself, to men. Behold the entire world takes delight in Mary's fruit.

The tree of life, hidden in the midst of Paradise, has surged forth in Mary and has spread its shadow over the universe; it has showered its fruits equally over peoples near and far.

Mary has woven a garment of glory and has given it to our first father. He had hidden his nakedness among the trees, but is now vested with purity, with virtue and with beauty. What his wife had knocked down, his daughter raises up; sustained by her, like the hero, he gets up.

Eve and the serpent had laid a trap, and Adam fell into it. Mary and her royal Son bent over and drew them back from the abyss.

The virginal vine had produced a bunch of grapes whose gentle weight had brought joy back to the afflicted. Adam and Eve in their anguish enjoyed the wine of life, and found full and firm consolation.

Hymn to the Blessed Virgin Mary

Saint Ephraem the Syrian

Pray Always and Everywhere

It is undoubtedly good not to sin! Nonetheless, let sinners not despair, but be sorry for their sins in such a way that by this sorrow they come to attain eternal bliss. It is good, then, as our Lord said, *to pray always and not lose heart* (Luke 18:1). And the Apostle insists: *pray without ceasing* (1 Thess 5:17), that is, at night, during the day, in fact, all the time. And not only when you are in a church, while the rest of the time you do not think about it at all. But while you are working, while you sleep, while you are on a journey, while you eat, while you drink or are resting, do not cease to pray, for you do not know when the moment will come when your soul will be recalled. Don't wait until Sunday comes, or a feast day or a holy day, or a visit to a church; but, as the prophet David said, pray *in any place on earth* (Ps 102:22).

So, do pray, whether you are in a church, or in your home or in the countryside; whether you are tending to your flocks, constructing a building or attending a meeting. Wherever you can, get down on your knees; and when this is not possible, call on God mentally, in the afternoon, in the morning or at noon. For if you put prayer ahead of any other activity, and when you get out of bed in the morning you direct your first thoughts to God, then sin will have no power over you.

Prayer preserves temperance, puts a brake on anger, moderates high spirits, leads to modesty, accepts injury without hate, destroys envy, facilitates piety. Prayer is strength for the body, and a sure guide in the good administration of family affairs, a foundation for rights and of laws, the upholder of society, the sepulchre for war and the guardian of peace.

Prayer is the seal of virginity, it guards matrimony, provides a refuge for travellers, looks after those who are asleep, gives confidence to those on guard, gives fertility to the harvest, and provides a safe haven for sailors. Prayer is a protection for those in prison, a respite for those enchained, consolation for those who are depressed, tumultuous for the cheerful, balsam for those in tears, a crown for spouses, rest for the dying.

Prayer is a dialogue with God, an honour proper to the angels. Prayer brings good nearer, keeps evil at a distance, and facilitates the conversion of sinners. Prayer obtained a whale as a seat for Jonah; it drew Ezechiel back from the gates of death and brought him back to life; it converted into dew the flames of fire which threatened the three young men in Babylon. On the strength of prayer Elias entreated heaven so that for three years and six months it should not rain.

Don't you see, my brethren, how valuable prayer is? There is nothing in human life which is more precious. Never consent to being separated from her, or ever abandon it. But, as Our Lord said, let us pray so that our work may not be in vain.

Obstacles to prayer

But when you go to pray, if you have a grudge against someone, forget about it, so that your heavenly father can forgive you your sins (cf Matt 6:14). Beloved, do realise that if we are in enmity with someone, in vain do we raise up our hearts to God while we are at work. For once again the Lord says, *When you are offering your gift at the altar, if you remember that your brother or sister has something against you, leave your gift there before the altar and go; first be reconciled to your brother or sister; and then come and offer your gift* (Matt 5:23-24). What is clear is that if you do not act like this, your offerings will be worthless; but if you do carry out the Lord's mandate, then you will be able to go to him and boldly say: 'Lord, forgive my offences, as I have forgiven my brother, as you commanded. I, who am a sinner, have forgiven.' And he, who loves humankind in a special way, will reply: 'If you have pardoned, I too will forgive you; if you have cast it out of your mind, I too will forget about it; for I have power on earth to forgive sins.' Forgive, and you will be forgiven. Don't you see how incomparable is God's graciousness, how immense is the goodness of the Lord?

Fruits of prayer

Prayer, then, is a consistent armour, infinite treasure, unending patrimony, a sheltered port, a basis for tranquillity; cause, source and root of innumerable goods, more powerful than a whole kingdom... And when I speak of prayer, I am not referring to a careless prayer, done in any old way, but prayer which is done with effort, leading to compunction and with a clear mind: this is prayer which leads one to Heaven. Water, if it is allowed to, spreads on a plain and simple surface and covers a vast area, but it cannot rise to any height. If it is restrained and contained in one's cupped hands, it can be taken from the lowest to the highest places. So too the human mind. If it is let loose, it spills over and strays; but if it is completely concentrated and is aware of its great poverty and weakness, it is raised on high through clear and abundant prayer.

Look, the prayer which is heard most is the one which is based on self-effacement, as the Prophet gives us to understand when he goes to speak with God: *entering crestfallen, I call out and he hears me*. Let us then, temper our conscience, humble our spirit with the recollection of our offences, not so as to fall into anguish but to be vigilant and to position oneself so as to be able to receive the celestial gifts.

For someone could wonder: 'Where am I going to place my trust? I am full of iniquity; I am incapable of even opening my mouth.' This is a diabolical temptation, a pretext for cowardice: what does the devil want but to close off the routes which lead towards God! Don't you trust in anything? This is the great trust: not to trust oneself; while to have confidence in oneself is to open the gates to perdition. For the greater the good works you may do, and the freer from evil you may believe yourself to be, if you place all your confidence in yourself, in vain have you done all your prayer.

On the other hand, although your conscience may be weighed down by the heaviest of sins, if this leads you to be convinced that you are the last among men, you will be able to abandon yourself totally into God's arms. For it is not humility for a sinner to confess being a sinner, but knowing his misery and his needs, is proud of nothing to such a degree that he can join Paul in saying: *even though I have nothing on my conscience, it is not because of this that I am justified*. And in another place he says, *Christ Jesus came into the world to save sinners – of whom I am the foremost* (1 Tim 1:15). This is humility: when he who has carried out great deeds does not become conceited, but considers himself the most miserable among all men. Not only does God receive and embrace those who present themselves as helpless, but also those who openly confess their sins: he is pleased with them and fills them with good will.

How to pray

And so, I ask, exhort and beseech you to open your heart to God diligently. It is certainly not a matter of publicly confessing your sins, but of laying bare your conscience to God: show him your injuries and ask him for the medicine. Present them to him so that he does not scold you but cures you; for although you would like to keep them to yourself, He knows and sees all things. Speak to him, then, and you will end up winning: expose your miseries and you will be cleaned of all your misdemeanours and you will be freed from public disgrace on judgement day.

The three young men thrown into the fire for their belief in the name of the Lord still proclaim: *we have sinned and broken your law in turning away from you; in all matters we have sinned grievously* (Dan 3:29). And what about us? If we, like them, exclaim, 'How can I be so bold as to speak?,' we too will win Our Lord's favour.

The power of prayer was stronger than the strength of the fire; it held back the lion's anger, ended wars, quietened confrontations, took the brunt of tempests, expelled demons, opened the gates to heaven, broke away the chains of death, cured illnesses, eradicated violence, rebuilt devastated cities, brought completely to an end the mockery of men and plagues sent from on high.

But, let me insist that I am not referring to prayer which consists only in moving one's lips, but a prayer which comes from the depths of the soul. The deeper the trees are rooted, the stronger can be the winds they are buffeted by without being uprooted, for their roots are firmly grasping the bowels of the earth. So too with prayer born and rooted in the intimacy of the soul: not only do they reach the heights, but they cannot be felled by any wilful distraction. For as the Prophet said: *Out of the*

depths I cry to you, O Lord (Ps 130:1).
  To Him be glory for ever and ever. Amen.

Sermone de oratione, I-II, 1-2, 4

Saint Ephraem the Syrian

A HYMN TO MARY

Let us turn our gaze to Mary again. When Gabriel entered into her chamber and began to speak with her, She asked: *How can this be?* (Luke 1:34). The servant of the Holy Spirit replied to her saying: *for nothing will be impossible with God* (Luke 1:37). And She, firmly believing what she had just heard, said: *Here I am, the servant of the Lord* (Luke 1:38).

At that instant the Lord descended upon Her, and entered into Her, and made his resting place in Her, without anyone being aware of it. He was conceived without risk to her virginity. he became a baby within her womb, while the entire world was filled with him. ... When you hear the word of God being spoken about, keep silent; may the announcement of Gabriel be impressed upon your spirit. Nothing is difficult for his lofty Majesty, who has come down to be born among us, from us, for us.

Today, Mary is heaven for us, because she takes us to God. The Highest has made himself anonymous, and has taken up residence in Her. He has made himself little in the Virgin Mary so as to make us great... The judgements of the prophets and of the just have been fulfilled in Mary. Light has surged from Her for us, and the darkness of paganism has disappeared.

Mary has many names. It is a great joy for me to call her by those names. She is the fortress in which the powerful King of Kings resides. But he did not leave from there in the same way in which he entered. In Her he took on flesh, and then emerged. She is also a new heaven, because the King of Kings lives there. There he entered and later came out dressed for the exterior world. She is the fountain which brings forth living water for the thirsty. Those who have enjoyed this drink bear fruit one hundred-fold.

The new king

This day is not like the first day of creation. On that occasion creatures were called into being. On this day the earth has been renewed and blessed with reference to Adam, because of whom it had been cursed. Adam and Eve, through sin, had brought death to the world. But the Lord of the world has given us a new life in Mary. Life, which has killed death, entered through the same gate where death entered. Mary's arms have carried Him whom the cherubims support. This God, whom the universe cannot contain, has been clasped by Mary. The king – in whose presence the angels, spiritual creatures, tremble – is in the bosom of the Virgin Mary, making her caress him as a babe. Heaven is the throne of his Majesty, and he seats himself on Mary's knees. The earth is his footstool, and he hops onto her like a child. His extended hand points to the limits of the earth, and on dust he plays like a little boy.

O Happy Adam, who in the birth of Christ you have rediscovered the glory you had lost. Have you ever seen clay serving as the dress of the potter? Who has seen fire enclosed in swaddling clothes? God has debased himself to all of this for love of man. Thus has the Lord humiliated himself out of love for his servant, who had been blindly praised, and on the advice of the murderous Evil One, had trampled on the divine command. The author of the Commandment humiliated himself to raise us up.

Let us give thanks to divine mercy, who has come down upon the inhabitants of the earth so that this sick world may be cured by the Divine doctor. Praise be to him and to the Father who sent him. And praise be to the Holy Spirit for ever and ever.

Hymn for the Birth of Christ

Saint Zeno of Verona

Zeno was born in Mauritania, and spent most of his life in northern Italy. He was bishop of Verona, and is today considered the Patron of that city. Zeno is remembered for his fight against the decadence of paganism, his struggle against the Arian heresy and against certain abuses which had filtered into Christian communities. Zeno is included in the Roman Martyrology on 12 April, martyred under Gallienus in 380.

He spent all his energy in the care of the faithful. His vigorous sermons, compiled after his death, are a witness to this. They state the central truths of the faith and exhort the practice of the Christian virtues. Many of these sermons were directed to catechumens as an immediate preparation for baptism. They reveal that Zeno was a great orator with a deep knowledge of Christian and pagan works.

Among his brief sermons or *tractatus* the one dedicated to the three theological virtues merit special attention. It is one of the first systematic works of ecclesiastical literature on faith, hope and charity.

St Zeno teaches in a clear and succinct way that these theological virtues are the basis of Christian life and may not be separated from one another, for they form the weft of our union with God.

Saint Zeno of Verona

FAITH, HOPE AND CHARITY

There are three things which are fundamental for Christian perfection: faith, hope and charity. These three virtues are so interwoven with one another that each one is necessary for the others.

If one does not progress in hope, of what use is faith? If one does not have faith, how can hope be born? And if one's faith and hope are denied charity, each will be useless, for faith does not operate without love, nor hope without faith. Consequently, the Christian who wishes to be perfect has to be well grounded in the three: if one of them is missing, he will not attain perfection in his work.

Hope
In the first place we are offered hope of future things. Without this the value of things present cannot have any meaning. Worse is to follow. Take away hope and entire humanity is paralysed. Take away hope and all the arts, skills and virtues cease. Take away hope and all is destroyed. What is the child doing beside his teacher if he cannot expect his classes to be fruitful? Which sailor will venture to the ocean amongst the waves, if there is no profit to be expected or no hope of the ship reaching its destination? Which soldier will scorn not only the discomforts of a cruel winter or a torrid summer, but his very self, if he is not able to cherish hopes of future glory?

Which farmer will scatter seed if he cannot conceive of reaping the harvest as a reward for his sweat? Which Christian will adhere to Christ through faith, if he does not believe that the time will ever come when he will receive the eternal happiness promised to him?

My brethren, we must therefore tenaciously embrace hope. Among all the virtues, let us guard it most carefully, and may we constantly grow in it. Hope is an immovable foundation of our life, both an unconquered bastion and a lance against the assaults of the devil, impenetrable armour plate of our soul. Hope is profitable and true knowledge of law, terror of devils, strength of martyrs, splendour and rampart of the Church.

Hope is God's servant, Christ's friend, invited guest of the Holy Spirit. The present and the future are subject to her. The present because she ignores it; the future because she knows beforehand that it belongs to her. She does not fear that it will not come to pass, for it has always been within the ambit of her power. Abraham, *hoping against hope, believed that he would become the father of many nations* (Rom 4:18). 'Against hope' means to say that it seemed impossible and could not be foreseen. But it is made possible by this hope when one trusts in God's word without any doubt and with great firmness. For the Lord says *all things can be done for the one who believes* (Mark 9:22); and Abraham *believed in the Lord, and the Lord reckoned it to him as righteousness* (Gen 15:6). He is righteous for having been faithful, for the righteous man believes (cf Gal 3:6). He is faithful because he believed in God: if he did not have faith he would neither be just nor could he be the father of peoples. It is clear for this reason that the nature of hope and faith are one and inseparable: if either one is lacking in man, the two die.

Faith

Faith, strictly speaking, is for ourselves. The Lord has said, *Your faith has made you well* (Mark 10:52). If it is ours, then, we should treasure it as our own, so that with good reason we can hope for things which we do not yet possess. No one honours the deserter with the booty of a triumphant campaign. And it is even written that *to those who have more will be given, and they will have an abundance; but from those who have nothing, even what they have will be taken away* (Matt 13:12).

It was through faith, my brethren, that Enoch obtained from God the favour of being bodily taken up, against the law of nature. Through faith Noah saved himself and could find no one to speak about the flood which had taken place. Through faith Abraham became friends with God; through faith Isaac was distinguished from the others (cf Heb 11:5, 7, 8, 20). Through faith Joseph had Egypt submit itself to his authority (cf Gen 41-42). This faith made a glass wall in the Red Sea for Moses (cf Exod 14:22). It brought to a standstill the sun and the moon, so that, giving up their normal course, they submitted themselves to Joshua's command (Josh 10:12-13); it gave the defenceless David a victory over Goliath (cf 1 Kings 17); and Job was not discouraged when frequently attacked by serious evils (Job 1-2). Faith was the medicine in Tobias' blindness (cf Tob 11); it was Daniel's saving when the lions' mouths were shut (cf Dan 6:22); and for Jonah, the whale became a boat (cf Jonah 2). Faith was the only winner in the courageous actions of the Maccabean family of brothers (cf 2 Mach 7), and she made the fire harmless in the case of the three young men (cf Dan 3).

This same faith led Peter to walk on the sea (cf Matt 14:29) and was the cause of the Apostles being able to cure many people of their ulcers and contagious diseases, giving a clear skin to the deformed leper. It is through this faith, I would add, that they were able to order the blind to see, the deaf to hear, the dumb to speak, the lame to walk, to strengthen the paralysed, to make demons flee from the people they possessed. Relatively frequently during the funeral itself, they brought the dead person back to life, so that all could see; what until that moment had been tears of sorrow now turned to tears of joy.

Charity

But, my brethren, it is a long job to detail all the acts of faith, above all because charity presents us with some even more prodigious acts. It is logical that this be the case, for charity is raised up above all the other virtues in such a way that she is truly queen of all of them.

Although faith triumphs with all kinds of marvellous deeds, and hope offers a great number of good things, neither one nor the other can be sustained without love. Not faith, if one does not love oneself, nor hope, if it is not loved. Moreover, faith is useful only for oneself; charity for every one. Faith does not struggle for nothing; charity is given even to those who are ungrateful. Faith is not transferable to someone else; with charity it is an understatement to say that it reaches out to another person, for it benefits all people. Faith is that of a few; charity that of all.

I would add to this that hope and faith exist in time, while charity knows no limits (cf 1 Cor 13). It grows all the time, and the more it is practised by those who mutually love one another, greater is the union between the two. Charity makes no distinction between people, for she does not know adulation. Charity seeks no honours because she is not ambitious; she has no fixation on sex because for her the two are but one; she does not practise only at certain times because she is not capricious. She is not envious because she is not aware of what envy is; she is not puffed up because she fosters humility; she does not think evil of anyone because she is simple and straightforward; she is not driven by anger because she receives harsh words joyfully; she does not cheat because she is a guardian of the faith; she is not in want of things, because she experiences no needs other than those of her being.

Charity preserves the fields, the cities, the peoples; she maintains peace treaties. She keeps the swords of kings fast by their sides. She scorches out wars, erases arguments, empties privileges, avoids courts, eradicates hatred, snuffs out anger. Charity goes across seas, circumscribes the world, distributes essential goods among nations through mutual agreements. What nature has denied some areas, charity supplies. The charity of conjugal love unites two people into just one flesh with a venerable sacrament. She gives to existing humanity everything that is born. Through charity one loves one's own spouse, children show that they are proud of their origins, and their parents live as true parents. We owe to her the fact that others become our neighbours and friends, just as close or even closer than our own selves. That we love our servants as our children and that they happily serve us as their masters, we owe to charity. She enables us to love not only acquaintances and friends, but also those whom we have never seen. To charity we owe, finally, our recognition of the virtues of our predecessors through books, or to our recognition of books through their virtues.

Tractatus de spe, fide et caritate, 1-IV

Saint Zeno

JOB, A TYPE OF CHRIST

As far as can be understood, dear brothers, Job was a type of Christ, and a comparison between them shows the truth of this. God himself called Job a righteous man. And God is righteousness itself, the source from which all who are blessed drink, and of him it is said: *for you the sun of righteousness shall rise.*

Job is called truthful. And the Lord is the very truth as he said in the gospel: *I am the way and the truth.*

Job was a rich man. But what is richer than the Lord. All the rich are his slaves and to him belongs the whole world and every creature, as holy David says: *The earth is the Lord's and the fulness thereof, the world and those who dwell therein.*

The devil tempted Job three times. In the same way, as the evangelist tells us, he tried to tempt the Lord. Job lost everything that he owned. And the Lord left behind his heavenly goods for love of us and made himself poor that he might make us rich.

The raging devil brought Job's sons to destruction. So, in their madness, the people of the Pharisees slew the prophets, the sons of the Lord.

Job was infected with ulcers. And the Lord, taking our flesh, was befouled with the filth of the sins of the whole human race.

Job's wife urged him to sin. And the synagogue did its best to make the Lord follow the corrupt observances of their elders.

It is told that Job's friends insulted him. So, too, did the priests and worshippers insult the Lord. Job sat upon a dunghill full of worms. The Lord also moved about on the real dunghill of the filth of this world amidst men seething with all manner of vices and lusts, which are the real worms.

Job recovered both his health and his position. But the Lord at his resurrection held out to those who believe in him not merely health but immortality, and took back to himself dominion over all nature as he himself bears witness when he says: *All things have been delivered to me by my father.*

Job begot new sons to replace those he had lost. The Lord too begot holy sons, the apostles, in place of the prophets.

Job blessed, rested in peace. But the Lord remains blessed for ever before all ages, from all ages and throughout all ages.

Sermon 15:2

Saint Cyril of Jerusalem

Cyril was born in 314 A.D. He was ordained to the priesthood by St Maximus. Towards the middle of the fourth century he was consecrated bishop of Jerusalem. He was a great adherent to the faith of the Church solemnly declared at the Council of Nicaea. As a consequence, for nearly a quarter of a century the Arians persecuted him, sending him into exile on three occasions, beginning in 357.

After 378, when he was able to return definitively to his diocese, he spent the rest of his life in the spiritual reform of the people of his diocese, helped in this task from 380 by St Gregory of Nyssa. He attended the Council of Constantinople in 381, and died at the age of 72 on 18 March 386.

Of his works which have been preserved are the *Catechesis*, among the most precious in Christian antiquity. They comprise an Introductory address, 18 instructions delivered in Lent to those preparing for baptism. Another five take the term *mystagogical* as they deal with the sacraments or sacred mysteries, whose detailed explanation was reserved to those who had been baptised; they were delivered during Easter week. They seem to have been spoken *ex tempore*, and written down afterwards. Their style is admirably clear, dignified and logical. In the third of this series, St Cyril describes the nature of the effects of Confirmation, which gives the faithful a spiritual age of majority and converts them into soldiers of Christ.

Other extant works include a sermon on the Pool of Bethzatha, and a letter to Emperor Constantius. St Cyril's teachings on the Blessed Sacrament are of primary importance.

Saint Cyril of Jerusalem

THE HOLY CHRISM

But you have an anointing from God and you know all things, etc... that we may have confidence and may not shrink ashamed from him at his coming (1 John 2:20-28).

Baptized into Christ and *clothed with Christ* (Gal 3:27), you have been shaped to the likeness of the Son of God (cf Rom 8:29). For God in *predestining us to be adopted as his sons* (cf Eph 1:5), has *conformed us to the body of the glory* (Phil 3:21) of Christ, as *partakers* (Heb 3:14) of Christ. Therefore, you are rightly called *Christs*, i.e., *Anointed ones*: it was of you that God said: *Touch not my Christs* (Ps 104:15). Now, you became Christs by receiving the antitype of the Holy Spirit; everything has been wrought in you *likewise* because you are likenesses of Christ.

He bathed in the river Jordan and, after imparting the fragrance of His Godhead to the waters, came up from them. The Holy Spirit visited Him in essential presence, like resting upon like (cf Sir 13:16). Similarly for you, after you had ascended from the sacred streams, there was an anointing with chrism, the antitype of that with which Christ was anointed, that is, of the Holy Spirit. Concerning this Spirit the blessed Isaiah, in the prophetical book which bears his name, said, speaking in the person of the Lord: *The Spirit of the Lord is upon me because he has anointed me. He has sent me to preach glad tidings to the poor* (cf Is 61:1).

The ointment of anointing

For Christ was not anointed by men with material oil or balsam; His Father, appointing Him Saviour of the whole world, anointed Him with the Holy Spirit as Peter says: *Jesus of Nazareth, whom God anointed with the Holy Spirit* (cf Acts 10:38). The prophet David also made a proclamation: *Your throne, O God, is forever and ever: the sceptre of your kingdom is a sceptre of uprightness. You have loved justice, and hated iniquity: therefore God, your God, has anointed you with the oil of gladness above your fellows* (Ps 44:7-8).

As Christ was really crucified and buried and rose again, and you at Baptism are privileged to be crucified, buried, and raised along with Him in a likeness, so also with the chrism. Christ was anointed with a mystical oil of gladness; that is, with the Holy Spirit, called *oil of gladness* because He is the cause of spiritual gladness; so you, being anointed with ointment, have become partakers and fellows of Christ.

Beware of supposing that this ointment is mere ointment. Just as after the invocation of the Holy Spirit the eucharistic bread is no longer ordinary bread, but the Body of Christ, so this holy oil, in conjunction with the invocation, is no longer simple or common oil, but becomes the gracious gift of Christ and the Holy Spirit, producing the presence of His deity. With this ointment your forehead and sense organs are sacramentally anointed, in such a way that while your body is anointed with the visible oil, your soul is sanctified by the holy, quickening Spirit.

You are anointed first upon the forehead to rid you of the shame which the first human transgressor bore about with him everywhere; so you may *reflect as in a glass the splendour of the Lord* (2 Cor 3:18). Then upon the

THE HOLY CHRISM   133

ears, to receive ears quick to hear the divine mysteries, the ears of which Isaiah said: *The Lord gave me also an ear to hear* (cf Is 50:4), and the Lord Jesus in the Gospels: *He who has ears to hear, let him hear* (Matt 11:15). Then upon the nostrils, that, scenting the divine oil, you may say: *We are the incense offered by Christ to God, in the case of those who are on the way to salvation* (2 Cor 2:15). Then on the breast, that *putting on the breastplate of justice you may be able to withstand the wiles of the Devil* (Eph 6:14). For as Christ after His Baptism and the visitation of the Holy Spirit went forth and overthrew the adversary, so must you after holy Baptism and the mystical Chrism, clad in the armour of the Holy Spirit, stand firm against the forces of the Enemy and overthrow them, saying: *I can do all things in the Christ who strengthens me.*

Consequences of receiving the Chrism

Once privileged to receive the holy Chrism, you are called Christians and have a name that bespeaks your new birth. Before admission to Baptism and the grace of the Holy Spirit you were not strictly entitled to this name but were like people on the way towards being Christians.

You must know that this Chrism is prefigured in the Old Testament. When Moses, conferring on his brother the divine appointment, was ordaining him high priest, he anointed him after he had bathed in water, and thenceforward he was called *Christ* (Lev 8:5), (*anointed*), clearly after the figurative Chrism. Again, the high priest, when installing Solomon as king, anointed him after he had bathed in Gihon (1 Kings 1:38). But what was done to them in figure was done to you, not in figure but in truth, because your salvation began from Him who was anointed by the Holy Spirit in truth. Christ is the beginning of your salvation, since He is truly the *first handful* of dough and you *the whole lump* (cf Rom 11:16): and if the first handful be holy, plainly its holiness will permeate the lump.

Keep this Chrism unsullied; for it shall teach you all things if it abide in you, as you heard the blessed John declaring just now as he spoke about the Chrism. For this holy thing is both a heavenly protection for the body and salvation for the soul. It was of this anointing that in ancient times the blessed Isaiah prophesied saying: *And the Lord shall make unto all people in this mountain* (elsewhere also he calls the Church a mountain, as when he says: *And in the last days the mountain of the Lord shall be manifest...* (Is 2:2),) and *they shall drink wine, they shall drink gladness, they shall anoint themselves with ointment* (Is 5:6). To alert you to the mystical meaning of *ointment* here, he says: *All this deliver to the nations: for the counsel of the Lord is upon all the nations* (Is 25:7).

Anointed, then, with this holy oil, keep it in you unsullied, without blame, making progress through good works and becoming well-pleasing to *the trail-blazer of our salvation* (Heb 2:10; 2 Cor 5:9), Christ Jesus, to whom be glory forever and ever. Amen.

Third Lecture on the mysteries

Saint Cyril of Jerusalem

THE DIGNITY OF MAN

After the knowledge of this august and glorious and all-holy faith, next know yourself for what you are, that you are a man, twofold in nature, composed of soul and body, and that the same God is the creator of the soul and the body. Know also that this soul of yours is free, self-determining, the fairest work of God, made according to the image of its Creator, immortal because of God who makes it immortal, a living being, rational, imperishable, because of Him who has conferred these gifts; having power to do as it will. For it is not according to your birth that you sin, nor is it according to fortune that you fornicate, nor as some foolishly say, do the conjunctions of the stars compel you to cleave to wantonness. Why, to avoid confessing your own evil deeds, do you ascribe the blame to the guiltless stars? Pay no attention henceforth to astrologers, for Scripture challenges them saying: *Let the astrologers come forward to save you*(Is 47:13), and further on: *Behold they all shall be consumed by fire as stubble and they shall not deliver their soul from flame* (cf Is 47:14, Sept).

Learn this also, that before the soul comes into the world, it has committed no sin; but though we came into the world sinless, we now of our own choice commit sin. Listen not, I pray you, to anyone who gives a perverse interpretation of the words: *If I do what I do not wish* (Rom 7:16), but remember Him who says: *If you are willing, and obey, you shall eat the good things of the land;*

but if you refuse and resist, the sword shall consume you (Is 1:19-20).

Freedom and immortality

The soul is immortal, and all souls are alike, both of men and women; only their bodily members are differentiated. There is not a class of souls sinning by nature and a class of souls acting justly by nature. But both act from choice, since the substance of souls is of one kind and alike in all. I realize that I am talking at length; but what is to be put above salvation? Are you unwilling to take the trouble to receive provision for the way against the heretics? Are you unwilling to learn the twists in the road, to avoid falling down the precipice through ignorance? If your teachers count it no little gain for you to learn these things, ought not you, the learner, gladly receive the multitude of the things that are told you?

The soul possesses freedom; and though the devil can make suggestions, he does not have the power to compel against the will. He brings to your mind the thought of fornication; if you will, you accept it; if you will not, you do not accept it. For, if you committed fornication by necessity, then why did God prepare Gehenna? If you acted justly by nature and not by choice, why did God prepare ineffable crowns? The sheep is meek, but it has never been crowned for its meekness; for its meekness comes not from choice but from nature.

You have been taught, beloved, the lore of the soul. Now receive as best you can the doctrine concerning the body also. Let no one tell you that this body of ours is a stranger to God; for those who believe that the body is something alien readily abuse it to fornication. Yet what is it that they complain of in this wonderful body? For what does it lack in comeliness? What is there in its structure

The Dignity of Man

that is not wrought skilfully?

Do not tell me that the body is the cause of sin. For, if the body is the cause of sin, how is it that a corpse does not sin? Put a sword in the right hand of one just dead and no murder takes place. Let all kinds of beautiful women pass before the body of a young man recently dead and no desire of fornication arises. Why? Because the body of itself does not sin, but the soul through the body. The body is the soul's instrument, its cloak and garment. If then it is given up to fornication by the soul, it becomes unclean; but if it dwells with a holy soul, it becomes a temple of the Holy Spirit. It is not I who say these things. No, it is the Apostle Paul who has said: *Do you not know that your members are the temple of the Holy Spirit, who is in you?* (1 Cor 6:19). Defile not, then, your flesh in fornication. Stain not your fairest garment. But if you have stained it, now cleanse it by repentance; for it is the time for purification.

Chastity in marriage and virginity

Let this doctrine of chastity be heeded above all by those who are single and virgins, those who are establishing in the world an angelic mode of life, and after them, by the rest of the people of the Church. A great crown is laid up for you, brethren; barter not a great dignity for petty pleasure. Listen to the Apostle saying: *Lest there be any immoral, or profane person, such as Esau, who for one meal sold his birthright* (Heb 12:16). Once enrolled in the angelic books for your profession of chastity, take care that you are not blotted out thereafter for practising fornication.

Again, because you practise chastity, do not be puffed up with conceit against those who live in the humbler state of matrimony. *For let marriage be held in honour, and let the marriage bed be undefiled* (Heb 13:4), as the Apostle says. For you who keep your purity, have you not been born of married persons? Do not, therefore, because you possess gold, condemn the silver. But let those be of good cheer also, who, being married, use marriage rightfully; who order their marriage according to law, not making it wanton by uncontrolled licence; who have entered into marriage for the sake of begetting children, not for self-indulgence.

Let not those who have been married only once find fault with those who have indulged in a second marriage. For, while continence is a noble and admirable thing, it is also allowable to enter upon a second marriage, that the weak may not commit fornication. For, *it is good for them if they so remain, even as I,* says the Apostle. *But if they do not have self-control, let them marry, for it is better to marry than to burn* (1 Cor 7:8-9). But let all other things be put far away, fornication, adultery, and every kind of licentiousness; and let the body be kept pure for the Lord, that the Lord also may respect the body.

Let the body eat to live and be a ready servant; not, however, that it may be given up to luxuries.

Catechesis IV, 18-26

Saint Cyril of Jerusalem

THE HOLY SPIRIT

There is One Holy Spirit, the Advocate. As there is One God, the Father, and there is no second Father, and as there is one Only-begotten Son and Word of God, and He has no brother, so there is one only Holy Spirit, and there is no second Spirit equal in honour to Him. The Holy Spirit is a mighty Power, a being divine and inscrutable. He is living and rational, the Sanctifier of all things made by God through Christ. He enlightens the souls of the just. He inspired the prophets. He inspired the Apostles in the New Testament. Let them be abhorred who dare to divide the operation of the Holy Spirit. There is One God, the Father, Lord of the Old and the New Testament, and One Lord Jesus Christ, who was prophesied in the Old, and came in the New Testament, and One Holy Spirit, who heralded Christ through the Prophets, and when Christ came, descended and showed him forth.

Let us return to the Sacred Scriptures and *drink water from our own cisterns and running water from our own wells* (cf Prov 5:15). Let us drink of the living water, *springing up unto life everlasting* (John 4:14). The Saviour *said this of the Spirit whom they who believed in him were to receive* (John 7:39). Consider what He says: *He who believes in me,* and not simply this, but *as the Scripture says* – He has referred you back to the Old Testament – *from within him there shall flow rivers of living water* (John 7:38); not visible rivers merely watering the earth with its thorns and trees, but enlightening souls. Elsewhere He says: *But the water I shall give him shall become in him a fountain of water, springing up into life everlasting* (John 4:14); a new kind of water, living and springing up, springing up for those who are worthy.

Why has He called the grace of the Spirit water? Because all things depend on water; water produces herbs and living things; water of the showers comes down from heaven, and coming down in one form, has manifold effects; one fountain waters the whole of Paradise; one and the same rain comes down on all the world, yet it becomes white in the lily, red in the rose, purple in the violets and hyacinths, different and many-coloured in manifold species; thus it is one in the palm tree and other in the vine, and all in all things, though it is uniform and does not vary in itself. For the rain does not change, coming down now as one thing and now as another, but it adapts itself to the things receiving it and becomes what is suitable to each.

Similarly the Holy Spirit, being One and of One Nature and indivisible, imparts to each man His grace *according as he will* (1 Cor 12:11). The dry tree when watered brings forth shoots; so too the soul in sin, once it is made worthy through penance of the grace of the Holy Spirit, flowers into justice. Though the Spirit is One in nature, yet by the will of God and in the name of the Son, He brings about many virtuous effects. For He employs the tongue of one man for wisdom; He illumines the soul of another by prophecy; to another He grants the power of driving out devils; to another the gift of interpreting the Sacred Scripture. He strengthens the self-control of one man, teaches another the nature of almsgiving, and still another to fast and mortify himself, another to despise the things of the body; he prepares another man for martyrdom, acting differently in different men. To one through the Spirit is given the utterance of wisdom; and to another the utterance of knowledge, according to the same Spirit; to another faith, in the same Spirit; to another the gift of healing, in the one Spirit; to another the working of miracles; to another prophecy; to another the distinguishing of spirits; to another various kinds of tongues. But all these things are the work of one and the same Spirit, who divides to everyone according as he will (1 Cor 12:7-11).

The Holy Spirit's actions effect what is good and salutary. First of all, His coming is gentle, the perception of Him fragrant, His yoke light; rays of light and knowledge shine forth before His coming. He comes with the heart of a true guardian; He comes to save, to cure, to admonish, to strengthen, to console, to enlighten the mind, first of the man who receives Him, then through him the minds of others also. As a man previously in darkness and suddenly seeing the sun gets the faculty of sight and sees clearly what he did not see before, so the man deemed worthy of the Holy Spirit is enlightened in soul, and sees beyond human sight what he did not know. Though his body is upon the earth his soul beholds the heavens as in a mirror.

Whenever a goodly thought on chastity or virginity occurs to you as you sit here, it is due to His teaching. Has it not often happened that a maiden, on the very threshold of the bridal chamber, has fled away, through the inspiration of His teaching on virginity? Or that a man distinguished at court has scorned wealth and honour, on being taught by the Holy Spirit? Is it not true that often a young man on beholding beauty has closed his eyes and fled the sight, and thus escaped defilement? How did this come to pass, you ask? The Holy Spirit taught the young man's soul. Covetous desires abound in the world; yet

Christians live in poverty. Why? Because of the prompting of the Holy Spirit. The Holy Spirit, the Good Spirit is truly worthy of honour, and it is fitting that we are baptised into Father, Son and Holy Spirit. A man still encumbered with the body wrestles with many cruel demons; often the demon, unconquerable by iron bonds, is conquered by the man through prayer, by virtue of the Holy Spirit within him. The simple breathing of the exorcist becomes as fire to the invisible foe.

We have from God, therefore, a strong Ally and Protector, a mighty Teacher and Champion in our behalf. Let us not fear the demons nor the devil, for our Defender is mightier; let us but open up the doors to Him; for He goes about seeking those worthy, seeking to whom He may impart His gifts.

Catechesis XVI

Saint Cyril of Jerusalem

TRUE TO THE FAITH

The faith which the Church hands down to you has all the authority of the Scriptures behind it. This is the faith, and none other, which you must learn to proclaim and in which you must persevere. Our spiritual life must not be put at risk through ignorance. And since there are some who do not read the Bible, either because they are too busy or because they are illiterate, the essence and core of our faith has been captured, and can be memorised, in the few short lines of the Creed.

Keep this faith ever by your side to help you on your way and close your ears and have nothing to do with any other, even if I myself should change my allegiance and preach another faith to you or an angel of darkness be transformed into an angel of light to lead you into error... To begin with, simply take the words as they stand at their face value, put your faith in them and commit them to memory. Later, as opportunity offers, you can take the propositions one by one and study them as truths of the Sacred Scriptures...

Pay attention then, brethren, to the truths of the Faith now being handed down to you and write them deep in your hearts. Keep a careful watch and be on your guard against foes and heretics intent on perverting your faith and plundering it. You must, as it were, deposit this gift of faith in the bank of safe-keeping and God will demand of you an account of your investment.

In the presence of God, who gives life to all things

and of Christ Jesus who in His testimony before Pontius Pilate bore witness to that great claim, I charge you to keep the faith unstained until the appearing of our Lord Jesus Christ.

Saint Hilary of Poitiers

Hilary belonged to a noble pagan family. He was born in Poitiers around 315. The facts about his life being uncertain and fragmentary do not allow us to put a date on his conversion to Christianity. It is likely that he received baptism as an adult, when having taken up the study of Scripture he found the truth he was looking for, and gave up idolatry.

Around 350 he was chosen to be bishop of Poitiers. He fought the Arian heresy with all his strength. But Emperor Constantine, the protector of this heresy, exiled him to Phrygia in Asia Minor. During these four years in exile Hilary displayed such gifts of thought and action that he came to be called the "Athanasius of the West'.

In 360, at the insistence of the Arians, who considered his presence in the East to be inopportune, he was allowed to return to Gaul. A year later he convoked a Council in Paris. This led to a decisive blow against Arianism in the west. Hilary died in Poitiers, probably in 368.

Hilary's fight against Arianism was also evident in his abundant writings. They can be divided into three: dogmatic, historico-polemical, and exegetical.

His *Commentary on the Gospel of St Matthew* was written during the early years of his episcopate, for the priests of his diocese. This exegetical work is presented in the form of a continuous commentary in which the most significant passages of the first gospel are examined in depth. The exegetical method followed by St Hilary begins the principle that every expression of Scripture presents, in addition to the immediate literal meaning, an allegorical one which can be seen only after a detailed examination of the text. Balancing these two meanings, Hilary safeguards the historicity of the gospel facts and tries to discover the prophetic significance of the words and actions of Christ.

Saint Hilary of Poitiers

WORKERS FOR THE HARVEST

When he saw the crowds, he had compassion for them, because they were harassed and helpless... (Matt 9:36)

We need to scrutinise the significance of these words not any less than the significance of these facts for, as we have said, the key to understanding their significance lies as much in the words as in the deeds. The Lord feels compassion for the harassed and helpless multitudes, like sheep scattered without a shepherd. He also says that the harvest is good, but the workers few, and that we need to ask the lord of the harvest to send many workers to the harvest (cf Matt 9:37-38). And, calling his disciples, he gave them the power to cast out unclean spirits and to cure all illnesses and sufferings (cf Matt 10:1). Although these facts refer to the present, we need to consider their significance for the future.

No aggressor had attacked the multitudes; yet they were prostrate without any adversity or misadventure having overtaken them. Why, then, does he feel compassion seeing them *harassed and helpless*? Clearly, the Lord had pity on a multitude tormented by the violence of an unclean spirit that had them under its dominion, on a multitude ill under the burden of the Law, because they did not yet have a shepherd who would restore the protection of the Holy Spirit to them (cf 1 Pet 2:25). In spite of the fruit of this gift being abundant, no one had gathered it in. Its abundance far exceeded the number of those who had received it, for although all took want they wanted, it continued to be available in superabundance, to be dispensed with generosity. And as it was necessary for many to distribute it, he exhorts the lord of the harvest to send many workers to the harvest. That is to say, to ask for many followers to benefit from the gift of the Holy Spirit that he had prepared, a gift which God distributes through prayer and petition. To show that this harvest and the multitude of followers should spread from the twelve Apostles, he called them to Himself and gave them the power to cast out demons and to cure all illnesses. With this power received as a gift, they could expel the cause of evil and cure the illness.

It is helpful to draw in the significance of these precepts, considering them one by one. He exhorts them to keep a distance from the haunts of the gentiles (cf Matt 10:5), not because he was not going to send them to save the pagans too, but rather that they refrain from the deeds and the way of living which accompanied pagan ignorance. He also forbade them from entering Samaritan towns. But did he Himself not cure a Samaritan woman? What he really exhorts them not to do, is to join in meetings with the heretics, for perversion in no way differs from ignorance. He sends them *to the lost sheep of the house of Israel* (Matt 10:6); yet, these sheep behave cruelly towards him, with tongues of vipers and claws of wolves. Since it is the Law which should be the first to receive the Gospel, Israel was to have fewer excuses for her crime, for she would have received greater attention as regards the exhortation.

The power of the strength of the Lord is transmitted in its entirety to the Apostles. Those who had been formed in Adam to the likeness and image of God, now received in a perfect way the image and likeness of Christ (cf 1 Cor

15:49). This power differed in no way from that of the Lord, and those who had previously been made from dust, were not transformed into heavenly beings (cf 1 Cor 15:48). They ought to preach that the kingdom of heaven is at hand (cf Matt 10:7); which is to say, that one now receives the image and likeness of God through communion in the truth, which allows all the saints, described by name from the heavens, to reign with the Lord (cf 1 Cor 4:8). They ought to cure the sick, raise the dead, heal lepers, cast out demons (cf Matt 10:8). All the evils caused in Adam's body at Satan's instigation, ought to be healed at the same time through participation in the Lord's power. And to achieve in a complete way the likeness to God, according to the prophecy of Genesis (cf Gen 1:26), they received the order to give freely what they had freely received (cf Matt 10:8). They ought to offer freely the service of a gift which they had received *gratis*.

He forbids them to keep any gold, silver or money in their girdles; to take any provisions for the journey, to take two tunics, or sandals or staff in their hands; *for labourers deserve their food* (Matt 10:10). I think there is nothing wrong in having a treasure in one's belt. What could the significance of this prohibition from having gold, silver or copper coins in their own girdles? The girdle is a garment indicating service, and one takes it off to work. We are encouraged, then, not to be mercenary in our service, to avoid the prize of our apostolate being the possession of gold, silver or of copper.

No bag for your journey (Matt 10:10). That is to say, we have to leave aside concern for temporal goods, since every earthly thing is prejudicial, from the moment when our heart goes to where our treasure is stored. *No two tunics (ibid)*. It is enough for us to be dressed with Christ once (cf Gal 3:27), without putting on immediately another suit, like heresy or the Mosaic Law, as a result of our intellect becoming perverted. *No sandals* (Matt 10:10). Could it be that the weak feet of men could bear being bare? Really, where we have to be barefoot is on holy ground, as Moses was told (cf Exod 3:5), not covered with the thorns and stings of sin; and we are told not to have any other footwear when entering, other than that received from Christ. *No staff in hand* (Matt 10:10), that is to say, the laws of a foreign power, for we have the staff from the root of Jesse (cf Is 11:1). No power proceeds from Christ other than the one referred to earlier.

According to the address you have just heard, we have been helpfully supplied with grace, viaticum, dress, sandals, power, to travel to the ends of the earth. Working under these conditions we will be worthy of our remuneration (cf Matt 10:10). That is to say, thanks to the fulfilment of these prescriptions, we will receive the reward of heavenly hope.

In Matthaeum commentarium, 10, 1-5

Saint Gregory Nazianzen

Gregory was born in 329 in Azianus, an area belonging to the family in the outskirts of Nazianzen in Cappadocia (Asia Minor). He completed his literary studies in Caesarea of Cappadocia, Caesarea of Palestine, Alexandria and Athens. He was baptised on his return to his native city. At Caesarea of Cappadocia he met Basil the Great, and a lifelong friendship developed. After considerable soul-searching he dedicated himself to the monastic life.

At Christmas 361 he was ordained to the priesthood. Ten years later, Basil, metropolitan of Cappadocia, consecrated him bishop of Sasima. However, he never took possession of his see. After a short period as head of the church at Nazianzen, he returned to Selucia of Isauria.

When Demophilus the Arian prelate was evicted, the Christians at Constantinople led by Theodosius asked him to take charge of the ecclesiastical re-organisation of the capital, which since 351 had been in Arian hands. The human and religious talent with which Gregory was gifted and the memorable addresses he delivered during these years, assured him of high prestige.

In May 381, the First Council of Constantinople was convoked. Arianism was condemned here. Disgusted by dissension, he resigned the see and returned to Nazianzen, until a new bishop was named for that city in 384. His mission fulfilled, he returned to the estate where he was born, to dedicate himself to contemplation and to writing books until his death in 390.

Gregory was affectionate and tender by nature, simple and humble, of sensitive temperament, lively and cheerful by disposition, yet constitutionally timid. Within a few months of Basil's death in 379 he embarked upon the difficult and arduous work in Constantinople. Cardinal Newman, in his appreciation of Gregory's character, suggests that it was the example of his friend's heroic spirit which inspired Gregory to take an active part in re-establishing the Catholic faith in the Eastern capital of the empire.

St Gregory's literary work can be classified into letters, prayers and poems. He did not write any biblical commentary. In both prose and poetry he shone above his contemporaries with the perfection of his style.

Gregory ranks as one of the greatest theologians of the early Church. This is based not only on his reputation among his contemporaries, but also for his five *Theological Discourses*. The third of these is dedicated to a defence of the Catholic doctrine of the Trinity and a demonstration of its consonance with the early doctrine of the Unity of God. He insisted on the principle of reverence in treating of the mysteries of the faith – a principle entirely ignored by his Arian opponents. In his exposition of the Trinitarian doctrine there are many passages which seem to anticipate the fuller teaching of the *Quicumque vult*.

Saint Gregory Nazianzen

THE CHRISTIAN VIRTUES

The three virtues of faith, hope and charity are attractive (cf 1 Cor 13:13). Abraham is certainly an example of faith; it was because of her that he was praised as a just man (cf Gen 15:6). As regards hope, Enosh was the first who was led to invoke the name of the Lord through hope (cf Gen 4:26); and with him all the just who suffer tribulation in hope. An example of charity is the blessed Apostle, who for the cause of Israel did not hesitate to suffer grave accusations against himself (cf Rom 9:3) ...

Hospitality is attractive. Among the just, Lot is an example, when he lived in Sodom (cf Gen 19:3) as an alien among the vices of the rest of the inhabitants of the town. And among the sinners, Rahab the prostitute (cf Josh 2:1 ss) who offered Joshua's spies a bed with no intention of sinning; having diligently protected her guests, she won praise and salvation.

Fraternal love is attractive, and Jesus himself is an example of it; he not only agreed to be called our brother, but also bore torture for our eternal health. Kindness towards human beings is attractive, and once again Jesus gives evidence of this, for he not only created man to do good works (cf Eph 2:10), joining his image to our flesh to guide us to the highest virtues and obtain for us the supreme goods, but he also became a man for us.

Longanimity is attractive, as He himself testifies, for he not only refused the help of legions of angels against his violent attackers (cf Matt 26:53), but he scolded Peter for drawing his sword (cf Matt 26:52) and even restored and healed the ear of the injured attacker. Stephen later showed the same virtue, imitating Christ as a disciple, when he cried out aloud pleading for those who were stoning him (cf Acts 7:59).

Meekness is attractive. Moses (cf Num 12:3) and David (cf Ps 131:1) are examples, praised above all others by Scripture for this virtue; and especially the Master of them all, who neither disputes nor screams, nor shouts in the squares (cf Is 42:2; 53:7), nor resists his executioners...

It is attractive to punish the body. Paul will convince you about this, for he ceaselessly fought and subjected it to punishment (cf 1 Cor 9:27). He, with the example of Israel, inspired a holy terror in those who trusted in themselves and complied with their bodies' needs. May Jesus himself convince you, with his fasts, his submission to temptation and his victory over the tempter (cf Matt 4:1 ss).

It is attractive to pray and to keep vigil. Jesus can give you testimony for this virtue, for he keeps vigil and makes petitions before his Passion (cf Matt 26:36).

Chastity and virginity are attractive too. Paul gives them credit when he determines the norms concerning these virtues, finding equitable solutions in the controversy over virginity and matrimony (cf 1 Cor 7:25). Jesus, too, believes this: he was born of a Virgin, to adorn the act of generation with honour, and to put the honour of virginity ahead of it.

It is attractive to practise temperance. May the authority of David move you: even when the three warriors managed to get hold of quite a lot of water from the well of Bethlehem, by no means would he drink it (cf 2

Sam 23:15-17). He poured it out to the Lord, not wishing to slake his thirst at the risk of his warrior's lives.

Recollection and peace are attractive. So I am taught by Mount Carmel, with Elijah (cf 1 Kings 18:42), the desert of John the Baptist (cf Luke 1:80) and finally that mountain (cf Matt 14:23) which Jesus frequently visited and where we know he spent more time in recollection.

Being short of resources is attractive. Elijah, who lodged in the house of the widow (cf 1 Kings 18:9), is an example. John dressed with camel's hair (cf Matt 3:4); and Peter fed on the poorest of food.

Humility is attractive. Examples abound; but by far the best are those of our Saviour and Lord, who not only lowered himself to the condition of a slave (cf Phil 2:6), and exposed his countenance to the mockery of saliva and slaps, and was counted among the criminals (cf Is 50:6; 53:12) while he purified the world from the stains of sin, but he also wanted, in doing the work of a slave, to wash the feet of the disciples (cf John 13:5).

Poverty and detachment from riches is attractive. Zacchaeus is an example, as he donates his estate when Christ enters his home (cf Luke 19:8)...

And to summarise my lesson, if contemplation is attractive, equally attractive is action. While the first raises us from this world to penetrate the Holy of Holies, redirecting our mind to its pure life, the other welcomes Christ and shows the intensity of one's love through deeds in his service.

Each one of these virtues forms part of the one way to salvation, which leads to some of the happy and eternal mansions. There are, certainly, many ways of living a virtuous life, and as many dwelling places beside God (cf John 14:2), each of which are distinguished from the others and allocated to each one according to his own merits and worthiness. Consequently, may this person cultivate this virtue, that person another, another person several virtues, and another, if its possible, all the virtues. In any case, work in such away that you make progress, and try to make an effort to advance more, persevering in the footsteps of Him who, when he showed us the true way, directed our steps and, making us pass through the narrow gate, leads us to the fullness of heavenly bliss.

As regards charity, according to Paul and on the authority of Christ himself, it has to be extended to become the summary and the goal of the Law and the Prophets. It is the first and greatest commandment (cf Matt 22:36 ss). I find that its principal work is rooted in welcoming the needy with kind love, in such a way that the misfortunes of our neighbour move us and hurt us. For there is no other devotion more pleasing to God as that of mercy. There is certainly no perfection which belongs more appropriately to God than the mercy and truth which precede him like heralds (cf Ps 89:15). And he prefers the offering of mercy than that of simple justice (cf Hos 12:7). There is no other better virtue for man than that kindness which will be paid by the kindness of Him who repays with justice and offers his mercy in abundant measure (cf Is 28:17).

Oratio XIV, de pauperum amore, II-V

Saint Gregory Nazianzen

TRUE GOD AND TRUE MAN

He was wrapped up in swaddling clothes; but at his resurrection he cast away the cloths in the sepulchre.

He lay in the manger, but later he was feted by the angels (cf Luke 2:7), pointed to by a star and adored by the Magi (cf Matt 2:2).

Why do you marvel at what you have seen with your eyes, while you do not observe what is perceived by the mind and the heart?

He was obliged to flee to Egypt; but he put to flight the errant ways of the Egyptians.

He had no comeliness, nor human beauty (cf Is 53:2) among the Jews; but, according to David, his countenance was the most handsome of all of the sons of man (cf Ps 44:3); and even at the summit of the mountain, in a brilliant way, he shines and comes to be more luminous than the sun (cf Matt 17:2), giving us a glimpse of future splendour.

He was baptised (cf Matt 3:16) as man, but as God bore sins upon himself, not because he was in need of purification, but so that those very waters might produce holiness.

He was tempted as a man; but as God he achieved victory. He commands us to have confidence in Him as the one who has overcome the world.

He suffered hunger (cf Matt 4:1-2), but he fed many thousands of people (cf Matt 14:21), and He has himself been changed into the bread which gives life and Heaven (cf John 5:41). He suffered thirst (cf John 19:28), but exclaimed: *Let anyone who is thirsty come to me, and let the one who believes in me drink* (John 7:37). He also promised to make fountains of living water flow for those who had faith.

He felt fatigue (cf John 4:6), but makes himself a repose for those who are tired and oppressed (cf Matt 11:28). He felt overcome by sleep (cf Matt 8:24) but walks lightly on the sea, calms the winds and saves Peter who is at the point of being drowned by the waves (cf Matt 14:25).

With a fish he pays his taxes (cf Matt 17:23), but he is the King of tax-collectors. He is called a Samaritan and one possessed by the devil (cf John 8:48), but takes salvation to him who, while he was going down from Jerusalem, was attacked by bandits; He is recognised by the demons (cf Mark 1:24; Luke 4:34), but he expels them and directs legions of evil spirits to cast themselves into the sea (cf Mark 5:7); he sees the prince of devils throw himself from the sky, almost like lightning.

He is attacked with stones, but he is not captured (cf John 8:59).

He makes petitions, but welcomes those who ask him for things. He weeps, but he dries away tears. He asks where Lazarus has been buried, because He is truly a man; but he raises Lazarus from the dead to life, because he is truly God.

He is sold, and cheaply too: for thirty pieces of silver (cf Matt 16:15). But meanwhile he redeemed the world at a great price – with his blood (cf 1 Pet 1:19; 1 Cor 6:20). He led to his death like a sheep (cf Is 53:7); but he gives Israel, and now the whole world, to graze.

He is dumb as a lamb (cf Ps 57:71), but he is the Word itself, proclaimed in the desert by the voice of one who cried out (cf (John 1:23). He was humbled and hurt by anguish (cf Is 53:4-5), but overcomes all infirmities and sufferings (cf Matt 9:35).

He is taken down from the log where he had been hung, but with that log he restores life, and gives salvation even to the thief (who hangs from the wood), and covers over everything which is uncovered.

Vinegar is given to drink, and gall for nourishment (cf Luke 23:33); Matt 27:34) – but, to whom? To Him who changed water into wine (cf John 2:7). He savoured that bitter taste, He who was sweetness itself and everything appetising (cf Song 16).

He entrusted his soul to God, but retained the faculty of taking it up again (cf John 10:18). The veil is rent (and the higher potencies are made manifest) and the rocks are broken to pieces, but the dead are raised up (cf Matt 27:51).

He dies, but he gives life back and defeats death with his own death.

He is honoured with a sepulchre; but he rises from a tomb.

He descends to hell, but accompanies souls to the heights, and rises to heaven, and he will come to judge the living and the dead and examine the words of men.

Oratio, 29, 19-20

Saint Gregory Nazianzen

PREPARING FOR DEATH

May we indeed be the kind of men we hope to be by the mighty mercy of our generous God. He asks little, He gives much, in this world and the next, to those who love Him sincerely, to us if by our love and hope in Him we bear all things, sustain all things and give thanks to Him for all things (for Scripture tells us that the trials of this life are often the weapons of salvation). We are also to commend our souls to Him and the souls of those who have travelled the common way of humanity and arrived more promptly before us at their destination.

O God, Lord and Creator of all and especially of mankind: God, Father and Ruler of Your children! Arbiter of life and death, Guardian and Benefactor of our souls, all things are made by You and all things are transfigured and transformed by Your Word when their time comes according to Your wisdom and providence. Take to Yourself now, I pray You, our brother Caesarius, the forerunner of us who remain. Take us also to Yourself in Your own good time, once our allotted span of life has been completed.

May the fear of the Lord make us prepared and yet unperturbed, so that at our death we shall not be drawing back and loath to depart, not dragged and torn from this life as men enthralled by the world and the flesh but rather going out readily and willingly to the life of eternal happiness in Christ Jesus Our Lord to whom be glory for ever and ever. Amen.

Saint Gregory Nazianzen

TIME AND ETERNITY

Are you still in the flower of youth? If so you should fight courageously against all sinful movements of the soul and then reap the harvest which comes from not having given in to those inclinations to which such an age is exposed. Instead you will give proof of mature prudence in a young and virile body, and you will get more pleasure from this victory than from any trophy won in the games, because then your prize will be before the whole world, a prize beyond compare.

Are you entering old age? If so, do not allow your spirit to grow old, and look forward to death as a time of your certain liberty; you will go forth from this life fully content with that situation which comes afterwards, where none are children nor are there any old people, but all are perfect adults in the state of perfection.

Do you have beauty of body? Then see to it that the beauty of your soul can stand comparison with it. Has the flower of beauty passed? Has it closed, so that now it cannot be seen, perhaps even seeming ugly to the sight? Well, it will still be wonderful in beauty amongst the things which are not visible. Like the rose which is changed later into a berry neither flowering nor perfumed. He who was the most beautiful of all the sons of men (cf Ps 44:3) wastes no time in contemplating exteriors, but turns His eyes to what is within.

Have you good health? Then make use of that

strength of body. You must warn, reprove, pass the night in vigils, sleeping on the ground, weakening and debilitating the grossness of the body. You must discuss heavenly things and earthly, meditate with attention on death.

Are you suffering some illness? You must fight and should this not avail, you will really gain the victory – that of never having to fight again.

Saint Basil the Great

Basil the Great was one of the most distinguished Doctors of the Church. He was born in Caesarea of Cappadocia around 330 A.D. He was one of ten children, his maternal grandfather having died a martyr. Under the care of his father and maternal grandmother, Basil was formed in the habits of piety and study. He went to Constantinople, distinguished for its teachers of rhetoric and philosophy, and then to Athens. Here he became the inseparable companion of St Gregory of Nazianzen.

He returned to Caesarea in 356, where he began to practise his profession. He soon gave up teaching, to dedicate himself entirely to the service of God. He retired to the desert and was joined by companions. In 358, with St Gregory of Nazianzen he wrote two *Rules* which were to have a decisive influence in monastic life in the East. In 364 he was ordained to the priesthood; and in 370 he succeeded Eusebius as Bishop of Caesarea, metropolitan of Cappadocia and exarch of the diocese of Pontus.

St Basil's great concern was the unity of the Church and his fight against semi-Arianism. One can say that he laid the foundations of the great movement which led to the Council of Constantinople, which brought order and peace to the universal Church.

He was a great theologian, a good administrator and an organiser. These are reflected in his writings. Basil was a great contemplative, a man of prayer. His literary work comprises dogmatic, ascetical and liturgical treatises. He is considered among the eight major Fathers of the Church. He died in 379 A.D.

Saint Basil the Great

IN THE PRESENCE OF GOD

I recognized your letter just as men recognize the children of friends from their unmistakable resemblance to their parents. For, you say that the environment is not important in implanting in your soul a desire to live with us until you learn something of our customs and our manner of life. This disposition of mind was characteristically yours and worthy of your soul, which regards all things here below as nothing in comparison with the promised happiness reserved for us hereafter.

But, I hesitate to write what I myself do in this solitude, night and day, seeing that, although I have left the distractions of the city, which are to me the occasion of innumerable evils, I have not yet succeeded in forsaking myself. I am like the inexperienced seafarers, distressed and ill because of their lack of skill in sailing. They ascribe their discomfort to the size of the boat and its consequent tossing upon the sea; even upon changing to a dinghy or a light boat, they still complain of their distress, not recognizing that they take the nausea and the bile along with them.

Such is our situation. Since we carry around with us our innate passions, we are everywhere subject to the same disturbances. Therefore, we have not profited much from this solitude. This is what we should do and it would have enabled us to follow more closely in the footsteps of Him who showed the way to salvation. For He says, *If anyone wishes to come after me, let him deny himself, and take up his cross, and follow me* (Matt 16:24).

A monastic life

We should try to keep the mind in tranquillity. For the eye which is continually gazing about, at one time darting to one side and again to the other, frequently casting glances hither and yonder, is not able to see clearly what is lying before it, but must fix its gaze firmly on that object, if a clear image of it is to be obtained. So, too, the mind of man is incapable of perceiving the truth clearly, if it is distracted by innumerable worldly cares. Wild desires, unruly impulses, and passionate yearnings greatly disturb him who is not yet united in the bonds of wedlock. And a tumultuous throng of different cares awaits him who already has taken a wife: the longing for children, if he is childless; the solicitude for their training, if he has children; the watchfulness over his wife, the care of his home, the protection of his servants, the losses on contracts, the contentions with his neighbours, the lawsuits, the business risks, the farm work. Each day, as it comes, brings its own shadow for the soul, and the nights, taking over the troubles of the day, beguile the mind with the same phantasies.

There is but one escape from these distractions, a complete separation from the world. Withdrawing from the world, however, does not mean mere bodily absence, but implies a disengagement of spirit from sympathy with the body, a renunciation of city, home, personal possessions, love of friends, property, means of livelihood, business, social relations, and learning acquired by human teachings; also, a readiness to receive in one's heart the impressions produced there by divine instruction. And this disposition follows the unlearning of worldly teachings which previously held possession of the heart. Just as it is not possible to write in wax without first smoothing down the letters already engraved upon it, so it is impossible to impart the divine teachings to the soul without first removing from it the conceptions arising from worldly experiences.

Now, solitude provides us with the greatest help toward this achievement, quieting our passions, and giving leisure to our reason to uproot them completely from the soul. Just as animals, if they are stroked are more easily subdued, so desires, wraths, fears, and griefs, the venomous evils of the soul, if they have been lulled to sleep by silence and have not been kept aflame by constant provocation, are more easily overcome by reason.

Living in the presence of God

A life of piety nourishes the soul with divine thoughts. What, then, is more blessed than to imitate on earth the choirs of angels; hastening at break of day to pray, to glorify the Creator with hymns and songs, and, when the sun is brightly shining and we turn to our tasks, to accompany them everywhere with prayer, seasoning the daily work with hymns, as food with salt? For, the inspirations of the sacred songs give rise to a joyousness that is without grief. Silence, then, is the beginning of purification in the soul, since the tongue is not busied with the affairs of men, nor the eyes looking around at fair complexions and graceful forms, nor the ears lessening the harmony of the soul by listening to melodies made for fleeting pleasure or to the sayings of wits and jesters, a course of action which tends especially to weaken the spiritual timbre of the soul. When the mind is not engaged by external affairs, nor diffused through the senses of the whole world, it retires within itself. Then, it ascends spontaneously to the consideration of God. It does not drag the soul down either to the thought of sustenance or to a solicitude for bodily apparel, but enjoys freedom from earthly cares, it turns all its zeal to the acquisition of eternal goods – pondering how to attain temperance and fortitude, justice and prudence, and all other consequent virtues, all of which prompt the earnest man to fulfil properly each separate duty.

Reading of the Bible

Meditation on the divinely inspired Scriptures is also a most important means for the discovery of duty. The Scriptures not only propose to us counsels for the conduct of life, but also open before us the lives of the blessed handed down in writing as living images for our imitation of life spent in quest of God.

Accordingly, by a continual practice of that virtue in which he perceives himself deficient, each one finds, just as he would in some public apothecary shop, a suitable remedy for his infirmity. One who aspires to a perfect chastity reads constantly the story of Joseph and from him learns the beauty of chaste habits, finding Joseph not only self-controlled in regard to sensual pleasures, but also a habitual lover of all virtue.

Fortitude he learns from Job, who, in spite of having suffered great reverses in life, being changed in an instant from a rich man into a poor one, and from the father of beautiful children into a childless man, remained the same, always preserving untarnished his nobility of soul. And not even when his friends, coming to console and taking advantage of his unfortunate condition, aggravated his sufferings was he provoked to anger.

In turn, if one considers how he may be meek and at the same time high-spirited, so as to use wrath against sin but gentleness toward men, he will find David noble in the brave deeds of war but gentle and dispassionate in the punishment of enemies. Such, also, was Moses, who rose up in great wrath against those offending God, but endured with a meek spirit the slanders against himself.

Prayer

Prayers, too, following reading, take hold upon a fresher and more vigorous soul already stirred to a longing for God. And prayer which imprints in the soul a clear conception of God is an excellent thing. This abiding of God in our memory is the indwelling of God. Thus we become in a special manner the temples of God when earthly thoughts cease to interrupt our continual remembrance of Him, and unforeseen passions to agitate the mind, and when the lover of God, fleeing all these, withdraws with Him and, driving out the passions which tempt him to incontinence, spends himself in the practices which lead to virtue.

Epistola II, 2-4

Saint Basil the Great

THE ACTION OF THE HOLY SPIRIT

Who is there who can hear the names of the Holy Spirit and not feel exaltation in his soul, and not lift up his thoughts to that supreme nature? For he is called the Spirit of God, the Spirit of Truth, who proceeds from the Father, the upright Spirit, the guiding Spirit. His chief and distinguishing name is Holy Spirit, for it is the name which clearly expresses, better than any other, the incorporeal, free of matter and indivisible. It is for this reason that Our Lord, teaching that the incorporeal cannot be comprehended, said to the woman who thought God is to be adored in a place: *God is spirit* (John 4:24).

Thus, on hearing Spirit, it is not right to understand it as a nature circumscribed by a place, subject to changes, similar to a creature in every way. Rather, one has to force our thoughts to what is highest within us, thinking about an intelligent substance, infinite as regards power, not located in a place by its size, not subject to the measure of time, and which gives generously of what it possesses.

All creatures turn to the Spirit for their sanctification. All who live virtuously seek him, and are refreshed and helped towards their own natural end by his influence. He is the source of holiness, the light of our understanding, for to every mind he offers his own light for the discovery of truth.

Though by nature he is inaccessible, yet through his generosity men can receive him in themselves. He fills all creatures with his power, but only those who are worthy can participate in him. But all do not share him in the same measure: he distributes his power in proportion to men's faith.

He is simple in essence, but manifold in power. He is present to each in his fullness, and in his fullness is present everywhere. He is divided, and does not suffer by the division. All share in him, but he remains whole, like a beam of sunshine whose kindly influence benefits each creature as though it were present to that creature alone, and shines over land and sea and dissolves in the air.

So too the Spirit is present like the sun to each individual who is capable of receiving him, and emits an influence which is sufficient to help them all, but is not divided. And they profit by sharing in him according to their natures, not according to his power.

Through him hearts are raised on high, the weak are led by the hand, those who are advanced gain perfection. He it is who shines on those whose hearts are purified and stainless and makes them truly spiritual through the common union they have with him.

Even as bright and shining bodies, once touched by a ray of light falling on them, become even more glorious and themselves cast another light, so too souls that carry the Spirit, and are enlightened by the Spirit, become spiritual themselves and send forth grace upon others.

This grace enables them to foresee the future, to understand mysteries, to grasp hidden things, to receive spiritual blessings, to have their thoughts fixed on heavenly things, so that their perseverance in God unfailing, so do they acquire likeness to God, so – most sublime of all – do they themselves become divine.

Liber de Spiritu Sancto, IX, 22-23

Saint Basil the Great

CONFIGURED TO CHRIST

The economy of our God and Saviour concerning men consists in coming again to call us after the fall and leading us back into his friendship after the separation produced by the disobedience. So, the coming of Christ in the flesh, his gospel preaching, his sufferings, the cross, the sepulchre, the resurrection, have made it possible for man, saved by Christ, to recover his adopted filiation.

For the perfection of this life, it is necessary to imitate Christ not only in the examples of benignity, humility and patience which he showed us in his life, but also in the way he died, as stated by St Paul, that imitator of Christ: *becoming like him in his death, that if possible I may attain the resurrection from the dead* (Phil 3:10-11).

In death

How are we to imitate him in his death? Burying ourselves with Him in baptism (cf Rom 6:4-5). How is the burial to be and what fruits follow from such an imitation? First, it is necessary to make a radical departure from one's past life. And this is only possible through a new generation (cf John 3:3). The very word regeneration signifies a principle of a second life, in such a way that, before achieving it, it is necessary to put an end to the previous one. For just as those who have reached the finishing line in the stadium before beginning a lap of honour, stop and rest for a moment, so it seems necessary for death to intervene in the change of life, in such a way that the first one finishes and then the second one begins.

How do we descend into hell? By imitating through baptism the burial of Christ, for the bodies of those to be baptised are buried in water. And baptism symbolically demonstrates leaving behind the works of the flesh, according to the Apostle: *In him also you were circumcised with a circumcision made without hands, by putting off the body of flesh in the circumcision of Christ; and you were buried with him in baptism, in which you were also raised with him through faith in the working of God, who raised him from the dead* (Col 2:11-12). In a certain way it happens that through baptism the soul is cleaned from the filth which comes from the carnal senses, according to what is written: *Wash me and I shall be whiter than snow* (Ps 50:7).

In Life

Thus we are cleaned from one and all of the stains, not according to Jewish custom but through the one saving baptism which we know, since one is death in favour of the world, and one too is the resurrection from the dead, and baptism is a figure of the two. So the Lord who gives life established with us the baptismal covenant, which carries upon it the image of death and life. The water is symbolic of death, while the Spirit provides the seal of life. This solves the problem which was raised as to why water and Spirit are connected. It results from the fact that baptism has two purposes.

First, the destruction of the body of sin to prevent it bearing fruit in death. Second, life in the Spirit (cf John 3:5) and the fruit borne in holiness. The water is the symbol of death and receives the body as it were into a tomb. The Spirit provides life-giving force and brings back our souls from the death of sin to the life they once enjoyed.

This is the meaning of being born again of water and the Holy Spirit. Death is brought to an end in the water and then the Spirit brings us to life.

By three immersions and as many invocations, the great mystery of baptism is performed. So the appearance of death is conveyed, and through the handing over of divine knowledge the baptised are enlightened. Therefore if there is any grace in the water, it is not because of any power the water may possess but because it derives from the power of the Spirit. For baptism is not the removal of dirt from the body but an appeal to God from a clear conscience (cf 1 Pet 3:21). For this reason the Lord, to prepare us for the risen life, lays before us all the gospel precepts. We must avoid anger, endure evil, be free from the love of pleasure and the love of money. So by our own choice we shall achieve those things which are the natural endowments of the world to come.

Through the Holy Spirit paradise is restored. We can ascend to heaven and regain our sonship. We can address God as our Father with confidence; we can share in the grace of Christ; we can be called children of the light and sharers in eternal glory. In a word, we can become full of all manner of blessings in this world and in that to come. We can observe, as in a glass, the beauty of the goods stored up for us in the future but now anticipated in faith, as though they were already here. If the earnest is such, what must the perfect thing be? If the first fruits are such, what must the consummation be?

From here it is easy to see the difference between the grace of the Spirit and the baptism of water: John baptised with water for penance, and Our Lord Jesus Christ baptised in the Holy Spirit: *I baptise you with water for repentance,* says St John the Baptist, *but he who is coming after me is mightier than I, whose sandals I am not worthy to carry; he will baptise you with the Holy Spirit and with fire* (Matt 3:11). He calls baptism of fire that trial which will take place at the judgement, according to the Apostle: *the fire will test what sort of work each man has done* (1 Cor 3:13). And a little earlier he had said: *the Day of the Lord will disclose the work of each one, because it will be revealed with fire* (1 Cor 3:13).

And not a few, in their struggle for piety, really submitting themselves and not simply imitating death for Christ's cause, also acquire the symbols which arise from water in the order of salvation, precisely through having been baptised in their own blood. I state this not despising the baptism by water, but to condemn the arguments of those who mix what ought not to be mixed and of those who make comparisons with what is incomparable.

Liber de Spiritu Sancto XV, 35-36

Saint Gregory of Nyssa

St Gregory was born into a deeply religious family, who were not very rich in worldly goods. His date of birth is not known. His mother was a martyr's daughter; two of his brothers became bishops, like himself. Gregory refers to Basil, one of these brothers, as 'our father and master'. The training Basil gave him was an antidote to his pagan schooling.

After consecration in 371 Gregory spent some time in rhetoric. He was appointed to the see of Nyssa, near Caesarea. On his arrival there he began to meet with difficulties. He was arrested by the governor, Demosthenes, and was later deposed. Under the new emperor, Gratian, he was reinstated (378). Gregory took an active part in the Council of Constantinople (381). He died around 385.

Most of his writings deal with Sacred Scripture. He was an ardent admirer of Origen. He belongs to a group known as the Cappadocian Fathers, which reveals his intellectual characteristics, ever in quest of allegorical interpretations and mystical meanings hidden away beneath the literal sense of texts.

In theology he follows the teaching of St Basil and St Gregory of Nazianzen, defending the unity of the divine nature and the trinity of persons. He wrote a defence of the Nicene creed against Arianism, a work of prime importance in that controversy. He also delivered a great many sermons and homilies.

Saint Gregory of Nyssa

THE DIGNITY OF MAN

In this beautiful domicile of the universe, the great and excellent creature we call man had not yet appeared. It was not appropriate for the sovereign to appear *before* the subjects he was to command. It was logical, for the empire was to be created first and then the emperor proclaimed. That is to say, after the Maker of all things had prepared creation in its entirety in the manner of a royal palace.

The palace is the land, the islands, the seas and, finally, the sky, extended over all things like an arched roof. And in this palace riches of all kinds are collected together; riches in all of creation, such as the plants and trees in her, and those that feel, and breathe and grow in her. And among these riches one has to count those things which, because of their elegance or beauty of their colours, men consider precious – for example, gold, silver and precious stones, which men covet; these too which appear abundantly, God hid as royal treasures, in the depths of the earth.

Creation of man

He then made man appear in the world, so that he could be on the one hand a witness to those marvels; and on the other hand, to be lord and master. And because of the beauty and greatness of what he could see, man would be able to recognise, more effectively than any speech could transmit, the ineffable power of Him who had done all of this. Here then is the reason why man was the last to be introduced into the world, after everything else had been created. It is not that he was squeezed in to a little corner as something to be despised. Rather, he had scarcely been born when the royalty of creation, which he was to subject, fell upon him.

A good host does not introduce his guest into a house before the food is served. Everything is first prepared with decorum; the house, the dining room, the table is splendidly decorated; and once everything is ready the guest is brought into the house. So too the Lord, our affluent and splendid host. After he had elegantly adorned his house and prepared a great banquet in which no delight was missing, he finally introduced man. It was not for man to acquire what might be missing, but to enjoy what was there present. God made man consist, by his very nature, of two parts, thus joining the spiritual with the earthly. It would thus be more natural and proper to enjoy the two spheres: to enjoy God, through the more divine part of his nature, and the goods of the earth, through the senses which are also earthly.

We cannot gloss over the fact that creation, to put it crudely, had been put together quickly. The depths of the earth and the universe appear at a simple command of God, apparently without any skill. But the creation of man is preceded by preparation. The artist, through the painting of the Word, sketches his future work beforehand; he tells us how it has to be and from which original a copy is to be made, for what end it is to be created, what he will do when he is born and over whom he will rule. Everything is argued out by the Word beforehand, so that man receives a dignity which is prior to his birth, and, before he received his being he possessed sovereignty over all other creatures. This is why Scripture records what God said:

The Dignity of Man

Let us make humankind in our image, according to our likeness; and let them have dominion over the fish of the sea, over the birds of the air, and over the cattle, and over all the wild animals of the earth, and over every creeping thing that creeps the earth (Gen 1:26).

O marvel! The sun is created, but no preparation has preceded it. The same with the heavens, which have no equal in beauty in creation. All this marvel arises at the command of a single word, without Scripture telling us from where, or how, or any other thing. And this happens with each and every other creature: the stars, the air which separates them, the sea, the land, the animals, the plants – they are all produced by a simple word from God. It is only for the formation of man that the Creator of the universe prepares with some deliberation, and has available previously the material for his work, and determines the exemplar of beauty to which he has to aspire; and pointing out the end for which he is to be born he manufactures a nature which corresponds and is proper to the actions man has to carry out and is in accord with the goal which he has been given.

Dignity of man

Just as in human things the manufacturer gives the material he is working on the form most suitable for the use it will be put to, so the highest Maker made our nature as a kind of instrument which will be able to carry out royal duties. And as man was perfectly suited to this, he was gifted not only with excellent qualities as regards the soul, but also in the very figure of his body. The soul shows its sublime royal dignity, far from private meanness, by the way it recognises nothing as its superior and does everything in accordance with its own judgement. She, by her own wish, as the ladyship she is, governs her own self.

Other than the king, no one else has such power.

It is human practice for those who work on images of the emperor to attempt in the first place to reproduce their figure; then, decorating these in fine clothes they express imperial dignity. It is already in common usage and custom to refer to the statue of the emperor as emperor. Human nature, too, created to be lord of all other creatures, because of the similarity he carries within him to the King of the universe, was raised like a living statue and takes part in the dignity and the name of the original. He is not dressed in fine clothes, nor does he show his dignity with his scepter and a crown with diadems, for the original does not wear these signs either. Instead of fine clothes he is dressed in virtue, which is the most regal of dresses; instead of a scepter, he supports himself and is supported by the blessing of immortality; and in place of diadems he wears the crown of justice. So that in reproducing faithfully the beauty of the original, the soul shows in everything its royal dignity.

De hominis opificio, II-IV

Saint Gregory of Nyssa

THE CHRISTIAN IS ANOTHER CHRIST

Paul, better and more clearly than all others, showed what Christ is. He showed by the things he did what type of person the one who bears Christ's name must be. He imitated Him so clearly as to show his Lord having been formed in himself. Through a most exact imitation, the very form of his soul was transformed into its prototype so that it seemed no longer to be Paul living and speaking but Christ Himself living in him.... *It is no longer I who live but Christ who lives in me* (Gal 2:20).

He made known to us what the name of Christ means, saying that Christ is the power and wisdom of God. But he also called Him Peace and Light unapproachable in which God dwells, Sanctification and Ransom, High Priest and Passover Lamb, propitiation for souls, splendour of glory and image of the divine hypostasis, ... spiritual Food and Drink, Rock and Water, the Foundation of our faith ..., image of the unseen God, the great God, the Head of the Body of the Church, ... the First-born of the dead and the First-born of many brothers, the Mediator between God and man and the Only-Begotten Son crowned with glory and honour, the Lord of glory and Ruler of all that exists, ... the King of righteousness, the Prince of peace and universal Monarch who possesses His royal power without end.

He also added many other titles, the number of which is not easily counted. If these are all compared with one another ..., they give us a certain image of the meaning of the name of Christ. They show us as much of His inexpressible greatness as our souls are able to understand. Our good Master has granted us fellowship with that greatest, most divine and first of all names, so that those who have been honoured with the name of Christ are called Christians.

It necessarily follows that all the meanings expressed by such a word be perceived likewise in us, so that our name may not be a false one but may receive confirmation from our way of life.

Homily to Olympos on Perfection

Saint Ambrose

Ambrose was born around 340 A.D. in Trier, where his father was Prefect of the Gallic areas. He studied rhetoric and was put in charge of this in the prefecture of Syrmio. After his father's death, Ambrose began his linguistic studies in Rome. In 370 he was appointed consul of Liguria and Emilia, with his seat in Milan. 'Go', said the prefect, with unconscious prophecy, 'conduct thyself not as a judge but as a bishop.' A few years later the Arian bishop, who had been illegally occupying the Milanese see, died.

As one responsible for public order, Ambrose would have mediated in the ensuing polemics between the Arians and the Catholics over the then vacant episcopal see of the city. With this in mind he gathered together the bishops and people, and urged calm. On finishing his address he was, by acclamation, declared Bishop of Milan (374). A few days later he was baptised and consecrated bishop.

Later, under the direction of Simplician, he completed his doctrinal formation. The systematic study of the Bible (of which Augustine was witness to his intensity and assiduousness) and meditation of the Word of God were the sources for his untiring activity as pastor and preacher. His power as an orator is attested by the conversion of Augustine, a skilled rhetorician.

St Ambrose has left us abundant literary work, with treatises of an exegetical, ascetical, moral and dogmatic nature, in addition to letters, hymns and various discourses. He died in the year 397.

He was one of the most illustrious Fathers and Doctors of the Church, and fittingly chosen, with Augustine, John Chrysostom and Athanasius, to uphold the venerable Chair of the Prince of the Apostles in the tribune of St Peter's in Rome.

Among the exegetical works, the *Treatise of the Gospel of St Luke* is perhaps best known. Originally they were sermons preached to the people in 377-378; later in 379 they were edited in the form of a treatise. In this work St Ambrose collects interpretations of the Greek Fathers, adopting them with great care to the specific requirements of his own environment.

Explanatio psalmorum XII is one of his exegetical works. It is not a unified work as regards composition nor organic as regards them. It is a collection of commentaries he made of twelve psalms. A common characteristic of these twelve is that they all prefigure and announce the coming of Christ: they are messianic. We do not know the reasons behind this choice. In fact, the dates of the composition of the various commentaries are varied. The *explanatio* on Psalm I was probably delivered around 390. What seems clear is that among the literary works in Scripture, those on the psalms are, for St Ambrose, the highest, almost a summary of all the others.

SAINT AMBROSE

THE BODY OF CHRIST

Then follows your coming to the altar. You began to come. The angels observed. They saw you approaching, and that human condition which before was stained with the shadowy squalor of sins, they saw suddenly shining bright. So they said: *Who is this that comes up from the desert whitewashed?* (cf Cant 8:5). So the angels also marvel. Do you wish to know how they marvel? Listen to the Apostle Peter saying that those things that have been conferred on you which the angels also desired to see (cf 1 Pet 1:12). Listen again. It says: *The eye has not seen, nor ear heard what things God has prepared for them that love him.* (cf 1 Cor 2:9).

Then recognise what you have received. The holy Prophet David saw this grace figuratively and desired it. Do you wish to know how he desired it? Again hear him as he says: *You shall sprinkle me with hyssop, and I shall be cleansed; you shall wash me, and I shall be made whiter than snow.* (Ps 50:9). Why? Because snow, although it is white, quickly grows dark with a little filth and is corrupted; if you hold fast what you have received, that grace which you have received will be lasting and perpetual (cf Rev 3:11).

You came, then, wanting. As you had seen all that grace, you came to the altar wanting to receive the sacrament. Your soul says: *And I will go in to the altar of God, to God who gives joy to my youth* (Ps 42:4) You laid aside the old age of sins, you took on the youth of grace.

The heavenly sacraments have bestowed this upon you. Finally, again, hear David as he says: *Your youth will be renewed like the eagles* (Ps 102:5). You have begun to be a good eagle, which seeks heaven, and disdains earthly things. Good eagles are about the altar, for *Wheresoever the body shall be, there shall the eagles also be gathered together* (Matt 24:28; Luke 17:37). The form of the body is the altar, and the body of Christ is on the altar. You are the eagles renewed by the washing away of transgression.

You have come to the altar; you have seen the sacraments placed on the altar; and indeed you have marvelled at the creature itself. Yet the creature is customary and known.

Someone may perhaps say: *God furnished the Jews so much grace; manna rained upon them from heaven; what more has He given His faithful; what more has He allotted to these to whom He promised more?* (cf Exod 16:14-15).

The Consecration

You perhaps say: *My bread is usual.* But that bread is bread before the words of the sacraments; when the consecration has been added, from bread it becomes the flesh of Christ. So let us confirm this, how it is possible that what was bread is the body of Christ.

By what words, then, is the consecration and by whose expressions? By those of the Lord Jesus. For all the rest that are said in the preceding are said by the priest: praise to God, prayer is offered, there is a petition for the people, for kings, for the rest (cf 1 Tim 1:1-2). When it comes to performing a venerable sacrament, then the priest uses not his own expressions, but he uses the expressions of Christ. Thus the expression of Christ performs this sacrament.

Do you wish to know how it is consecrated with

THE BODY OF CHRIST

heavenly words? Accept what the words are. The priest speaks. In the Canon of the Mass he says: *Perform for us this oblation written, reasonable, acceptable, which is a figure of the body and blood of our Lord Jesus Christ. On the day before He suffered He took bread in His holy hands, looked toward heaven, toward you, holy Father omnipotent, eternal God, giving thanks, blessed, broke, and having broken it gave it to the Apostles and His disciples, saying: 'Take and eat of this, all of you; for this is my body, which shall be broken for many'* (cf Matt 26:26; Mark 14:22; Luke 22:19; 1 Cor 11:24). Take note.

Similarly also, on the day before He suffered, after they had dined, He took the chalice, looked toward heaven, toward you, holy Father omnipotent, eternal God and giving thanks He blessed it, and gave it to the Apostles and His disciples, saying: 'Take and drink of this, all of you; for this is my blood' (cf Matt 26-28; Mark 14:23-24; Luke 22:20). Behold! All these words up to *Take* are the Evangelist's, whether body or blood. From then on the words are Christ's: *Take and drink of this, all of you; for this is my blood.*

Look at these events one by one. It says: *On the day before He suffered, He took bread in His holy hands.* Before it is consecrated, it is bread; but when Christ's words have been added, it is the body of Christ. Finally, hear him as He says: *Take and eat of this, all of you; for this is my body.*

And before the words of Christ, the chalice is full of wine and water. When the words of Christ have been added, then blood is effected, which redeemed the people. So behold in what great respects the expression of Christ is able to change all things. Then the Lord Jesus Himself testified to us that we receive His body and blood. Should we doubt at all about His faith and testimony?

Now return with me to my proposition. Great and

venerable indeed is the fact that manna rained upon the Jews from heaven. But understand! What is greater, manna from heaven or the body of Christ? Surely the body of Christ, who is the Author of heaven. Further, he who ate the manna died; he who has eaten this body will effect for himself remission of sins and *shall not die forever* (cf John 6:49-58; 11:26).

So you should not say indifferently *Amen*, but already confess in spirit that you receive the body of Christ. Therefore, when you ask, the priest says to you: *the body of Christ*, and you say: *Amen*, that is, *truly*. What the tongue confesses let the affection hold.

De sacramentis, IV, 5-9, 14, 21-25

Saint Ambrose

ON FRIENDSHIP

Governed by rules

Friendship which fosters good customs is the only kind which is worthy of praise. Friendship should be preferred above riches, above honours, above power, but not above virtue. Rather, friendship has to be governed by rules of moral uprightness. Such was the friendship between Jonathan and David. Because of the affection he had for David, Jonathan paid no attention to his father's anger or to the danger to his own life (cf 1 Sam 20:20 ss). Such too was the friendship of Ahimelech: to carry out his duties which were consequent on hospitality, he preferred to face death than to betray his friend on the run (cf 1 Sam 22:6).

Scripture, too, dealing with friendship, states that virtue ought never to be insulted by love for a friend: nothing has to be preferred to virtue.

Corrections made to friends

If you notice some defect in a friend, correct him in secret; if he does not listen to you, reprimand him openly. Corrections do good. They are of greater benefit than a mute friendship. If the friend feels offended, correct him just the same. Insist without fear, although the bitter taste of a correction upsets him. The Book of Proverbs says: *Well meant are the wounds a friend inflicts, but profuse are the kisses of the enemy* (Prov 27:6). Correct the errant friend then, and do not abandon the innocent friend.

Friendship has to be constant and persevering in its affections: we do not change friends as children do, for they allow themselves to be carried away by the free and easy wave of feelings.

Open your heart to your friend, so that he be faithful and so that he is united to the joy of life. A faithful friend, really, is *life-saving medicine, an elixir of life* (Sir 6:16). Respect him as one would like to be respected. Do not fear winning him over with your favours, because friendship does not allow pride. This is why Wisdom says: *be not ashamed to protect a friend* (Sir 22:25). Do not abandon him at the moment of need. Do not forget about him. Do not deny him your affection. For friendship is the support to life. We carry one another's burdens, as the Apostle taught those who were united, forming just one body in charity (cf Gal 6:2). If the prosperity of one is beneficial to all his friends, why in his adversity is he not going to receive the help of all his friends? Let us help him out with our advice. We link our efforts to his. We participate in his affliction.

Sacrifices, a consequence of friendship

Out of loyalty to a friend, we are prepared to make big sacrifices, if such become necessary. To defend the cause of an innocent friend, one may well have to face enmity. Quite frequently one may be insulted when trying to reply to those who attack him or when dealing with allegations made against the friend. Do not be concerned about this, for the voice of the just person says: *if harm should come to me because of a friend, I shall bear it* (Sir 22:26). True friends are proven in adversity. For in prosperity everyone appears to be a fast friend. Just as patience with and compassion for a friend in misfortune are needed, when he is successful it is good to be demanding, cautioning and correcting the arrogance which can perhaps fill him with pride. How well the saintly Job expressed it in the midst of his afflictions: *Have pity on me, have pity on me, O you my friends, for the hand of God has touched me* (Job 19:21). It was not a simple petition, but a reprimand. Job was asking his friends to *have pity on me* while they spoke unjustly of him. It was as if to say: this is the time to show mercy, but instead you are afflicting and speaking badly of a man with whom you should be sympathising.

My children, be faithful to true friendship with your brethren, for there is nothing more beautiful in human relations. It is certainly a great consolation in this life to have a friend to whom one can turn and open one's heart and relate what weighs on one's mind. It helps a great deal to have a loyal person who rejoices with you in prosperity, shares in your sorrow in adversity and sustains you in difficult moments. How beautiful is the friendship between the three Hebrew lads. The saintly David did well when he said: *Saul and Jonathan, beloved and lovely! In life and in death they were not divided* (1 Sam 1:23).

Friendship and faith

This is fruit of friendship: out of affection for a friend, faith is not destroyed. For one cannot be a friend of a person if one is unfaithful to God. Friendship is the guardian of piety and master of equality. It makes the superior equal to the inferior. It raises the inferior to the level of the superior. There cannot be true friendship between people who have very different customs; mutual love leads them to become identified with one another. The inferior does not lack the authority to correct, nor the superior the humility to accept the correction. One listens to the other as an equal; the other reproaches and admonishes as a friend, not with pride but with sincere affection.

The warning does not have to be harsh, nor the correction offensive. If it is true that friendship leaves no room for adulation, it is also true that it brooks no insolence. Who is a friend but a loving companion with whom one is intimately united even to fusing one's soul with his and forming one heart. In him you abandon yourself as confidently as one would in another 'oneself'. You fear nought from him, and you ask him nothing untoward for yourself. For friendship is not mercenary, but shines with dignity and beauty. It is a virtue, not a consumer commodity, for it is acquired not by money but by love. It is not offered at an auction to the highest bidder, but arises from the challenge of being for mutual benefit. It is for this reason that the poor make better friendships than the rich. And so, while those with abundant resources frequently find themselves without true friends, the poor have them in abundance.

Where there is flattery or false adulation there is no friendship. It is not uncommon that one is "understanding" towards a rich person out of adulation. But this hardly happens when one is dealing with a needy person. The friendship offered to a poor person is more sincere, since there is less self-interest.

What is there which is more precious than friendship, which is common to angels and men? The Lord Jesus himself says: *Make friends for yourselves out of dishonest wealth, so that when it is gone, they may welcome you into their eternal homes* (Luke 16:9). He himself has converted us from slaves to friends, as he clearly stated: *You are my friends if you do what I command you* (John 15:14). He has left us the model we are to imitate. We have, then, to share in the goodwill of a friend, reveal to him confidentially what we have in our heart, and not to ignore anything which he carries in his. We open our soul out to him, and he to us. In this respect Our Lord has declared, *I have called you friends because I have made known to you everything that I have heard from my Father* (John 15:14). The true friend then, hides nothing from his friend. He uncovers his whole being, just as Jesus laid bare the mysteries of the Father to the hearts of the Apostles.

De officiis ministrorum, III, 124-135

Saint Ambrose

Interior Martyrdom

Many are my persecutors and my adversaries, yet I do not swerve from your decrees (Ps 119:157).

The worst persecutors are not those who are known as such, but those who are not seen. And of this type there are many! For just as a persecuting king promulgates many laws to cause harassment and the persecutors spread to all the provinces and are in all the cities, so the devil launches many of his followers to persecute all souls, not only on the outside but also internally.

Of these persecutions it has been said: *All who want to live a godly life in Christ Jesus will be persecuted* (2 Tim 3:12). The Apostle wrote *all*; he made no exceptions. For how can there be exceptions when the Lord himself experiences the attempts at persecution? Avarice persecutes; ambition persecutes; lust persecutes; pride persecutes and so do the pleasures of the flesh. Don't forget that the Apostle said: *Flee from fornication!* (1 Cor 6:18). And what do you flee from, but what persecutes you: the bad spirit of lust, the bad spirit of avarice, the bad spirit of pride.

The persecutors to fear are those who, without the terror of the sword, frequently destroy the spirit of man; those who with flattery, rather than with wonder, subject the souls of the faithful. These are the enemies you have to guard against. These are the most dangerous of tyrants, the ones who beat Adam. Many souls, crowned in public persecutions, have fallen in these hidden persecutions.

Disputes without, says the Apostle, *fears within* (2 Cor 7:5).

Be warned that the battle which takes place in the interior of man is tough, so that you engage in a duel against yourself and against your passions. The Apostle himself hesitates, doubts, is attacked and shows that he is subject to the law of sin and limited by his body of death. He would not be able to escape it had he not been liberated by the grace of Jesus Christ (cf Rom 7:23-25).

Suffering martyrdom in daily circumstances

Just as there are many persecutions, so too there are many martyrs. You are a daily witness to Christ. You are a martyr for Christ if you suffer the temptation of the spirit of lust, but fearful of the future judgement of Christ, you have not thought about profaning the purity of soul and body.

You are a martyr for Christ if you were tempted by the spirit of avarice to confiscate the goods of those below you or not to respect the rights of defenceless widows. But you judged that it was better to achieve riches through the contemplation of divine precepts, than to commit an injustice. Christ wishes to remain close to such witnesses: *Learn to do good; seek justice, rescue the oppressed, defend the orphan, plead for the widow. Come now, let us argue it out* (Is 1:17-18).

You are a martyr for Christ if you suffer the temptation of the spirit of pride, but seeing yourself weak and helpless, you turn with a pious spirit, and you love humility more than arrogance. Furthermore, you can witness not only in word but also in deed. For who is a more faithful witness than the one who confesses that Jesus was made incarnate, and at the same time keeps the commandments of the gospel? For the one who listens but does not put it into effect denies Christ. Although he confesses it in words, he denies it in deeds. For there are many who say: *Lord, Lord, did we not prophesy in your name, and cast out demons in your name, and do many deeds of power in your name?* (Matt 7:22); that day he will tell them, *Go away from me you evil-doers* (Matt 7:23). For he who has made himself reliable through his works, confesses to Jesus Christ, and is a true witness.

How many people are hidden martyrs for Christ each day, confessing the Lord Jesus with their deeds! The Apostle recognised this martyrdom and faithful witness to Christ when he stated: *This is our boast: the testimony of our conscience* (2 Cor 1:12)...

Many are my persecutors and my adversaries. Christ perhaps says this, and says it through the voice of each one of us: the foe persecutes him within us. If you claim that no one persecutes you, sideline Christ, who suffered temptation to overcome it. Where the devil sees him, he prepares traps, there he prepares the tricks of temptation, there he plots his deceit, so as to reject him if possible. But where the devil fights, there too is Christ; where the devil besieges, there Christ is confined and defends the walls of the spiritual fortress. Thus he who retreats in the face of the arrival of the persecutor, also expels the defender. So, when you hear, *many are my persecutors and my adversaries,* do not fear, for you too can say: *If God is for us, who is against us* (Rom 8:31). This states the truth that through the testimonies of our Lord, one distances oneself from the twists and turns of the paths of vice.

In Psalmum CXVIII expositio, Sermo XX, 45-48, 51

Saint Ambrose

DIVINE MERCY

Which one of you, having a hundred sheep and losing one of them, does not leave the ninety-nine in the wilderness and go after the one that is lost until he finds it (Luke 15:4). A little earlier you learned that we need to banish negligence, to avoid ignorance, and also to acquire devotion and not to give oneself over to worldly business, nor to give preference to fragile goods over those which last for ever. Since human weakness does not allow it to maintain a straight line in the midst of such a corrupt world, this good doctor has offered you the prescription, even against error, and this merciful judge has offered you the hope of a pardon. And so, not without reason, has St Luke narrated three parables in order: that of the sheep which was lost and then found, that of the drachma which was mislaid and was located, and that of the son who had died and was brought back to life. All of this so that, having been taught the lesson of the triple remedy, we can cure our wounds, for *a threefold cord is not easily broken* (Eccl 4:12).

Who, then, is this father, this shepherd, this mother? Could they not, perhaps, represent God the Father, Christ and the Church? Christ carries you on his shoulders, the Church seeks you out, and the Father receives you. One, because he is Shepherd, continues carrying you; another, as Mother, ceases not to search for you; and then the Father comes back to dress you. The first, as a work of his mercy; the second, looking after you; and third, reconciling yourself to him. Each one of them matches these qualities perfectly well: the Redeemer comes to save, the Church assists, and the Father reconciles. The same mercy is present in all divine activity, although the grace varies according to our merits. The Shepherd calls out to the tired sheep, the drachma which had been lost is found, and the son, on his own initiative, returns to the father, fully repentant of his errors, which he accuses himself of. We see then, that with complete justice it is written, *You save animals and humans alike, O Lord* (Ps 36:7). And who are these animals? The prophet stated that the seed of Israel would be the seed of humans, and that the seed of Judah would be the seed of animals (cf Jer 31:27). Israel is therefore saved as a man would be, and Judah fetched as an animal. As regards myself, I would prefer to be a son rather than a sheep, for although the latter is sought for by the shepherd, the son receives the welcome of his father.

The lost sheep

Let us recall then, that the sheep which had perished in Adam was saved by Christ. The shoulders of Christ are the arms of the Cross. On them I place my sins, and on this noble gibbet I have rested. This sheep is one as regards genus, but not as regards species: *because we who are many are one body* (1 Cor 10:17), although we are many members. And so it is written, *you are the body of Christ and individually members of it* (1 Cor 12:27). For *the Son of man came to seek out and to save the lost* (Luke 19:10), that is to say, for all, since *for as all die in Adam, so all will be made alive in Christ* (1 Cor 15:22).

We are referring to a rich shepherd, and we do not form even one per cent of his property. He has numerous flocks of angels, archangels, dominions, powers, thrones (cf Col 1:16), and many others whom he has left on the mountainside: being spiritual beings, with good reason they delight in the redemption of men. Moreover, each one who feels that his conversion will be a cause of great joy for the choirs of angels – who sometimes have the duty to exercise their patronage and on other occasions to keep one away from sin – is certainly very suitable for progressing in good. Make an effort, then, to be a joy for these angels who are filled with rejoicing on your conversion.

The lost drachma

Not without reason, too, did that woman who found the drachma rejoice (cf Luke 15:8-10). And this drachma, which carries the imprint of the figure of the prince, is not something of little value. The riches of the Church consist in possessing the image of the King. We are his sheep. Let us pray so that we may become worthy of placing ourselves in the waters which give life (cf Ps 22:2). I have said that we are sheep: let us ask for the pasture; and as we are sons and daughters, let us run towards the Father.

The son brought back to life

Let us not fear having squandered our spiritual inheritance on worldly pleasures (cf Luke 15:11-32). The Father once again gives to the son the treasure he once possessed, the treasure of faith, which never diminishes. Although he might have given everything, he who had not lost what he had received had everything. And do not be afraid that you may not receive, because God *does not delight in the death of the living* (Wis 1:13). Truly, he will come out running to meet you, his arms will be all-embracing – for *the Lord lifts those who are bowed down* (Ps 146:8) – and He will give you a kiss, a sign of affection and of love; he will order his servants to dress you, to put a ring on you and give you sandals. You still are fearful for the affront you have caused, but He returns to you the dignity which you had lost. You fear punishment, and He kisses you. Finally, you fear being scolded, but He entertains you with a banquet.

Expositio evangelii segundum Lucam VII, 207-212

Saint Ambrose

THE RICHES OF THE PSALMS

Although the beauty of God is exhibited in all the books of Sacred Scripture, it is particularly sweet in the book of Psalms. Moses himself, who described the features of the Patriarchs in unaffected language, when he came to lead the peoples of the Fathers across the Red Sea in a memorable undertaking, and saw Pharaoh drowned with his troops, was inspired to great heights (for he had achieved feats which he knew to be beyond his capability). Triumphantly he intoned a canticle to the Lord (cf Exod 15). Miriam, too, taking a tambourine in her hand, exhorts other women saying: *Sing to the Lord, for he has triumphed gloriously; horse and rider he has thrown into the sea* (Exod 15:22)...

History instructs. The Law teaches. Prophecy announces. Correction reprimands. Morals advise. In the book of Psalms, the way for progress for all men is to be found, and there lies the medicine for the health of all. Whosoever reads it, will find the way to cure the wounds of one's own defects with a specific prescription. Whoever takes the trouble to look at it will find, as on a training ground for virtues, various kinds of exhibitions. And one can choose for oneself, whatever one considers most suitable. The prize is thus more easily within one's grasp.

Examples of virtue

If one is keen to look into features of his ancestors and wants to imitate them, he will find in one psalm (cf Ps

68:9 ss) the whole development of the family history. With a little reading he can enrich his mind with a treasure of knowledge... If another studies the value of the law, which is summarised in its entirety in the bond of charity – *for the one who loves another has fulfilled the law* (Rom 15:8) – he will read in the psalms the depth of love King David showed when he risked great dangers to discard the ignominy of all his people. In it one will recognise that the glory of charity is not inferior to the triumph of virtue. If one fears the violence of corrections, let him listen to the words of the psalm: *O Lord do not rebuke me in your anger, or discipline me in your wrath* (Ps 6:1). Let him learn to moderate the judgement of a furious judge. If another seeks an example of patience, let him read in the psalms: *if I have repaid my ally with harm...* (Ps 7:4), and see the psalm has foreseen the spirit of the evangelical precept and has preceded it in virtue...

And what will I say about the value of prophecy? What others had announced a little enigmatically, appears only to have been clearly and openly promised by David. Thus, the Lord Jesus would be born of his lineage, just as the Lord had said to him: *One of the sons of your body I will set on your throne* (Ps 132:11). Jesus then, is not only born in the psalms, but he also suffers the salvific passion of his body, he dies, rises, ascends to heaven, and sits at the right hand of the Father. This, which no man could bring himself to say, was announced only by this prophet; and later, the Lord himself stated it in the Good News.

Furthermore, hagiographers have always quoted in their writings examples taken from the book of Psalms or some preceding text; but the psalms, on the other hand, do not contain anything which is not original. What is more pleasing than the psalm? David, himself, has said: *Praise the Lord! How good it is to sing praises to our God; for he is gracious, and a song of praise is fitting* (Ps 147:1). And it's true. For the psalm is a blessing for the whole people; it is praise for God, the applause of all, universal words, the voice of the Church, a melodious profession of faith, a devotion permeated with authority, a recognition of freedom, a clamour of joy, an exclamation of good cheer. Anger is tempered, worry rejected, sadness taken away. A weapon at night, a teacher in the day; a shield in fear, a celebration in holiness, an image of serenity, a foretaste of peace and concordance, like a zither which produces just one melody from a variety of disparate sounds. The dawn of a new day brings the sound of the song of a psalm, and with the song of a psalm comes the setting of the sun...

In a psalm, doctrine competes with beauty. One sings it both for pleasure and one learns from it. The hardest pieces of advice are not remembered except for those given gently. But once they have entered the heart, they are never forgotten. What is it that is not to be found in the reading of the psalms? In them I read: *a song for the loved one* (Ps 45:1), and I am set alight by the longing of sacred love. In them I recognise the wine-press of the divine mysteries. In them I examine the grace of divine revelation, the witnesses to the resurrection, the gifts of the promises. In them I learn to avoid sin and not to be ashamed to do penance for my faults. Such a great kind, such a great prophet, plucking chords with the plectrum of the Holy Spirit, has made the sweetness of celestial music resound all over the earth. At the same time, while he – modulating various rhythms with the lye and zither, made from the skins of animals – has raised to heaven the sounds of praises to God, he has also taught us that we should first die to sin, for only then can we make this body of ours rhyme with works of virtue, through which the gratitude of our devotion can reach God...

David, then, teaches us that it is good to sing internally and to recite the psalms quietly, just as Paul sang, saying: *I will pray with the spirit; I will also pray with the mind; I will pluck chords with the spirit; I will pluck chords also with the mind* (cf Rom 6:2,10). He has taught us to model our actions and our lives on the highest realities, so that the pleasure of sweetness does not excite the passions of the body, which do not rescue our soul but enchain it.

The same holy prophet recalled that he would sing the psalms for the redemption of his own soul: *I will sing praises to you with the lyre, O Holy One of Israel. My lips will shout for joy, when I sing praises to you; my soul also which you have rescued* (Ps 71:22-23).

Explanatio Psalmorum XII, 1, 4, 7-12

Saint Ambrose

THE MERCY OF CHRIST

Moderation alone has propagated the Church, purchased at the price of the Lord's blood. It is the imitation of the heavenly gift and the redemption of all people. It rules by such healthy discretion that the ears of men are able to bear it, their minds do not flee from it and their spirits are not terrified of it.

Whoever is striving to amend the imperfections of human weakness must bear them on his own shoulders and in some way compensate for them, not reject them. Indeed, that shepherd in the gospel is said to have carried the exhausted sheep, not to have cast it aside.

Solomon says, *Do not be excessively just* (Sir 7:16). Moderation must temper justice. How can someone present himself to you to be cured whom you hold in disdain, who feels himself to be despised, who does not consider that he will be an object of compassion for his physician?

Therefore, the Lord Jesus took compassion on us in order that he might call us to Himself and not scare us away. He comes as someone gentle, someone humble and then He says, *Come to me all you who labour and I will refresh you* (Matt 11:28). Thus the Lord Jesus refreshes. He neither excludes nor casts away. He rightly chose such disciples who, as messengers of the Lord's will, would gather together God's people, not disdain them.

It is clear, then, that they are not to be considered disciples of Christ who believe that hard and proud principles are to be preferred to gentle and humble ones. They seek God's mercy themselves, but deny it to others. Such are the teachers of the Novatians, (*Editor's Note: Novatians refused pardon to those guilty of grave sins after Baptism*), who call themselves pure. They deny that it is necessary for these, who have fallen away by collusion with the pagans, to be returned to communion. They say that they are paying reverence to God, to whom alone they reserve the power of forgiving sins.

On the contrary, no one does greater harm than he who wishes to rescind the Lord's commandments and take back the gift which has already been given. Indeed, since the Lord Jesus Himself has said in the gospel, *Receive the Holy Spirit. Whose sins you shall forgive, they are forgiven and whose sins you shall retain, they are retained* (John 20:22-23), who is it who honours the Lord more, the one who obeys His commands, or the one who resists them?

On Penance, 1.1-3; 2.5,6

Saint Ambrose

THE VISITATION OF OUR LADY

When the angel was announcing the mysteries to the Virgin Mary, he also told her, as a precedent, to help her believe, that an old barren woman had conceived. This is to show that God can do everything that pleases Him.

When Mary heard this she hurried off to the hill country ... not because she disbelieved the oracle, or was uncertain about the messenger, or doubted the precedent offered, but because she was overjoyed with desire, eager to fulfil a duty of piety, and impelled by gladness.

Where could she that was filled with God hasten to, except to the heights? There is no such thing as delay in the working of the Holy Spirit. The arrival of Mary and the blessings of the Lord's presence are also speedily declared.

As soon as Elizabeth heard the greeting of Mary, the babe leaped in her womb; and she was filled with the Holy Spirit. Notice the choice of words and their precise meaning. Elizabeth was the first to hear the voice; but John was the first to experience grace. She heard according to the order of nature; he leaped because of the mystery. She recognised the arrival of Mary; he, the arrival of the Lord. The woman recognised the woman's arrival; the child, that of the child. The women speak of grace; the babies make it effective from within to the advantage of the mothers who, by a double miracle, prophesy under the inspiration of their babies.

The infant leaped. The mother was filled with the Holy Spirit. The mother was not filled before the son, but after the son was filled with the Holy Spirit, he filled his mother too. John leaped and the spirit of Mary rejoiced. As John leaped, Elizabeth is filled, but we know that Mary was not filled but her spirit rejoiced. For He who cannot be comprehended was working in His mother's womb in ways beyond comprehension. Elizabeth was filled with the Spirit after she had conceived, and Mary before. *Blessed are you*, she said, *who believed*.

Personal belief

But you too, who have heard and have believed, are blessed. Every soul who has believed both conceives and generates the Word of God and recognises His works. Let the soul of Mary be in each one of you to magnify the Lord. Let the spirit of Mary be in each one to exult in God. According to the flesh one woman is the mother of Christ, but according to faith, Christ is the fruit of all men.

Every soul, indeed, receives the Word of God, provided it remains unstained and free from sin and preserves its chastity in unviolated modesty. The soul who has been able to reach this state magnifies the Lord, as Mary's soul magnified the Lord and her spirit rejoiced in God her Saviour. The Lord is magnified, as you have also read elsewhere, *Magnify the Lord with me*, not that human words can add anything to the Lord, but because He is magnified in us. Christ is the image of God; hence, any good or religious deed a soul has performed magnifies the image of God in whose likeness the soul was made. And as it magnifies His image it has some share in His greatness and is thereby ennobled.

Commentary on the Gospel of St Luke

Saint Ambrose

THE UNTIMELY FRIEND

Suppose one of you has a friend, and you go to him at midnight and say to him, 'Friend, lend me three loaves of bread...' (Luke 11:5).

Frequent prayer

From this passage one may infer the precept of praying at every moment, not only during the day, but also at night. See how this man, who has gone to his friend in the middle to the night to ask for three loaves of bread and perseveres in his request, does not ask in vain.

What do these three loaves signify, but a type of heavenly nourishment? You, if you love the Lord your God, will obtain it not only for yourself but also for others. And who could be a better friend to us than He who gave his body for us?

It was of Him that David, in the middle of the night, asked for bread and got it. He really asked for it, for he says: *At midnight I rise to praise you* (Ps 119:62). He merited this bread, which he later placed before us so that we could eat it. He also asked for it when he says: *Every night I flood my bed with tears* (Ps 6:7). he did not fear awakening from sleep someone who is always awake.

Taking our cue from Scripture, let us night and day ask with insistent prayer for the forgiveness of our sins. For if that great saint, who was so busy with governing his kingdom turned to the Lord to praise him seven times a day (cf Ps 119:164), and was prompt to offer sacrifices in the early morning and in the evening, what should we be doing? Should we not be asking with greater insistence, given our frequent falls that are a consequence of the fragility of our soul and body? Tired by the journey, fatigued by the passage through this world and the torturous nature of this life, there will always be for our nourishment the bread that strengthens the hearts of men.

The Lord commands us to be on our guard, not only in the middle of the night, but at all times, for he may call on us in the afternoon, or in the second or the third watch. So *blessed are those slaves whom the master finds alert when he comes* (Luke 12:37). If you want God's power to guard you and to defend you, you should always be on guard. For we are always surrounded by a lot of cunning and the tendency of the body to become drowsy; and if the soul falls off to sleep it will lose the vigour of its strength.

The experience of John and Paul

Shake off your drowsiness, so that you can call at Christ's door, at which Paul also called, so that it be opened. Not content with his own petitions, he asked all the people for their help, so that the door might be opened for him to speak of the mystery of Christ (cf Col 4:3).

Perhaps this is the door which John saw open. For when he gazed at it he said: *After this I looked, and there in heaven a door stood open! And the first voice which I had heard came speaking to me like a trumpet, said, 'Come up here and I will show you what must take place after this.'* (Rev 4:1). The door stood open for John, and also for Paul, so that they could receive the bread which we eat. Paul persevered in calling out, opportunely and inopportunely (cf 2 Tim 4:2), so as to revitalise, with an abundance of spiritual food, the gentiles exhausted and weary of the journey through this world.

This passage, first by way of a command, and then as an example, prescribes for us frequent prayer, the hope of achieving the goal of our petitions and the special art of persuading God. For he who promises something, ought to offer a hope of that promise being fulfilled, so that one offers obedience to advice and faith in that promise: a faith, which bearing in mind human generosity, rightly acquires hope in eternal generosity, provided one is asking for things which are just, so as to avoid prayer becoming an occasion of sin (cf Ps 109:7).

Paul, moreover, did not feel ashamed to ask often for the same thing. It might appear to us as if he did not trust in the Lord's mercy, or to complain proudly that he had not received it with his first prayer. *Three times I appealed to the Lord about this* (2 Cor 12:8), he says. In this way he wanted to point out to us that frequently God does not grant us what we ask for, because what we consider to be advantageous, he judges to be useless.

Expositio Evangelii secundum Lucam, 7, 87-90

Saint Cromacious of Aquileya

Cromacious was born in Aquileya, a town in northern Italy, about the year 340 A.D. He was present as a presbyter in the synod which took place in the town in 381, and which ended semi-arianism in the provinces of Illirico. On the death of Bishop Valerianus in 388, Cromacious was elected his successor to the see of Aquileya.

St Cromacious dedicated himself to the pastoral care of his flock for the twenty years of his episcopate, preaching and administering the sacraments. He corresponded with St Ambrose, St Jerome and St John Chrysostom, who appreciated the holiness of this bishop of Aquileya.

St Cromacious died in 407 or 408, a little before the second invasion of Italy by Alaric's forces.

Precious little of his homiletic activity survives to the present day. The authenticity of 43 sermons or fragments of sermons are recognised as being from his lips. Most of them are commentaries on St Matthew's Gospel. St Cromacious also encouraged St Jerome and St Rufinus of Aquileya in their work of translation, urging them to put their linguistic talent to the service of the Church. This is how St Jerome came to translate the books of Sacred Scripture into Latin. Rufinus, for his part, translated some of the works of Origen and the History of the Church by Eusebius of Caesarea.

Saint Cromacious of Aquileya

THE BEATITUDES

This meeting and gathering of people on market-day offers us the possibility of proposing to you, dear brothers, some words of the Gospel. For the realities of this world are a figure of the spiritual, and the things of the earth are an image of those of Heaven. Indeed, our Lord and Saviour frequently taught us about the heavenly realities by referring to the things of the earth, as for example: *The kingdom of heaven is like a net which was thrown into the sea* (Matt 13:7); and also: *The kingdom of heaven is like a merchant who goes in search of fine pearls* (Matt 13:45).

A salesman for God

Thus, if the mission of the merchant is to allow each one, according to his interests, to put on sale what he does not need or to buy what he does need, it will not be out of place for me to offer you the merchandise which the Lord has entrusted to me, particularly by preaching. For, although I am most vile and unworthy, he has chosen me from among those servants to whom he has distributed talents for them to use and make a profit. Where there are, by the grace of God, so many and such fine listeners, merchants there certainly will not be lacking. For it is more necessary to seek heavenly gain precisely where material interests are not neglected.

Dearest brothers, I wish to offer you the precious pearls of the beatitudes taken from the Gospel. Open the gates of your heart, purchase and take avid possession, and joyfully become their owners.

The Beatitudes

The first rungs

While the multitudes gathered from the various regions, our Lord and our God, only-Begotten Son of the Highest Father, who being God deigned to become Man, took his disciples with him. That is to say, he went up the mountain with his Apostles and began to teach them saying: *Blessed are the poor in spirit for theirs is the kingdom of heaven. Blessed are the meek, for they shall inherit the earth* (Matt 5:3,4) ... Our Lord, Our saviour, establishes extremely solid steps of precious stones, by which saintly souls and faithful can climb, can rise to this supreme good, which is the kingdom of heaven. I want then, dearest brothers, to point out briefly what these steps are. Pay attention with all your heart and mind, because God's things are of no little importance.

Blessed are the poor in spirit for theirs is the kingdom of heaven (Matt 5:3). My brothers, this is a splendid principle of celestial doctrine. The Lord begins not through fear, but through beatitude. He raises not fear but desires. Like an umpire or a promoter of a contest of gladiators, he offers an important prize to those who fight in the spiritual stadium, so that they do not fear fatigue. And with the prize in view, do not tremble before the dangers. *Blessed,* then, *are the poor in spirit for theirs is the kingdom of heaven.*

The Lord has not simply said, without being more specific, that it is the poor who will be rich. He has been more specific: it is the poor *in spirit*. We cannot just call any poverty 'blessed'; for frequently it is a consequence of disgraceful behaviour, depraved customs, and even divine rage. Blessed, then, is spiritual poverty, that is to say, that of those men who willingly make themselves poor for God, renouncing the goods of this world and spontaneously donating their own riches. It is these who are justly called blessed, because they are poor in spirit, and because theirs is the kingdom of heaven. Through voluntary poverty they attain the riches of the kingdom of heaven.

The next steps

Our Lord continues: *Blessed are those who mourn, for they shall be comforted* (Matt 5:5). What can be this salutary weeping for us? Clearly not that which results from losing our goods, or as a result of the death of our loved ones, or the loss of the honours of this world. These things do not sadden those who have come to be poor in spirit. Crying is healthy if the tears are shed for one's own sins, recalling God's judgement. In the midst of the innumerable concerns and difficulties of this world, the soul was not able to think about itself. But now, free from cares and with serenity, it looks at itself more closely, examining its actions by day and by night. The injuries from past faults then begin to appear. These are then followed by beneficial weeping and tears, and very useful in immediately attracting heavenly consolation. For he who has said, *Blessed are those who mourn, for they shall be comforted*, is truthful.

Let us move on then, brethren, to the fourth step. *Blessed are those who hunger and thirst for righteousness, for they shall be satisfied* (Matt 5:6). After repentance, after weeping and shedding tears for sins, what other hunger and what other thirst can be born, but that for justice! How joyful one becomes when light begins to dawn for one who has spent the night in darkness, and how one wishes to eat and drink after swallowing bitter bile. So, too, the soul of a Christian – having expiated for one's own sins, with sorrow and with tears – hungers and thirsts only for the justice of God, and rightly will enjoy being satisfied with what he desires.

The fifth and sixth steps

Let us now move to the fifth step. *Blessed are the merciful for they shall obtain mercy* (Matt 5:7). No one can give anything to anyone if he himself has not previously been given it. Thus having obtained mercy and an abundance of justice, the Christian begins to have compassion on those who are unhappy, and he begins to pray for the sins of others. He becomes merciful even towards his enemies. With this goodness, a fine reserve of mercy is prepared for the Lord's coming. Thus it is said, *Blessed are the merciful for they shall obtain mercy*.

And the sixth step. *Blessed are the pure in heart, because they shall see God* (Matt 5:8). The following are certainly already clean of heart and can see God: the poor of spirit, the meek, those who have wept for their own sins, those who have been nourished by justice, and the merciful who even in adversity maintain the eye of their heart so clear and clean that they can see the inaccessible clarity of God without the heat of malice and without obstacle. Purity of heart, and uprightness of conscience, will not put up with a cloud before the Lord.

I continue, my brothers. *Blessed are the peacemakers, for they shall be called sons of God* (Matt 5:9). Great is the dignity of those who work for peace, for they are considered to be the children of God. It is certainly good to re-establish peace among brothers who look for judgement on matters concerning interest, vainglory and rivalry. But this does not merit more than a modest reward, because, to give an example, our Lord has said: *Who made me a judge or divider among you?* (Luke 12:14). And in another place: *How can you believe who seek glory from one another and do not seek the glory that comes from the only God?* (John 5:44).

We have to realise that there is a kind of work for

peace which is of better quality and more noble. I refer to that which, with regular teaching, brings peace to pagans, God's enemies; that which corrects sinners, and through penance, reconciles them with God; that which brings rebel heretics back to the straight path; that which brings about unity and peace in those who were in disagreement with the Church. Such workers for peace are not only blessed, but are also worthy of being called children of God. Having imitated the Son of God himself, Christ, whom the Apostle calls *our peace* and *our reconciliation* (cf Eph 2:14-16; 2 Cor 5:18-19), allows them to participate in his name.

Blessed are those who are persecuted for righteousness sake, for theirs is the kingdom of heaven (Matt 5:10). There is no doubt, brethren, that the companion of a good deed done is always envy. And that is not to mention the cruelty of persecutors when one begins to practise justice rigorously, to combat arrogance, to advise unbelievers to make peace with the Lord; when, further, one begins to dissent from another who lives in a worldly way and in error, immediately do persecutions erupt; it is inevitable that hate is aroused and that rivalry defames. Thus does Christ finally lead his followers to the final rung, to this peak, to those heights, not only so that they may resist in suffering, but that they may find joy in dying.

At the top of the ladder

Blessed are you, he says, *when men revile you and persecute you, and utter all kinds of evil against you falsely on my account. Rejoice and be glad, for your reward is great in heaven, for so men persecuted the Prophets who were before you* (Matt 5:11-12). Brethren, it is a perfect virtue, having carved out works of great justice, to be reviled for the truth, to be afflicted with torments, and at the end mortally injured but not terrified, following the example of the Prophets, who harassed by injustice, merited being likened to the sufferings and rewards of Christ.

This is the highest rung, of which Paul, looking to Christ, said: *One thing I do, forgetting what lies behind and straining forward to what lies ahead, I press on toward the goal for the prize of the upward call of God in Christ Jesus* (Phil 3:13-14). And even more clearly to Timothy: *I have fought the good fight, I have finished the race* (2 Tim 4:7). And as one who has climbed every step, he adds: *I have kept the faith. Henceforth there is laid up for me the crown of righteousness* (2 Tim 4:8).

Having completed the race, there was nothing more for Paul to do but to achieve gloriously, through tribulation and suffering, the highest rung which is martyrdom. The word of the Lord exhorts us then in an opportune way: *Rejoice and be glad, for your reward is great in heaven*; and He shows clearly that this reward increases as the persecutions increase.

Jacob's ladder

Brethren before your eyes are the *eight rungs* of the gospel, constructed, as I have said, with precious stones. Behold Jacob's ladder which starts on earth and whose top touches heaven. He who climbs it finds the gate of heaven, and having entered it, will have endless joy in the presence of the Lord, eternally praising Him with the holy angels.

This is our trade; this is our spiritual merchandise. Blessed by God, we give what we have. We offer poverty of spirit to receive the riches of the kingdom of heaven which has been promised to us. We offer our meekness to possess the earth and paradise. We weep for our own sins and those of others to merit the consolation of the Lord's goodness. We hunger and thirst for justice, to be satisfied most abundantly. We show mercy to receive true mercy. We live like workers for peace, to be called children of God. We offer a pure heart and a chaste body, to see God with a clear conscience. We do not fear persecution for justice, so as to merit the kingdom of heaven. We welcome cheerfully and joyfully, the insults, torments, death itself – if it comes to that – for God's truth, to receive in heaven a great reward with the Apostles and Prophets.

And so that the end of my address ties in with the beginning: if commercial travellers are cheered up by temporary and fragile profits, how much more should we be joyful and congratulate one another having today found the Lord's pearls, with which there is no compare in this world. To merit buying them, obtaining them and possessing them, we have to ask for help, grace and strength from God Himself.

To him be glory for ever and ever. Amen.

Sermo de octo beatudinibus

Saint Cromacious of Aquileya

A LIFE-GIVING CATCH

As Jesus walked by the sea of Galilee, he saw two brothers ... (Matt 4:18). The gospel text ends with the expression: *Immediately they left the boat and their father, and followed him* (Matt 4:22).

Happy were these fishermen whom the Lord had called, not from among the doctors of the Law, not from among the scribes, nor from among the wise of this world. He called them to the great task of divine preaching and to the grace of apostolate; and they were privileged to be the first.

Criteria for divine selection

Such an election was certainly worthy of Our Lord and would be a very great asset for their preaching. The praise and admiration which would arise at the announcement of the presence of each one, would be even more marvellous considering the humble condition of those called to fulfil the apostolic mission. Despised by the world, they were destined to conquer it, not with the wisdom of beautiful words but with the humble preaching of faith. This was to be the way to liberate the human race from the error of death, as the Apostle indicated when he wrote: *that your faith might not rest in the wisdom of men, but in the power of God* (1 Cor 2:5). And also, *God chose what is foolish in the world to shame the wise; God chose what is weak in the world to shame the strong; God chose what is low and worthless, despised in the world, even things that are not, in order to bring to nothing things that are* (1 Cor 1:27-28).

He has not chosen the rich or the nobility of this world, so that there be no conjecture on the gospel preaching. He has not chosen from among the worldly wise so that no one may believe that its persuasive power over men had been entrusted to the wisdom of the world. On the contrary, He has chosen some poor fishermen, illiterate, inexperienced and ignorant, in order to show that the convincing strength of the Gospel is based on the grace of our Saviour. Men, humble in respect of their profession, but noble in respect of their faith and obedience of the mind, completely dedicated to the Lord; despised by the men of this world, but of inestimable worth in heaven; ignoble by birth, noble through Christ, whose names are not inscribed in the book of heraldry here below, but in the book of life possessed by the angels; poor by this world's standards, but rich by God's. The Lord, who knows the human heart well, knows that he must choose not those who seek to possess the wisdom of this world but those who seek the wisdom of God; not those who seek the riches of this life, but those who ardently seek to possess the treasures of Heaven.

Response to calling

Their willingness manifests itself in the way in which they follow Our Lord. As soon as they hear the invitation, *Come and follow me*, they leave their nets and family trade, and follow Him. The attitude that they have displayed enables us to recognise them as true sons of Abraham: just as he promptly obeyed the voice of God, so too they followed Our Lord. Indeed, in an instant they forewent the possibility of earthly gain, to win eternal advantages; they left an earthly father, to acquire a

A Life-Giving Catch

celestial father. For these things they well merit to have been chosen.

Divine games: hunting and fishing

The Lord chose fishermen, changing the quality of their trade: from fishing of a human kind they were to be led into fishing of a heavenly kind. They were going *to fish* for men sunk in the deepest depths of error; they *would fish* in order to bring them to salvation. The Lord said to them, *Follow me, and I will make you fishers of men* (Matt 4:19). It is nothing more than the fulfilment of the prophecy made by God through the prophet Jeremiah who proclaimed: *I am sending for many fishermen, says the Lord, and they shall catch them. And afterwards I shall send for many hunters* (Jer 16:16). For this reason the Apostles are not simply *fishermen* but also *hunters*. Fishermen, in so far as using the nets of the gospel preaching they bring to the shore, as if they were tiny fish, men who have been uprooted from a worldly life. Hunters, in that they 'capture' men and offer them salvation; men who were immersed in the errors of this world, just like savages living like beasts in the forest: they capture them as in a heavenly hunt, so to speak, in order to save them.

As a result of the preaching of the Apostles, believers are 'captured' each day in order to be offered eternal life. Observe how these fish, the ones caught by the Apostles, differ from material fishing. The first is heavenly fishing. Let me explain. Fish taken from the water die immediately. But precisely the reverse happens when – to continue the imagery – men are fished: they may attain to life eternal. This is what Our Lord said to Peter after the latter made that abundant catch of fish. Do not fear, he said, it will be you who gives life (cf Luke 5:10).

He was not talking of a new promise. The prophet

Ezechiel had spoken of it clearly, when he anticipated the call of the Apostles as evangelical fishermen who would capture fish to give them life. *Wherever the river goes every living creature which swarms will live, and there will be very many fish; for this water goes there, that the waters of the sea may become fresh, so that every thing may live where the river goes. Fishermen will stand beside the sea ... it will be a place for the spreading of nets; the fish will be of very many kinds, like the fish of the Great Sea* (Ezech 47:9-10).

A supernatural catch

What a marvellous catch! What extraordinary fishermen, who fish not to take away life but to give it!

We said a little earlier, that in earthly reality fish taken from the sea, die. On the other hand, in our case (one truly speaks of a spiritual catch,) those fish that are *not* caught, die.

It is clearly seen that one is speaking of life-giving fish in the sacred text just quoted. Note that the Prophet says that the waters will go far; and that every fish that comes to the river will be saved and have life. Be careful nonetheless, not to interpret this detail wrongly. The Prophet is not referring to ordinary water, even less the water we find in an ordinary river. He is alluding to the water of salvation at Baptism and the river of the preaching of the Gospel: it is here that the faithful will attain life.

Do you want to know the properties of the water of which we have spoken? Who can truly understand how it heals, and cures wounds, and gives life? You will find the explanation in the Gospel where Our Lord says: *Whoever drinks of the water I shall give him shall never thirst; the water that I shall give him will become in him a spring of water welling up to eternal life* (John 4:13-14).

I shall put to you another question: Do you want to

know which is the river that gives eternal life? Listen once more to the prophets: *There is a river whose streams make glad the city of God* (Ps 45:4).

In conclusion: we are drawn out from the sea of this age by such fishermen; by them we are uprooted from the abyss of error, when we are reborn in the waters of Baptism; we are purified in the waves of the gospel river, to be able to persevere throughout our life.

Tractatus 16, On the Gospel of St Matthew, 1-3

Saint Jerome

St Jerome was born at Studon (Dalmatia) about 340; he died in Bethlehem on 30 September 420.

At the age of 19 he went to Rome, where he studied Grammar, Rhetoric and Philosophy. He was baptised there and became interested in ecclesiastical matters. He began his theological studies in Trier and continued in Aquileya. Around 374 he set out on a pilgrimage to Jerusalem.

He was taken ill and settled at Antioch. From 374-379 Jerome led a hermit's life in the desert at Chalcis, southwest of Antioch. There he learned Hebrew; later he came to master Latin and Greek.

In 382 he returned to Rome. Pope Damasus asked him to revise the text of the Latin version of the Bible. The Vulgate is the fruit of this work. It continues to be used in the Latin Church. Pope Damasus died (384) and Jerome's position became very difficult, as his earlier harsh criticism had made many enemies.

He was compelled to leave Rome and he went to Bethlehem (386). He settled in a monastery, supported by two Roman ladies who had followed him to Palestine. There he set up four monasteries, three of them for women, a school and a hospice for pilgrims. He spent 34 years at Bethlehem, dedicating himself to the study of the Scriptures, to the spiritual direction of a number of souls, and to defending the faith against various controversies.

It was here that he wrote most of his commentaries on the Bible, as well as various treatises of an apologetic-dogmatic character.

Saint Jerome

THE FIGURE OF THE PRIEST

Detachment

A clergyman, who is a servant in Christ's Church, should first know the meaning of his name. When he has that accurately defined, he should then strive to be what he is called. For since the Greek *kleros* means *lot* or *portion*, the clergy are so named, either because they are the Lord's portion, or else because the Lord is theirs. Now he who himself is the Lord's portion, or has the Lord for his portion, must so bear himself as to possess the Lord and be possessed by Him. He who possesses the Lord and says with the prophet: *The Lord is my portion* (Psalm 123:26), should have nothing outside the Lord. For if he has anything except the Lord, the Lord will not be his portion. For example, if he has gold and silver, land and inlaid furniture, with portions such as these the Lord will not deign to be his portion. If I am the Lord's portion and in the line of His inheritance, I receive no portion among the other tribes (cf Deut 32:9); but like the Priest and the Levite I live on tithes, and serving the altar am supported by the altar offerings. Having food and raiment I shall be satisfied with them, and naked shall follow the naked cross.

So I beseech you and *again and yet again my words repeat* (Virgil, *Aeneid*, III:436), do not think that clerical orders are but a variety of your old military service; that is, do not look for worldly gain when you are fighting in

Christ's army, lest, having more than when you first became a clergyman, you hear it said of you: *Their portions shall not profit them* (Jer 12:13). Let poor men and strangers be acquainted with your modest table, and with them Christ shall be your guest. Avoid, as you would the plague, a clergyman who is also a man of business, one who has risen from poverty to wealth, from obscurity to a high position. *Evil communications corrupt good manners* (1 Cor 15:33). You despise gold; the other loves it. You trample money underfoot; he pursues it. You delight in silence, peacefulness, solitude; he prefers talking and effrontery, the markets and the streets and the apothecaries' shops. When your ways are so diverse, what unity of heart can there be between you?

Refined ways of practising chastity

A woman's foot should seldom or never cross the threshold of your humble lodging. Show all maidens and all Christ's virgins the same disregard or the same affection. Do not remain under the same roof with them. Do not place your trust in the chastity you have practised in the past. You cannot be a more saintly man than David, or more wise than Solomon. Remember always that a woman drove the tiller of Paradise from the garden that had been given him.

If you are ill let one of the brethren attend you, or else your sister or your mother or some woman of universally approved faith. If there are no persons marked out by ties of kinship, or reputation for chastity, the Church maintains many elderly women who by their services can both help you and benefit themselves, so that even your sickness may bear fruit in almsgiving. I know of some whose bodily recovery coincided with spiritual sickness. There is danger for you in the ministrations of one whose face you are continually watching.

If in the course of your clerical duties you have to visit a widow or a virgin, never enter the house alone, and let your associates be men whose fellowship brings no disgrace. If a reader or acolyte or psalm-singer comes with you, let their character, not their dress, be their adornment. Let them not wave their hair with curling tongs but let their outward looks be a guarantee of their chastity. Never sit alone and without witnesses with a woman in a quiet place. If there is anything intimate she wants to say, she has a nurse or some elderly virgin at home, some widow or married woman. She cannot be so cut off from human society as to have no one but yourself to whom she can trust her secret. Beware of men's suspicious thoughts, and if a tale can be invented with some probability, avoid giving the scandalmonger his opportunity.

Frequent gifts of handkerchiefs and ties, pressing a woman's dress to your lips, tasting her food beforehand, writing her fond and flattering *billets-doux*, all of this a holy love knows nothing. *My honey, my light, my darling* – lover's nonsense like this, and all such wanton playfulness and ridiculous courtesy, makes us blush when we hear it on the stage, and seems detestable even on the lips of worldlings. How much more loathsome is it then in the case of monks and clergymen who adorn the priesthood with their vows and their vows with the priesthood! I say this not because I fear such errors in you or in any holy man, but because in every order, in every rank and sex, both good and bad people are to be found, and to condemn the bad is to praise the good.

On giving doctrine

Read God's Book continually; never let the sacred volume be out of your hand. Learn, so that you may teach.

Hold fast to the words of faith, according to sound doctrine, so that you may be able thereby to exhort and refute the gainsayers. *Continue in the things that you have learned and have been assured of, knowing from whom you have learned them* (Tit 1:9; 2 Tim 3:14); and *Be ready always to give an answer to every man who asks of you a reason of the hope and faith that are in you* (1 Pet 3:15). Your deeds must not belie your words, lest, when you are speaking in church, some one may say to himself: *Why do you not practise what you preach?* A teacher, fond of good living, may fill his own stomach and then discourse on the benefits of fasting. Even a robber can possibly accuse others of greed. But in a priest of Christ mind and mouth should be in harmony.

Obedience to the bishop

Be obedient to your bishop, and respect him as your spiritual father. Sons love, slaves fear. *If I be a father,* says Scripture, *where is mine honour? And if I am a master, where is my fear?* (Mal 1:6). In your case one and the same man has many titles to your respect: he is monk, bishop, uncle. But even bishops should realize they are priests, not lords; they should give to clergymen the honour that is their due, so that the clergy may offer them the respect proper to bishops. The orator Domitius made a telling point when he said: *Why should I treat you as leader of the Senate, when you do not treat me as a senator?* (cf Cicero, *De Oratore*, III.1).

We should recognize that a bishop and his priests are like Aaron and his sons. There is but one Lord and one Temple; there should be also but one ministry. Let us always remember the charge which the apostle Peter gives to priests: *Feed the flock of God which is among you, taking the oversight thereof not by constraint but willingly as*

THE FIGURE OF THE PRIEST

God would have you; not for filthy lucre but of a ready mind; neither as being lords over God's heritage but being examples to the flock, and that gladly, that when the chief shepherd shall appear you may receive a crown of glory that does not fade away (1 Pet 1:2).

Visiting families

It is part of your duty to visit the sick, to be acquainted with people's households, with matrons, and with their children, and to be entrusted with the secrets of the great. Let it therefore be your duty to keep your tongue chaste as well as your eyes. Never discuss a woman's looks, nor let one house know what is going on in another. Hippocrates, before he will instruct his pupils, makes them take an oath and compels them to swear obedience to him. *To hold my teacher in this art equal to my own parents ... I will keep pure and holy both my life and my art... Whatsoever I shall see and hear in the course of my profession ... I will never divulge.* This oath exacts silence from them, and prescribes for them their language, gait, dress, and manners. How much greater an obligation is laid on us who have been entrusted with the healing of souls!

We ought to love every Christian household as though it were our own. Let them know us as comforters in their sorrows rather than as guests in their days of prosperity. A clergyman soon becomes an object of contempt, if, as often he is invited to dinner, he does not refuse.

Epistola 52 ad Nepot presby, 55,7,15

SAINT JEROME

TO GIVE FRUIT

A man going on a journey, summoned his slaves and entrusted his property to them. To one he gave five talents, to another two, to another one, to each according to his ability (Matt 25:14-15). There is little doubt that this man, this father of a family, is Christ himself. For before ascending victoriously to his father after the Resurrection, having called the Apostles, he entrusted the gospel doctrine to them, giving to one more, and to another less. This was not out of largess or parsimony, but according to the strengths of those who received them. This is similar to the Apostle's statement that he had fed with milk those who were not ready for solid food (1 Cor 3:2). With equal joy Christ welcomes the man with five talents who returned with ten, as the one who started with two and returned with four... For he does not consider the amount of profit but the effort made by the will. In the five, as in the two and the one talent, we discover the various graces which we find are given to each one of us. One can see the first in the five senses, the second in the intelligence and deeds, and the third in reason, which distinguishes men from animals.

The one who had received five talents went off at once and traded with them, and made five more talents (Matt 25:16). Having received the five earthly senses, he replicated the news of heavenly things, knowing the Creator through creatures, spiritual things through corporeal, invisible through visible, and eternal through contingent things.

The one who had two talents, made two more talents (Matt 25:17). This too replicated, in the knowledge of the Gospel, the truths with which he had learned the Law. Or that he understood well the characteristics of future beatitude, through knowledge and the deeds of earthly life.

But the one who had received the one talent went off and dug a hole in the ground and hid his master's money (Matt 25:18). The bad servant, dominated by earthly works, sensuous living and the pleasures of the world, neglected and stained the precepts of God. Another evangelist says that this servant wrapped the money in piece of cloth (cf Luke 19:20). That is to say, living among pleasures, he rendered the teaching of the father of the family ineffective.

On his return...

After a long time the master of those slaves came and settled accounts with them. The one who had received five talents came forward bringing five more talents saying: 'Master, you handed over to me five talents; see, I have made five more talents' (Matt 25:19-20). Much time will have to pass between the Ascension and the second coming... *His master said to him, 'Well done, good and trustworthy slave, you have been trustworthy in a few things, I will put you in charge of many things. Enter into the joy of your master.' And the one with two talents also came forward saying, 'Master, you have handed over to me two talents, see, I have made two more talents.' His master said to him 'Well done, good and trustworthy slave, you have been trustworthy in a few things, I will put you in charge of many things. Enter into the joy of your master'* (Matt 25:21-23).

The two slaves, both the one who had five talents and

obtained five more, and the one with two talents who obtained two more, received exactly the same praise from the head of the family. It is noteworthy that everything we possess in this life, although it may appear to be big and in abundance, is always small and little in comparison to future benefits. *Enter*, he says, *into the joy of your master*, and receive *what no eye has seen, nor ear heard, nor the human heart conceived, what God has prepared for those who love him* (1 Cor 2:9). What bigger present could one give a faithful slave than to live by his Lord and contemplate his glory?

The one who had received one talent also came forward, saying, 'Master, I knew you were a harsh man, reaping where you did not sow, gathering where you did not scatter seed, so I was afraid and went and hid your talent in the ground. Here you have what is yours' (Matt 25:24-25). What is written in the psalm, *seek excuses for your sins* (cf Ps 140:4), is also applicable to this slave. For, to laziness and negligence he added the sin of pride. He who simply ought to have confessed his cowardice and pleaded with the master, actually calumniates him, maintaining that he acted prudently in not seeking profit, for he was afraid to lose the capital amount.

But his master replied, 'You wicked and lazy slave! You knew, did you, that I reap where I did not sow, and gather where I did not scatter? Then you ought to have invested my money with the bankers, and on my return I would have received what was my own with interest. So take the talent from him, and give it to the one with ten talents' (Matt 25:26-28). He is silent under the penalty, though he had something in his defence. And the slave is called wicked, because he has calumniated the Lord; lazy, because he has not wished to double the talent. He is first condemned for pride, and then for negligence. If you knew – He is, in effect, saying – that I am tough and cruel, and I want things which are not mine, to the point where I reap where I have not sown, why has this thought not implanted fear into you, that I would immediately ask for what was mine, and demand that you lent the bankers my money and my silver?

Money and silver

Both one thing and the other – money and silver – are implied in the Greek word *argyrion*. It is written: *The promises of the Lord are promises that are pure silver refined in a furnace on the ground, purified seven times* (Ps 12:6). Money and silver refer to the preaching of the Gospel and the divine word. These should be given to bankers and dealers. This refers to other learned men (as the Apostles in fact did, when they ordained bishops and presbyters in every province), and to all those believers who can double or repay with interest, for they can carry out in deeds what they have learned by word.

The servant has his talent taken away and given to the one who already had ten, so that we may realise that a greater reward is given to the one who has greater dealings with the Lord's money. And this, within the concept that the Lord is equally pleased by the work of the one who doubled the five talents and the one who doubled the two talents.

This is why the Apostle says, *Let the elders who rule well be worthy of double honour, especially those who labour in preaching and teaching* (1 Tim 5:17). With the statement which the bad slave made, *reaping where you did not sow, gathering where you did not scatter seed*, we understand that the Lord also accepts the noble lives of the pagans and the philosophers who have acted justly, and rejects those who have worked unjustly. In the end, then, when comparing those who have fulfilled the natural law with those who have violated the written law, these latter will be condemned.

For to all those who have, more will be given, and they will have an abundance; but from those who have nothing, even what they have will be taken away (Matt 25:29). Many, although they may be naturally wise and clever, are perhaps also negligent and lackadaisical, and thus squander their natural resources. These people, when compared with someone who is a little slower but who works industriously and makes up for the fewer gifts which he has received, will find that they will lose their natural gifts and see the reward which had been promised to them passed on to others.

We can also understand it in this way: whoever has faith and is inspired by good will in the Lord, will receive remuneration from the just Judge even though through human frailty he has carried out fewer good works. On the other hand, he who did not have faith will lose even the virtues which he had possessed by nature. It is justly said that *even what they have will be taken away*; for everything that one has without faith in Christ, is not to be attributed to the one who has used it badly, but to Him who has given those natural gifts, even to the bad slave.

In evangelium Matthaei commentarii, IV, 25, 14-30

Saint John Chrysostom

St John Chrysostom is one of the four great Fathers of the Eastern Church and the best representative of the school of Antioch. He was born in Antioch around 350 into a noble Christian family.

While still a youth John dedicated himself to the study of theology with Diodorus of Tarsus as his master. After some time on penitential retreat in the desert, he returned to Antioch where he was ordained in 386 by Bishop Flavian. He was given the job of preaching at the principal church in Antioch, a post he held for twelve years. John's splendid eloquence won him the nickname *Chrysostom*, 'the golden mouth'.

As Bishop of Constantinople his zeal led him from the very beginning to change the customs of society, guiding it towards faithfully fulfilling the precepts of the Gospel. He died on 14 September 407 in exile.

He composed famous sermons, which are all-time masterpieces of oratory. He prepared them with consummate skill, and looked especially to the care of the faithful. Although some of his sermons lasted up to two hours, it was clear that these were much appreciated, for on a number of occasions the congregation would break out into applause. As a true doctor of souls he understood the fragility of the human condition, but he also did not hesitate to tackle egoism, lust, arrogance and other vices wherever he came across them.

Among the sermons he delivered are a number of

panegyrics; one of particular interest was preached in honour of St Ignatius of Antioch, a predecessor of his in that see, who had suffered martyrdom. Chrysostom demonstrates what a privilege it is to have the relics of a saint so close and the benefit, to souls, of devotion to a saint.

The sermon on Pentecost is among those dedicated to liturgical feasts, and is of undoubted authenticity.

Saint John Chrysostom

THE RELICS OF THE SAINTS

The war waged against the Church in an earlier period was terrible. It was as if the most horrible tyrannical power had got hold of the earth, and snatched people away from the very middle of the squares. And this, not because they were the culprits for any crime, but because they walked along the paths of truth, free from the general misconduct around them. They had not joined in the worship of demons; they had recognised the true God and they adored his Only-Begotten Son. They really should have been crowned and honoured; but precisely for that reason they were punished and difficulties heaped on those who had embraced the faith, especially those who were the leaders of the Church. For the devil, ever cunning and skilful in setting up these plots, hoped that after capturing the shepherds, it would be easier to scatter the sheep.

Christ permits difficulties

He who knows how to trap the cunning in their own slyness, wanted to show that it was not men who governed the churches, but it is He who at all times is pastor to those who have faith. So in allowing this to happen, he would show that in spite of eliminating the leaders of the churches, not only would religion not be impaired and preaching not be extinguished, but that it would actually increase. The devil, and all his assistants, would realise that our religion is not a human enterprise, and that it teaches that its roots are in heaven. He would come to realise that it is God who leads the Church at all times, and finally, that no one who wages war against Him can ever emerge victorious.

The martyrdom of Ignatius

But this was not the only plot the devil contrived; he added another which was not immediately obvious. It is this. He did not allow the bishops to suffer martyrdom in their diocesan cities, but led them to distant lands before taking their lives. With this he achieved two objectives. He had them deprived of aid and assistance from their friends, and he also had them exhausted from the weariness of the journey. This is exactly what happened to our saint. But the enemy did not know that in taking Jesus as a companion on the journey, the difficulties and sufferings were followed by renewed strength, and that he was training the churches and giving them greater signs of life.

The fact is that people from all over rushed to the towns through which the bishop was due to pass. They anointed the athlete and gave him the viaticum in abundance, uniting themselves to the combatant with their prayers and emissaries. What they perceived was not simply something which they needed for consolation. They saw a quickness of step of the one going to his death – a quickness proper to one who is called to his heavenly dwelling. They saw the fervour and joy with which he went towards a change in home, towards his ascent to heaven. On this journey he gave a lesson not only by word but also in deed...

Rooted as you are in the faith, by the grace of God, you would need no example. But the Romans needed something which would be of greater help, because their impiety was even bigger. The reason why Peter and Paul were sacrificed, followed by Ignatius, is this: to purify with their blood that city which was stained by the blood offered to idols; to give witness, with deeds, to the resurrection of the crucified Christ, convincing the inhabitants that it was not possible to neglect our present life by taking so much pleasure in it; rather they had to be firmly convinced that they had to rise and reach Jesus Christ and to contemplate him in heaven.

But really the strongest proof of the resurrection of Christ is the strength of the power he shows after suffering a violent death. It is a power which convinces men, for the love of God, to treat with true detachment one's country, one's family, friends, relatives and one's own life; to prefer the whip, dangers and death itself to the pleasures of the present. This could not be represented as a heroic feat of a person who was dead and already laid out in a tomb, but rather the work of one who has risen and lives. Otherwise, what reasonable explanation can there be for the reaction of the Apostles who had lived with him, who had turned into playthings of fear, who had acted treacherously towards Him and in fleeing, had abandoned him. But when he died, not only Peter and Paul, but Ignatius too, who had not even seen him or had any kind of relationship with him, all showed such devotion and dedication to his person, that they gave their lives out of love for him?

St Ignatius thought of the wild beasts not as one who was going to be uprooted from life, but with the joy of one who is called to a better state and to be more spiritual. Where can this be seen? By the very words he uttered when he heard the sentence of his punishment: 'I wish – he said – I could rejoice being with wild beasts.'

That is the way of those who are in love. Whatever they suffer they receive with pleasure, seeing their wishes granted when their sufferings are all the more difficult.

This is what happened with our saint. Not only did he earnestly try to imitate the Apostles in the way he died, but also in the fervour with which he did so. Having heard that the Apostles had left the presence of the Sanedhrin rejoicing after being flogged (cf Acts 5:41), he wanted to imitate his teachers not only in death, but also in the joy of dying.

Once his life came to an end in Rome, or rather, when he went up to heaven, he returned to us once again with a crown. Here, too, one can see the divine kindness in bringing him to us, and granting a martyr to two cities: Rome received his blood when he shed it and you have been honoured with his relics. They rejoiced in his martyrdom, and you in his episcopacy. The Romans saw him struggle and win, and in the end, receive a crown; you have had him continually at your side. For a short period God took him away from you, but gave you greater glory later, thanks to him. Just as those who take money on loan and return it with interest, so God having taken this precious treasure for a short while, returned him to you with greater glory. You sent a bishop and you received a martyr; you sent him amidst prayers and you received him amidst crowns.

And not only have you received gifts, but so have all those cities through which he passed. What will their sentiments be when they see his relics pass their way? What pleasure will they feel? What pride will theirs be? What blessings will they shower on the victor? When a competitor has defeated all his opponents and leaves the arena victorious, the spectators do not allow him to touch the ground with his feet, but carry him home on their shoulders amidst infinite acclamation...

Devotion to a saint

If the occasion of his translation has lifted up these

cities, how much more will Ignatius enrich our city! As an inexhaustible treasure which enriches those who take his side, our blessed Ignatius grants those who turn to his intercession a multitude of blessings, of trust, of thoughts of generosity of great value.

So, not only today, but daily, we will turn to him to harvest these spiritual goods. They will be truly great if we go with faith. And, not only the bodies of the saints, but also their graves are filled with spiritual graces. After Elisha's times (cf 2 Kings 13:21), when a dead person was touched to his grave the chains of death were broken and he came to life again. How much more will happen now, when grace is more abundant and the work of the Holy Spirit is more effective, if one touches the tomb of a saint to draw forth virtue bountifully. This is just why God has left us the relics of the saints. It is as if he wants to lead us by the hand to have the same zeal as they had, and to prepare for us a gate of salvation and certain consolation against the evils which continue to afflict us.

If someone is discouraged or ill, overtaken by his weakness or some other temporal calamity, or weighed down by his sins, I exhort him to come here full of faith and see how all of that will be off-loaded and he will go back full of joy. Just the sight of the tomb of a saint will lighten his conscience. But it is not only for those who are harassed to come here. He who is in full spirit and cheerful, or occupies an important position or exercises authority or feels filled with the confidence of God, he should not value this gift any the less. For if he comes and looks at this saint, he will continue to have the goods which he enjoys, surely and certainly. He will learn to moderate his own soul with the memory of his virtues and will not allow his conscience to make use of any opportunity to become vain...

In summary, this treasure is of use to every one. It is a refuge for those who have stumbled, so that they may be freed of their temptations. It is for those who are enjoying prosperity, so that their goods remain stable and good. It is for the sick so that they may regain their health; and it is for the saints, so that they do not fall ill.

Bearing all this in mind, may we have greater esteem for the time we spend here than any other recreation or pleasure. Drawing on both joy and its good use, we will manage to become colleagues and guests of the saints, through their prayers and through the grace and mercy of Our Lord Jesus Christ, for whom be the glory with the Father and the Holy Spirit, now and forever. Amen.

Panegyric in honour of St Ignatius of Antioch

Saint John Chrysostom

THE PRESENCE OF THE HOLY SPIRIT

On Pentecost Sunday
 The gifts which have descended from heaven to the earth for the benefit of human kind have indeed been many. Among them some refer exclusively to today. Let us look to see which of them are earlier, which are those of today, so that we are more clearly aware of the difference.

He rained down on them manna to eat, and gave them the grain of heaven (Ps 78:24). Man ate the bread of heaven: a great thing, this, and proper to the goodness of God. Fire from heaven was then sent which consumed from the altar the burnt offering which had been prepared (cf 1 Kings 18:38); then the Jewish people who had gone astray were scolded. When almost every one was suffering from hunger, rain was sent with an abundance of wheat.

These events are great and admirable; but those of today's feast are greater still. No manna, no fire, no rain, has been sent to us; but a stream of spiritual gifts: torrents have descended from heaven, not to saturate the earth to produce fruits, but to induce human nature to offer the Farmer the harvest of the virtues of men.

Those who receive just one drop of this rain become transformed to such an extent that it seems as though the earth is filled with angels. Not because they have been transformed into celestial creatures, but because through their human body the strength of incorporeal powers has worked. For the latter have not descended, but in a most wonderful way those who were here below have risen to the power of those on high. Rain did not fall on pure souls disengaged from the flesh, but upon men who, retaining their nature, resembled angels by the splendour of their soul.

One then understands that the punishment – *you are dust and to dust you shall return* (Gen 3:19) – was not so bad after all. For he has left us on earth the power of the Holy Spirit, who has had to work marvels through men. It remained to be seen how the a tongue of clay ruled the demons, and how a hand of clay cured illnesses; a hand of clay, and even the shadow of bodies of clay – which is even more worthy of admiration – overcame death, incorporeal beings, the demons. Just as when the sun breaks out at dawn, darkness disappears, and wild beasts hide in their dens and bandits seek hiding places in the hills, so too when Peter appears and lets his voice be heard, the darkness of error fades away, the devil retreats, the demons take fright, bodily pains disappear, spiritual illnesses are healed, all badness is rejected and virtue extends to all parts.

Ten days ago our nature rose to the royal throne; today the Holy Spirit descends to our nature. The Lord raised our first-fruits to heaven and sent us the Holy Spirit, who is also Lord; and thus one can distinguish the Gift from Him who sends it, for the Father, the Son and the Holy Spirit divided among themselves the cause of our salvation. Ten days had hardly passed since the ascension of Christ, when he sent us spiritual presents, the gift of reconciliation. And so that no one could doubt what Christ did as soon as he arrived in heaven and so that there is no question of us not being reconciled to the Father and to show himself as the propitiatory victim, he immediately sent us the gift of reconciliation.

Once enemies are reconciled and united, immediately do gifts begin to flow. We send our faith and we have received the gifts of the Holy Spirit; we send our obedience and we have received justification...

The evangelist says: *The Holy Spirit had not yet been sent because Jesus had not been glorified* (John 7:59). As Christ had not yet been crucified, the Holy Spirit had not been given to men, for being glorified is worth as much as being crucified: although the action is, in itself, ignominious, Christ calls it glorious, because he suffered for those he loved.

Why was the Holy Spirit not given before the Passion? Because all the earth was covered in sin, offences, hate and ignominious activities – for all of which the Lamb was sacrificed to take away the sin of the world. As Christ had not yet been crucified, reconciliation had not yet taken place. This is why Christ also said, *It is to your advantage that I go away; if I do not go away, the Paraclete will not come to you* (John 16:7). If I do not go away, he says, and reconcile you with the Father, I will not send you the paraclete... Thus when you see the Holy Spirit being sent copiously, you can be certain that reconciliation has taken place.

The Holy Spirit in action today

But someone may say: Where is the Holy Spirit now? For he was certainly around when the signs were there – when the dead were raised and lepers cured. But how are we to know that the Holy Spirit is given to us now? Fear not! I will show you that the Holy Spirit is also in us. If this were not the case, how could those who are going to receive the light of faith this sacred night be freed from sin? For we cannot effectively free ourselves from sin – it is the Holy Spirit who does, as Paul teaches: *For we ourselves, were once foolish, disobedient, led astray, led by various passions and pleasures, passing our days in malice and envy, despicable, hating once another. But when the goodness and loving kindness of God our Saviour appeared, he saved us, not because of any works of righteousness that we had done, but according to his mercy, through the water of rebirth and renewal by the Holy Spirit* (Tit 3:3-5). And elsewhere he says, *You certainly were iniquitous, but you were washed, you were sanctified, you were justified* (1 Cor 6:11). How? This is exactly what we wanted to know: if the Holy Spirit has been involved in the process of getting rid of our iniquity. Here is the answer: *You were sanctified, you were justified in the name of the Lord Jesus Christ and in the Spirit of our God*. Do you see how the Holy Spirit has erased away all this horror?

There remains no doubt, then, about his action and his presence. For if he does not forgive sins, in vain do we receive Baptism. If the Holy Spirit were not to act, we would not be able to say 'Lord Jesus', *for no one can say 'Jesus is Lord' except by the Holy Spirit* (1 Cor 12:3). Just as we could not invoke Jesus, we would not be able to call upon God the Father, according to the same Apostle: *Because you are children, God has sent the Spirit of his Son into our hearts, crying 'Abba, Father!'* (Gal 4:6). When you call upon the Father, remember that you have been able to do this because of the Holy Spirit, who has moved your soul to make this invocation.

Were the Holy Spirit not to act, the Church would not have the gifts of wisdom and knowledge: *To one is given through the Spirit the utterance of Wisdom, and to another the utterance of knowledge* (1 Cor 12:8). Were the Holy Spirit not to act, the Church would not have shepherds and doctors, for they are of the Holy Spirit, as Paul also says: *the Holy Spirit has made you overseers, to shepherd the*

Church of God (Acts 20:28). If the Holy Spirit were not present in your father and doctor, when he rose to the seat a little while ago and gave peace to all of you, you would not have been able to respond with one voice: *and with your Spirit*. And you did it not simply because he rose to his chair, or because he speaks to you, or because he prays with you, but because he approaches the Sacred Table to offer that wonderful sacrifice, (and what I am going to say now is well known to those who take part in the sacraments), and before the oblation he asks God for grace for you, and you acclaim: *and with your Spirit*. By what you yourselves confess, the one who appears there seems to do nothing and the gifts which are offered are not the work of human nature. But, because of the Holy Spirit, the grace present blossoms over everything and works the mystical sacrifice. For, although we see a man, it is God who works through him. Don't limit yourself, then, to the nature of what you see, but be attentive to invisible grace: nothing which takes place in this sacred sanctuary is by human endeavour.

If the Holy Spirit were not to act, the Church would not subsist; but as the Church subsists, there is no doubt that the Holy Spirit is within here.

Homilia I de Sancta Pentecostes, 2-4

SAINT JOHN CHRYSOSTOM

THE NATURAL LAW

I am going to try to show you that man, by himself, has knowledge of virtue.

Examples from the Old testament

Adam committed the first sin, and hid immediately after committing it. Well, if he did not know that he had done something wrong, why did he hide? For in those days neither the Scriptures nor the Law of Moses were in existence. From where, then, did he recognise his action to be a sin and consequently to go into hiding? And, not only did he hide, but when he was accused, he tried to shift the blame onto someone else, saying, *The woman you gave to be with me, she gave me fruit from the tree, and I ate* (Gen 3:12). And she, in turn, shifted the blame onto the serpent.

We see similarities in the story of Cain and Abel. They were the first to offer the first-fruits of their work. I want to prove to you that man is not only capable of recognising sin, but he also recognises virtue. Adam showed that man knows sin to be an evil, while Abel showed that man knows virtue to be a good. If Abel offered his sacrifice it was not because he had learned it from anyone, nor because he had heard about some law that had spoken of first-fruits. He – his conscience – was his own teacher. I will not move on to later times in history, but will dwell on the first men on earth, when there were no writings, no laws, no prophets, no teachers,

THE NATURAL LAW

no precedent. Adam was there, on his own, with his children, and so we realise that knowledge of good and evil is a primary gift of nature.

The Greeks

The Greeks nonetheless, do not agree with this. Let me also argue against them, and continue with the theme of conscience, with the procedure we used when dealing with creation. We will not tackle them only on the basis of Scripture, but also with arguments from reason. Paul has already won his battle with them on this topic.

What do the Greeks say? 'We don't have a law which conscience could know by itself', they say, 'nor did God infuse anything of the sort in our nature.' Tell me then, where did their legislators seek inspiration to establish their laws concerning marriage, murder, wills, avarice and many more things? The current legislators have perhaps been inspired by their predecessors, these latter by earlier legislators and these by even earlier men. But as regards those who first passed the legislation, what inspired them? It's clear! It was their conscience! Because they aren't going to say that they had had dealings with Moses or that they had listened to the prophets. They would not be gentiles if they had! No. Clearly the ancients passed laws that were inspired by the law of God infused in man at creation, and as a result they were able to invent the arts and all the rest.

The New Testament

Surely they established tribunals and determined penalties. Which is what St Paul says. Many gentiles went to argue with him thus: How could God judge men before Moses' time when he had not yet sent them a legislator, or proposed a law, or sent them a prophet, or an apostle or an evangelist? What right did He have to ask them for an account of their deeds? But listen to Paul's reply, It shows them that they did have a law that was known to them, and they had clear knowledge of what they ought to be doing: *When Gentiles who do not possess the law do instinctively what the law requires, these, though not having the law, are a law to themselves. They show that what the law requires is written on their hearts* (Rom 2:14-15).

The Natural Law is written in our hearts

How can something be written without letters? *Because their own conscience bears witness; and their conflicting thoughts will accuse or perhaps excuse them on the day when, according to the Gospel, God, through Jesus Christ, will judge the secret thoughts of all* (Rom 2:15-16). And a little earlier: *All who have sinned apart from the law will also perish apart from the law, and all who have sinned under the law will be judged under the law* (Rom 2:12). What does 'perishing apart from the law' mean? That the law will not be the one to accuse them; it is their conscience and their reason that will. But not having the law of their conscience, they could hardly perish in sin. How would they perish if they sinned outside the law? When the Apostle says that they sinned outside the law, he does not mean to say that they had no law at all, but rather, while they did not have a law in writing, they did have the natural law.

In another passage the Apostle writes, *Glory and honour and peace for those who do good, the Jew first and also the Greek* (Rom 2:10). When speaking like this he was referring to much earlier times than the coming of Christ. And he calls Greek, or gentile, not to idolatry but to the adoration of a single God, and not tied by necessity to Judaic observances of the Sabbath, of circumcision, on

THE NATURAL LAW

various purifications. In the final analysis, he is dealing with a gentile who can practise all the virtues and religion. For speaking of the gentiles he says, *There will be anguish and distress for everyone who does evil, the Jew first and also the Greek* (Rom 2:9). Here he refers to one who, as a Greek, is free from Judaic observances. But if one has not heard the law nor been educated with the Jews, how can one be the target of the indignation and anger, of tribulation and anguish – is it not a case of operating badly? He says it because they have it within their conscience which gives it a reference point, teaches it, and above all instructs it.

How does one prove this? By the fact that the gentile himself punishes those who sin; by the fact that he makes laws and establishes tribunals. Paul makes it clear when he says of those who live in evil: *Though they know God's decree that those who do such things deserve to die, they not only do them but even approve of those who practise them* (Rom 1:32). And how, it will be asked, did they come to know that God wishes to punish with death those who live in evil? By the fact that they punish those who sin. For if they did not consider murder to be a crime, they would not sentence a convicted assassin. If they do not think that adultery was an evil, let them absolve from all punishment the adulterer who falls into their hands.

Take the case of sins against other promulgated laws and guided sentencing; and you are a strict judge. What excuse can you have as regards the matter in which you yourself sin, with the weakness of not knowing what ought to be done. You have committed adultery like another. What reason is there for punishing the other person and expecting yourself to be pardoned? If you did not know adultery was an evil, you could not really punish the other. But if you punish the other and expect to escape punishment yourself, what logic is there if for equal sins the punishment is unequal?

In conclusion, God has to pay each one according to his deeds. And if he established the natural law, and later the written law, so as to ask us for an account of our sins and to crown us with our virtues, let us order our lives with great care. For we will appear before a strict tribunal, knowing that after receiving the natural and written law, after so much preaching and continuous exhortation, if we still disregard our health, there will be no forgiveness for us.

Homiliae ad populum Antiochenum, XII, 4-5

Saint John Chrysostom

LIKE SALT AND LIGHT

To teachers, priests and leaders

You are the salt of the earth (Matt 5:13).

Implying that He includes all this of absolute necessity. For *not for your own life apart,* says He, *but for the whole world, shall your account be. For not to two cities, nor to ten or twenty, nor to a single nation am I sending you, as I sent the prophets; but to earth, and sea, and the whole world; and that in evil case.* By saying, *You are the salt of the earth*, He signified all human nature to have *lost its savour*, and to be decayed by our sins. For which cause, you see, He requires of them such virtues, as are most necessary and useful for the superintendence of the common sort.

For first, the meek, yielding, merciful, and righteous person shuts not up his good deeds to himself only, but also provides that these good fountains should run over for the benefit of others. And he who is pure in heart, and a peacemaker, and is persecuted for the truth's sake: he orders his way of life for the common good. Think not then, He says, that you are drawn on to ordinary conflicts, or that for some small matters you are to give account. *You are the salt of the earth.*

What then? Did they restore the decayed? By no means; for neither is it possible to do any good to that which is already spoilt, by sprinkling it with salt. Therefore they did not do this. But rather, the things that had been before restored, and committed to their charge, and freed from that ill-savour, these they salted, maintaining and preserving them in that freshness, which they had received of the Lord. That men should be set free from the rottenness of their sins was the good work of Christ. But their not *returning* to it again any more was the object of these men's diligence and travail.

You see how by degrees He indicates their superiority to the very Prophets? In that they are teachers, not of Palestine, but of the whole world; and not simply teachers, but awful ones too. For this is the marvellous thing, that not by flattering, nor soothing, but by sharply bracing them, as salt, even so they became dear to all men.

Now marvel not, He says, if leaving all others, I discourse to you, and draw you on to so great dangers. For consider over how many cities, tribes, and nations, I am to send you to preside. Wherefore I would have you not only be prudent yourselves, but that you should also make others the same. And such persons, in whom the salvation of the rest is at stake, have great need to be intelligent: they ought so much to abound in virtue, as to impart of the profit to others also. For if you do not become such as this, you will not suffice even for your own selves.

Be not then impatient, as though my sayings were too burdensome. For while it is possible for others who have lost their savour to return by your means, you, if you should come to this, will with yourselves destroy others also. So that in proportion as the matters are great, which you have put into your hands, you need so much the greater diligence.

Therefore He says, *But if the salt have lost its savour, wherewith shall it be salted? It is thenceforth good for nothing, but to be cast out, and to be trodden under foot of men* (Matt 5:13).

For other men, though they fall never so often, may

possibly obtain indulgence: but should this happen to him, the teacher is deprived of all excuse, and will suffer the most extreme vengeance.

Thus, lest at the words, *When they shall revile you, and persecute you, and say all manner of evil against you* (Matt 5:11), they should be too timid to go forth: He tells them, unless you are prepared to combat with all this, you have been chosen in vain. For it is not evil report that you should fear, but lest you should prove partners in dissimulation. For then, *You will lose your savour, and be trodden under foot:* but if you continue sharply to brace them up, and then evil is spoken of, rejoice; for this is the very use of salt, to sting the corrupt, and make them smart. And so their censure follows of course, in no way harming you, but rather testifying your firmness. But if through fear of it you give up the earnestness that becomes you, you will have to suffer much more grievously, being both evil spoken of, and despised by all. For this is the meaning of *trodden under foot.*

A higher image

After this He leads on to another, a higher image.

You are the light of the world (Matt 5:14).

Of the world again; not of one nation, nor of twenty states, but of the whole inhabited earth. And *a light* to the mind, far better than this sunbeam: as they were also a spiritual *salt*. Before they were *salt*, now *light*: to teach you how great is the gain of these strict precepts, and the profit of that grave discipline. How it binds and permits one not to become dissolute; and causes clear sight, leading men on to virtue.

In what follows, He requires that boldness of speech which was due on their part: *Neither do men light a candle and put it under the bushel, but on the candlestick, and it gives light unto all that are in the house. Let your light so shine before men, that they may see your good works, and glorify your Father which is in Heaven* (Matt 5:15-16).

For I, it is true, have kindled the light; but as for its continuing to burn, let that come of your diligence: not for your own sakes alone, but also for their sake, who are to profit by these rays, and to be guided to the truth. Since the calumnies surely shall not be able to obscure your brightness, if you are still living a strict life, and as becomes those who are to convert the whole world. Show, therefore, a life worthy of his grace; that even as it is everywhere preached, this light may everywhere accompany it.

Bringing all things to Christ

Next He sets before them another sort of gain, besides the salvation of mankind, enough to make them strive earnestly, and to lead them all to diligence. He says: You shall not only amend the world if you live aright, but you will also give occasion for God to be glorified; if you do the contrary, you will both destroy men, and make God's Name be blasphemed.

In Matthaeum homiliae, 15, 10-11

Saint John Chrysostom

A CHRISTIAN'S BATTLE

The time which preceded baptism was a period of training and exercises, when falls and failures found their remedy. From today the arena is open to you. The combat begins. You are under the public gaze. And not only of human kind. Multitudes of angels are also witnesses to your struggles. As St Paul writes in his letter to the Corinthians: *We have become a spectacle to the world, to angels and to mortals* (1 Cor 4:9). The angels, then, gaze on us and the Lord of the angels is the one who presides over the struggle. For us this is an honour and an assurance. For if He who has given his life for us is the judge of this struggle, what pride and what confidence we can have!

Christ is on our side

In the Olympic games, the referee stands between the two opponents, without favouring one or the other, awaiting the outcome. If the referee places himself between the two combatants it is because he is neutral. But in the battle where the devil confronts us, Christ does not remain indifferent: he is entirely on our side. How can this be? You see that no sooner has he entered the ring than he anoints us, while he chains up the devil. He has anointed us with the oils of joy, and him he has bound with unbreakable ties to paralyse his assaults.

If I hit a stumbling block, he stretches out his hand towards me, he lifts me from my fall, and puts me back on my feet. For it is written: *Tread on snakes and scorpions, and over all the power of the enemy* (Luke 10:19).

The devil holds the threat of hell. If I achieve a victory, I receive a crown. But he, when he wins, he is punished. Let me give you an example so that you may see how he is tormented, above all, when he is the victor. He defeated Adam, causing him to stumble. What was the reward for his victory? *Upon your belly you shall go, and dust you shall eat all the days of your life* (Gen 3:14). If God has punished the material servant so severely, what punishment will he inflict on the spiritual serpent! If such has been the condemnation of the instrument, it is clear that one equally terrible sentence awaits the one who directed it. As the good father who lays his hands on the murderer of his son, in addition to punishing him destroys his sword, so Christ, on meeting the murderous devil, not only reprimands him but shatters his sword.

Our weapons and our armour

Let us be filled with confidence, then, and give up everything to confront his assaults. Christ has clothed us with weapons which are of greater splendour than gold, more resistant than steel, which burn better than any flame, and are more slight than a puff of breath. They possess such qualities that we do not double over under their weight. They give us wings; they lighten our members. If you want to embark on a flight into the skies, they will be no obstacle to you.

They are weapons of a totally new nature, for they have been forged for a battle as yet unseen. I, who am no more than a man, see that I am obliged to aim blows at the devil. I, who am dressed in flesh, am to fight against incorporeal beings.

God has prepared an armour-plate too for me, which

is not made of metal but of justice. He has prepared for me a shield made not of bronze but of faith. I have a sharp sword – the word of God – in one hand. The enemy shoots arrows while I have a sword. He is an archer, I a lancer. This is an indication to us of how wary he is, for the archer dares not come close; he would rather shoot from afar.

The Blood of Christ

But what? Has God not given you more than some armour? He has also prepared some food which is more powerful than any arms, so that you may not become demoralised in combat. It is important that your victory be one of a man overflowing with contentment. If the enemy sees you returning from the banquet of the Lord, he will flee faster than the wind, as one who has seen a lion breathing fire from his mouth. If you show him your tongue tinted with the Precious Blood, he will not be able to seize you. And if you show him your reddened mouth, like a wretched animal he will, at great speed, beat a retreat.

Would you like to know where the strength of this blood comes from? Let us return to the old narratives, to what happened in Egypt, to what prefigured it. God was going to inflict the tenth plague on Egypt. He wanted to slay their first-born, because they kept a hold on his – first-born – chosen people. How could he avoid hurting the Jews as they lived in the same areas as the Egyptians. Observe the power of the figure so as to come to know the power of the reality behind it.

The punishment sent by God was going to come from heaven, and the exterminating angel was to do the rounds of the houses. What did Moses order? *Slaughter a lamb without blemish*, he said, *and paint the two doorposts with its blood* (cf Exod 12:21-25). What does this mean? That the blood of an irrational animal can save the life of men gifted with reason. Yes, Moses would reply. Not because it was blood but because it pre-figured the blood of the Lord. The statues of the emperors, which have neither soul nor intellect, protect men gifted with a soul and intelligence and those who have sought refuge beside them, not because these are made of bronze but because they represent the emperor. So, too, this blood bereft of soul and intelligence, has saved men gifted with a soul, not because it was blood but because it pre-figured the blood of the Lord.

That day the exterminating angel saw the blood on the lintel and doorposts, and he did not enter. In the present case, if the devil now sees, not the blood of the figure of the lamb indicating the doors, but the real Blood on the lips of the faithful marking out the gate of the sanctuary of Christ into which it has been converted, he has all the more reason for refraining from getting involved. For if the figure held the angel back, the real thing will be all the more powerful in routing the devil.

Catecheses III, 8-15

Saint John Chrysostom

THE DIGNITY OF THE PRIESTHOOD

When you behold the Lord immolated and lying on the altar, and the priest standing over the sacrifice and praying, and all the people purpled by that precious blood, do you imagine that you are still on earth among men, and not rather rapt in heaven; and casting away all wordly thoughts from your mind, do you not contemplate with a clean heart and pure mind the things of heaven? O miracle! O goodness of God! He that sits above with the Father, is at that moment in the hands of all (2 Cor 3:10), (*Editor's Note: There is an allusion here to an ancient form of distributing Holy Communion. The sacred particle was placed in the hand of the communicant*), and gives Himself to all who desire to embrace and receive Him. At that moment all do this with the eyes of faith.

Do these things seem to you deserving of contempt, or of such a nature that any one could despise them? Do you want to learn from another miracle the excellence of that holiness? Picture to yourself Elias, and the immense multitude standing around, and the victim laid on the altar, and all in stillness and deep silence, while the prophet alone prays; and the fire forthwith descends from heaven upon the altar (3 Kings 18). All this is wonderful and awe-inspiring.

Pass from then to the sacrifice which is now offered, and you will behold what is not only wonderful, but what exceeds all admiration. For the priest stands bringing down not fire, but the Holy Spirit, and he prays long not that fire may descend from heaven and consume the oblation, but that grace may descend upon the victim, and through it inflame the souls of all and render them brighter than fire-tried silver.

Who then, unless he has completely lost his reason and senses, could despise this most awful ministry? Don't you know that the soul of man could not endure the fire of that sacrifice, but all would have utterly perished were it not for the abundant assistance of the grace of God?

For if you consider what it is for a man yet clothed in flesh and blood to approach that pure and blessed nature, you will easily understand to what a dignity the grace of the Holy Spirit has raised priests. For by them these things are accomplished, and others not inferior to these pertaining to our redemption and salvation.

The power of forgiveness

For they who have their abode and sojourn upon earth have been entrusted with a heavenly ministry, and have received a power which God has not granted to angels or archangels. For was it not said to them, *Whatsoever you shall bind on earth, shall be bound also in heaven, and whatsoever you shall loose, shall be loosed*? They who rule on earth have the power of binding, but they can bind the body only.

But this bond reaches to the soul itself, and transcends the heavens; and what priests do upon earth God ratifies above, and the master confirms the sentence of his servants. What then has He given but all power in heaven? *Whose sins,* He says, *you forgive they are forgiven them, and whose sins you retain they are retained* (John 20:23). What power could be greater than this? *The Father has given all power to the Son* (John 5:22).

Now I see that all this power has been placed in the

The Dignity of the Priesthood

hands of his priests by the Son, and they are raised to such a dignity as though they were already lifted up to heaven, elevated above human nature, and set free from its passions.

Duties of the priest

It is manifest folly to despise so great a ministry, without which we could obtain neither salvation nor the good things that have been promised. For as no man can enter into the kingdom of heaven unless he be born again of water and the Holy Spirit (John 3:5); and except he eats the flesh of the Lord, and drinks his blood, he shall be excluded from everlasting life (John 6:54); and as all these things are ministered only by the consecrated hands of priests, how could anyone without them either escape the fire of hell or obtain the crown that is prepared?

It is to priests that spiritual birth and regeneration by baptism is entrusted. By them we put on Christ, and are united to the Son of God, and become members of that blessed head. Hence we should regard them as more august than princes and kings, and more venerable than parents. For the latter begot us of blood and the will of the flesh, but priests are the cause of our generation from God, of our spiritual regeneration, of our true freedom and sonship according to grace.

The priests of the Jews had power to cleanse from leprosy, or rather not to cleanse, but to pronounce cleansed (Lev 14:3). Yet you know what emulation there was then to obtain the priestly office. But our priests have received power not to declare cleansed, but in reality to cleanse, not the leprosy of the body, but the uncleanness of the soul. Hence they who should despise such an office, would be more abominable than Dathan and his fellows (Num 16), and deserving of severer punishment.

Parents and priests

God has given to priests greater power than to our natural parents not merely to impose penance, but also to confer favours; and so much greater as the future life excels the present. For our parents begot us to the present life, but priests to the life to come; and the former cannot ward off from their children the death of the body, nor hinder disease from attacking them, whereas the latter often preserve souls that are ill and about to die, in some cases by imposing a lighter penance, and in others by hindering them from falling, and that not merely by means of instruction and admonition, but also by means of prayer. And not only in our regeneration have they the power to remit sin; but they have also the power to remit the sins committed after regeneration.

Moreover, parents according to nature can be of no assistance to their children if they chance to offend anyone in dignity and power. But priests have often reconciled them, not with kings or princes, but with God himself, even when he is incensed against them.

De sacerdotio, III, 4-6

Saint John Chrysostom

BEGINNING AGAIN

It does not surprise anyone to learn that those who do not believe in the Resurrection live negligently and have no fear of being judged. On the other hand it is silly that we, for whom the life to come is more certain than the present one, live so miserably that the thought of that life leaves no impression on us. If those of us who are believers act like unbelievers – and at times we even live worse than them (for among the pagans there are many who shine in virtue) – what consolation and what kind of forgiveness awaits us?

Many merchants, whose businesses have failed, have not allowed this to discourage them. They have resumed their activity, in spite of the fact that the earlier threat had not come from their own negligence but because of the violence of the winds. And we, who can look confidently to the end, and know perfectly well that if we do not want to, we do not have to sink or suffer any difficulty, could we not once more put our shoulder to the wheel and begin to trade like before? Are we to remain idle, with our hands folded? Although sometimes I do wish that those hands remained only folded, and not raised against our very selves!

For this is what sometimes happens, and it is the height of madness. If a boxer, turning aside from his opponent, were to direct his fists at his own head and cut his own cheeks, would we not count him among the madmen? The devil has sprung a trap on us and thrown us to the ground. It is for us to get up and not allow ourselves to be dragged down once again. Let us not hurl ourselves against ourselves nor add our own punches to that of the devil.

David's example

Blessed David had a fall similar to your own; and then another, that of murder. And then, what? Did he stay there, laid out flat? Did he not get up immediately and confront the enemy? So it was. And so valiantly did he defeat him that, after his death, he was the protector of his descendants. That is why Solomon, who had committed a serious crime which merited a hundred deaths, was told by God that out of love for David, he would allow his kingdom to remain intact: *I will surely tear the kingdom from you and give it to your servant. I will not do it in your lifetime.* Why? *For the sake of your father David. I will take it out of the hand of your son* (1 Kings 11:13).

Out of love for David too, God deigned to help Hezekiah, who although a good man personally, was in great danger: *I will defend this city to save it for my own sake, and for the sake of my servant David* (2 Kings 19:34).

Such is the strength of repentance. If David had thought to himself what you are now thinking, that it is now too late to placate God; if he had said to himself, 'God has showered me with such high honours, he has given me prime position among the prophets, he has entrusted to me the command of my peoples, he has delivered me from countless dangers... If I have offended him after having received such great favours, and I have committed the gravest of crimes, how can he now treat me favourably?' Had David reasoned in this way, not only would he not done what he did, but he would have lost everything he had.

It is not only the injuries to the body but also those to the soul which, if they are not taken care of, lead to death.

Nevertheless, on occasions we reach such a state of stupidity that we make every effort to look after the body, but pay no attention to the soul. It is natural for an incurable illness to attack the body. But we don't despair, and in spite of what the doctors say, and repeat to us, that there is no medical cure, we insist once and again that they at least try to give us some relief. On the other hand, in the soul there is no incurable disease, for the spirit is not subject to the needs of nature. But we still neglect its illnesses and despair of its cure, as if we were dealing with someone else's ailments. Where the nature of an illness should lead us to despair, we make every effort as if we held out great hopes of cure; where there is no reason for being sad, we give up and become neglectful, as if we had been given a hopeless prognosis. It is to that extent that we care for the body at the expense of the soul.

Really, this is not the way even to save the body. The person who neglects the primary and puts all his energies into the secondary, destroys and loses both. He who retains the proper hierarchical order, trying to safeguard and look after the primary, albeit neglecting a little the secondary, manages to save the former and with it the latter. This is what Christ wanted us to understand when he said, *Do not fear those who kill the body but cannot kill the soul; rather fear him who can destroy both body and soul in hell* (Matt 10:28).

Nineveh repents

Are you convinced that one ought never to despair of the illnesses of the soul as if they were incurable. Or will it be necessary to resort to further arguments?... You can still return to virtue and be reconciled with the highest life.

Listen to what follows.

The Ninevites were not discouraged when they heard what the Prophet said, and he clearly threatened them saying: *Forty days more, and Nineveh shall be overthrown!* (Jon 3:4). They certainly were not sure that they would be able to placate God; they suspected the opposite, as the Prophet's words were absolutely categorical and unconditional. Nevertheless, they carried out penances, saying, *Who knows? God may relent and change his mind; he may turn from his fierce anger so that we do not perish. When God saw what they did, how they changed from their evil ways, God changed his mind about the calamity that he had said he would bring upon them; and he did not do it* (Jon 3:9-10).

If crude and uneducated men could understand this, so much more has to be the case with us who have been instructed in the divine truths, and who have seen copious examples in word and in deed. For the Prophet Isaiah quotes, *My thoughts are not your thoughts, nor are your ways my ways, says the Lord. For as the heavens are higher than the earth, so are my ways higher than your ways, and my thoughts than your thoughts* (Is 55:8-9).

Ad Teodorum lapsum, 1, 14-15

Saint John Chrysostom

PRAISE OF MARY, MOTHER OF GOD

I see the joyful assembly of the holy ones who have eagerly come together, called by Mary, the holy and ever-virgin Mother of God. Although I was labouring under much grief, the presence of the holy fathers has transformed this into joy. Now the sweet words of the psalmist David have been fulfilled for us: *How good, how delightful it is when brothers live in harmony!* (Ps 132:1).

We greet you, therefore, holy and mystical Trinity, who have gathered us all together in this church of Mary, the Mother of God. We greet you Mary, Mother of God, venerable treasure of the whole world, inextinguishable lamp, crown of virginity, sceptre of orthodoxy, indestructible temple... mother and virgin...

We greet you, who held in your holy, virginal womb, the one who cannot be contained. Because of you, the Trinity is worshipped and adored. Because of you the cross is venerated and adored throughout the whole world. Because of you heaven rejoices, the angels and archangels delight and demons are put to flight. Because of you, the devil, the tempter, has fallen from heaven, and fallen creation is taken up to heaven...

What more needs to be said? Because of you, the Only-Begotten Son of God has shone as a light on those who sit in darkness and in the shadow of death (cf Luke 1:79). Because of you the dead are raised and kings rule through the grace of the Holy Trinity.

Who can sing adequately the praise of Mary? She is

both virgin and mother... Behold now, the universe rejoices. Let us tremble and worship the undivided Trinity. Let us praise the ever-virgin Mary...

Homily 4 at the Council of Ephesus

Saint John Chrysostom

ON FRIENDSHIP AND THE EDUCATION OF CHILDREN

In war and on the battlefield, the soldier who only looks to save himself by fleeing, loses both himself and his companions. The valiant person, on the other hand, who struggles to save the others, also saves himself. Our religion is a war, and the toughest of all wars, and a struggle, a battle. We form a battle-front as our King has commanded, willing to shed our blood, looking for the salvation of all, encouraging those who have been firm and raising up those who have fallen.

It is true that in this battle many of our brothers lie on the ground riddled with wounds and dripping blood. There is nobody to look after them: not the villagers around, no priest, nobody; no protector, no friend, no brother. Each one can look only to himself. This is the source of the pettiness in the atmosphere in which we live.

Helping friends in the Faith

The greatest freedom and glory comes to us when we are not concerned only about ourselves. If we are weak, and men and the devil can so easily knock us down, it is precisely because we seek ourselves, because we do not protect one another like a shield, because we do not surround others – those near us – with the charity of God. On the contrary, we seek other reasons for friendship: relations, neighbours, social intercourse... Any reason at all is good enough to make friends, except religion, when this ought to be what most unites us to the others. Nowadays, quite the reverse happens: we prefer to have Jews and pagans as friends rather than the sons of the Church.

'It's true', you tell me. 'What happens is that my brother in the faith is a scoundrel, while the other person, Jew or gentile, is good and honest.'

What are you saying? Are you calling your brother a scoundrel, when you have been commanded not even to call him 'raca', 'silly'? Are you not ashamed, are you not embarrassed, to publicly denigrate your brother, who is a member of your body, who came from the same womb and shares the same table as you do ...?

'But he really is a scoundrel! And there is no one who can stand him!'

Well then, become a friend of his, so that he stops being the way he is, so as to convert him, to fill him with virtue.

'But he takes no notice of me', you reply. 'He does not heed any advice.'

How do you know that? Have you spoken to him and tried to correct him?

'I have exhorted him often', you reply.

How often?

'Many times. Once and again.'

And is this many times? Even if you had done this all your life, you ought not to have got tired or to have lost hope. Don't you see how God exhorts us throughout life, through the prophets, the apostles, the evangelists? And we? Is it that we fulfil everything He asks of us and pay attention to him in everything? Not at all! And has this stopped Him from exhorting us? Has He kept silent?...

Concern for our spouse and the children

But how are we going to accuse ourselves for neglecting others if we have not taken notice even of our own family, of our wife, of the children, of the servants? We concern ourselves with certain aspects instead of others, as if we were drunk. For example, the more servants the better, and we want them to serve us better; we want the children to receive a fat inheritance one day; we want our wife to have gold, luxurious dresses and pearls... We are concerned not with our inner selves, but with other things, just as we are not concerned about our spouse and the children but rather things for the spouse and things for the children. We behave like the one who, with his house in ruins, with walls swaying, is not concerned with shoring it up or reinforcing them, but with building a great fence around the house...

If a bear, outwitting his guards, escapes from his cage, we immediately shut the gates and run into the streets for fear of falling into the clutches of the beast. And here, it is not a beast but many thoughts which, like wild beasts, tear our soul to pieces. And we are not aware of it. In the cities great care is taken to ensure that the wild animals are in special areas, well locked away in their cages, and they are not let near the city council, or the tribunal, or near the imperial palace. If we have them well tied up, and a good distance from these places ...

Discipline for children

We have, however, men who are worse than the most savage animals. Such is the majority of our young people. Allowing themselves to be led by a savage concupiscence, how they jump about, kick about and run around unbridled, without having the least idea of their duties. The ones to blame are their parents. When one is dealing with horses, one sends them to the grooms who will look after them well, and not let them grow without taming them: from the beginning they bridle them and place a harness on them. But when it is a matter of young children, they are let loose everywhere, for a long time; so they lose their chastity, they are stained with dishonesty and games, and waste their time taking part in or attending corrupt shows. The parents' duty is to seek a chaste and prudent wife for them, before they are given over to impurity...

'It's better to wait', you tell me, 'until they gain prestige and shine in public activities.'

Yes. But you take no account of his soul, and consent to it being dragged down onto the ground. Its like that because the soul is considered an accessory, because the important things are neglected and effort is made with what is secondary. Everything is thus confused and disorderly.

Riches that can shackle

When the Lord, speaking of children, says, *Their angels always behold the face of My Father*, and *this is My Father's will*, He made those responsible for them take their task more seriously.

See what a protective wall He puts around them. He holds out the threat of fatal punishment for those who cause them to fall. To those who serve them and take care of them, following His example and that of His Father, He promises great blessings.

Let us follow that example, let us never refuse to undertake what may seem tedious or beneath us, for the sake of our brothers. However insignificant and worthless is the one whom we are to serve, however laborious is the work involved, even if we have to cross mountains and precipices, let us put up with everything to save our

FRIENDSHIP AND CHILDREN

brothers.

God has such an eager care for the soul that He did not spare His own Son. And so, from the moment we leave our homes in the morning we must have as our one objective and chief preoccupation to save those in spiritual danger.

Don't you know that the best favour you can do your son is to safeguard him from the impurity of fornication?

Nothing is worth as much as the soul: *What does it profit a man if he gains the whole world and suffers the loss of his own soul?* The love of money corrupts and degrades everything. Once it invades souls, like a tyrant invading a citadel, it casts out the fear of God. And so we neglect our children's salvation and our own; we have only one aim, to become richer and leave our wealth to others, who will pass it on to their descendants, who in turn will pass it on to others after them; in fact we become mere transmitters of our own money and possessions, but not masters of them.

An absurd consequence follows: free men are of less worth than slaves. For we set value on slaves, if not as persons, at least for their usefulness to us; but free men do not enjoy even this consideration; they are of less value in our estimation than these slaves.

Why do I say this? Because children are less valued than cattle; because we take greater care of horses and donkeys than we do of children. If a man has a mule, he is very concerned to have the best driver, and not one who is reckless or a thief or a drunkard or incompetent. But if we have to appoint a tutor to care for a child's soul, we accept quite at random the first fellow who comes along. Yet there is no greater art than this.

What can equal the work of training the soul, of forming the young mind? The man who has this art must be more painstaking than any painter or sculptor. But we take no account of this; we are concerned only to provide him with a training in language, and once again it is the acquisition of money that prompts us. He is taught how to speak, not in view of communication, but in order to make money. Indeed if it were possible to become rich even without this, we should pay no attention to it. See the great tyranny of money: it has seized control of all things; it has bound them like a gang of slaves or beasts and pulls them wherever it wants.

But what do we gain from making accusations against it? We can only attack with words, but it defeats us in action. Despite this, we shall not stop attacking it with our words. If any progress is made, we shall both gain, you and me; but if you remain simply as you are, we at least have fulfilled our duty.

May God cure you of this disease and so give us something to be proud of in you. To Him be glory and power for ever and ever. Amen.

In Matthaeum homiliae 59, 6-7

Saint John Chrysostom

WE HAVE FOUND THE MESSIAH!

When Andrew had been with Jesus, and had learned so much from him, he did not keep this treasure to himself. He made haste and ran to his brother, to share with him what he had learned.

Notice what he said to him: *We have found the Messiah* (which means Christ). Notice the way in which he shows here what he had learned in such a short space of time. He shows both the power of the Master in convincing them that He was the Messiah and their own zeal and persistence, for they had been concerned about this from the beginning.

Andrew's words are those of one waiting for the Messiah to come from heaven, full of joy that he has come, and hurrying to tell the great news to the others. This action of sharing his spiritual gains with others was born of brotherly love, family ties, and genuine affection.

Peter's reaction

But notice the eager and obedient spirit of Peter. The moment he heard the news he hurried at once to Jesus with his brother. *He brought him to Jesus*, says John. Let no one condemn Peter's impetuosity in accepting the message without any security. His brother had probably told him everything, carefully and at length. Moreover, it is a characteristic of the evangelists to tell a great deal in a few words, in the interests of brevity. In any case, John does not say that Peter believed at once, but only that

Andrew brought him to Jesus. He put Peter into His hands so that he could learn everything from Jesus Himself. The other disciple was there also, and was a party to all that happened.

No delay in bringing a friend to Christ

John the Baptist said, *This is the Lamb*, and *He baptises in the Spirit*, and left the clarification of this teaching to be expounded by Christ. Andrew, who was not capable of giving a full explanation, had all the more reason for doing as John did. He brought his brother to the source of light itself, in so much haste and joy that he would not brook the slightest delay.

Homilies on the Gospel of St John

Saint John Chrysostom

LEARNING TEMPERANCE

Listen to the voice of Paul, with great earnestness forbidding these things, and then you will perceive the absurdity of them. What then does he say? *Not with broidered hair, or gold, or pearls, or costly array* (1 Tim 2:9). Of what favour then can you be worthy when, in spite of Paul's prohibiting the married woman to have costly clothing, you extend this effeminacy even to your shoes, and have no end of contrivances for the sake of this ridicule and reproach? Yes. For first a ship is built, then rowers are mustered, and a man for the prow, and a helmsman, and a sail is spread, and an ocean traversed. And, leaving wife and children and country, the merchant commits his very life to the waves, and comes to the land of the barbarians, and undergoes innumerable dangers for these threads, that after it all you may take them and sew them into your shoes, and adorn the leather. What can be worse than this folly?

The madness of some young people

But the old ways are not like these, but such as become men. I, for my part, expect that in process of time the young men among us will wear even women's shoes, and not be ashamed. And what is more grievous, men's fathers seeing these things, are not much displeased, but do even account it an indifferent matter.

Do you want me to add what is still more grievous; that these things are done even when there are many poor?

Do you want me to bring before you Christ, hungry, naked, wandering everywhere, in chains? And how many thunderbolts must you not deserve, overlooking him in want of necessary food, and adorning these pieces of leather with so much diligence? And He indeed, when He was laying down the law to his disciples, would not so much as suffer them to have shoes at all; but we cannot bear to walk, I say not barefoot, but even with feet shod as they ought to be.

What then can be worse than this unseemliness, this absurdity? For this marks a soul, in the first place effeminate, then unfeeling and cruel, then curious and idly busy.

Who is curious about the beauty of threads, and the bloom of colours, and the tendrils made of such woven work, when he is able to look to heaven? Will he admire the Beauty there, when he is excited about a kind of beauty that belongs to pieces of leather, and is bending to the earth? And whereas God has stretched out the heavens and lit up the sun, drawing your looks upwards, you constrain yourself to looking downwards, to the earth, like the swine, and obey the devil.

And the young man goes about bending double towards the earth, he that is required to seek wisdom concerning the things in heaven; priding himself more on these trifles than if he had accomplished some great and good work, and walking on tiptoe in the forum, and hereby begetting to himself superfluous sorrows and distresses, lest he should stain them with the mud when it is winter; lest he should cover them with the dust, when summer is come.

You may indeed laugh at hearing this. But I am inclined to weep for these men's madness, and their earnest care about these matters. For in truth they would rather stain their body with mud, than those pieces of leather.

They become triflers then in this way, and fond of money again in another way. For he who has become used to being frantic and eager upon such matters, requires much expense for his clothes and for all other things, and thus a large income.

And if he has a munificent father, his thraldom becomes worse, his absurd fancy more intense; but if a parsimonious one, he is driven to other unseemliness, by way of getting together a little money for such expenses.

Hence many young men have even sold their manhood, and have become parasites to the rich, and have undertaken other servile offices, purchasing thereby the fulfilment of such desires.

So then, this man is sure to be at once fond of money, and a trifler, and about important things the most indolent of all men; and that he will be forced to commit many sins, is hereby evident. And that he is cruel and vain-glorious, neither this will anyone gainsay. Cruel, in that when he sees a poor man, through the love of finery he makes as though he did not even see him, but while he is decking out these things with gold, overlooks the one perishing of hunger: vain-glorious, since even in such little matters he trains himself to hunt after the admiration of the beholders.

For I suppose no general prides himself so much on his legions and trophies, as our profligate youths on the decking out of their shoes, on their trailing garments, on the dressing of their hair; yet surely all these are works of other persons, in their trades. But if men do not cease from vain boasting in the works of others, when will they cease from it in their own?

And although I know that many of the young will not so much as pay attention to what I have said, I ought not therefore to keep silence. For those fathers who still understand and are still sound, will be able to force them, even against their will, to a becoming decency.

Do not say then, *this is of no consequence, that is of no consequence;* for this, this has ruined all. For even now you ought to train them, and through these things which seem trifling, make them serious, great of soul. Then we shall find them sensible in great things too. For what is more ordinary than the learning of letters? Nevertheless it is through this that men become rhetoricians, and sophists, and philosophers; and if they know not their letters, they will never have that knowledge.

And this we address not only to young men but also to women, and to young girls. For they too are liable to similar charges, and much more so, since seemliness is a thing appropriate to a virgin.

Pray for young people

All of you then pray with us, that the young men of the Church above all things may be enabled to live orderly, and to attain an old age becoming them. Since for those surely who do not so live, it were well not to come to old age at all. But for them that have grown old even in youth, I pray that they may attain also to the very deep of grey hairs, and become fathers of approved children, and may be a joy to them that gave them birth, and above all surely to the God that made them, and may exterminate every distempered fancy, not that about their shoes, or about their clothes only, but every other kind also.

For as untilled land, such is also youth neglected, bringing forth many thorns from many quarters. Let us then send forth on them the fire of the Spirit, and burn up these wicked desires, and let us break up our fields, and make them ready for the reception of the seed, and let the young men see us with more sober minds than the old elsewhere.

With these things then in our minds, let us emulate that blessed Joseph, who shone through all these trials, that we may attain the same crowns with him; may we all attain them by the grace and love towards man of our Lord Jesus Christ, with Whom be glory unto the Father, together with the Holy Spirit, now and always, and world without end. Amen.

In Matthaeum homiliae 49, 5-8

Saint John Chrysostom

JOSEPH, A JUST MAN

Joseph, her spouse, as he was a just man (Matt 1:19).

The concept of *just* here signifies the man who possesses all the virtues. By *justice* one at times understands only one virtue in particular, as in the phrase: the one who is not avaricious is just. But *justice* also refers to virtue in general. And it is in this sense, above all, that Scripture uses the word *justice*. For example, it refers to: *a just man and true* (cf Job 1:1), or the two were just (cf Luke 1:6). Joseph, then, being just, that is to say good and charitable, *thought about repudiating her in secret*.

The Gospel lets us know what this man was thinking of doing just before he got to know the mystery, so that there can be no doubt as to what happened once he did know... Joseph was so pure and noble that he did not wish to afflict the Virgin Mary in any way. If, on the one hand, to keep her in the house would involve breaking the Law, to dismiss her and hand her over to the tribunal would be to put her to death. But Joseph did neither of the two. His way of acting was superior to the old law.

Then, *while Joseph was considering these things, behold an angel of the Lord appeared in his dreams* (Matt 1:20). Why did he not appear visibly as he did with the shepherds, with Zachary and Mary herself. The reason is that the faith of St Joseph was such that he did not need a similar vision. As regards Mary, who had to receive such a powerful message – more incredible than the one which had been given to Zachary – she not only had to know about the mystery before it came to pass, but an extraordinary vision was also need. With respect to the shepherds, rough and tough men, they needed a more impressive vision. But Joseph... welcomes wholeheartedly that revelation.

When he heard how the angel spoke to him, it was a clear sign for him that the angel had come on God's behalf. For only God can know the secrets of the heart. Notice the consequences which follow: the wisdom and virtue of Joseph become apparent. At the same time, the Angel's revelation coming at an appropriate time helps to strengthen his faith. And finally, the gospel narrative raises no doubts or suspicions when it tells us what his sentiments were, for we know them to be typical of a person in such circumstances.

How did the angel convince Joseph? Listen and admire the wisdom of his words. The Angel arrives and says: *Joseph, son of David, do not fear to take Mary your wife* (Matt 1:20). He reminds Joseph about David, from whom Christ is to come. And he does not allow Joseph to be thrown off balance from the moment he refers to the name of his most glorious ancestor, and the promise made to his lineage. Why, otherwise, would he call him, *son of David*?

Do not fear, he adds. God does not always act like this. When Abimalec began to have illicit thoughts about a relationship with Sarah, God spoke to him using strong and threatening language, although Abimalec did not know at the time that Sarah was Abraham's wife. Here, God speaks sweetly. What a difference there is between Joseph's and Abimalec's dispositions! Joseph's behaviour certainly warranted no reproach...

And what do the words *receive Mary* mean? None other than that Joseph had to continue keeping Mary in his house, for he had thought of separating from her. Keep your spouse, the Angel says, whom you had thought of leaving, for it is God who has given her to you, not her parents. She has been given to you not for marriage, but for her to be with you, and to be united to you, through my words. She is entrusted to Joseph now, as Christ will later entrust her to his disciple.

For what has been conceived in her is the work of the Holy Spirit. Marvellous words which surpass all human reasoning and are beyond the laws of nature. How was a man going to believe these things which he had never heard of?

She will give birth to a son, he continued, *and you will name him Jesus.* Although the Child has been conceived by the Holy Spirit do not think that you aren't required for service within the divine economy. Although you have not taken part in his conception, and Mary will always remain a virgin, I am giving you a job proper to a father – to name the recently-born. It will be you who imposes the name, and although he is not your son, you will take the place of a father. For this reason, the Angel concludes, with the imposition of the name, I am uniting you in an intimate way with the one who is to be born.

But so that no one may imagine that we are talking about a true paternity, listen to the precision with which the Angel speaks. *A son will be born,* he says. He does not say: 'a son will be born to you', but he says generically that Mary will give birth to Jesus not for Joseph, but for all men.

In Matthaeum homiliae, 4 (PG 57, 40-54)

Saint Augustine of Hippo

St Augustine was born in Tagaste (Numidia) in the north of Africa; he died on 28 August 430 as bishop of Hippo. On his conversion from the life-style he was leading and on receiving baptism, Augustine decided to give up teaching rhetoric in Milan and withdraw on his own. But Providence led him first to the priesthood in 391. He then began to help the ageing bishop of Hippo. Later he received the episcopal consecration.

His activity as bishop was directed principally to defending the faith against numerous schisms and heresies: manicheism, arianism, donatism, pelagianism ... The treatises he wrote – dogmatic, apologetic, exegetic and moral – are numerous. He wrote letters in reply to people who had consulted him on very varied questions. There is hardly any aspect of Christian doctrine which Augustine has not dealt with, with theological vigour and burning piety.

But all this work did not prevent him from the tender care of the faithful of his diocese. The large number of sermons which have come down to us are witness to this. In them he speaks about fundamental questions of Christian doctrine in a careful but simple style, so that his congregation would understand.

In 416 he was close to finishing his treatise *On the Trinity* and *The City of God* was already at an advanced stage. But he then began his commentary on the fourth gospel. St Augustine spent two years explaining to the faithful the full text of St John. These sermons were taken down in shorthand and then corrected by the author. They have come down to us entitled *Treatise on the Gospel of St John*. These treatises are, above all, a sign of pastoral concern for his flock; he tried to strengthen them in their faith and encouraged them with good customs. He uses many examples, analogies, allegories and metaphors.

His *Sermons* are the fruit of almost forty years of uninterrupted preaching in Hippo and Carthage. They are very rich in content and are a model of eloquence and clarity; they have the ability to put Christian people into immediate contact with the gospel scenes, and then to draw practical conclusions for ordinary life.

SAINT AUGUSTINE

EPISCOPAL SERVICE

He who presides over a people ought to be aware all the time that he is, above all, a servant to many. And this is not meant to be taken as a disgrace. It is not a dishonour, I repeat, to be the servant to many, because not even the Lord of lords scorned the possibility of serving us.

Christ teaches the Apostles to serve
From the dregs of the flesh a certain desire for greatness had infiltrated into the disciples of Christ, our Apostles, and the smoke of vanity had begun to reach his eyes. For, according to what we read in the Gospel, *a dispute also arose among them as to which one of them was to be regarded as the greatest* (Luke 22:24). But the Lord, a doctor who was present, tackled that tumour. When he saw the evil that had given rise to that disagreement, putting some children in front of them, he said to the Apostles: *unless you change and become like children, you will never enter the kingdom of heaven* (Matt 18:3). What he recommends is humility in the person of a child. But he did not want his followers to have a childish mentality, as the Apostle says in another place, *Do not be children in your thinking* (1 Cor 14:20). And he adds, *rather be infants in evil, but in thinking be adults*. Speaking to the Apostles and strengthening them in holy humility, after having proposed to them the example of a child, he tells them:

whoever wishes to be great among you must be your servant... (Matt 20:26).

Bishops at the service of their flocks

To put it briefly: we are your servants; your servants, but at the same time servants like you. We are your servants, but we all have the one Lord. We are your servants, but in Jesus, as the Apostle says: *we proclaim ourselves your slaves for Jesus' sake* (1 Cor 4:5). We are your servants for him, who also makes us free. He tells those who believe in Him: *If the Son makes you free, you will be free indeed* (Matt 20:26). Will I doubt becoming a servant for Him who, if he does not free me, will mean that I remain in slavery with no redemption? He has placed us at your head and we are your servants; we preside, but only if we are useful. Let us examine, then, how the bishop who presides can be a servant. It is just like it was with the Lord when he said to his Apostles: *whoever wishes to be great among you must be your servant* (Matt 20:26). But he immediately consoled them, in case their human pride irritated them with the use of this word referring to service. He used himself as an example in fulfilling what he had exhorted them to do...

Christ's example

What do these words of his, *just as the Son of Man came not to be served but to serve* (Matt 20:28) mean? Listen to how he continues: *(he) came not to be served but to serve, and to give his life as a ransom for many*. Here we are told how the Lord served. Here we learn what he commanded us to do as servants. He gave his life as a ransom for many: he redeemed us. Which of us is capable of redeeming another? We have been redeemed with his blood and with his death. With his humility we have been raised up, for we had fallen. But we too have to offer our grain of sand to help his members, as we have been transformed into his members: He is the head, we are the body...

A good bishop

It is certainly good for us to be good bishops who preside as they ought to and not only in name: this is good for us. A great reward is promised those who act like this. But, if we are not like that but – and as God does not want us to be – bad; if we seek honour for ourselves, if we neglect the precepts of God without taking into account your salvation, we can expect an anguish greater than the great rewards promised us. The higher the place we occupy, the greater is the danger we find ourselves in.

May the Lord grant me, with the help of your prayers, to be and to persevere until the end, in the way those who are my well-wishers wish me to be; and to be and to do what he, who has called me and commands me, wants of me. May He help me to do what he orders me to do. But whoever the bishop is, your hope must not be rooted in him. I leave my person aside. I speak to you as a bishop: I want you to be the cause of my joy, and not of vanity. I will not greet anyone at all whom I find placing his hope in me. He needs to be corrected, not confirmed. He has to change, not to remain where he is. If I cannot bring this to his attention, it would cause me sorrow; if, on the other hand, I can do it, it wouldn't.

I am now speaking in the name of Christ to you, the people of God. I am speaking to you in the name of the Church of God. I am speaking to you just as any other servant of God: your hope lies not in us, it does not lie in men. If we are good, we are servants. If we are bad, we are servants. But if we are good, we are faithful servants,

servants to the truth.

Look and see how we serve you: if you are hungry and do not wish to be ungrateful, observe carefully as to where the food is dispensed from. Don't concern yourself with the plate on which is placed what you are eager to eat. *In a large house* of the father of a family, *there are utensils not only of gold and silver, but also of wood and clay* (2 Tim 2:20). There are utensils of silver, of gold and of clay. You should look only at the bread, and from whom the bread has come, and who has given it to the one who is serving it to you. Look at Him whom I am speaking about, the Giver of this bread which is being served to you. He is the Bread: *I am the living bread that came down from heaven* (John 6:51). It is in this way that we serve to you Christ, in his stead. We serve you in Him, and under his command, so that He might reach you; let Him be the judge of our service.

Sermo 340A, 1-9 (PL 38, 1482-1484)

Saint Augustine

THE WEDDING AT CANA

The miracle indeed of our Lord Jesus Christ, whereby He made the water into wine, is not marvellous to those who know that it was God's doing. For He who made wine on that day at the marriage feast, in those six water-pots, which He commanded to be filled with water, the self-same does this every year in vines.

For even as that which the servants put into the water-pots was turned into wine by the doing of the Lord, so in like manner also is what the clouds pour forth changed into wine by the doing of the same Lord. But we do not wonder at the latter, because it happens every year: it has lost its marvel by its constant recurrence. And yet it suggests a greater consideration than that which was done in the water-pots. For who is there that considers the works of God, whereby this whole world is governed and regulated, who is not amazed and overwhelmed with miracles? If he considers the vigorous power of a single grain of any seed whatever, it is a mighty thing, it inspires him with awe. But since men, intent on a different matter, have lost the consideration of the works of God, by which they should daily praise Him as the Creator, God has, as it were, reserved to Himself the doing of certain extraordinary actions, that, by striking them with wonder, He might rouse men as from sleep to worship Him.

The marvels of creation

A dead man has risen again; men marvel: so many

are born daily, and none marvels. If we reflect more considerately, it is a matter of greater wonder for one to be who was not before, than for one who was to come to life again. Yet the same God, the Father of our Lord Jesus Christ, does by His word all these things; and it is He who created that governs also. The former miracles He did by His Word, God with Himself; the latter miracles He did by the same Word incarnate, and for us made man. As we wonder at the things which were done by the man Jesus, so let us wonder at the things which were done by Jesus God.

By Jesus God were made heaven, and earth, and the sea, all the garniture of heaven, the abounding riches of the earth, and the fruitfulness of the sea – all these things which lie within the reach of our eyes were made by Jesus God. And we look at these things, and if His own spirit is in us they in such manner please us, that we praise Him that contrived them; not in such manner that turning ourselves to the works we turn away from the Maker, and, in a manner, turning our face to the things made and our backs to Him that made them.

And these things indeed we see; they lie before our eyes. But what of those we do not see, as angels, virtues, powers, dominions, and every inhabitant of this fabric which is above the heavens, and beyond the reach of our eyes? Yet angels, too, when necessary, often showed themselves to men. Has not God made all these too by His Word, that is, by His only Son, our Lord Jesus Christ?

The human soul

What of the human soul itself, which is not seen, and yet by its works shown in the flesh excites great admiration in those that duly reflect on them – by whom was it made, unless by God? And through whom was it made, unless through the Son of God? Not to speak as yet of the soul of man: the soul of any brute whatever, see how it regulates the huge body, puts forth the senses, the eyes to see, the ears to hear, the nostrils to smell, the taste to discern flavours – the members, in short, to execute their respective functions! Is it the body, not the soul, namely the inhabitant of the body, that does these things? The soul is not apparent to the eyes, nevertheless it excites admiration by these its actions.

Direct now your consideration to the soul of man, on which God has bestowed understanding to know its Creator, to discern and distinguish between good and evil, that is, between right and wrong: see how many things it does through the body! Observe this whole world arranged in the same human commonwealth, with what administrations, with what orderly degrees of authority, with what conditions of citizenship, with what laws, manners, arts! The whole of this is brought about by the soul, and yet this power of the soul is not visible. When withdrawn from the body, the latter is a mere carcass: first, it in a manner preserves it from rottenness. For all flesh is corruptible, and falls off into putridity unless preserved by the soul as by a kind of seasoning.

But the human soul has this quality in common with the soul of the brute; those qualities rather are to be admired which I have stated, such as belong to the mind and intellect, wherein also it is renewed after the image of its Creator, after whose image man was formed. What will this power of the soul be when this body shall have put on incorruption, and this mortal shall have put on immortality? If such is its power, acting through corruptible flesh, what shall be its power through a spiritual body, after the resurrection of the dead? Yet this soul, as I have said, of admirable nature and substance, is a thing invisible, intellectual; this soul also was made by God Jesus, for He is the Word of God. *All things were made by Him, and without Him was nothing made.*

When we see, therefore, such deeds wrought by Jesus God, why should we wonder at water being turned into wine by the man Jesus? For He was not made man in such manner that He lost His being God. Man was added to Him, God not lost to Him. This miracle was wrought by the same who made all those things. Let us not therefore wonder that God did it, but love Him because He did it in our midst, and for the purpose of our restoration. For He gives us certain intimations by the very circumstances of the case.

The sacramental effects

I suppose that it was not without cause He came to the marriage. The miracle apart, there lies something mysterious and sacramental in the very fact. Let us knock, that He may open to us, and fill us with the invisible wine: for we were water, and He made us wine, made us wise; for He gave us the wisdom of His faith, whilst before we were foolish. And it appertains, it may be, to this wisdom, together with the honour of God, and with the praise of His majesty, and with the charity of His most powerful mercy, to understand what was done in this miracle.

The Lord, on being invited, came to the marriage. What wonder if He came to that house to a marriage, having come into this world to be with human beings.

Tractate VIII

Saint Augustine

TRIBUTE TO MARY

While he was still speaking to the crowds, his mother and his brothers were standing outside, wanting to speak to him. Someone told him, 'Look, your mother and your brothers are standing outside, wanting to speak to you.' But to the one who had told him this, Jesus replied, 'Who is my mother, and who are my brothers?' And pointing to his disciples he said, 'Here are my mother and my brothers! For whoever does the will of my Father in heaven is my brother and sister and mother.' (Matt 12:46-50).

Maternal affection

Why did Christ piously scorn his mother? It did not concern just any mother, but a virgin Mother. Mary, in effect, had received the gift of fertility without detriment to her integrity: she was a virgin at conception, a virgin at birth and forever. Nevertheless, the Lord relegated such an excellent Mother so that maternal affection would not be a barrier to fulfilling a job which had begun.

What was Christ doing? He brought the good news to the people, he destroyed the old man and built up the new, he freed souls, unchained prisoners, illuminated darkened intellects, and carried out every kind of good work. His whole being was consumed in this holy enterprise. And just at that moment someone announced the affections of the flesh. You have already heard Jesus' reply; why am I going to repeat it? May mothers pay attention, so that their affection does not make the good work of their sons difficult. And if they try to impede them or to place obstacles so as to delay what they cannot prevent, they will be despised by their sons. Worse, I am inclined to say that they will be scorned, scorned out of piety. If the Virgin Mary was treated like that, why does a woman – be she married or widowed – have to get annoyed when her son, keen to do good, neglects her? You will say to me: 'Are you comparing my son with Christ?' I will reply: 'No. No, I am not comparing him with Christ, nor you with Mary. Christ did not condemn maternal affection, but showed with his towering example that one has to leave behind one's own mother to carry out the work of God...

Mary is a most blessed disciple

Is it possible that Mary – chosen so that from her salvation would be born for us, and created by Christ before Christ was created in her – did not fulfil the will of the Father? There is no doubt that she did, and did so perfectly. Mary, who through faith believed and conceived, was more a disciple of Christ than simply as the Mother of Christ. She received more happiness as a disciple than as a Mother.

Mary was already blessed before giving birth, because she carried the Teacher in her womb. Check to see if what I am saying is true. On seeing the Lord walking among the multitude and working miracles, a woman exclaimed, *Blessed is the womb that bore you and the breasts that nursed you* (Luke 11:27). What does the Lord reply so that we would not seek happiness in the flesh? *Blessed rather who hear the word of God and keep it* (Luke 11:28). But Mary is blessed because she heard the word of God and kept it: she retained the truth in her mind better than the flesh in her womb. Christ is Truth, Christ is Flesh. Christ Truth was in the soul of Mary; Christ Flesh was enclosed in her womb; but what is found in the soul is better than what is conceived in the womb.

Mary is most holy and most blessed. The Church, nevertheless, is more perfect than the Virgin Mary. Why? Because Mary is a part of the Church, a holy member, excellent, super-eminent, but a member of the entire body. The Lord is the Head, and Christ is Head and body. What will I then say? Our Head is divine: we have God for our Head.

Being sons, daughters and mothers of Christ

You, dearly beloved, are also members of Christ, you are the body of Christ, See how you are what He said you would be: *Here are my mother and my brothers* (Matt 11:49). How will you be the Mother of Christ? Our Lord himself replies: *Whoever does the will of my Father in heaven is my brother and sister and mother* (Matt 12:50). Look! Understand the bit about the brother and the sister, for this legacy is unique; and discover in these words the mercy of Christ: Being the only-Begotten, he wanted us to be the heirs of the Father, co-heirs with him. His inheritance is such, that it cannot decrease even if it is shared by a multitude. Understand well then, that we are brothers of Christ, and that the holy and faithful women are his sisters. But how are we to understand that we are also mothers of Christ? Am I inclined to say that we are? Yes, I am inclined to say so. If earlier I stated that you are brothers of Christ, how can I now not state that you are his mother? Can I now deny Christ's words?

We know that the Church is the Spouse of Christ, and also, although this is more difficult to understand, that she is his Mother. The Virgin Mary foreshadowed her as a type of the Church. Why, I ask you, is Mary the Mother of Christ, other than because she gave birth to the members of Christ? And you, members of Christ, who has given birth to you? I hear the voice in your hearts saying 'Mother Church!' Just like Mary, this holy and honourable Mother while she gives birth, is also a virgin.

You are the proof of the first statement: you have been born of Her, like Christ, of whom you are members. Divine testimonies of her virginity are not lacking. Come to the front of the people, blessed Paul, and be my witness. He raises his voice to say what I would like to state: *I promised you in marriage to one husband, to present you as a chaste virgin in Christ. But I am afraid that as the serpent deceived Eve by its cunning, your thoughts will be led astray from a sincere and pure devotion to Christ* (2 Cor 11:2-3). Preserve virginity in your souls, which is the integrity of the catholic faith. Where Eve was corrupted by the word of a serpent, there the Church ought to be a virgin with the grace of the Omnipotent.

Consequently, the members of Christ give birth in the mind, as Mary gave birth to Christ in her womb, remaining a virgin. In this way will you be mothers of Christ. This relationship ought not to be strange or to cause repugnance: you were sons, but also mothers. On being baptised, you were born as members of Christ, you were sons of the Mother. Bring those you can to the font of Baptism now; and just as you were sons with your birth, you will be able to become mothers of Christ, leading those who are about to be born.

Sermo 72A, 3, 7-8

Saint Augustine

THE MORAL VIRTUES

As to virtue leading us to a happy life, I hold virtue to be nothing other than perfect love of God. For the fourfold division of virtue I regard as taken from four forms of love. As for these four virtues (I wish everyone felt their influence in their own minds as they have the names of the virtues in their mouths!), I should have no hesitation in defining them:

- temperance is love giving itself entirely to that which is loved;
- fortitude is love readily bearing all things for the sake of the loved object;
- justice is love serving only the loved object, and therefore ruling rightly;
- prudence is love distinguishing with sagacity between what hinders it and what helps it.

The object of this love is not anything, but only God, the chief good, the highest wisdom, the perfect harmony. So we may express the definition thus:

- temperance is love keeping itself entire and incorrupt for God;
- fortitude is love bearing everything readily for the sake of God;
- justice is love serving God only, and therefore ruling well all else, as subject to man;
- prudence is love making a right distinction between what helps it towards God and what might hinder it.

Temperance

First, then, let us consider temperance, which promises us a kind of integrity and incorruptibility in the love by which we are united to God. The office of temperance is in restraining and quieting the passions which make us pant for those things which turn us away from the laws of God and from the enjoyment of His goodness; that is, in a word, from the happy life. For there is the abode of truth; and in enjoying its contemplation, and in cleaving closely to it, we are assuredly happy; but departing from this, men become entangled in great errors and sorrows. For as the apostle says, *The root of all evils is covetousness; which some having followed, have made shipwreck of the faith, and have pierced themselves through with many sorrows.* And this sin of the soul is quite plainly, to those rightly understanding, set forth in the Old Testament in the transgression of Adam in Paradise.

Paul then says that covetousness is the root of all evils; and the old law also intimates that the first man fell by covetousness. Paul tells us to put off the old man and put on the new. By the old man he means Adam who sinned, and by the new man him whom the Son of God took to Himself in consecration for our redemption. For he says in another place, *The first man is of the earth, earthly; the second man is from heaven, heavenly. As is the earthly, such are they also that are earthly; and as is the heavenly, such are they also that are heavenly. And as we have borne the image of the earthly, let us also bear the image of the heavenly,* that is, put off the old man, and put on the new.

The whole duty of temperance, then, is to put off the old man, and to be renewed in God – that is, to scorn all bodily delights, and popular applause, and to turn the whole to things divine and unseen.

The man, then, who is temperate in such mortal and transient things has his rule of life confirmed by both Testaments, that he should love none of these things, nor think them desirable for their own sakes, but should use them as far as is required for the purposes and duties of life, with the moderation of an employer instead of the ardour of a lover. These remarks on temperance are few in proportion to the greatness of the theme, but perhaps too many in view of the task on hand.

Fortitude

On fortitude we must be brief. The love, then, of which we speak, which ought with all sanctity to burn in desire for God, is called temperance, in not seeking for earthly things, and fortitude, in bearing the loss of them. But among all things which are possessed in this life, the body is, by God's most righteous laws, for the sin of old, man's heaviest bond, which is well known as a fact, but most incomprehensible in its mystery. Lest this bond should be shaken and disturbed, the soul is shaken with the fear of toil and pain; lest it should be lost and destroyed, the soul is shaken with the fear of death. For the soul loves it from the force of habit, not knowing that by using it well and wisely its resurrection and reformation will, by the divine help and decree, be without any trouble made subject to its authority. But when the soul turns to God wholly in this love, it knows these things, and so will not only disregard death, but will even desire it.

Then there is the great struggle with pain. But there is nothing, though of iron hardness, which the fire of love cannot subdue. And when the mind is carried up to God in this love, it will soar above all torture and glorious, with wings beauteous and unhurt, on which chaste love rises to the embrace of God. Otherwise God must allow the lovers of gold, the lovers of praise, the lovers of women, to have more fortitude than the lovers of Himself, though love in those cases is rather to be called passion or lust. And yet even here we may see with what force the mind presses on with unflagging energy, in spite of all alarms, towards what it loves; and to learn that we should bear all things rather than forsake God, since those men bear so much in order to forsake Him.

Instead of quoting here authorities from the New Testament, where it is said, *Tribulation works patience; and patience, experience and experience, hope;* and where, in addition to these words, there is proof and confirmation of them from the example of those who spoke them; I will rather summon an example of patience from the Old Testament, against which the Manichaeans make fierce assaults. Nor will I refer to the man who, in the midst of great bodily suffering, and with a dreadful disease in his limbs, not only bore human evils, but discoursed of things divine.

But these Scriptures present to me a woman of amazing fortitude, and I must at once go on to her case. This woman, along with seven children, allowed the tyrant and executioner to extract her vitals from her body rather than a profane word from her mouth, encouraging her sons by her exhortations, though she suffered in the tortures of their bodies, and was herself to undergo what she called on them to bear. What patience could be greater than this? And yet why should we be astonished that the love of God, implanted in her inmost heart, bore up against tyrant, and executioner, and pain, and sex, and natural affection.

THE MORAL VIRTUES

Justice

What of justice that pertains to God? As the Lord says, *You cannot serve two masters,* and the apostle denounces those who serve the creature rather than the Creator. Was it not said before in the Old Testament, *You shall worship the Lord your God, and Him only shall you serve*? I need say no more on this, for these books are full of such passages. The lover, then, whom we are describing, will get from justice this rule of life, that he must with perfect readiness serve the God whom he loves, the highest good, the highest wisdom, the highest peace; and as regards all other things, must either rule them as subject to himself, or treat them with a view to their subjection. This rule of life is, as we have shown, confirmed by the authority of both Testaments.

Prudence

With equal brevity we must treat of prudence, to which it belongs to discern between what is to be desired and what to be shunned. Without this, nothing can be done of what we have already spoken of. It is the part of prudence to keep watch with most anxious vigilance, lest any evil influence should stealthily creep in upon us. Thus the Lord often exclaims, *Watch;* and He says, *Walk while you have the light, lest darkness come upon you.* And then it is said, *Know you not that a little yeast leavens the whole lump?* And no passage can be quoted from the Old Testament more expressly condemning this mental somnolence, which makes us insensitive to destruction advancing on us step by step, than those words of the prophet, *He who despises small things shall fall by degrees.* On this topic I might discourse at length did our haste allow of it. And did our present task demand it, we might perhaps prove the depth of these mysteries, by making a mock of which profane men in their perfect ignorance fall, not certainly by degrees, but with a headlong overthrow.

Conclusion

I need say no more about right conduct. For if God is man's chief good, which you cannot deny, it clearly follows, since to seek the chief good is to live well, that to live well is nothing else but to love God with all the heart, with all the soul, with all the mind. And, as arising from this:

- that this love must be preserved entire and incorrupt, which is the part of temperance;
- that it give way before no troubles, which is the part of fortitude;
- that it serve no other, which is the part of justice;
- that it be watchful in its inspection of things lest craft or fraud steal in, which is the part of prudence.

This is the one perfection of man, by which alone he can succeed in attaining to the purity of truth. This both Testaments enjoin in concert; this is commended on both sides alike.

De moribus Eccl Catholicae

Saint Augustine

On Prayer

Seek, and you shall find (Matt 7:7).

So that you might not think that this too was cursorily given, see what He added further, see with what He finished. *Knock, and it shall be opened unto you:* see what He added. He would have you ask that you may receive, and seek that you may find, and knock that you may enter in. Seeing then that our Father knows already what is needful for us, how and why do we ask? Why seek? Why knock? Why weary ourselves in asking, and seeking, and knocking, to instruct Him who knows already?

In another place the words of the Lord are, *Men ought always to pray, and not to faint* (Luke 18:1). If men *ought always to pray,* how does He say, *Use not many words*? How can I always pray, if I so quickly make an end? Here You bid me to finish quickly; there *always to pray and not to faint:* what does this mean? Now that you may understand this, *ask, seek, knock.* For this reason is it closed, not to shut you out, but to exercise you. Therefore, brethren, we ought to exhort to prayer, both ourselves and you. For we have no other hope amid the manifold evils of this present world than to knock in prayer, to believe and to maintain the belief firm in the heart, that your Father does not give you only what He knows is not expedient for you. For you know what you do desire; He knows what is good for you.

Imagine yourself under a physician, and in weak health, as is the very truth; for all this life of ours is a weakness; and a long life is nothing else but a prolonged weakness.

Imagine yourself then to be sick under the physician's hand. You have a desire to ask your physician leave to drink a draught of fresh wine. You are not prohibited from asking, for it may chance to do you no harm, or even good to receive it. Do not then hesitate to ask; ask, hesitate not; but if you receive not, do not take it to heart. Now if you would act thus in the hands of a man, the physician of the body, how much more in the hands of God, who is the Physician, the Creator, and Restorer, both of your body and soul?

Two kinds of blessings

There are then two kinds of blessings, temporal and eternal. Temporal blessings are health, substance, honour, friends, a home, children, a wife, and the other things of this life in which we are sojourners. We put up then in the hostelry of this life as travellers passing on and not as owners intending to remain. But eternal blessings are, first, eternal life itself, the incorruptibility and immortality of body and soul, the society of Angels, the heavenly city, glory (cf Matt 17:19-20) unfailing, Father and fatherland, the former without death, the latter without a foe.

Let us desire these blessings with all eagerness; let us ask with all perseverance, not with length of words, but with the witness of groans. Longing desire prays always, though the tongue be silent. If you are ever longing, you are ever praying.

When does prayer sleep? When desire grows cold. So, then, let us beg for these eternal blessings with all eager desire. Let us seek for those good things with an entire earnestness. Let us ask for those good things with all assurance. For those good things do profit him that has

ON PRAYER

them, they cannot harm him. But those other temporal good things sometimes profit, and sometimes harm.

Poverty has profited many, and wealth has harmed many; a private life has profited many, and exalted honour has harmed many. And again, money has profited some, honourable distinction has profited some; profited them who use them well; but from those who use them ill, the not withdrawing them has harmed them more.

Temporal blessings

And so, Brethren, let us ask for those temporal blessings too, but in moderation, being sure that if we do receive them, He gives them, who knows what is expedient for us. You have asked, and what you have asked, has not been given you? Trust your Father, who would give it you, were it expedient for you. Judge in this case by yourself. For just as your son, who knows not the ways of men, regards you, so too you, who do not know the things of God regards the Lord. Your son cries a whole day before you, to give him a knife, or a sword. You refuse to give it to him; you will not give it, you disregard his tears, lest you should have to bewail his death. Let him cry, and beat himself, or throw himself upon the ground, that you may set him on horseback; you will not do it, because he does not know how to govern the horse and he may be thrown and be killed. To whom you refuse a part, you are reserving the whole; so that he may grow up, and possess the whole in safety, you do not give him that little thing which is full of peril to him.

And so, Brethren, we say, pray as much as you are able. Evils abound, and God has willed that evils should abound. Would that evil men did not abound, and then evils would not abound. Bad times! Troublesome times! This men are saying. Let our lives be good; and the times are good. We make our times; such as we are, such are the times. But what can we do? We cannot, it may be, convert the mass of men to a good life. But let the few who do give ear live well; let the few who live well endure the many who live ill. They are the corn, they are in the floor; in the floor they can have the chaff with them, they will not have them in the barn. Let them endure what they would not, that they may come to what they would. Are we sad, and do we blame God? Evils abound in the world, in order that the world may not engage our love.

Detachment from worldly goods

Great men, faithful saints were those who despised the world with all its attractions. We are not able to despise it even disfigured as it is. The world is evil. Yes, it is evil, and yet it is loved as though it were good. But what is this evil world? For the heavens and the earth, and the waters, and the things that are therein, the fish, and birds, and trees, are not evil. All these are good: but it is evil men who make this evil world. As we cannot be without evil men, let us, as I have said, while we live pour out our groans before the Lord our God, and endure the evils, that we may attain to the things that are good.

Let us not find fault with the Master of the household; for He is loving to us. He bears us, and not we him. He knows how to govern what He made. Do what He has bidden, and hope for what He has promised.

Sermo 80, 2, 7-8

Saint Augustine

INVOCATION TO THE LORD

I call upon You, O God the Truth, in whom and by whom and through whom all those things are true which are true.

O God, Wisdom, in whom and by whom and through whom all those are wise who are wise.

O God, True and Supreme Life, in whom and by whom and through whom all those things live which truly and perfectly live.

O God, Happiness, in whom and by whom and through whom all those things are happy which are happy.

O God, the Good and the Beautiful, in whom and by whom and through whom all those things are good and beautiful which are good and beautiful.

O God, Intelligible Light, in whom and by whom and through whom all those things which have intelligible light have their intelligible light.

O God, whose domain is the whole world unknown to sense.

O God, from whose realm law is promulgated even in these regions.

O God, from whom to turn away is to fall, to whom to turn is to rise again, in whom to abide is to stand firm.

O God, from whom to depart is to die, to whom to return is to be revived, in whom to dwell is to live.

O God, whom no one loses unless deceived, whom no one seeks unless admonished, whom no one finds unless he is purified.

O God whom to abandon is to perish, whom to heed is to love, whom to see is to possess.

O God, to whom Faith moves us, Hope raises us, Charity unites us.

O God, through whom we overcome the enemy, You do I pray.

O God, through whom we obtain that we do not altogether perish.

O God, by whom we are admonished to be ever watchful.

O God, through whom we discern the good from the evil.

O God, through whom we flee evil and follow after good.

O God, through whom we are not overcome by afflictions.

O God, through whom we fittingly serve and fittingly rule.

O God, through whom we learn that that is alien to us which once we thought was meet for us, and that is meet which we used to think was alien.

O God, through whom we cling not to the charms and lures of evil.

O God, through whom deprivations do not abase us.

O God, through whom what is better in us is not under the dominion of our lower self.

O God, through whom death is swallowed up in victory.

O God, who does convert us, stripping us of that which is not and clothing us with that which is.

O God, who makes us worthy to be heard.

O God, who strengthens us; who leads us into all truth.

O God, who speaks to us of all good things; who does

not drive us out of our mind, nor permits that anyone else do so.

O God, who calls us back to the way; who leads us to the gate; who grants that it is opened to those who knock.

O God, who gives us the bread of life.

O God, through whom we thirst for the cup, which when it is drunk we shall thirst no more.

O God, who does convince the world of sin, of justice, and of judgement.

O God, through whom we are not shaken by those who have no faith.

O God, through whom we denounce the error of those who think that the merits of souls are nothing before You.

O God, through whom we do not serve weak and beggarly elements.

O God, who does cleanse us, who does make us ready for divine reward, graciously come to me.

Whatever I have said, come to my aid, You, the one God, the one, eternal, true substance in whom there is no strife, no disorder, no change, no need, no death; where there is supreme harmony, supreme clarity, supreme permanence, supreme fullness, supreme life; where there is no deficiency and no excess; where the One begetting and the One begotten is One.

O God, who is served by all things which serve, who is obeyed by every good soul.

O God, by whose laws the poles revolve, the stars follow their courses, the sun rules the day, and the moon presides over the night; and all the world maintains, as far as this world of sense allows, the wondrous stability of things by means of the orders and recurrences of seasons: through the days by the changing of light and darkness, through the months by the moon's progressions and declines, through the years by the successions of spring, summer, autumn, and winter, through the cycles by the completion of the sun's course, through the great eras of time by the return of the stars to their starting points.

O God, by whose ever-enduring laws the varying movement of movable things is not suffered to be disturbed, and is always restored to a relative stability by the controls of the encompassing ages.

O God, by whose laws the choice of the soul is free, and rewards to the good and chastisements to the wicked are meted out in accord with inexorable and universal destiny.

O God, from whom all good things flow even unto us, and by whom all evil things are kept away from us.

O God, above whom, beyond whom, and without whom nothing exists.

O God, under whom everything is, in whom everything is, with whom everything is.

O God, who has made man to Your image and likeness, a fact which he acknowledges who knows himself.

Hear, hear, O hear me, my God, my Lord, my King, my Father, my Cause, my Hope, my Wealth, my Honour, my Home, my Native Land, my Salvation, my Light, my Life.

Hear, hear, O hear me, in that way of Yours, well known to a select few.

You alone do I love; You alone do I follow; You alone do I seek; You alone am I ready to serve, for You alone have just dominion; under Your sway do I long to be.

Order, I beg You, and command what You will, but heal and open my ears, so that with them I may hear Your words.

Heal and open my eyes so that with them I may perceive Your wishes.

INVOCATION TO THE LORD

Banish from me my senselessness, so that I may know You.

Tell me where I should turn that I may behold You; and I hope I shall do all You have commanded me.

Look, I beseech You, upon Your prodigal, O Lord, kindest Father; already have I been punished enough; long enough have I served Your enemies whom You have beneath Your feet; long enough have I been the plaything of deceits. Receive me Your servant as I flee from them, for they took me in as a stranger when I was fleeing from You.

I realise I must return to You. Let Your door be open to my knocking. Teach me how to come to You. Nothing else do I have but willingness. Nothing else do I know save that fleeting and perishable things are to be spurned, certain and eternal things to be sought after. This I do, O Father, because this is all I know, but how I am to reach You I know not. Do You inspire me, show me, give me what I need for my journey.

If it is by faith that they find You who have recourse to You, give me faith; if it is through virtue, give me virtue; if it is by knowledge, give knowledge to me. Grant me increase of faith, of hope, and of charity.

O how marvellous and extraordinary is Your goodness.

To You do I appeal, and once more I beg of You the very means by which appeal is made to You. For, if You should abandon us, we are lost; but You do not abandon us, because You are the Supreme Good whom no one ever rightly sought and entirely failed to find. And, indeed, every one has rightly sought You whom You have enabled to seek You aright. Grant that I may seek You, my Father; save me from error. When I seek You, let me not find anything else but You, I beseech You, Father. But, if there is in me any vain desire, do You Yourself cleanse me and make me fit to look upon You.

With regard to the health of this my mortal body, so long as I am ignorant of its usefulness to me or to those whom I love, I entrust it to You, O wisest and best of Fathers, and I shall pray for it as You shall in good time advise me. This only I shall ask of Your extreme kindness, that You convert me wholly to You, and that You allow nothing to prevent me when I wend my way to You. I beg You to command, while I move and bear this my body, that I may be pure, generous, just, and prudent; that I may be a perfect lover and knower of Your Wisdom; that I may be worthy of Your dwelling place, and that I may in fact dwell in Your most blessed kingdom. Amen. Amen.

Soliloquies

Saint Augustine

CHRIST DIED FOR ALL

Christ is the true mediator, whom in the secret of your mercy you have shown to men and sent to men, that by His example they may learn humility. The Mediator between God and men, the man Christ Jesus, appeared between sinful mortals and the immortal Just One: for like men He was mortal, like God He was just. The wages of justice being life and peace, through the union of His own justice with God He was to make void the death of those sinners whom He justified by choosing to undergo death as they do.

How much You have loved us, O good Father, who spared not even Your own Son, but delivered Him up for us wicked men! How you have loved us, for whom He who thought it not a robbery to be equal with You became obedient even unto the death of the cross, He who alone was free among the dead, having power to lay down His life and power to take it up again: for us He was to you both Victor and Victim, and Victor because Victim: for us he was to You both Priest and Sacrifice, and Priest because Sacrifice; turning us from slaves into Your sons, by being Your Son and becoming a slave.

Rightly is my hope strong in Him, who sits at Your right hand and intercedes for us; otherwise I should despair. For many and great are my infirmities, many and great; but Your medicine is of more power. We might well have thought Your Word remote from union with man and so have despaired of ourselves if He had not been made flesh and dwelt amongst us.

Terrified by my sins and the mass of my misery, I had pondered in my heart and thought of flight to the desert; but You forbade me and strengthened me, saying: *Christ dies for all; that they also who live, may now not live to themselves but with Him who died for them.* See, Lord, I cast my care upon You, that I may live: and I will consider the wondrous things of Your law.

You know my unskilfulness and my infirmity: teach me and heal me. He, Your only One, in whom are hidden all the treasures of wisdom and knowledge, has redeemed me with His Blood.

Confessions

Saint Augustine

LOVE FOR OUR SEPARATED BRETHREN

Brothers, we exhort you most of all to show this charity not only towards one another but also to those who are outside our communion, whether they be pagans who do not know Christ or Christians separated from the body. Let us grieve for them, brethren, as though for our own brothers. They are our brothers whether they wish to be or not. They will only cease to be our brothers when they will have ceased to say 'Our Father'.

Let them say, 'Why do you seek us? Why do you want us?' We will answer, 'You are our brothers.' Let them say, 'Go away. We have nothing in common with you.' We absolutely do have something in common: we profess one Christ, we ought to be united in one Body under one Head.

I therefore entreat you, brethren, through the very depth of that love by whose milk we are nourished and by whose bread we are fortified; I entreat you through Our Lord Jesus Christ and through His meekness. It is now time that we employ great charity in their regard and overflowing mercy in beseeching God on their behalf, that He finally grant them a sober understanding to look and see that they have nothing at all to say against the truth.

Nothing is left to them except the infirmity of animosity which is all the weaker the more strength it considers itself to have. I entreat you on behalf of the weak, of those who reason according to the flesh, of those who are crude and carnal, of those who nevertheless are our brothers and celebrate the same Sacraments. Even though they do not celebrate them together with us, they are the same. They respond with the same *Amen* which, even though they do not say it together with us, is the same. Pour out the depth of your love to God on their behalf.

Commentary on the Psalms, Ps 32:29

Saint Augustine

THE BOAT IN A TEMPEST

And when he entered into the boat his disciples followed him. And, behold, a great tempest arose in the sea, so that the boat was covered with waves; but he was asleep. And they came to him and awakened him, saying: Lord, save us, we perish. And Jesus said to them: Why are you fearful, O you of little faith? Then rising up, he commanded the winds and the sea; and there came a great calm. But the men wondered, saying: What manner of man is this, for the winds and the sea obey him? (Matt 8:23-27).

A living faith

By the Lord's blessing, I will address you upon the lesson of the Holy Gospel which has just been read, and take occasion thereby to exhort you that, against the tempest and waves of this world, faith sleep not in your hearts. *For the Lord Christ had not indeed death nor sleep in His power, and perchance sleep overcame the Almighty One as He was sailing against His will?* If you believe this, He is asleep in you; but if Christ be awake in you, your faith is awake.

The Apostle says, *that Christ may dwell in your hearts by faith.* This sleep then of Christ is a sign of a high mystery. The sailors are the souls passing over the world in wood. That ship also was a figure of the Church. And all, individually indeed are temples of God, and his own heart is the vessel in which each sails; nor can he suffer shipwreck, if his thoughts are only good.

Anger

You have heard an insult, it is the wind; you are angry, it is a wave. When therefore the wind blows and the wave swells, the ship is endangered, the heart is in jeopardy, the heart is tossed to and fro. When you have heard an insult, you long to be avenged; and, avenged you have been, and so rejoicing in another's harm you have suffered shipwreck.

And why is this? Because Christ is asleep in you. What does this mean, Christ is asleep in you? You have forgotten Christ. Rouse Him up then, call Christ to mind, let Christ awake in you, give heed to Him. What did you wish? To be avenged. Have you forgotten, that when He was being crucified, He said, *Father, forgive them, for they know not what they do?* He who was asleep in your heart did not wish to be avenged. Awake Him up then, call Him to remembrance. The remembrance of Him is His word; the remembrance of Him is His command. And then will you say if Christ, awake in you, What manner of man am I, who wish to be avenged! Who am I, who deals out threats against another man? I may die perhaps before I am avenged.

And when at my last breath, inflamed with rage, and thirsting for vengeance, I shall depart out of this body, He will not receive me, who did not wish to be avenged. He will not receive me, who said, *Give, and it shall be given to you; forgive, and it shall be forgiven you.* Therefore will I refrain myself from my wrath, and return to the repose of my heart. Christ has commanded the sea, tranquillity is restored.

Temptations

Now what I have said as to anger, holds fast as a rule in all your temptations. A temptation has sprung up. It is the wind. You are disturbed. It is a wave. Wake up Christ then, and let Him speak with you. *Who is this, since the winds and the sea obey Him? Who is this, whom the sea obeys? The sea is His, and He made it. All things were made by Him.*

Imitate the winds then, and the sea rather; obey the Creator. At Christ's command the sea gives ear; and are you deaf? The sea hears, and the wind ceases: and do you still blow on? What! I say, I do, I devise; what is all this, but to be blowing on, and to be unwilling to stop in obedience to the word of Christ? Let not the wave master you in this troubled state of your heart. Yet since we are but men, if the wind should drive us on, and stir up the affections of our souls, let us not despair; let us awake Christ, that we may sail on a tranquil sea, and so come to our country.

Sermon XIII

SAINT AUGUSTINE

WITH CHRISTIAN PURITY

Holy Communion

For my flesh is meat indeed, and my blood is drink indeed. He that eats my flesh... (John 6:55).

As we heard when the Gospel was being read, the Lord Jesus Christ exhorted us by the promise of eternal life to eat His Flesh and drink His Blood. You who heard these words, have not all as yet understood them. For those of you who have been baptised and the faithful do know what He meant. But those among you who are still called Catechumens, or Hearers, could have been hearers when it was being read; but could they be understanders too? Accordingly our discourse is directed to both.

Let them who already eat the Flesh of the Lord and drink His Blood, think What it is they eat and drink, lest, as the Apostle says, *They eat and drink judgement to themselves* (1 Cor 11:29). But they who do not yet eat and drink, let them hasten when invited to such a Banquet. Throughout these days the teachers feed you, Christ daily feeds you, that His Table is ever ordered before you. What is the reason, O Hearers, that you see the Table, and come not to the Banquet? And could it be, just now when the Gospel was being read, that you said in your hearts, 'We are thinking what it is that He said, *My Flesh is meat indeed, and My Blood is drink indeed* (John 6:55). How is the Flesh of the Lord eaten, and the Blood of the Lord drunk? We are thinking what He said.' Who has closed it against you, that you do not know this? There is a veil over it; but if you will, the veil shall be taken away. Come to the (baptismal) profession, and you have resolved the difficulty.

For what the Lord Jesus said, the faithful know well already. But you are called a Catechumen, are called a Hearer, and are deaf. For the ears of the body you have open, seeing that you hear the words which were spoken; but the ears of the heart you have are still closed, seeing you understand not what was spoken. I plead, I do not discuss it. Easter is at hand. Give in your name for baptism. If the festivity arouse you not, let the very curiosity induce you: that you may know the meaning of, *Whosoever eats My Flesh and drinks My Blood dwells in Me, and I in him* (John 6:56). That you may know with me what is meant, *Knock, and it shall be opened unto you* (Matt 7:7): and as I say to you, *Knock, and it shall be opened unto you,* so do I too knock, open you to me. When I speak aloud to the ears, I knock at the breast.

Chastity

But if the Catechumens, my Brethren, are to be exhorted not to delay to approach to this so great grace of regeneration; what great care ought we to have in building up the faithful, that their approaching may profit them, and that they eat and drink not such a Banquet unto their own judgement? Now that they may not eat and drink unto judgement, let them live well. Be exhorters, not by words, but by your conduct; that they who have not been baptised, may in such wise hasten to follow you, that they perish not by imitating you. Do you who are married keep the fidelity of the marriage-bed with your wives. Render what you require. As a husband you require chastity from your wife; give her an example, not words. You are the head, look where you go. For you ought to go where it may not be dangerous for her to follow: yes, you ought to walk yourself where you would have her follow.

You require strength from the weaker sex. Lust of the flesh you both have: let the one who is the stronger, be the first to conquer. Yet, many men are conquered by the women, which is to be lamented. Women preserve chastity, which men will not preserve; and in that they preserve it not, would wish to appear men: as though he was in sex the stronger only that the enemy might more easily subdue him. There is a struggle, a war, a combat. The man is stronger than the women, the *man is the head of the woman* (Eph 5:23). The woman combats and overcomes; do you succumb to the enemy? The body stands firm, and does the head lie low?

But those of you who have not yet wives, and who yet already approach to the Lord's Table, and eat the Flesh of Christ, and drink His Blood, if you are about to marry, keep yourselves for your wives. As you would have them come to you, such ought they also to find you. What young man is there who would not wish to marry a chaste wife? And if he were about to espouse a virgin, who would not desire she should be unpolluted? You look for one unpolluted, be unpolluted yourself. You look for one pure, be not yourself impure. For it is not that she is able, and you are not able. If it were not possible, then could not she be so. But seeing that she can, let this teach you, that it is possible. And that she may have this power, God is her ruler.

But you will have greater glory if you shall do it. Why greater glory? The vigilance of parents is a check to her, the very modesty of the weaker sex is a bridle to her; lastly, she is in fear of the laws of which you are not afraid. Therefore it is then that you will have greater glory if you shall do it; because if you do it, you fear God. She has many things to fear besides God, you fear God alone. But

He whom you fear is greater than all. He is to be feared in public, He in secret. You go out, you are seen; you go in, you are seen; the lamp is lighted, He sees you; the lamp is extinguished, He sees you; you enter into your closet, He sees you; in the retirement of your own heart, He sees you. Fear Him, Him whose care it is to see you; and even by this fear be chaste. Or if you will sin, seek for some place where He may not see you, and do what you would.

But you who have taken the vow already, chasten your bodies more strictly, and suffer not yourselves to loosen the reins of concupiscence even after those things which are permitted; that you may not only turn away from an unlawful connection, but may despise even a lawful look. Remember, of whichever sex you are, whether men or women, that you are leading on earth the life of Angels: *For the Angels are neither given in marriage, nor marry* (Matt 12:30). This shall we be, when we shall have risen again. How much better are you, who before death begin to be what men will be after the resurrection! Keep your proper degrees, for God keeps for you your honours.

The resurrection of the dead is compared to the stars that are set in heaven. *For star differs from star in glory,* as the Apostle says; *so also is the resurrection of the dead* (1 Cor 15:41-42). For after one manner virginity shall shine there, after another shall wedded chastity shine there, after another shall holy widowhood shine there. They shall shine diversely, but all shall be there. The brilliancy unequal, the heaven the same.

Receiving Communion worthily

With your thoughts then on your degrees, and keeping your professions, approach the Flesh of the Lord, approach to the Blood of the Lord. Whosoever knows himself to be otherwise, let him not approach. Be moved to compunction rather by my words. For they who know that they are keeping for their wives, what from their wives they require, they who know that they are in every way keeping continence, if this they have vowed to God, feel joy at my words; but they who hear me say, *Whosoever of you are not keeping chastity, approach not to that Bread,* are saddened. And I should have no wish to say this; but what can I do? Shall I fear man, so as to suppress the truth? What, if those servants do not fear the Lord, shall I therefore too not fear? As if I do not know that it is said, *You wicked and slothful servant* (Matt 25:26); you should dispense, and I require.

I have dispensed, O Lord my God; in your Sight, and in the sight of your Holy Angels, and of this your people. I have laid out your money. I am afraid of your judgement. I have dispensed what You do require. Though I should not say it, You would do it. Therefore I rather say, I have dispensed, do You convert, do You spare. Make them chaste who have been unchaste, that in your Sight we may rejoice together when the judgement shall come, both he who has dispensed and he to whom it has been dispensed. Does this please you? May it do so!

Whosoever of you are unchaste, amend yourselves, while you are alive. For I have power to speak the word of God, but to deliver the unchaste, who persevere in wickedness, from the judgement and condemnation of God, I have no power.

Sermon LXXXII

Saint Augustine

ETERNAL LIFE

Our hope, brethren, is not of this present time, nor of this world, nor in that happiness whereby men who forget God are blinded. We ought to know this above all things, and as a Christian realise, that we were not made Christians for the good things of the present time, but for something else which God at once promises, and man does not yet comprehend. For of this good it is said, *That eye has not seen, nor ear heard, neither has it entered into the heart of man, what things God has prepared for them that love Him* (1 Cor 2:9).

Because so great, so excellent, so ineffable a good as this did not come through man's understanding; it required God's promise. For man who is blind of heart does not now comprehend what has been promised him; nor can he be shown now, what he will be one day. Let us consider the situation of an infant, who is able to understand the words of someone speaking to it, when it cannot speak, or walk, or do anything. It is feeble; we see it is unable to stand, and requires the assistance of others. If it were only able to understand what it was being told: *just as you see me able to walk, work and speak, so too you yourself will be able to do in a few years*, the infant would be able *to see* what was promised. But in view of its own present inabilities it would not *believe* what was being promised; and yet he would *see* what was promised.

But with us infants, as it were, clothed in this feeble flesh, what is promised is at once great but is unseen. So faith is required that we believe what we do not see, and that we may manage to see what we believe. Whoever denies this belief comes to think that he is not to believe what he does not see. But when what he did not believe in does comes about, he is put to shame; and being confounded, is separated; and being separated is condemned.

But whoever has believed will stand at the right hand and shall stand with great confidence and joy among those to whom it shall be said: *Come, blessed of my Father receive the Kingdom which has been prepared for you from the beginning of the world* (Matt 25:34). But Our Lord made an alternative end when he declared *these shall go into everlasting burning but the righteous into life eternal* (Matt 25:46). This is the life eternal which is promised to us.

Search for eternal life

Since men love to live on this earth, life is promised them; and because they have an overwhelming fear of dying, eternal life is promised to them. What do you love? To live. This you shall have. What do you fear? To die. You shall not suffer it. It would seem to meet the needs of human frailty that it should be said, *You shall have eternal life.* This the mind of man can comprehend; in its present state it can in some way comprehend what is to be. But because of the imperfection of its present condition how far can it comprehend it? Because he lives and does not wish to die, he loves eternal life; he wishes to live always, never to die. Even they who are tormented with punishments, have a wish to die, but cannot. It is no great thing, then, to live long, or to live for ever. But to live a good life is a great thing. Let us love eternal life. May we know how greatly we ought to strive for eternal life when we see men who love the present life (which lasts but for a time and must be brought to an end) so labour for it, that when the fear of death comes they will do whatever they can to put off death.

How does a man strive when death threatens? By flight, by concealment, by giving all that he has, and by redeeming himself with toil, by endurance of torments and discomfort, by calling in physicians, and whatever else a man can do? See how after exhausting all the possibilities and his means, he is able only to contrive to live a little longer; to live always he is not able. If then men strive with such great efforts, at so great a cost, with such earnestness, with such watchfulness, with such care, so that they may live a little longer, how should they strive that they may live for ever?

And if those who by all means strive to put off death, and live a few days longer, are called wise, how foolish are those who live in such a way as to lose the day eternal.

Eternal life

When eternal life is promised, let us set before our eyes a life of such a kind as to remove from it everything unpleasant which we suffer here. For it is easier for us to find what is not there, than what is there. Here we live; we shall live there also. Here we are in health when we are not sick, and there is no pain in the body; there we shall be in health also. And when things go well with us in this life, we suffer no scourge; there we shall suffer nothing. Take, then, the case of a man living here below, in sound health, suffering no scourge. If anyone were to grant him the possibility that he should be like that for ever and that this good estate should never cease, how greatly would he rejoice? How greatly transported, how would he contain himself in joy without pain, without torment, without end of life?

If God had promised us only this, which I have mentioned, which I have just now set out in such words as I was able, at what price ought it to be purchased? If it were to be sold, how great a sum ought it to fetch? Would all that you have suffice, even though you possessed the whole world? Yet it is to be sold. Buy it if you can.

Do not be uneasy for a thing so great, because of the amount to be paid. Its price is no more than what you have. To procure any great and precious thing you would get ready gold or silver or money; or any increase of cattle or fruit which might be produced from your lands, to buy this great and excellent thing which would allow you to live happily on this earth. Buy this too if you can. Do not look for what you have but for what you are. The price of this thing is yourself. Its price is what you are yourself. Give your own self and you shall have it. Why are you troubled? Why are you uneasy? What are you going to seek for your own self or to buy yourself? Give your own self, such as you are, to that thing, and you shall have it. But you will say *I am wicked and perhaps it will not accept me*. By giving yourself to it you will become good. The giving of yourself to this faith and this promise: this is to become good.

For what is it that the good are to receive? Now I am revealing that which I did not reveal above; and yet in revealing it I do not reveal it. For I said that there we shall be in sound health, shall be safe, shall be living, shall be without scourges, without hunger and thirst, without failing, without loss of our eyes. All this I said; but what we shall have in addition I did not say.

We shall see God. Now this will be so great, yes so great a thing will it be, that in comparison to it, all the rest is nothing. I said that we shall be living, that we shall be safe and sound, that we shall suffer no hunger and thirst, that we shall not fall into weariness, that sleep will not oppress us. All this, what is it to that happiness we shall have when we shall see God? Because God cannot be manifested as He is, whom nevertheless we shall see. Therefore, *what eye has not seen nor ear heard* (1 Cor 2:9): this the good shall see. This shall the godly see. This the merciful shall see. This shall the faithful see; this shall be seen by those who have a good lot in the resurrection of the body, for they have had a good obedience in the resurrection of the heart.

The resurrection of the body and life eternal

When is He to manifest Himself to those who love Him? After the resurrection of the body, when *the ungodly shall be taken away so that he shall not see the Glory of God*. For then *when He shall appear, we shall be like Him; for we shall see Him as He is* (1 John 3:2): this is life eternal. For all that we said before is nothing to that life.

What is it to be alive? What is it to be in good health? To see God is a great thing. This is life eternal; this He Himself has said: *but this is life eternal that they may know You, the only true God and Jesus Christ whom You have sent* (John 17:3).

This is life eternal that they may know, see, comprehend, acquaint themselves with what they had believed, may perceive that which they were not able to comprehend.

Sermon 77

Saint Augustine

In Praise of Charity

The love with which we love God and our neighbour contains in itself all the greatness and depth of the other divine precepts. This is what the unique heavenly Teacher teaches: *You shall love the Lord your God with all your heart, and with all your soul and with all your mind... You shall love your neighbour as yourself* (Matt 22:37-40). So if you don't have the time to study each page of the scriptures, or to lift the veil which covers the words and discover the secrets of the scriptures, practise charity which encompasses everything. In this way you will possess what you have learned and what you have not yet deciphered. If you have charity, you already know a principle which contains what you perhaps do not understand. Charity is made manifest in those passages of scripture which are open to your intelligence, and it is hidden in those passage which are unclear. If you put this virtue into practice in your customs, you will possess all the divine revelations, whether or not you understand them.

So, my brethren, pursue charity, the sweet and healthy bond of hearts. Without it, the richest person is poor; with it, the poorest is rich. Charity is what gives us patience in our affliction, moderation in prosperity, strength in adversity, joy in doing good deeds. She offers us a sure refuge in temptations, gives generous hospitality to the disadvantaged, gives joy to the heart when it meets with human truths, and lends patience to suffer traitors.

Some examples from the Bible

Charity led Abel to make pleasing sacrifices. She gave Noah a sure refuge during the flood. She inspired Moses with gentle sweetness in the midst of injury and great meekness to David in his tribulations. It deadened the devouring flames around the three young Hebrew boys in the fiery furnace, and gave strength to the Maccabeans in the torture of fire.

Charity was chaste in Susanna's marriage; it was chaste with Anna in her widowhood and with Mary in her virginity. It was the cause of the holy freedom in Paul when it came to correct, and that of humility in Peter to obey. It is human in Christians when it comes to repenting of their sins, and divine in Christ to forgive them. But what praise can I make of charity, after the Lord himself has done so, teaching us through the lips of his Apostle that it is the most excellent of all virtues? Pointing out to us the path of the highest perfection, he says: *If I speak in the tongues of mortals and of angels, but do not have love, I am a noisy gong or a clanging cymbal. And if I have prophetic powers, and understand all mysteries and all knowledge, and if I have all faith so as to remove mountains, but do not have love, I am nothing. If I give away all my possessions, and if I hand over my body so that I may boast, but do not have love, I gain nothing.*

Love is patient; love is kind; love is not envious or boastful or arrogant or rude. It does not insist on its own way; it is not irritable or resentful; it does not rejoice in wrongdoing, but rejoices in the truth. It bears all things, believes all things, hopes all things, endures all things (1 Cor 13:1-8).

How many treasures does charity contain! It is the soul of scripture, the strength of prophecies, the salvation of the mysteries, the foundation of science, the fruit of faith, the riches of the poor, and life of the death-bound. Can one imagine greater magnanimity than that of dying for the godless, or greater generosity than that of loving one's enemies?

Fruits of charity

Charity is the only one which is not saddened by the happiness of one's neighbour, because it is not envious. It is the only one which does not become self-centred in prosperity because it is not vain. It is the only one not to suffer remorse of conscience, because it does not act without reflection. Charity remains serene in the face of insults; it does good in the midst of hatred; in the midst of anger it stays calm; it is simple and innocent facing the tricks of its enemies; in injustice it grieves, and expands in the truth.

Imagine, if you can, something with greater fortitude than charity, not to avenge injuries, but rather to make restitution. Imagine someone more faithful, not through vanity, but for supernatural reasons, who looks to eternal life. For everything which one suffers in the present life is because one firmly believes in what has been revealed for future life. If one tolerates the bad things, it is because one hopes for the goods which God has promised in heaven; for this reason charity never ever ceases.

Seek charity. Meditating on it in a saintly way, try to produce the fruits of sanctity. And may everything which you find most excellent in her and which I may not have made mention of, shine in your customs.

Sermo 350, 2-3

Saint Augustine

WHEN CHRIST PASSES BY

And he said: No, lest perhaps gathering up the cockle you root up the wheat also together with it. Suffer both to grow until the harvest, and in the time of the harvest I will say to the reapers: Gather up first the cockle and bind it into bundles to burn, but the wheat gather into my barn. Another parable he proposed to them, saying: The kingdom of heaven is like to a grain of mustard seed which a man took and sowed in his field. Which is the least indeed of all seeds; but, when it is grown up, it is greater than all herbs and becomes a tree, so that the birds of the air come and dwell in the branches thereof.

Another parable he spoke to them: The kingdom of heaven is like to leaven which a woman took and hid in three measures of meal, until the whole was leavened. All these things Jesus spoke in parables to the multitudes; and without parables he did not speak to them (Matt 20:29-34).

Crying out to Christ

Now what is it, Brethren, *to cry out* to Christ, but to correspond to the grace of Christ by good works? This I say, Brethren, lest haply we cry aloud with our voices, and in our lives be dumb. Who is he that cries out to Christ, that his inward blindness may be driven away by Christ as He is *passing by,* that is, as He is dispensing to us those temporal sacraments, whereby we are instructed to receive the things which are eternal?

Who is he that cries out to Christ? Whoever despises

the world, cries out to Christ. Whoever despises the pleasures of the world, cries out to Christ. Whoever says not with his tongue but with his life, *The world is crucified to me, and I to the world,* cries out to Christ. Whoever *disperses abroad and gives to the poor, that his righteousness may endure for ever,* cries out to Christ. For let him that hears, and is not deaf to the sound, *sell that you have, and give to the poor; provide yourselves bags which wax not old, a treasure in the heavens that fails not.* Let him, as he hears the sound as it were of Christ's footsteps *passing by,* cry out in response to this in his blindness, that is, let him do these things. Let his voice be in his actions. Let him begin to despise the world, to distribute to the poor his goods, to esteem as nothing worth what other men love. Let him disregard injuries, not seek to be avenged, let him give his *cheek to the smiter.* Let him pray for his enemies. If any *one has his goods taken away,* let *him not ask for them again.* If he *has taken anything from any man,* let him restore four-fold.

When he shall begin to do all this, all his kinsmen, relations, and friends will be in commotion. They who love this world, will oppose him. What madness this! You are too extreme! What? Are not other men Christians? This is folly, this is madness. And other such like things do the multitude cry out to prevent the blind from crying out. The multitude rebuked them as they cried out; but did not overcome their cries. Let them who wish to be healed understand what they have to do.

Suppressing the cries to Christ

Jesus is now also *passing by;* let them who are by the way side cry out. These are they *who know God with their lips, but their heart is far from Him.* These are by the way side, to whom as blinded in heart Jesus gives His precepts.

For when those passing things which Jesus did are recounted, Jesus is always represented to us as *passing by*. For even to the end of the world there will not be wanting *blind men sitting by the way side*. Need, then, there is that they who sit by the way side should cry out. The multitude that was with the Lord would repress the crying of those who were seeking for recovery.

Brethren, do you see my meaning? For I know not how to speak, but still less do I know how to be silent. I will speak then, and speak plainly. For I fear *Jesus passing by* and *Jesus standing still;* and therefore I cannot keep silence.

Evil and lukewarm Christians hinder good Christians who are truly earnest, and wish to carry out the commandments of God which are written in the Gospel. This multitude which is with the Lord hinders those who are crying out, hinders those who are doing well, that they may not by perseverance be healed. But let them cry out, and not faint. Let them not be led away as if by the authority of numbers. Let them not imitate those who became Christians before them, who live evil lives themselves, and are jealous of the good deeds of others. Let them not say, *Let us live as these so many live.*

Why not rather as the Gospel ordains? Why do you wish to live according to the remonstrances of the multitude who would hinder you, and not after the steps of the Lord, *who passes by?* They will mock, and abuse, and call you back; do cry out till you reach the ears of Jesus. For they who shall persevere in doing such things as Christ has enjoined, and regard not the multitudes that hinder them, nor think much of their appearing to follow Christ, that is of their being called Christians. But who love the light which Christ is about to restore to them, more than they fear the uproar of those who are hindering them, they shall on no account be separated from Him, and Jesus will *stand still,* and make them whole.

To be brief; that I may conclude this Sermon, Brethren, with a matter which touches me very dearly, and gives me much pain, see what crowds there are which *rebuke the blind as they cry out.* But let them not deter you, whosoever among this crowd desire to be healed; for there are many Christians in name, and in works ungodly. Let them not deter you from good works. Cry out amid the crowds that are restraining you, and calling you back, and insulting you, whose lives are evil. For not only by their voices, but by evil works, do wicked Christians repress the good.

The actions of a good Christian

A good Christian has no wish to attend the public shows. In this very thing, that he bridles his desire of going to the theatre, he cries out after Christ, cries out to be healed. Others run together thither, but perhaps they are heathens or Jews? Ah! indeed, if Christians went not to the theatres, there would be so few people there, that they would go away for very shame. So then Christians run thither also, bearing the Holy Name only to their condemnation.

Cry out then by abstaining from going, by repressing in your heart this worldly concupiscence. Hold on with a strong and persevering cry to the ears of the Saviour, that Jesus may *stand still* and heal you. Cry out amidst the very crowds, despair not of reaching the ears of the Lord. For the blind men in the Gospel did not cry out in that quarter, where no crowd was, that so they might be heard in that direction, where there was no impediment from persons hindering them. Amidst the very crowds they cried out; and yet the Lord heard them. And so also do you even amidst sinners, and sensual men, amidst the lovers of the vanities of the world, there cry out that the Lord may heal you. Go not to another quarter to cry out to the Lord, go not to heretics, and cry out to Him there. Consider, Brethren, how in that crowd which was hindering them from crying out, even there were they who cried out made whole.

Sermo 88, 12-13, 17

SAINT AUGUSTINE

THE MIRACULOUS CATCH

The fishing of our Saviour is our salvation. Moreover, we notice two fishing incidents in the holy Gospel of our Lord, that is, times when the nets were lowered at His word: one earlier when He chose the disciples, and the other when He had risen from the dead. That earlier fishing incident showed what the nature of the Church is now; the one which took place after the Resurrection of the Lord showed what the nature of the Church is going to be at the end of this world. Finally, in that earlier fishing, He bade the nets to be lowered without saying in what direction; He simply ordered them to be lowered. The disciples obeyed; there was no direction specifying *to the right* nor was there any direction specifying *to the left*. For the fish represented men. If, therefore, He had said *to the right*, only the good were going to be included; if He had said *to the left*, only the wicked would be taken. In fact, it was because both good and bad were going to be mixed together in the Church that the nets were lowered without any distinction, so that fish might be taken indiscriminately, signifying the mixture of the good and the bad.

Near sinking
Furthermore, the statement is also made in the same passage that they took so many fish that the two boats were filled and were about to sink, that is, they were pressed down to the sinking point (cf Luke 5:1-7). As a

The Miraculous Catch

matter of fact, those two boats did not sink, but they were in danger of doing so. Why were they in danger? Because of the large number of fish. In this way it was pointed out that, by reason of the large number of people which the Church would gather, her discipline would be endangered. Besides, a statement was added to the account of the fishing relating that the nets were broken on account of the large number of fish. What did broken nets signify except future schisms?

Three points, therefore, were emphasised in that first fishing incident: the mixture of the good and the bad, the pressure of the crowds, and the severance of heretics. The mixture of the good and the bad was indicated because the nets were lowered neither to the right nor to the left; the pressure of the crowds, because so many were taken in that the boats were weighed down; the severance of heretics, because the number was so great that the nets were broken.

A clear directive

Turn your attention now to the account of the other fishing incident which was read aloud today. For that happened after the Resurrection of the Lord to indicate what the nature of the Church would be after our resurrection. The Lord said: *Cast the net to the right side* (John 21:6). Therefore, the number of those who will stand on His right hand was determined, for you remember that the Lord said that He will come with His angels, that all nations will be gathered before Him, that He will separate them as the shepherd separates the sheep from the goats, that He will set the sheep on His right side and the goats on the left, and that He will say to the sheep: *Come, receive the kingdom,* and to the goats: *Go into everlasting fire* (cf Matt 25:31-42).

Cast 'the net' to the right side. It is as if He were saying: *Now that I have risen again, I wish to show what the Church will be at the resurrection of the dead. Cast to the right side.* The nets were cast to the right, and the disciples were not able to raise them because of the large number of fish. In the previous incident the word *multitude* was used, but here a definite number was specified – both multitude and magnitude; there, however, the number was not mentioned. For now, before the resurrection takes place and before the good are separated from the evil, that which the Prophet predicted is being fulfilled, namely: *I have declared and I have spoken* (Ps 39:6). What is the meaning of: *I have declared and I have spoken?* It signifies: *I have lowered the nets.* And what then? *They are multiplied above number.* There is a number; they exceed that number. The number pertains to the saints who are destined to reign with Christ. Now persons can enter the Church in excess of that number; they cannot so enter the kingdom of heaven.

For this reason, I urge you to remove yourselves from the evil world of our day. For this reason, I urge you, who wish to live, not to imitate wicked Christians. Do not say: *How is it? Is he not a believer, and is he intoxicated? How is it? Is he not a believer, and has concubines? How is it? Is he not a believer, and does he daily perpetrate frauds? How is it? Is he not a believer, and does he consult astrologers?* Actually, you who now wish to be grain will then be found in the bread; you who now wish to be chaff will then be found in the great heap destined to be burned in a great conflagration.

The end of the world

What follows? He continues: *They hauled the nets to the shore* (John 21:11). Just now, when the Gospel was

THE MIRACULOUS CATCH

read aloud, you heard that Peter hauled the nets to the shore. When you hear *shore*, understand the end of the sea; when you hear *the end of the sea*, understand the end of the world. In the earlier fishing, the nets were not hauled to the shore; but the fish that were taken were poured into the boats. However, in this incident they hauled the nets to the shore. Hope for the end of the world. The end is going to come to the advantage of those on the right, to the disadvantage of those on the left.

And how many fishes were there? *They hauled in the nets which held one hundred fifty-three fishes.* In addition, the Evangelist notes a necessary detail: *And though they were so great*, that is, so large, *the net was not torn.* They will be great, but there will not be heresies; and it is for the very reason that they will be great that there will not be heresies. Who are the great? Read the words of the Lord Himself in the Gospel and you will find who are the great. For He says: *I have not come to destroy the Law and the Prophets, but to fulfil them* (Matt 5:17).

For amen I say to you that whoever does away with one of these least commandments, and so teaches men – does away with and so teaches; *does away with* by evil living, and *so teaches* by good instruction – *shall be called least in the kingdom of heaven* (Matt 5:19). But in what kingdom of heaven? In the Church which exists now, because it is also called the kingdom of heaven. For, if the Church which gathers in the good and the bad were not also called the kingdom of heaven, the Lord Himself, speaking in a parable, would not have said: *The kingdom of heaven is like a net cast into the sea that gathered in fish of every kind.* But, behold what follows! *The kingdom of heaven is like a net cast into the sea* – sagenae are nets – *that gathers in fish of every kind.* What then? They drag them to the shore. (The Lord said this in the parable.)

And when they have hauled the nets to the shore, they sit down and *gather the good fish into vessels, but they throw away the bad.* Moreover the Lord explained what He declared. What is it he says? *So will it be at the end of the world.* (Did you grasp the meaning of the word *shore*?) He continued: *The angels come and separate the wicked from among the just, and cast them into the furnace of fire, where there will be the weeping and the gnashing of teeth* (cf Matt 13:47-51).

Nevertheless, the Church is called the kingdom of heaven. And, inasmuch as the sea has both good and bad fish swimming about at the same time, in that kingdom of heaven, that is, in the Church of our times, he is called least who teaches good things but does evil, because such people are there also. Yes, such a one is there; he is there in the kingdom of heaven, that is, in the Church as she exists in our times. He teaches good things; he does evil. He is a member, but he is a hireling. *Amen I say to you,* the Lord says: *they have received their reward* (Matt 6:2). Such a person is of some good, for if they who teach good things and do evil were of no use, the Lord Himself would not have said to His people (cf Matt 23:2-4): *The Scribes and the Pharisees sit on the chair of Moses. Do what they say; do not what they do.* Why? *For they talk, but do nothing.*

The big fish

Therefore, let your Charity be attentive, for I desire to explain to you whom these great fishes represent: *Whoever has done away with one of these least commandments, shall be called least in the kingdom of heaven.* He will be there, but he will be least. *But whoever has carried them out and has so taught them, he shall be called great in the kingdom of heaven.* Behold, those are the great fishes

THE MIRACULOUS CATCH

taken on the right side. *Whoever has carried them out and has so taught them*: he has done good things; he has taught good things; he has not contradicted his own instructions by evil living, having a good tongue in spite of his evil life. Therefore, *whoever has carried them out and has so taught them, he shall be called great in the kingdom of heaven.*

And Scripture continues: *For I say to you that unless your justice exceeds that of the Scribes and Pharisees, you shall not enter the kingdom of heaven* (cf Matt 5:19-20). Now, how do you understand the words *kingdom of heaven* here? As that place of which the Scripture says: *Come, blessed of my Father, receive the kingdom* (cf Matt 25:34). *Unless your justice exceeds that of the Scribes and Pharisees* – what does *exceeds that of the Scribes and Pharisees* mean? Recall those Scribes and Pharisees who sit on the chair of Moses, of whom the Scripture says: *Do what they say; do not do what they do; for they talk, but do nothing* (cf Matt 23:1-5). Hence, the justice of the Pharisees is to talk and not to do. Let your justice exceed that of the Scribes and Pharisees so that you may both speak well and live well.

Sanctity

Now, therefore, what need is there of repeating the same statements about the number of the 153 fishes? You know all that. A gradually increasing number derives from ten and seven. Begin with one, go on to seventeen in such a way that you add all the intervening numbers, that is, add one to two, and it becomes three; add three, and it becomes six; add four, and it becomes ten. In this way add all the numbers up to seventeen, and the total is 153. Hence, our whole attention ought to be directed to nothing else except the significance of ten and seven, for therein lies the foundation of the 153.

Now, what is the significance of the ten and the seven? Understand the ten as in the Law. Ten precepts were given first; the Decalogue was inscribed by the finger of God on tablets. In the ten, understand the Law; in the seven, understand the Holy Spirit, for the holy Spirit is presented in sevenfold form. On that account, sanctification is not mentioned in the law until the seventh day. God made light; the Scripture does not say: *He sanctified it.* He made the firmament; it does not say: *He sanctified the firmament.* He separated the sea from the earth; He ordered the earth to bud forth; it does not say: *He sanctified it.* He made the moon and the stars; it does not say: *He sanctified them.* He ordered living things that swim and fly to come forth from the waters; it does not say: *He sanctified them.* He ordered four-footed animals and all creeping things to come forth from the earth; it does not say: *He sanctified them.* He made man himself; it does not say: *He sanctified him* (Gen 1:1-31).

We have reached the seventh day whereon He rested; and He sanctified it (cf Gen 2:3). By His rest, God sanctified our rest. Therefore, our complete sanctification will be there where we shall rest eternally with Him. But why should God rest, for He was not wearied by His work? If you were to accomplish things by a mere word, you would not be tired; if you should give a direction and should find it carried out immediately, you would stay at rest, you would remain fresh. He spoke a few words by which He made all things, and was He suddenly wearied?

Hence, understand that the Law is represented by the ten; understand that the Holy Spirit is represented by the seven. Let the Spirit be joined to the Law, because, if you have received the Law, and if you lack the help of the Spirit, you do not fulfil what is of the Law, you do not carry out what is commanded you. Moreover, man under the Law is held as a prevaricator. Let the Spirit be added, let Him help: that which is commanded is accomplished. If the Spirit is absent, the letter kills you. Why does the letter kill you? Because it will make you a prevaricator. You cannot excuse yourself on the plea of ignorance since you have received the Law. Now, because you have learned what you should do, ignorance does not excuse you; the Spirit does not help you: therefore, you are ruined.

But why does the Apostle say: *The letter kills, but the spirit gives life?* (2 Cor 3:6). How does the Spirit give life? Because He causes the letter to be fulfilled so that it may not kill. The sanctified are those who fulfil the law of God according to the gift of God. The Law can command; it cannot help. The Spirit is added as a helper, and the commandment of God is fulfilled with joy and delight. Certainly many observe the Law from fear, but those who keep the Law from fear of punishment would prefer that what they fear did not exist. On the contrary, those who observe the Law through love of justice rejoice even in that respect because they do not consider it hostile to them.

On that account the Lord says: *Come to terms with your opponent quickly while you are with him on the way* (Matt 5:25). Who is your opponent? The word of the Law. What is the way? This life. How is the word of the Law an opponent? It says: *You shall not commit adultery*, and you wish to commit adultery. It says: *You shall not covet your neighbour's goods,* and you wish to steal the property of another. It says: *Honour your father and your mother,* and you are insolent to your parents. The Law says: *Do not bear false witness,* but you do not refrain from lying. When you see that the Law commands one thing and you do another, the Law is your opponent. You have a destructive adversary; let it not enter into intimacy with you; come to an agreement while you are on the way. God is near at hand to reconcile you. How does God reconcile you? By forgiving your sins, and by implanting justice so that your words may become good.

Therefore, when you have come to terms with your opponent, that is, with the Decalogue of the Law through the Holy Spirit, you will arrive at the ten and the seven. When you have come to the ten and the seven, then the number will increase to 153. You will deserve to be crowned on the right side; do not remain in the left side to be condemned.

Sermon 251

Saint Peter Chrysologus

According to the *Liber Pontificalis* and a biography written in the ninth century, Peter was born at Imola around 380 A.D. He was baptised, educated and ordained deacon by Cornelius, Bishop of Imola, and was consecrated Archbishop of Ravenna between 425 and 429. His piety and zeal won for him universal admiration, and his oratory merited for him the title Chrysologus.

He shared the confidence of Leo the Great. In 445 he witnessed the death of St German of Auxerre. Four years later, after the Synod of Constantinople issued a decree of condemnation, Peter wrote to the monophysite Eutyches, a presbyter of Constantinople, asking him to submit to the decisions made by the Pope.

In addition to this letter, a collection of some 180 sermons are considered among his authenticated works. Most of these centre on the explanation of texts of Sacred Scripture read during the Mass. Others, very few in number, are directly dogmatic and refer, above all, to the Incarnation (defending the Catholic faith against the Arian, Nestorian and monophysite heresies), grace, Christian life and recognition of the primacy of the Papacy.

St Peter Chrysologus expended his best efforts in the spiritual formation of the faithful, in preparing Catechumens for baptism and in the conversion of pagans. He died in his native city on 3 December 450.

In the sermon below, the cure of the woman suffering

from an issue of blood (from the Gospel of St Matthew) is commented upon. It aims to instruct the faithful on the interior dispositions with which they ought to receive the Sacrament of the Eucharist.

Saint Peter Chrysologus

THE SYMBOLIC MEANING OF TWO MIRACLES

A gentlemanly borrower soon pays what he has promised. He does not tax his creditor's good will by frequently putting him off, or keep him in anxiety by long waiting. When the account of the ruler of the synagogue, or the related account which springs from it, that of the woman with the haemorrhage, was enticing us away from the customary brevity of our sermons, we preferred to cut our discourse in half lest it seem to start anew to such an extent as to overburden your patience to listen.

The woman with an issue of blood

The ruler of the synagogue hastened to meet the Lord, and fell prostrate on the ground. He explained his case, manifested his grief, excited the compassion of his Benefactor, and begged him to come with speed to effect a cure. In contrast, the Lord met the woman before He was entreated. While passing by, He gave her an occasion of recovering health; while silent himself, He understood the case of the silent woman, and saw her wound even when she was hiding it. With her it was in secret that the Lord carried on his important work of healing. And while He was making his way after being petitioned in public, her knowledge sprang from her faith, penetrated to his divinity, and discovered that great secret.

Oh, happy is that woman! In the midst of such a great multitude she was so much alone with Christ that only she was aware both of her restoration to health and his exalted power! Happy is she who found such access that no one could stop her. Happy she who by such a path struggled and crept up to her Creator, before she was upbraided by anyone because of her sore, and before she was free from its repugnance.

She knew that with men and through their power the way to full health was closed to her. Men are more accustomed to shrink away from wounds than to cure them. God cleanses human wounds; He does not despise them. He does not shrink from human sores, but heals them. Nor does He detest the suppurations from the human body; rather, He cleanses them. God cannot, He cannot, be soiled through contact with his creature.

But the Evangelist poses a problem when he states: *And Jesus instantly perceiving in himself that power had gone forth from him, turned to the crowd and said, Who touched my cloak?* While He was asking as if professing ignorance, did He perceive that power had gone forth from him, and fail to know to whom it had gone? Did He know that He had let it go forth, without knowing to whom? Did He, who was certain that health had been conferred, doubt about the beneficiary?

No. The Lord asked here, not because of any error of one in ignorance, but with the majesty of him who knows both the present and the future. He was not investigating something hidden to him; rather, He manifested that it was well known to him, in this way. He so asked his questions that He alone revealed the hidden matter to all those unaware of it. Not as an unknowing examiner, but as a questioner who knew everything beforehand, He drew his petitioner into the centre of attention. She was silent, making suggestions only by her thoughts, in ready waiting behind his back for the measures by which He exercised his powers. He made her stand before all so that she who had gained health for herself might also bring faith for all; that she who had his power might acknowledge his majesty; that she who had made him so fully known might not go away again unknown, herself, as she expected.

While she was blushing over her wound and with so much concern fearing him as God, the woman found her faith getting darkened. Clouds of confusion obscured the light in her mind. Therefore, the voice of her questioning Lord, like a salutary wind, drove the clouds away, dispersed the mists, and enlightened her faith. It made her who had recently been in darkness of the light brighter than the very sun. For, she shines throughout the whole world, is resplendent in the whole of the Church, and is glorious among its members. Is she, then, less than a sun? If she had returned unseen – give me leave to say it – she would have escaped her Physician, not tested him. She could have ascribed what she obtained to herself rather than to her Healer. She would have believed that she had drawn her cure from the hem of his garment, not from his penetrating understanding. For, what would she have believed to be truly his whose power she had experienced in her own case, but which in her wish she had deemed to be something outside him?

Before her cure, perhaps it was because of her shame that she kept herself hid, and because of her humility that she thought herself unworthy. But after her cure, why did she not of her own accord run up to give Him thanks, and honour, and glory for such a great deed? After she saw that the Lord persisted in his questioning, that the disciples said that jostling from the crowd was the reason why He had been touched, and that she could not remain hidden, after fear and trembling in her own conscience began to trouble her, she came into the midst of them all. She wanted to profess public belief in him whom she had privately recognised as her Physician, and to adore him as God, and to become herself a remedy for sickness as great as hers, both to present and future men. As the Evangelist narrates: *But the woman, fearing and trembling, knowing what had happened within her, came and fell down before him, and told him all the truth.*

The symbolic meaning

However, the historical narrative should always be raised to a higher meaning, and mysteries of the future should become known through figures of the present. Therefore, we should now unfold, by allegorical discourse, what symbolic teaching is contained beneath the outward appearance of the ruler of the synagogue, or his daughter, or the woman afflicted with the haemorrhage.

In respect to his divinity, Christ cannot be moved from place to place; but walking by means of his human nature He comes, strides, and hastens to the daughter of the ruler of the synagogue. Without doubt, she is the Synagogue, for Christ said: *I was not sent except to the lost sheep of the house of Israel.*

But, while Christ was hastening to her, his Church which was located out among all the nations was suffering a haemorrhage and losing the blood of the human race. The integrity of nature had been lost. While human skill kept trying to cure the weakness of the race, it increased it. For, the censure of human frailty, and the severity of the discipline of this world, did indeed continually shed the blood of nations. But it could not obliterate the enemy, nor check the wars of the citizens, nor blot out the insanity of crimes.

Therefore, as a result of such cares, this Church had a running wound. She saw that whatever substance she had possessed and still possessed was used up – that is, her soul, mind, power of discernment, ingenuity, toil, industry, and planning. (All these endowments can indeed be ascribed to her officials, the physicians trying to cure the sick.) When she perceived that Christ was present as He was passing by, she came up behind him because, soiled with blood, she did not deserve to look upon his face.

She came up behind him. That is, she follows the hearing of faith and getting very close she touches, so to speak, the very fringe of his garment. She does this while she is not honoured among the fathers, is not sanctified by the Law, does not publicly bring herself forward among the Prophets, does not receive honour even from the very Body of the Lord, while she is deemed a stranger even by the group of men reborn from Christ.

She follows Christ behind his back, that is, in this last age of time. She is established as sacred by a hidden bond of faith, and she has truly touched his cloak (which she found in the Sepulchre) through this, that she has faith in these insignia of the risen Lord, and preaches them. But, while Christ is employing his powers in the case of his Church, He is not paying attention to the ruler's daughter. And the Synagogue dies – in order that she, too, who has died through the Law and perished through nature, may return to life through faith.

While He was speaking, there came some from the house of the ruler of the synagogue, and they said, Do not trouble the Master, the girl is dead. Today, also, the Jews do not want Christ to be troubled. They desire him not to come. They have faithlessly destroyed their apprehension of his Resurrection, and proclaim that He is dead.

But I see how that, too, is consistent with our assertion! For, as Scripture tells, the daughter of the ruler of the synagogue spent twelve years in life. So, too, it is recounted, did this woman endure her sore for twelve years, since the health of life both were to be restored at the latest and fulfilled time. That number, twelve, rounds off the time of human life. To make a year, the number twelve is divided and applied to the months. Consequently, the Prophet indicates that Christ came in the acceptable year of the Lord. The Apostle, too, approves the teaching that Christ came in the fullness of time: *When the fullness of the time came, God sent his Son.*

Pray, brethren, that just as the Synagogue has died to itself and the Law, in order to live to Christ, so we, too, may die in our sins in order to live in Christ.

Sermon 36

SAINT PETER CHRYSOLOGOS

THE LORD'S PRAYER

Dearly beloved, you have received the faith by hearing; now listen to the formula of the Lord's prayer. Christ taught us to pray briefly. He wishes us to put our petitions forward quickly. Why will He not give Himself to those who entreat Him, since He gave Himself to those who did not ask Him. Or what delay in answering will He show, who, by formulating prayers, has thus anticipated His suppliants' desires?

The angels stand in awe at what you are going to hear today. Heaven marvels. Earth trembles. Flesh does not bear it, hearing does not grasp it, the mind does not penetrate it, all creation cannot sustain it. I do not dare to utter it, yet I cannot remain silent. May God enable you to hear and me to speak.

What is more awesome: that God gives Himself to earth, or that He places you in Heaven? That He himself enters a union with flesh, or that He causes you to enter into a sharing of the Divinity? That He Himself accepts death, or that He recovers from death? That He Himself is born into your state of slavery, or that He makes you to be free children of His own? That He takes your poverty upon Himself, or that He makes you His heirs, yes, co-heirs of His unique Self?

It is indeed more awesome that earth is transformed into a heaven, that man is changed by a deification and that those whose lot is slavery get the rights of domination. All this is indeed something to fill us with fear.

Nevertheless, the present situation has reference not to the one instructing but to the One who gives the command. Therefore, my little children, let us approach where charity summons, love draws, and affection invites us. May our hearts perceive God as our Father! Our voice should proclaim this, our tongue should utter it, our spirit should shout it aloud; and everything that is in us should be in tune with grace, not fear. For, He who has changed from a judge into a Father has wished to be loved, not feared.

Our Father, who art in heaven. When you say this, do not understand it to mean that He is not on earth, or that He who encompasses all beings is Himself contained in a place. But understand that you, whose Father is in heaven, have a lineage derived from heaven. So act, too, that you become your Father's image by your holy way of life. He who does not darken himself with human vices, but shines with virtues like God's, proves himself a son of God.

Hallowed be thy name. We are called by the name of Him whose offspring we are. Therefore, let us beg that His Name, which is holy in itself and by its very nature, may be treated as holy by us. For, God's Name either gets honoured because of our conduct, or blasphemed because of our misdeeds. Hear the Apostle's words: *For the name of God is blasphemed through you among the Gentiles* (Rom 2:24).

Thy kingdom come. Was there ever a time when God did not reign? Therefore we ask that He who always has reigned Himself may now reign in us, that we also may be able to reign in Him. The devil has reigned; sin has reigned; death has reigned; and the human race has long been captive. Consequently, we ask that God may reign in His kingdom, the devil may be subject, sin may fail, death may die, and the captive human race may be captured in such a way that we may reign as free men unto everlasting life.

Thy will be done on earth as it is in heaven. This is the kingdom of God, when no other will than God's prevails, either in heaven or on earth; when in the case of all men, God is the directing mind, God is living, God is acting, God is reigning, God is everything, so that, according to that statement of the Apostle: *God may be all in all of you* (1 Cor 15:28).

Give us this day our daily bread. He who gave Himself to us as a Father, who adopted us as His sons, who made us the heirs of His goods, who raised us up in name and gave us His own honour and kingdom, He has directed that we should ask for our daily bread. In the kingdom of God, in the midst of His divine gifts, why does man in his poverty beg? Is it only when asked that a Father so good, so kindly, so generous gives bread to His children: And what are we to make of His statement: *Do not be anxious about what you are to eat, or what you are to drink, or what you are to put on* (Matt 6:31). Is he telling us to ask for that about which He forbids us to think? What do we hold? The heavenly Father is encouraging us, as heavenly sons, to ask for heavenly bread. He said: *I am the bread that has come down from heaven* (John 6:41). He is the Bread sown in the Virgin, leavened in the flesh, moulded in His passion, baked in the furnace of the sepulchre, placed in the churches, and set upon the altars, which daily supplies heavenly food to the faithful.

And forgive us our trespasses, as we also forgive those who trespass against us. O man, if you cannot be without sin, and wish your whole debt to be forgiven you always, you yourself should forgive always. Forgive just as much as you want to be forgiven to yourself. Forgive as often as you want to be forgiven. Indeed, just because you want the whole debt to be forgiven to yourself, you yourself forgive the whole. O man, understand that by forgiving others you have given forgiveness to yourself.

And lead us not into temptation, because in the world life itself is a temptation. *The life of man upon earth is a temptation* (cf Job 7:1), Job says. Therefore let us ask Him not to leave us to our own will, but to hedge us about in our own every act with His fatherly kindness, and by His guidance from heaven to keep us firm on the path of life.

But deliver us from evil. From which evil? Surely, from the devil, from whom all evil comes. We ask that we be freed from evil, because he who has not been free from evil cannot enjoy the good.

If those not yet born (by baptism), those still remaining in the womb, ask for bread and seek the kingdom, why is there complaint because the Son of God always remained in the bosom of God the Father? If the Church begets – that is not a doctrine based on reason, it is a heavenly mystery. The fact that the Son of God has been in God the Father – that cannot be explained by human reasoning. God must not be appraised in a human manner. You have heard the name, God; do not think of anything earthly or anything human. You have heard: Father of Christ; believe that He is this through His substance. You have heard that He is your Father; believe that He is this through His grace. He eternally possessed the power that His Son should be existent; He recently allowed you to become His son. Therefore, so know that you are a son as not to become unaware of being a servant. So hear that you have been made into a likeness of Christ as to know yourself always as the servant of Christ.

Sermon 67, On Matt 6:9-13

Saint Peter Chrysologus

THE LIVING SACRIFICE OF ONE'S DAILY LIFE

This is a remarkable kind of piety, which requests both that it may request and give a present. For, today, the blessed Apostle is not asking for human gifts, but conferring divine ones, when he prays: *I exhort you, by the mercy of God* (Rom 12:1).

Turning to God's mercy
When a physician persuades the sick to take some bitter remedies, he does so by coaxing requests. He does not use a compelling command. He knows that weakness, not choice, is the reason why the sick man spits out the healthy medicines, whenever he rejects those which will aid him. Also, a father induces his son to live according to the severity of disciplinary control not by force, but by love. He knows how harsh discipline is to a youthful disposition.

If one sick in body is thus enticed by requests toward getting cured, and if a boyish disposition is with difficulty thus coaxed to prudence, is it strange that the Apostle, always a physician and a father, prays with these words, in order to entice human souls which bodily diseases have wounded to accept divine remedies? *I exhort you by the mercy of God.*

He is introducing a new kind of exhortation. Why does he not exhort through God's might, or majesty, or glory, rather than by His mercy? Because it was through that mercy alone that Paul escaped from the criminal state of a persecutor, and obtained the dignity of his great apostolate. He himself tells us this: *For I formerly was a blasphemer, a persecutor and a bitter adversary; but I obtained the mercy of God* (1 Tim 1:13). A little further on he continues: *This saying is true and worthy of entire acceptance, that Jesus Christ came into the world to save sinners, of whom I am the chief. But I obtained mercy to be an example to those who shall believe in him for the attainment of life everlasting* (1 Tim 1:15-16).

What God is asking of us

I exhort you, by the mercy of God. Paul asks – rather, God Himself is asking through Paul, because God has greater desire to be loved than feared. God is asking because He wants to be not so much a Lord as a Father. God is asking through his mercy, that He may not punish in His severity. Hear God asking: *I have spread forth my hands all the day* (Is 65:2). Is not He who spreads forth His hands asking by His very demeanour? *I have spread forth my hands.* To whom? To a people. And to what people? *To an unbelieving people,* yes, more, to a contradicting one. *I have spread forth my hands.* He opens His arms, He enlarges His heart, He proffers His breast, He invites us to His bosom, He lays open His lap, that He may show Himself a Father by all this affectionate entreaty.

Also hear God asking in another way: *O my people, what have I done to thee, or in what have I molested thee?* (Mich 6:3). Does He not say the following? 'If My divinity is something unknown, at least let Me be known in the flesh. Look! You see in Me your own body, your members, your heart, your bones, your blood. If you fear what is divine, why do you not love what is characteristically human? If you flee from Me as the Lord, why do you not run to Me as your Father? But perhaps the greatness of My Passion, which you brought on, confounds you. Do not be afraid. This cross is not Mine, but it is the sting of death. These nails do not inflict pain upon Me, but they deepen your love of Me. These wounds do not draw forth My groans; rather, they draw you into my Heart. The extending of My body entices you into My bosom; it does not increase My pain. As far as I am concerned, My blood does not perish, but it is something paid down in advance as a ransom price for you. Therefore, come, return and at least thus have experience of Me as a Father whom you see returning good things for evils, love for injuries, such great charities for such great wounds.'

Paul's exhortation

Let us now hear the contents of the Apostle's exhortation. *I exhort you to present your bodies.* By requesting this, the Apostle has raised all men to a priestly rank. *To present your bodies as a living sacrifice.* O unheard of function of the Christian priesthood, inasmuch as man is both the victim and the priest for himself! Because man need not go beyond himself in seeking what he is to immolate to God! Because man, ready to offer sacrifice to God, brings with himself, and in himself, what is for himself! Because the same being who remains as the victim, remains also as a priest! Because the victim is immolated and still lives! Because the priest who will make atonement is unable to kill! Wonderful indeed is this sacrifice where the body is offered without the slaying of a body, and the blood without bloodshed.

I exhort you, says the Apostle, *by the mercy of God, to present your bodies as a living sacrifice.* Brethren, Christ's sacrifice is the pattern from which this one comes to us. While remaining alive, He immolated His body for the life of the world. And He truly made his body a living sacrifice, since He still lives although He was slain. In the case of such a victim, death suffers defeat. The victim remains, the victim lives on, death gets the punishment. Consequently, the martyrs get a birth at the time of their death. They get a new beginning through their end, and a new life through their execution. They who were thought to be extinguished on earth shine brilliantly in heaven.

I exhort you, brethren, he says, *by the mercy of God, to present your bodies as a sacrifice, living, holy.* That is what the Prophet sang: *Sacrifice and oblation you would not, but a body you have perfected for me* (Ps 39:7). O man, be both a sacrifice to God and a priest. Do not lose what the divine authority gave and conceded to you. Put on the robe of sanctity, gird yourself with the belt of chastity. Let Christ be the covering of your head. Let the cross remain as the helmet on your forehead. Cover your breast with the mystery of heavenly knowledge. Keep the incense of prayer ever burning as your perfume. Take up the sword of the spirit. Set up your heart as an altar. Free from anxiety, move your body forward in this way to make it a victim for God.

God seeks belief from you, not death. He thirsts for self-dedication, not blood. He is placated by good will, not by slaughter. God gave proof of this when He asked holy Abraham for his son as a victim (cf Gen 22:1-18). For, what else than his own body was Abraham immolating in his son? What else than faith was God requiring in the father, since He ordered the son to be offered, but did not allow him to be killed?

The sacrifice of daily life

Therefore, O man, strengthened by such an example, offer your body. Do not merely slay it, but also cut it up into numerous members, that is, the virtues. For, your skills at practising die as often as you offer these members, the virtues, to God. Offer up faith, that faithlessness may suffer punishment. Offer a fast, that gluttony may cease. Offer up chastity, that lust may die. Put on piety, that impiety may be put off. Invite mercy, that avarice may be blotted out. That folly may be brought to naught, it is always fitting to offer up holiness as a sacrificial gift. Thus your body will become a victim, if it has been wounded by no javelin of sin.

Your body lives, O man, it lives as often as you have offered to God a life of virtues through the death of your vices. The man who deserves to be slain by a life-giving sword cannot die. May our God Himself, who is the Way, the Truth, and the Life, deliver us from death and lead us to life.

Sermon 108

Saint Peter Chrysologus

THE TRIUMPH OF FAITH

The holy Evangelist has told us today that within the very time of the Crucifixion the Apostles were concerned with the table; that they were gazing at foods, concerned about banquets, and forgetful of the Lord's Passion. He states: *He appeared to the Eleven as they were reclining at table* (Mark 16:14).

Reclining where? At the tomb of their Master, and then soon at table, these servants? Is this the loyalty of servants? Is this the charity of disciples? Is this the ardour of Peter? Is this the love of John who raised himself from Christ's own bosom? Is this the affection they gained through so long a time, and through such great gifts and virtues? Right after His Passion, when His death still burns the mind and His burial still haunts the memory, when His enemies are rejoicing and all Judaea scoffing – were the disciples then taking their meal with all the comforts of the banquet couches and all the pleasures of those who recline at table?

At the death of Moses the angels were present (Jude 9), and God Himself took care of his burial. The Jews kept their camp in one place, halted their journey, endured a dreadful delay in the desert, enjoined thirty days of mourning and honoured this body of a servant by these obsequies of thirty days (Deut 34:5-8). Therefore, did not the true Christ, the one Lord, the Creator of the world, the Redeemer of all men – did not He deserve tears from His disciples three days after His tragic passion and death, the death of the Cross?

The earth trembled, hell was disturbed, rocks were split, tombs were opened, the sun disappeared, the day was buried, everything became dark. And were the disciples alone feasting on delights, free from care, on high couches in one crowd, at perfect leisure? Is this, brethren, what the Master Himself found upon His return from below? *Therefore he appeared to the Eleven as they were reclining at table; and he upbraided them for their lack of faith and hardness of heart, in that they had not believed those who had seen him after he had risen* (Mark 16:14).

Reclining in grief

O faithful Peter, Peter so devoted, what shall we say about these words? *While they were reclining at table.* Were they also eating? Brethren, the whole case was not one of reclining at a feast, but of lying prostrate in grief. The Apostles were not a convivial crowd, but an assembly of mourners. The bread there was that of grief, not joy. The cups were filled with the bitterness of the Cross, not the sweetness of wine.

The disciples, says Scripture, *were shut within for fear of the Jews.* If they were in fear and shut within, they surely were not feasting. And if they were not enjoying a meal, that was not a home but a jail. Theirs was not a banquet couch, but a tomb. At that time, all the distress of the Lord's passion had passed over to His disciples. The whole lance of sorrow was piercing not only their sides, but their very hearts. Their hands and feet were held fast by the nails of the clinging grief. The bitter spirit of the Jews was then giving them vinegar and gall to drink. For them the sun had set and the day had waned. At that time severe temptation of thought was dashing them against the crags of infidelity to shipwreck their faith. Despair, which is worse than all evils

The Triumph of Faith

and is in adversity always the last one to arrive, was already laying them out in sombre tombs.

Consequently, as we mentioned, the Lord found the disciples not reclining to eat, not feasting, but lying in grief and buried. So He upbraided them for their lack of faith. They had given so much belief to their despair that they had none for the Resurrection foretold by the Lord, and none for His servants who announced its occurrence. Consequently, they retained nothing conducive to faith and salvation. Dead to the world, and buried as far as the world was concerned, they already believed that they all had but one abode, that is, one tomb.

Thus, when the Lord saw that they had withdrawn themselves from the world, He called them to the world. He sent them back into it by the words: *Go into the whole world and preach the gospel to every creature* (Mark 16:15). Come into the world, that you who think you now lie prostrate in one abode may quickly see the whole world lying subject to you.

Hope

Come into the whole world, preach the gospel to every creature. This is to say: You be the hope of all, you who have been the cause of despair to your very selves. Test how great your unbelief has been. Test it then when you will see the world believing what you preach – you who could not believe your own sight. Know how great is your hardness of heart. Know it then when you will perceive the wildest nations throughout the world acknowledging Me although they have not seen Me – Me whom you denied when I was before your eyes. You will observe men scattered all over the earth – men secluded on islands, or dwelling on cliffs, or living in remote deserts; superficial magi of the East, quarrelsome Greeks, and skilful Romans

– you will observe them seeking by faith alone the belief which you sought by inserting hand and finger into My open wounds. However, since I am sending you as witnesses of My Passion, Death and Resurrection, I have allowed you to scrutinise those wounds more carefully – in the hope that your own hesitation will become a source of strength for those who will believe you.

Faith

He who believes, He continues, *and is baptised will be saved* (Mark 16:16). Brethren, faith is to baptism what the soul is to the body. Hence it is that he who is generated from the font lives by faith: *He who is just lives by faith* (Rom 1:17). Therefore, everyone who lacks faith dies.

He who believes – believes that the Trinity is one God; that in the Father and Son and the Holy Spirit there is one Majesty with full equality; that the Godhead is distinct in regard to the Trinity, not confused in the unity; rather, that it is clearly one with respect to the Godhead, and three-fold with respect to the Persons; that God is the name of the Trinity; that the Father and the Son should not be thought such according to an order of dignity, but according to their relationship of love; that the Holy Spirit should not be regarded as a Being more or less inferior nor more or less exterior, since divinity cannot have exterior parts; that Christ became man in such a way that what is God remains, and He died in such a way that by His death He called the dead of the centuries back to life; that He arose not for His own sake, but for ours; that He raised us into heaven when He ascended there Himself; that He sits there to exercise the authority of judge, not as one weary and seeking rest; that He who, as far as movement goes, is already everywhere, will come, not in regard to place, nor will He who already possesses the whole world come to hold it fast, but He will come in order that the world may make itself more worthy to see its Creator.

Man should also believe in forgiveness of sins, because, although the heavenly region is very spacious, it does not admit the sinner. Neither should a man despair over the magnitude of his sins. For, if there is one sin which God cannot forgive, He is not omnipotent. Man should believe in the resurrection of the body, that is, that it is the man himself who arises. He who sins is to incur punishment and he who labours is to get a reward. He should believe in everlasting life, to keep a second death from occurring.

In addition to this, the greatest indication of firm faith consists in the following signs. The devils, that is, the ancient foes, get exorcised from human bodies. One language intelligible in many others comes forth from one mouth. Serpents grasped in the name of Christ lose the power of their venom. Through Christ, cups of poison have no power to harm those who drink them. Bodily diseases are cured at the touch of one who preaches Christ.

Pray, brethren, that in the present life we may always be aware of the medicine of faith. Pray that when we are awaiting Christ and He is on the point of coming, we may be free from anxiety and rejoice because of our good conscience.

Sermon 83

Saint Vincent of Lerins

Vincent of Lerins is an ecclesiastical writer in Southern Gaul in the fifth century. He died around 450 in the monastery at Lerins. St Eucherius of Lyons calls him a holy man, conspicuous for eloquence and knowledge

His work is better known than his life. *Commonitorium* was written around 434; it is his only certainly-known work extant. It offers the main rules for discerning catholic Tradition from heretical teachings. The word *Commonitorium*, often used as a title for works in that period, means notes put into writing to aid the memory, without being an attempt at an exhaustive treatise. In this work St Vincent proposes, with constant examples from Tradition and the history of the Church, to offer criteria so that the catholic faith may be preserved intact.

The *Commonitorium* is a jewel of patristic literature. His celebrated principle is that Christians should believe *quod ubique, quod semper, quod ab omnibus* – what all men have everywhere, at all times and believed must be regarded as true. Several Popes and Councils have confirmed with their own authority the perennial validity of this rule of faith.

Thus St Vincent does not resort to a complicated method. The rules he offers can be known and applied by all Christians. 'I do not cease to be surprised by the idiocy of some... who, not content with the rules of the faith once given and which were received once and forever, are constantly seeking new things, and are making an effort to add, change or subtract from religion; it is as if it were not a heavenly doctrine, for which it is enough to be revealed once for ever, but an earthly institution which cannot be perfected except by continuous change and even by correcting it.'

Saint Vincent of Lerins

PROGRESS IN CHURCH DOCTRINE

O Timothy, St Paul says, *keep that which is committed to your trust, avoiding the profane novelties of words* (1 Tim 6:20). It is worth while studying this text of the Apostle more thoroughly.

The exclamation *O* is at one and the same time an expression of foreknowledge and of love. He foresaw future errors and suffered pain in advance over their coming.

The *Timothy* of today is either, speaking generally, the Universal Church, or, in particular, the whole body of ecclesiastical superiors who ought to have for themselves and to administer to the people an integral knowledge of divine worship. What, then, does *keep that which is committed to you* mean? *Keep it,* he says, in the face of thieves and enemies, lest, while men are asleep, they oversow cockle among the good wheat which the Son of man had sown in His field (Matt 13:24 ff).

Keep that which is committed. What is *committed*? It is that which has been entrusted to you, not that which you have invented; what you have received, not what you have devised; not a matter of ingenuity, but of doctrine; not of private acquisition, but of public tradition; a matter brought to you, not created by you; a matter you are not the author of, but the keeper of; not the teacher, but the learner; not the leader, but the follower.

This deposit, he says, guard. Preserve the *talent* (Matt 25:15) of the Catholic faith unviolated and unimpaired.

What has been entrusted to you may remain with you and may be handed down by you. You received gold; hand it down as gold. I do not want you to substitute one thing for another; I do not want you shamelessly to put lead in the place of gold, or, deceitfully, copper. I do not want something that resembles gold, but real gold.

O Timothy, O priest, O interpreter, O doctor, if a gift of heaven has prepared you by mental power, experience, and knowledge, to be the Bezalel (cf Exod 31:2 ff) of the spiritual Tabernacle, to cut the precious gems of divine dogma, to put them together faithfully, to adorn them judiciously, to add glamour, grace, and loveliness, may that which was formerly believed with difficulty be made, through your interpretation, more understandable in the light. May posterity, through your aid, rejoice in the understanding of things which in old times were venerated without understanding.

Yet, teach precisely what you have learned; do not say new things even if you say them in a new manner.

Is progress possible?

The question may be asked: If this is right, then is no progress of religion possible within the Church of Christ? To be sure, there has to be progress, even exceedingly great progress. For who is so grudging toward his fellow men and so full of hatred toward God as to try to prohibit it? But it must be progress in the proper sense of the word, and not a change in faith. Progress means that each thing grows within itself, whereas change implies that one thing is transformed into another.

Hence, it must be that understanding, knowledge, and wisdom grow and advance mightily and strongly in individuals as well as in the community, in a single person as well as in the Church as a whole, and this gradually according to age and history. But they must progress within their own limits, that is, in accordance with the same kind of dogma, frame of mind, and intellectual approach.

An analogy

The growth of religion in the soul should be like the growth of the body, which in the course of years develops and unfolds, yet remains the same as it was. Much happens between the prime of childhood and the maturity of old age. But the old men of today who were the adolescents of yesterday, although the figure and appearance of one and the same person have changed, are identical. There remains one and the same nature and one and the same person. The limbs of infants are small, those of young men, large, yet they are the same. The joints of adult men are as many as those of young children; though some are developed only in maturity, they already existed virtually in the embryo. Hence, nothing new is later produced in old men that has not previously been latent in children.

Therefore, without any doubt, this is the legitimate and correct rule of progress and the established and most impressive order of growth: The course of the years always completes in adults the parts and forms with which the wisdom of the Creator had previously imbued infants. If, on the other hand, the human form were turned into a shape of another kind, or if the number of members of the body were increased or decreased, then the whole body would necessarily perish, or become a monstrosity, or be in some way disabled.

Progress in dogma

In the same way, the dogma of the Christian religion

ought to follow these laws of progress, so that it may be consolidated in the course of years, developed in the sequence of time, and sublimated by age – yet remain incorrupt and unimpaired, complete and perfect in all the proportions of its parts and in all its essentials (let us call them members and senses), so that it does not allow of any change, or any loss of its specific character, or any variation of its inherent form.

To give an example. In ancient times, our forefathers sowed the seeds of the wheat of faith in that field which is the Church. It would be quite unjust and improper if we, their descendants, gathered, instead of the genuine truth of wheat, the false tares of error (cf Matt 13:24-30). On the contrary, it is logically correct that the beginning and the end be in agreement, that we reap from the planting of the wheat of doctrine the harvest of the wheat of dogma. In this way, none of the characteristics of the seed is changed, although something evolved in the course of time from those first seeds and has now expanded under careful cultivation. What may be added is merely appearance, beauty, and distinction, but the proper nature of each kind remains.

May it never happen that the rose garden of the Catholic spirit be turned into a field of thistles and thorns. May it never happen that in this spiritual paradise darnel and poison ivy suddenly appear from growths of cinnamon and balsam. Whatever has been planted in the husbandry of God's Church (cf 1 Cor 3:9) by the faith of the fathers should, therefore, be cultivated and guarded by the zeal of their children; it should flourish and ripen; it should develop and become perfect.

For it is right that those ancient dogmas of heavenly philosophy should in the course of time be thoroughly cared for, filed, and polished; but it is sinful to change them, sinful to behead them or mutilate them. They may take on more evidence, clarity, and distinctness, but it is absolutely necessary that they retain their plenitude, integrity, and basic character.

If such a licence for impious fraud be granted only once, what terrible danger – I am afraid even to speak of it – would result, with religion being destroyed and abolished. If one tenet of Catholic dogma were renounced, another, then another, and finally one after the other would be abandoned, first by custom, and then as though by right. When, one segment after the other had been rejected, what else would the final result be, except that the whole would be likewise rejected?

On the other hand, once there is a beginning of mixing the new with the old, foreign ideas with genuine, and profane elements with sacred, this habit will creep in everywhere, without check. At the end, nothing in the Church will be left untouched, unimpaired, unhurt, and unstained. Where formerly there was the sanctuary of chaste and uncorrupted truth, there will be a brothel of impious and filthy errors. May divine compassion divert such shocking impiety from the minds of its children; instead, may the impious crowd itself be left in its madness!

The Church of Christ, zealous and cautious guardian of the dogmas deposited with it, never changes any phase of them. It does not diminish them or add to them; it neither trims what seems necessary nor grafts things superfluous; it neither gives up its own nor usurps what does not belong to it. But it devotes all its diligence to one aim: to treat tradition faithfully and wisely; to nurse and polish what from old times may have remained unshaped and unfinished; to consolidate and to strengthen what already was clear and plain; and to guard what already was confirmed and defined. After all, what have the councils brought forth in their decrees but that what before was believed plainly and simply might, from now on, be believed more diligently; that what before was preached rather unconcernedly might be preached from now on more eagerly; that what before was practised with less concern might from now on be cultivated with more care?

This, I say, and nothing but this, has the Catholic Church, aroused over the novelties of the heretics, again and again accomplished by the decrees of its councils, i.e., what it earlier received from our forefathers by tradition alone, it has handed down to posterity by authoritative decisions, condensing weighty matters in a few words, and particularly for the enlightenment of the mind, by presenting in new words the old interpretation of the faith.

Commonitorium, XXII-XXIII

Saint Vincent of Lerins

THE RULE OF FAITH

A tactic of heretics

Perhaps someone wants to ask me: Do the heretics also make use of the testimonies of Sacred Scripture? Indeed they do; and to a great degree. They go through each and every book of the Bible: Moses and the Books of Kings, the Psalms, the Apostles, the Gospels, the Prophets. They utter almost nothing of their own that they do not try to support with passages from the Scripture – whether they are among their own disciples or among strangers, in private or in public, whether in sermons or in writings, in private meetings or in forums.

Read the treatises of Paul of Samosata, of Priscillian, of Eunomius, of Jovinian, and of the rest of these pests, and you will discover an abundance of examples; there is scarcely a page that is not painted and illumined with texts from the Old and New Testaments. One must be on guard and fear them all the more because they are concealed under the protective shade of divine Law.

They know well that their putrid products would not easily please anyone if their vapours were emitted undisguised; therefore, they sprinkle them with the perfume of divine words, knowing too well that anyone who readily despises human errors would hesitate to set aside divine prophecies. Thus, they behave like those who have to prepare a bitter drink for their infants and first smear some honey around the rim of the cup so that the unsuspecting child may not be averse to the bitterness when he has first sipped the sweet taste, or like those who take great pains to embellish poisonous herbs and noxious juices with high-sounding medical names, so that no one suspects the poison while reading the labels on the mixture.

Our Lord's advice

That is why the Saviour exclaimed: *Beware of false prophets, who come to you in the clothing of sheep, but inwardly they are ravening wolves* (Matt 7:15). What does *the clothing of sheep* mean save the words of the Prophets and Apostles, which these men in their pretended lamb-like simplicity put on as a fleece, imitating the lamb unspotted (1 Pet 1:19), *who takes away the sin of the world?* What are *ravening wolves?* What but the fierce and insane doctrines of the heretics who invade the sheepfold of the Church wherever they can, and harass the flock of Christ. To approach the trusting sheep more deceitfully, they discard their wolf-like appearance, though keeping their wolfish ferocity, and cover themselves with quotations from the Bible as though these were fleece. Thus, no one who has first felt the softness of the wool will fear the sharpness of their teeth.

How does the Saviour continue? *By their fruits you shall know them* (Matt 7:16). This means: Once they begin not only to use the divine expressions but also to explain them, not only to present them but also to interpret them, then people will realise how bitter, how sharp, how fierce they are. Then will the poisonous breath of their new ideas be exhaled, then will *profane novelties* appear in the open, then will you see that *the hedge is broken* (Eccl 10:8), that the ancient bounds have been passed (Prov 22:28), that the dogma of the Church is lacerated, that the Catholic faith is harmed.

St Paul's warnings

Such were those whom the Apostle Paul attacked in the Second Epistle to the Corinthians, when he says: *For they are false apostles, deceitful workmen, transforming themselves into the apostles of Christ* (2 Cor 11:13). What does *transforming themselves into the apostles of Christ* mean? The Apostles quoted the divine Law; so did the heretics. The Apostles adduced the authority of the Psalms; so did they. The Apostles invoked texts from the Prophets; so did they. But, when they began to interpret in an inaccurate way what they had accurately quoted, it became easy to distinguish the simple-minded from the deceitful, the unsophisticated from the sophisticated, the upright from those of perverted mind; in short, the true apostles from the false. *And no wonder, for Satan himself transforms himself into an angel of light. Therefore it is no great thing if his ministers be transformed as the ministers of justice.*

According to the teaching of the Apostle Paul, whenever false apostles, false prophets, or false doctors quote passages from the Bible – in an attempt to support their errors with the aid of wrong interpretations – they are obviously imitating the cunning machinations of their master. Satan certainly would never have invented them if he had not known that there was no easier way to deceive people than by pretending to the authority of the Bible when wicked errors were to be fraudulently introduced.

How to discern good interpretations from bad

But someone may ask: If it is true that Satan and his disciples, of whom some are false apostles, some, false prophets, and some, false teachers, but all entirely heretical, make use of Scriptural passages, texts, and promises – what should Catholics, children of Holy Mother Church, do? How shall they discern in Holy Scripture truth from falsehood?

Here is the answer as we gave it at the beginning of this *Commonitorium*, in accordance with what holy and scholarly men have handed on to us. They will devote all their care and attention to interpreting the divine Canon according to the traditions of the Universal Church and the rules of Catholic dogma; within the Catholic and Apostolic Church they must follow the principles of *universality, antiquity, and consent*. If, at any time, a part is in rebellion against the whole, or some novelty against tradition, or if there is a dissension of one or a few involved in error against the consent of all or the vast majority of Catholics, then they should prefer the integrity of the whole to the corruption of a part.

Further, within the same universality, they should place traditional religion before profane novelty. Likewise, within tradition, before the inconsiderate attitude of a very few they should place, first the general decrees (if there are any) of a universal council, and, then, if this is less important, they should follow the concordant opinions of great and outstanding teachers. If, with God's help, these rules are cautiously and carefully observed, then we may with little difficulty control all the noxious errors of rebellious heretics.

Commonitorium, XXV, XXVI

Saint Maximus of Turin

The few details we have of the life of St Maximus of Turin come from references made by Gennadius of Marseilles and from facts gleaned from the sermons of the saint himself.

Maximus was born probably in about 380. He was the first known bishop of Turin, then a suffragan see of Milan. From one of his homilies we know that he occupied the episcopal see in the year 398. It was in this year that the bishops of northern Italy and of Gaul met for a synod in Turin. He died shortly after 465.

One hundred discourses of his homiletic works are still preserved. Their brevity leads one to think that they are either extracts or resumes. Most of them follow the liturgical cycle, although some are dedicated to commemorating the feats of some Turin saints and martyrs.

St Maximus understands preaching to be medicinal, to cure the wounds of the soul and to move one to conversion. Prayer, almsgiving and fasting are the weapons he recommends to the faithful, so as to fight like true Christians and to obtain the necessary help from God. The struggle against paganism, which was rife in the rural areas of his diocese, formed another of the central themes of his homilies. He demanded that Christians be coherent in their professed faith so that the pagans be converted.

Saint Maximus of Turin

ALWAYS GIVING THANKS TO GOD

I have repeatedly warned you to be more concerned about eternal life while you still take part in this brief life. But with sorrow I see that you ignore my teachings. I speak to you about fasting, and very few of you fast. I speak to you of almsgiving, and more eagerly than ever you rush into the arms of avarice. It does not surprise me that you neglect prayer and giving thanks to God when, with the first light of dawn you awaken and begin to think about nothing but eating. Once you have eaten you tumble into sleep, without recalling at all to give thanks to the Divinity who has given you the food to recover your strength and sleep that you may rest.

You, Christian! If you truly want to become one, remember whose bread it is that you eat, and thank him. You, yourself, when you have given someone a present, do you not expect him to thank you, and to bless the house from which that gift has come? And when you have not been thanked, how unappreciated you feel! Similarly, God patiently hopes that we will thank him for the food we have received from him, and that we will praise him when we are content with his gifts.

Accepting that we have received divine favours is a way of acknowledging them. If, on the other hand, when we receive them we keep quiet, and we forget about them through ingratitude or lacking in worthiness of such generosity, then we deprive ourselves of the opportunity of turning, in times of tribulation, to a God whose kindness we have not recognised; as we were not capable of giving thanks in prosperity, we become unable to turn to God in adversity. Having been too lazy to praise in good times, we will have to mourn the difficulties in stormy periods.

* * *

Last Sunday I turned to correct those who, while enjoying divine gifts, do not praise the Creator, and while using heavenly goods, do not recognise their author. Those who are servants and do not respect their God as Lord are ungrateful, I said. Being sons, they do not honour him as their Father. For God says through the Prophet: *'If I am a father, where is the honour due to me? And if I am a master, where is the respect due to me?'* (Mal 1:6). As a servant, then, pay the Lord the tribute of the gift of your respect; and as a son, show him the signs of your affections. For when you are not grateful you neither love nor venerate God; you come to be a a servant persistent in error and a proud son.

The true Christian ought to give thanks to his Lord and father and to try to give him glory at every moment, as the holy Apostle says: *Whether you eat or drink, whatever you do, do everything for the glory of God* (1 Cor 10:31). See what the Apostle says about the quality of the life of a Christian: one feeds oneself more in the faith of Christ than in gluttonous meals, for frequent invocation of the name of the Lord is more useful to man than frequent and abundant banquets: religion quenches more than the fat of animals! Do everything, he says, for the glory of God. All our actions ought to have Christ as a witness and as a companion. In this way, doing good at the hands of the one who is its Author, we will avoid evil as a consequence of his presence. We will be ashamed to do bad deeds because we are associated with Christ: He will help us with doing good and will guard us against evil.

When we wake up at the first light of dawn, the first thing we have to do is to thank the Saviour. And before doing anything else we ought to show him our love, because he has watched over us while we slept and rested. For, if it is not God who keeps watch over man while he sleeps, who does? For when man goes to sleep he loses all his strength and becomes a stranger to himself to such an extent that he is unaware as to where he has been and so is unable to look after himself. Clearly, the help of God is absolutely necessary for those who are asleep, for they cannot look after themselves. He guards them from insidious nights, for there is no other person who can do it. I also should be grateful to Him who looks after me while I sleep soundly. He welcomes those who go to bed into an embrace of rest; he envelops them in a treasure of peace; and he hides them from the light, protecting them with a veil of a shade, so that the malice of men, which can be confronted by kindness, is lost in darkness. Thus nightfall offers those who are exhausted a peace which humanity cannot offer. For when the enemy is unknown to men, unwillingly do they offer a peace which they do not desire.

We should give thanks to Christ when we awake, and do all the deeds of the day in the presence of the Saviour. Could it be that when you were a pagan you did not know how to scrutinise the signs to ascertain which were the most auspicious? Now it is much easier. Only in the presence of Christ is prosperity in all things to be found. He who sows with this sign will harvest the fruit of eternal life. He who begins to travel with this sign will reach Heaven itself. The name of Christ should preside over all our actions, and we should refer all the activities of our life to Him. This is what the Apostle says: *'In him we live and move and have our being'* (Acts 17:28). And when night falls, we ought to praise him and sign his glory, so that we may merit rest as winners in the duty to carry out our obligations and sleep be the victory-palm for our work

To get to this stage not only do we have the use of reason, but also the encouragement of the birds of the air. When dawn brings the first rays of light, even the smallest bird breaks into chirping before leaving its nest, so as to praise the Creator with its trills, for it cannot do so with words. The better they sing, the better they express their offering. They do the same as day come to an end. And what are these songs, but a deep rendition of their gratitude? This is the way the innocent little birds behave towards their Shepherd, for they can do so in no other way. For the birds of the air also have their shepherd, as the Lord says: *Look at the birds of the air, they neither sow nor reap nor gather into barns, and yet your heavenly Father feeds them* (Matt 6:26). And with what food do they feed on? The commonest. And if the birds give thanks for such poor food, how much more ought you to do for the wonderful meals which you receive!

Sermo LXXII, 3; LXXIII, 1-4

Saint Maximus of Turin

THE GOOD THIEF

As we made a reference to the thief, yesterday, let us examine who he is. For while Christ is worn down on the Cross, not only does he merit forgiveness of his sins, but also receives the prize of the glory of Paradise. And so, he who was condemned for breaking the law, is led to glory by his faith, converting the cross from being a punishing torment into an occasion of salvation for himself.

He believes that that man who is nailed to the Cross is Christ the Lord. Accompanying Him in his passion he thus comes to be his companion in Paradise too. This blessed thief attains the kingdom of heaven while he suffers torture. Here we have an offender who has the good fortune to be condemned on that day. Had this not been his sentence, he would not have obtained glory. Let us see why one who is guilty of so many offences is, in so short a time, promised Paradise by the Saviour; while others, who shed tears daily and fast frequently, only just manage to receive forgiveness for their sins.

We see several important reasons. Firstly, this thief was transformed so suddenly through the devotion of faith that he did not mind enduring the present punishment, and he asked for future mercy. He believed that it was more useful to be freed from eternal damnation than temporal torture. Actually, on recalling his own offences and fostering his own reparation, he began to be more concerned about what he feared he would have to suffer than his current pains. Had he not given importance to future events, having believed in Christ once and for all, he would have asked for relief from his present torture.

Secondly, what helped him to a greater extent to obtain this grace was that he believed that the Christ before his eyes on the Cross was the Lord. In this way the Passion, which was a cause of scandal for others, was for him an occasion of faith. As the Apostle says, the Passion of the Cross was a scandal for many: *We proclaimed Christ crucified, a stumbling block to Jews and foolishness to Gentiles* (1 Cor 1:23).

This man, who considered the Cross of Christ not as a scandal or a stumbling-block but as a source of power, merited Paradise in justice; the Apostle continues, *but to those who are the called, both Jews and Greeks, Christ is the power of God and the Wisdom of God* (1 Cor 1:24). The Lord justly grants Paradise to the one who confesses Him on the gibbet of the Cross, while Judas Iscariot committed treason in the Garden.

Admirable reality: the thief recognised Him whom the disciple had denied. Marvellous reality, I repeat: on the gibbet the thief honours Him whom Judas betrayed with a kiss. Judas had auctioned the greeting of peace; this man preaches the wounds of the crucified, saying: *Jesus, remember me when you come into your kingdom* (Luke 23:42).

Perfect exercise of true faith is also shown when one implores the Lord for his power of forgiveness, precisely when one has seen blood flow from His wounds; for it is when one contemplates our Lord's humanity, that one fears even more his divinity. It is when one sees him given over to death that he is given royal honours.

This faithful thief did not believe that Jesus had to die; he declared that He ought to reign. He did not think that he had to descend to hell; but he did confess that he had to rule the heavens. This faithful thief did not judge that he would be retained in the nether world; but he asks to be liberated.

The faithful thief believes that He is God and does not accept Him as an offender, even though he sees His open wounds and gazes at the way his Blood flows. He confesses that He is just and does not accept that He is a sinner. He told the other thief who had insulted the Lord: *We, indeed, have been condemned justly, for we are getting what we deserve for our deeds, but this man has done nothing wrong* (Luke 23:41).

He understands that Jesus has received these wounds because of the sins of others, and that Christ bears these injuries for the offences of others. He understands that these injuries to the Body of Christ are not Christ's injuries but those of a thief; and so he began to love Him more, for he recognises in His Body his own hurt. As the prophet says: *He has borne our infirmities and carried our diseases; yet we have accounted him stricken, struck down by God, and afflicted. but he was wounded for our transgressions, crushed for our iniquities; upon him was the punishment that made us whole, and by his bruises we are healed* (Is 53:4-5).

The crucified thief loved the Lord all the more, then, when he saw His wounds. This is surprising: the thief on the cross loves Christ more than Judas at Supper. The first believes in the Lord who is suffering; the latter, on the other hand, betrays him at the meal, as the prophet says: *Even my bosom friend in whom I trusted, who ate of my bread, has lifted the heel against me* (Ps 41:9).

This thief learned that the Lord had suffered the Passion because he wanted to and it was within his power to give his life up to death or to bring it back to life again, as He himself had said, *No one takes it from me, but I lay it down of my own accord. I have the power to lay it down* (John 10:18). And so he considered him to be free of the clutches of hell to such an extent that he implored Him to free him from them too.

Sermo LXXIV, 1-3

Saint Leo the Great

The date and place of Leo's birth are unknown. He was a native of Tuscany, and the earliest information we have reveals him as a deacon under Pope Celestine I (422-432). He was raised to the Chair of St Peter in 440. Next to that of Pope Gregory I, the pontificate of Pope St Leo the Great is the most important and significant in Christian antiquity.

It was a time when the Church was experiencing great obstacles to her progress following the increasing disintegration of the western empire, while the orient was profoundly agitated over dogmatic controversies. From the moment of his election, this great pope untiringly dedicated himself to the governing of the Church with far-seeing sagacity.

He fostered unity with the Roman see with all his strength. He tackled monophysitism which by then had spread to a greater part of the Christian world. His *Tomus ad Flavianum*, an encyclical letter written to the Patriarch of Constantinople, was of decisive importance in the definitions proposed by the Council of Chalcedon (451) where this heresy was condemned.

St Leo died on 10 November 461.

The very concern to expound Christian doctrine is reflected in the ninety-two homilies which are preserved from St Leo, almost all of them preached on the principal feasts of the liturgical year.

For St Leo, the members of Christ, configured with

Him through the sacraments, ought to imitate the life of Our Lord in the yearly cycle of celebration: the liturgy of the Church is presented as continuation of the salvific life of Christ in the members of his Mystical Body.

In the sermons delivered during Lent, he defines this liturgical period as one of a special fight against the devil, with the weapons of prayer, of fasting, and of the works of mercy. And he gives abstinence from food a deeply spiritual meaning: bodily fasting ought to be, above all, an expression of the rejection of vices.

The text we publish below is part of a homily preached to prepare the faithful for the celebration of the feast of Easter.

Saint Leo the Great

As Lent Begins

My dearest ones, *the earth is full of the steadfast love of the Lord* (Ps 32:5). And every faithful person finds in his own nature a doctrine which teaches him to honour God. Heaven and earth, the sea and everything it contains, proclaim the goodness and the omnipotence of their Author. And the admirable beauty of the elements placed at our service call for, from intellectual creatures, a merited act of thanksgiving. But when these days, which are especially marked out for the mystery of human redemption and immediately precede the paschal feast, come around, we are bound to prepare ourselves more diligently with pious purification.

The life of many, in every age, is innocent and a great number of people are pleasing to God because of their good works. Nevertheless, no one can be confident of the integrity of his conscience and come to think that in the midst of scandals and temptations which constantly surround human fragility, there is nothing which can harm him. Did the great prophet not say: *Who can say, 'I have made my heart clean; I am pure from my sin'?* (Prov 20:9). And further: *Clean me from what is hidden, O Lord, forgive your servant from what does not befit him* (Ps 18:13-14).

Examination

Experience shows that the person who resists concupiscence, who struggles against rushes of anger and comes to neutralise even his most secret thoughts, always finds something to correct when he comes to examine his heart; and, on the other hand, he falls often in unseen faults or finds himself burdened by those of the others. So, in this period it is necessary to examine more carefully what vices, illnesses or wounds need more severe treatment. In this way such people will not find themselves without the grace of this sacrament, whose effect is to destroy the works of the devil...

My dearest ones, what every Christian has to practise always, has now to be done with more faith and more love. In this way we will satisfy the apostolic instruction which commands us to fast for forty days, not only reducing our food intake, but principally abstaining from sin. As mortification has as its aim to cut out the focal points of carnal desires, no abstinence is so advantageous as the one which makes us abstemious of evil desires and free from immoral actions...

Good works

Nothing unites more and gives greater fruit to a holy and reasonable fast than those good deeds which are almsgiving. Under the title 'works of mercy' come those praiseworthy actions of goodness, thanks to which the souls of all the faithful can have the same value. Love, which is owed equally to God and to men, is never prevented by such obstacles as when it is not free to want the good. If the angels have said: *Glory to God in the highest heaven, and on earth peace among those whom he favours* (Luke 2:14), it is not only in virtue of kindness but also the good of peace, which brings happiness to those who, through their charity, feel sympathy for the misery which others suffer.

Good works are very varied, and this very variety gives true Christians, be they rich or poor, a part of the distribution of alms, in such a way that those who differ by the quantity of their good become equal at least through affections of the heart. Within sight of the Lord many throw into the collection boxes great amounts from their abundance, and a widow gives only two coins (cf Luke 21:2). Yet she deserves to be honoured with a testimony from Jesus Christ who said that such a small gift was preferred to the offerings of others, since in relation to the big amounts of those who were still left with a lot, what she gave was all she had, as she was so poor. And even if someone were to see himself reduced to such a poor situation that he could not give two coins to the poor, he will find in the Lord's precepts the way of carrying out these duties of charity. For he who gives a glass of water to the thirsty will receive his reward (cf Matt 10:42).

What opportunities the Lord has prepared for his servants so that they may obtain his kingdom, if just the giving of water, which is something common and free, receives such a reward! But the Lord does point out, and with good reason, that this glass of water has to be given in his name. For it is faith that makes precious these things which are ordinary in themselves; the gifts of the unfaithful, although they may be considerable, are useless for justification.

My dearest ones, you who want to celebrate the Passover of the Lord, should carry out these holy fasts, so that you come to the most holy of all feasts free from all turmoil. Love of humility expels the spirit of pride, source of all sin, and meekness contains those whom presumption inflates. Those who, with their offences, have irritated the courageous, reconciled among themselves may seek to enter in harmonious unity: *Do not repay anyone evil for evil* (Rom 12:17), but *forgive each other, just as the Lord has forgiven you* (Col 3:13). Suppress human enmities with peace. And if some of your subordinates have deserved to go to prison or to be put in chains, let them mercifully be let loose. We, who daily need the remedy to indulgence, should pardon without difficulty the faults of others. If we say to the Lord, our Father: *Forgive us our debts as we also have forgiven our debtors* (Matt 6:12), it is absolutely certain that when we forgive the offences of others, we prepare ourselves to receive divine clemency.

Through our Lord Jesus Christ, who with the Father and the Holy Spirit, lives and reigns for ever and ever. Amen.

Homilia 44

Saint Leo the Great

AN ASSAULT FOR HOLINESS

Dearly beloved, we are entering Lent, that is, a period of greater faithfulness in the Lord's service. It is as if we were entering into an assault for holiness. Let us prepare our souls, then, for violent attacks of temptations; for the more zealous we are for our salvation, the more violently do our opponents attack us.

But he who lives in our midst is stronger than the one who fights against us. Our fortitude comes from Him, in whom we have placed our trust. The Lord allowed himself to be visited by the tempter, so that we might receive, not only the strength of his help, but also the teaching of his example.

You have just heard it read: he overcame his adversary with the words of the Law, not with the power of his hands. There is no doubt that his Humanity obtained more glory and greater was his adversary's punishment, when he triumphed over the enemy of men as a mortal being and not as God. He has fought so as to teach us to go, after Him, into combat too. He has won so that we may also be winners in the same way. For, my dearest ones, there are no virtuous actions without temptations, no faith without trials, no assaults without an enemy, no victory without a battle.

Life develops amidst ambushes, in the midst of surprises. If we do not want to be caught off guard, we have to be vigilant. If we aim to win, we have to struggle. It was for this reason that Solomon, when he was wise, said: *My child, when you come to serve the Lord, prepare yourself for testing* (Sir 2:1). Filled as he was with the wisdom of God, he knew that there is no fervour without deeds and combat. Foreseeing the dangers, he warns us to be prepared to counter the attacks of the tempter.

My dearest ones, let us enter the stadium, instructed by divine teaching, listening to what the Apostle has to say to us concerning this conflict: *For our struggle is not against enemies of blood and flesh, but against the rulers, against the authorities, against the cosmic powers of this great darkness, against the spiritual forces of evil in the heavenly places* (Eph 6:12).

Who is the enemy?

Let us not be fooled! These enemies, who want us to lose, are very aware that everything we try to do for our salvation also works against them. So, each time we want to do good, we provoke the enemy. Between them and us there is a deep-seated opposition, fostered by the devil. This is because they have been dispossessed of the goods that the grace of God brings with it, and our effort to become more just, tortures them. When we lift ourselves up, they sink. When we come to replenish our strength, they lose theirs. Our medicine is their wounds, for the cure of our injuries contributes to their sadness: *Be alert then*, says the Apostle, *and fasten the belt of truth around your waist, and put on the breastplate of righteousness. As shoes for your feet put on whatever will make you ready to proclaim the gospel of peace. With all of these take the shield of faith, with which you will be able to quench all the flaming arrows of the evil one. Take the helmet of salvation, and the sword of the Spirit, which is the word of God* (Eph 6:14-17).

An Assault for Holiness

Our armament

My dearest ones, look and see what powerful lances and what unassailable defences we have been armed with, by this celebrated commander of so many victories, by this invincible instructor of Christian warfare. He has put a belt of chastity right around us, he has shod our feet with sandals of peace. For a soldier whose waist is not completely covered is soon defeated by the instigator of impurity, and he who is not shod is easily bitten by the serpent. He has given us the shield of faith to protect the whole body; he has placed on our head the helmet of salvation; into our hands he has put a sword, which is the word of truth. The hero of duels of the spirit can thus not only be protected from injury, but he can also inflict casualties on those who attack him.

Trusting in this armament, we enter, energetically and fearlessly, into the battle that is suggested to us. And in this stadium, in which one fights while fasting, we are not satisfied with simply abstaining from food. It's not much good if the body's strength is weakened but the soul's vigour is not increased through feeding. Let us mortify the exterior man a little, and restore the interior. Let us deprive the flesh of its bodily nourishment, and acquire the strength of soul with spiritual delicacies. May every Christian observe this carefully, and scrutinise with a deep examination the depths of his heart. Let him make sure that there is no discord, and check that no concupiscence has found lodging there. Through chastity, incontinence is kept a good distance away; through the light of truth the darkness of lies is scattered: pride is deflated; anger is made to subside; harmful lances are broken; a brake is put on defamation in speech; revenge is made to cease and injuries forgotten about. In a phrase: *Every plant that my heavenly Father has not planted will be uprooted* (Matt

15:13). For when the unwanted seeds have been weeded out of the field of our heart, then within us the seeds of virtue will be nourished...

Recalling our weakness that allows us to fall so easily into all kinds of error, may we not neglect the following fundamental prescription and so effective a means for curing our injuries: Let us forgive, so that we may be forgiven; let us grant the grace which we ourselves ask for. We will not seek revenge, since we ourselves are looking for pardon. We will not turn a deaf ear to the laments of the poor; we will, with diligent kindness, be merciful to those in poverty so that we ourselves may find mercy on the day of judgement.

Helped by the grace of God, he who tries with all his might to achieve this perfection, who faithfully fulfils the holy fast and, keeps a distance from the yeast of long-standing evil, will reach the Paschal bliss with the zenith of purity and sincerity (cf 1 Cor 5:8). Taking part in a new life (cf Rom 6:4) will merit the taste of joy in the mystery of human regeneration. Through Christ Our Lord, who with the Father and the Holy Spirit lives and reigns for ever and ever. Amen.

Homilia I in quadragesima, 3-6

Saint Leo the Great

THE BIRTH OF OUR LORD

Today, my dearest ones, Our Saviour is born. Let us rejoice. It isn't right to allow sadness any room when Life is born, taking away the fear of death and, with eternity promised us, filling us with joy. No one can consider himself excluded from such an invitation, for there is just one cause of our common joy. Our Lord is the destroyer of sin and death. While no one took away the guilt of sin, he came to free every one from sin. The saint exults because the reward has been brought closer. The sinner is cheered because he is invited to forgiveness. The pagan is enlivened because he is called to life.

When the fullness of time came (cf Gal 4:4), indicated by the inscrutable designs of divine counsel, the Son of God took on human nature so as to reconcile it with its Author and to vanquish the introducer of death, the devil, through the very nature which he had conquered (cf Wis 2:24). This fight, embarked upon for our good, was fought out according to all the best and most noble rules of fairness. For the all-powerful Lord engaged the impious enemy not in his own majesty but in our littleness, placing in opposition to him a human nature, mortal like our own, although free from all sin.

The Incarnation

In this birth these words, which apply to everyone else, were not fulfilled: *Who can bring a clean thing out of an unclean? There is not one* (Job 14:4). With such a singular birth he felt neither carnal concupiscence nor was he subject to the law of sin. A virgin, of the royal stock of David, was chosen, who conceived in her spirit prior to conception in her body. And so that she would not be shaken by the unusual effects of divine design, she learned through the words of an angel what the Holy Spirit was to carry out in her. In this way she felt that coming to be the Mother of God was not a danger to her virginity.

What reason was there for Mary not to believe the singular nature of that conception when it was promised to her that everything would be done by the power of the Most High? Mary believed. And her faith is seen to be corroborated by a miracle which had already taken place: the unexpected fertility of Elizabeth is a testimony that what has been made to happen in a sterile person can also happen in a virgin.

Thus, the Word, the Son of God, who in the beginning was in God, by whom all things were created, and without whom nothing could have been made (cf John 11:3) became man to free men from eternal death. Taking on the lowliness of our condition without reducing his majesty, he was humiliated in such a way that, remaining what he was and becoming what he was not, he linked the condition of a slave (cf Phil 2:7) to that which He had as equal to the Father, forming such a close union between the two natures, that the inferior was not absorbed by this glorification, nor was the superior reduced by the assumption. Conserving the properties of each nature and reuniting them in a single person, the majesty has been vested with humility; strength with weakness, eternity with temporality.

Hypostatic union

To pay the debt due to our condition, the unchanging

nature is united to a nature which can suffer; true God and true man are linked in the unity of one Lord. In this way the one and only mediator between God and man (cf 1 Tim 2:5) can die, as our cure requires, in virtue of one of the two natures and to rise in virtue of the other. The birth of the Saviour, then, rightly did not disturb the integral virginity of his Mother. The arrival into the world of one who is Truth, was the safeguard of her purity.

The Birth

Such a birth, my dearest ones, was fitting for the strength and wisdom of God, who is Christ (cf 1 Cor 1:24), so that in Him, there was a similarity to us through humanity, and we were given the advantage of his divinity. If he were not God, he would not be able to offer a remedy. If he were not man, he would not have been able to give us an example. This is why the angels announced, singing joyfully: *Glory to God in the Highest*, and proclaiming: *Peace on earth to men of goodwill* (Luke 2:14). They see that the heavenly Jerusalem is being raised up in the midst of the nations of this world. What joy this ineffable work of divine goodness should cause in the little world of men, if such joy is caused in the sublime sphere of the angels!

And so, my dearest ones, let us give thanks to God the Father, through his Son in the Holy Spirit, who through the immense mercy with which he has loved us, has suffered for us. Being dead through sin, he raised us to life in Christ (cf Eph 2:5) so that we might become a new creature in Him, a new work of his hands. Let us then leave aside the old man and his activities (cf Col 3:9). Let those of us who have been allowed to participate in the birth of Christ renounce the works of flesh.

O Christian, recognise your dignity, for you take part

in divine nature (cf 2 Pet 1:4). Do not return to the old weakness of your depraved life. Recall what kind of Head and what kind of Body you are a member of. Be aware that having rooted out the power of darkness, you have been moved to the kingdom and clarity of God (cf Col 1:13). By the sacrament of Baptism you were converted into a temple of the Holy Spirit. Do not banish such a welcome guest with sinful actions. Do not offer yourself once again as a slave of the devil, for you have cost the Blood of Christ, who has redeemed you according to his mercy, and will judge you according to the truth. He, who with the Father and the Holy Spirit, reigns for ever and ever. Amen.

Homilia 1 de Nativitate Domini

Saint Leo the Great

THE VIRGIN MOTHER

Original sin

From the moment when the evil of the devil poisoned us with the natural venom of his envy, the all-powerful and clement God, whose nature is Goodness, whose will is power, whose action is merciful, pointed to the remedy by which his mercy would provide relief to us mortals. He did this from the beginning of the world, when he told the serpent that from a Woman would be born a son so strong as to split his arrogant and malicious head (cf Gen 3:15). That is to say, Christ would take on our flesh, being God and Man; and being born of a Virgin, with his birth He would condemn him who had stained human kind.

The devil deceived man with his cunning. He then withdrew, seeing that man had been dispossessed of the heavenly gifts, stripped of the privilege of immortality, and groaning under the weight of the terrible death sentence. He rejoiced at having had some consolation in the evil deeds he committed, and having made God – who had created men in a state with such fine honours – change his approach towards them to satisfy the requirements of due severity.

My dearest ones, a formula with a very committed approach was needed. God, who does not change, and whose will does not cease to be good, could carry out the first requirements of his goodness – through an even deeper mystery – so that man, dragged down towards evil by the cunning and malice of the devil, would not perish, frustrating the divine plan.

The Redemption

My dearest ones, when the time came for the redemption of man, Our Lord Jesus Christ came down from the heights of his heavenly seat. He came into the world in a new way, with a new birth, without leaving aside the glory of his Father. In a new way, because, earlier, he was invisible by nature; now, he made himself visible in our nature. Incomprehensible before, he has wanted to become comprehensible. He who was before time, has begun to be within time. Lord of the universe, he has taken the condition of a slave (cf Phil 2:7), guarding the splendour of his majesty. The God who cannot suffer has not turned away from being a human being subject to suffering; immortal he submits himself to the law of death.

He was born by a new birth; conceived by a virgin, given birth by a virgin, without attacking the integrity of motherhood. Such an origin was worthy of one who was to be a Saviour of men... For the Father of this God who is born in the flesh, is God, as the angel testified to the Blessed Virgin Mary: *The Holy Spirit will come upon you, and the power of the Most High will overshadow you, therefore the child to be born of you will be called holy, the Son of God* (Luke 1:35).

Reasons for this Birth

Disparate origin, but common nature. For a virgin to conceive, for a virgin to give birth and remain a virgin is humanly unique; but it reveals the power of God. Here we do not consider the condition of birth, but in the free decision of the one who is to be born, being born in the way he wanted to. Do you want to know the reason for this

THE VIRGIN MOTHER

origin? He confesses that his power is divine. The Lord Jesus Christ has come to take away our corruption, so as not to become its victim. He has come so that we are not overcome by our vices, but rather to cure them. He decided to be born in a new way, thus bringing to our human bodies the new grace of purity without sin. He specified that the integrity of the Son safeguard the unequalled virginity of his Mother, and that the power of the divine spirit showered upon her (cf Luke 1:35) maintain this cloistered state of chastity and this haven of holiness which she enjoyed. For he has decided to raise what has fallen, to restore what has deteriorated, and to grant the power of magnified strength to dominate the seduction of the flesh, so that virginity, incompatible in others – because of the transmission of life – would come to be imitated in others, thanks to the new birth.

But, my dearest ones, does it not seem that the Lord has chosen to be born of a woman for a deeper reason than any of these? It is so that the fact may be made known that salvation has been born for human kind, for the devil himself might be unaware of this. Not knowing His conception as work of the Holy Spirit, the devil might not believe that Christ was born in a way different from other men. In fact, seeing Christ with a nature identical to others, he thought that Christ's origin was similar to theirs. He did not know that Christ was free from all ties of sin, He whom he saw as subject to the law of death. For God, who in his justice and in his mercy had many ways of raising up his chosen people (cf Ps 85:15), has preferred to choose the way which allows him to destroy the work of the devil, not with a powerful intervention, but with a justly weighed response.

Praise God in all his works (cf Wis 39:19) and all his judgements, my dearest ones. May no doubt cloud your faith in the integrity of the Virgin Mary and in the virgin birth. Honour with a holy and sincere obedience the sacred and divine mystery of the restoration of the human species. Embrace Christ, who is born in our flesh, so that you merit seeing Him reigning in majesty, this very God of glory, who with the Father and the Holy Spirit lives in the divinity for ever and ever. Amen.

Homilia II in nativitate Domini, 1-3, 6

Saint Leo the Great

SPIRITUAL CHILDHOOD

Some lessons from Christ's childhood

Dearly beloved, it is very useful for us to recall what the Saviour has done for men. We make the ideal which we wish to imitate the object of our faith and of our veneration. In the economy of the mysteries of Christ, the miracles are graces and stimuli which reinforce doctrine. This enables us to follow the example of the actions of Him whom we confess to in a spirit of faith.

Even these very moments lived by the Son of God, born of the Virgin, his Mother, can instruct us for our spiritual progress. Our hearts see the humility proper to humanity and divine majesty appear in one and the same person. Heaven and the celestial armies call to their recently-born Creator, lying in a cradle. This Child, this baby, is Lord and Chancellor of the world. He who cannot be enclosed by any limits, is contained in his entirety on the lap of his Mother. In this is to be found the cure to our wounds, and to being lifted up from our previous position of being flat on our faces.

The remedies prescribed for our cure have become a norm of life. From what was a medicine prescribed for the dead, the guideline for our customs has emerged. When the three Magi were led by the shining new star to adore Jesus, they did not see him exorcising devils, or raising the dead, or giving sight to the blind, or curing the lame, or giving the power of speech to the dumb, or any other action which would have revealed his divine power. And this, not without good reason. They saw a Child who was silent, serene, entrusted to the care of his Mother. No sign of his power showed in him: the great spectacle that was on display to them was his humility. Thus the sight of the Holy Child, the Son of God, presented to their gaze a lesson which was to be proclaimed later. What the sound of his voice did not yet preach, was taught to them by the simple fact of seeing Him.

The whole victory of the Saviour, who subdues the world and the devil, began with humility and was consummated in humility. The appointed period for him had begun in persecution, and in persecution too it would end. Suffering for the Child has not been wanting, but he who had been called to suffer has not missed the sweetness of childhood. For the Only-Begotten Son of God – simply by the humiliation of his majesty – has willingly accepted being born as a man and thus allowed himself to be put to death by man.

The Humanity of Christ

Through the good offices of his humility, the omnipotent God has turned our hopeless cause to the good. He has displayed death and the author of death (cf 1 Tim 1:10) without rejecting the sufferings his persecutors would make him undergo. He bore the cruelties of those who raged their anger against him with great gentleness and out of obedience to his Father. If he has done all this for us, how much more humble and patient we ourselves will have to be. We have to bear in mind, too, that if trial comes our way, this has only happened because we have merited it. Who would boast of having a chaste heart and of being clear of any stain of sin. And, as St John says, *if we say we have no sin, we deceive ourselves, and the truth is not in us* (1 John 1:8). Who would be free of fault to such an extent that justice would have nothing to reproach him about or for divine mercy to forgive him?

For this reason, dearly beloved, the practice of Christian wisdom does not consist in a surfeit of words, or the ability to argue, in the desire for praise or glory, but in sincere and voluntary humility. This is what the Lord Jesus Christ has chosen. This is what he has taught, from the bosom of his mother to the torture of the Cross, to be the true strength. When the disciples began arguing among themselves, as the evangelist relates: *Who is the greatest in the kingdom of heaven? Calling to him a child, he put him in the midst of them and said, 'Truly I say to you, unless you turn and become like little children, you will never enter the kingdom of heaven. Whoever humbles himself like this child, he is greatest in the kingdom of heaven'* (Matt 18:1-4).

Love for childhood

Christ loves childhood. He himself has lived through it in body and soul. Christ loves childhood, mistress of humility, norm of innocence, model of sweetness. Christ loves childhood, I repeat. He directs the behaviour of adults towards it; towards it he directs an old spirit. He attracts by his own example those whom he raises to the eternal kingdom.

But if we want to be able to understand perfectly how it is possible to come to such an admirable conversion, and what kind of transformation we have to undergo to reach the age of childhood, let us allow St Paul to instruct us. He says: *Do not be children in your thinking; be babes in evil, but in thinking be mature* (1 Cor 14:20).

It is not, then, a matter of returning to play the games of little children, nor of going to the imperfections of the beginnings of life, but of taking something which is also useful for the age of maturity. That is to say, may our interior agitations pass away quickly. May we not retain any bitterness for offences committed against us. May we not covet honours, but love to be united to others. And may we look after the equality which conforms to nature. It is a great good that we do not stimulate or take delight in evil, for to inflict injury and retaliate is proper to the wisdom of this world. On the other hand, not to repay evil with evil (cf Rom 12:17) is proper to spiritual childhood, overflowing with Christian equanimity and evenness of mind.

The suffering of the Holy Innocents

The mystery of today's feast, dearly beloved, invites us to this similarity with children. It is the humility taught to you by the Child-Saviour being adored by the Magi. To demonstrate that glory which he has prepared for those who imitate him, he has consecrated those born at the same time as him, to martyrdom. Born in Bethlehem, like Christ, they have been associated with him by his age and his suffering. The faithful, then, should love humility and avoid all forms of pride. Each one should prefer his neighbour to himself (cf 1 Cor 4:6) and *let no one seek his own good, but the good of his neighbour* (1 Cor 10:24). When everyone is filled with the spirit of benevolence, in no place will there be any trace of the venom of envy. For, *every one who exalts himself will be humbled, and he who humbles himself will be exalted* (Luke 14:11).

This is the evidence given by Our Lord Jesus Christ, who with the Father and the Holy Spirit, lives and reigns for ever and ever. Amen.

Homilia 7 in Epiphania Domini

Saint Leo the Great

IN THE LIKENESS OF GOD

Dearly beloved, if we faithfully and wisely consider the start of our creation, we will find that man was formed in the likeness of God, so as to imitate our Author. The natural dignity of our lineage consists precisely in that the beauty of divine goodness shines in us, as in a mirror. To this end, the grace of the Saviour helps us, in such a way what was lost by Adam was made up for by Christ.

The cause of our health is none other than the mercy of God, whom we would not have loved if he had not previously loved us, and if he had not enlightened the shadows of our ignorance. This had already been foretold to us by the Lord, through the prophet Isaiah: *I will lead the blind by a road they do not know; by paths they have not known I will guide them. I will turn the darkness before them into light, the rough places into level ground. These are the things I will do and I will not forsake them* (Is 42:16). And later: *I was ready to be sought out by those who did not ask, to be found by those who did not seek me* (Is 65:1).

Love and Truth

John the Apostle shows how all this has been fulfilled: *We know that the Son of God has come and has given us understanding so that we may know him who is Truth; and we are in him who is Truth, in his Son Jesus Christ* (1 John 5:20). And also, *We love because he loved us first* (1 John 4:19). When God loves us, he restores us to his likeness, and to find in us the image of his goodness, he grants us the ability to do what He does, illuminating our intellects and setting our hearts aflame, so that we love not only Him, but also everything He loves.

When men share similar customs, it leads to a close friendship (although, admittedly similarity in customs and desires can also lead to evil effects). How much more, then, should we desire and force ourselves not to compromise in those things which God loves! For the Prophet had said: *For a moment lasts his anger, for a lifetime his love* (Ps 29:6) – divine majesty will in no way be in us if we do not try to fulfil the will of God.

The Lord says: *You will love the Lord your God with your whole heart and with your whole soul ... Love your neighbour as yourself.* This is the way the faithful soul receives the unfading charity of its Author and Rector, and submits its whole will to Him, in whose deeds and judgement there are no gaps of the truth of justice, nor of compassion of clemency...

Prayer, fasting and almsgiving

Three works pertain principally to religious actions: prayer, fasting and almsgiving, which have to be exercised all the time, but especially in those periods consecrated by apostolic traditions, as we have received them.

During this tenth month a custom of ancient standing refers; so we try to fulfil with greater diligence the three works to which I have just referred. For through prayer one seeks God's propitiation, through fasting the concupiscence of the flesh is extinguished, and through almsgiving sins are forgiven (cf Dan 4:24).

At the same time, the likeness of God is restored within us if we are always prepared for divine praise, if we are constantly solicitous for our purification and if we continuously obtain the sustenance of our neighbour.

This triple observance, dearly beloved, synthesises the effects of all the virtues, brings us to the image and likeness of God, and inseparably unites us to the Holy Spirit. It happens thus: through prayer, an upright faith lasts; in fasts, innocent life; and in almsgiving, kindness.

Homilia XII in ieiunio decimi mensis, 1-2, 4

Saint Cyril of Alexandria

Cyril was born of an Alexandrian family. He accompanied his uncle bishop Theophilus, to Constantinople (403) which deposed St John Chrysostom. In 412 Cyril succeeded his uncle as Patriach of Alexandria, but only after a riot between his supporters and those of his rival, Timoteus.

In the winter of 427-28, Nestorius became Patriarch of Constantinople, and Cyril soon heard of his heretical teachings. Cyril taught him the use of the term *theotokos* in his Paschal letter for 429. There was correspondence between the two for a number of years.

St Cyril was a man of great courage and force of character. We can often discern that he controlled and schooled his natural vehemence, and he listened with humility to the severe admonitions of his master and adviser, St Isidore.

For Pope Celestine II, Cyril was not only the senior prelate of the East but also the inheritor of the tradition of Athanasius and Peter; he gave him his authority to excommunicate Nestorius. As Legate of Celestine, Cyril presided over the Council of Ephesus (431) which solemnly defined that the Blessed Virgin Mary is truly the Mother of God, since she gave birth to the Word according to his human nature.

He died in June 444 after an episcopate lasting 32 years.

St Cyril is one of the most eminent figures of ancient

Christian literature. He composed many treatises, dogmatic letters and sermons. His theological thinking, firmly anchored in Sacred Scripture and in the living Tradition of the Church, is deep and precise in its logic. He edited exegetical commentaries on almost all the books of the Old and New Testaments, and wrote dogmatic treatises against the Arians. Cyril's principal fame rests upon his defence of the Catholic doctrine against Nestorius, as he gave body and soul to refuting these errors and expressing the true faith.

From among the numerous writings, we publish some paragraphs of two of his homilies in which St Cyril weaves burning praise of the Mother of God.

Saint Cyril of Alexandria

THE MOTHER OF GOD

Hail Mary, Mother of God, Virgin Mother, Morning Star, Vessel of Honour.

Hail Mary, Virgin and Handmaid. Virgin by the grace of Him who was born of You without detriment to your virginity. Mother by reason of Him you carried in your arms and suckled with your breast. Handmaid, because of Him who took the form of a slave. The King entered your city, or to put it more clearly, into your womb; and later left as he wished, leaving your gates still closed. You have conceived as a virgin, and have given birth in a divine way.

Hail Mary, Temple in which God is received, or rather, holy Temple, as the prophet David exclaimed, *Holy is your temple, admirable in goodness* (Ps 65:4).

Hail Mary, most precious jewel of all the earth. Hail Mary, chaste dove. Hail Mary, the lamp always alight, for the Sun of Justice has been born of you.

Hail Mary, seat of Him who in no place can be contained. In your womb you contained the Only Begotten Word of God, and without seed and without plough, you made an ear sprout that will not wither.

Hail Mary, Mother of God, for whom the angels muster choir and the archangels exult, singing high hymns.

Hail Mary, Mother of God, through whom the Magi adored, guided by a brilliant star.

Hail Mary, Mother of God, through whom the embellishment of the twelve apostles was selected.

Hail Mary, Mother of God, for whom John, yet still

in his maternal womb, jumped for joy and adored the luminary of eternal light.

Hail Mary, Mother of God, through whom that ineffable grace, which the Apostle spoke about, gushed forth: *Glory to God in the Highest, and peace on earth to men of good will* (Luke 2:14).

Hail Mary, Mother of God, through whom glowed the true light, Jesus Christ Our Lord, of whom the gospel states, *I am the light of the world* (John 8:12).

Hail Mary, Mother of God, through whom shone the light over those who worked in darkness and in the shadow of death: *the people who sat in darkness have seen a great light* (Is 9:2). And what is the light but Our Lord Jesus Christ, *the true light who enlightens every soul born into the world* (John 1:9).

Hail Mary, Mother of God, through whom came the victor over death and the exterminator of hell.

Hail Mary, Mother of God, through whom has been shown the Creator of our first parents and Healer of their fall, the King of the heavenly kingdom.

Hail Mary, Mother of God, through whom the beauty of the Resurrection flowered and shone.

Hail Mary, Mother of God, through whom the waters of the River Jordan were changed into the baptism of holiness.

Hail Mary, Mother of God, through whom John and the Jordan were sanctified, and the devil rejected.

Hail Mary, Mother of God, through whom the faithful spirits are saved. Hail Mary, Mother of God, through you the waves of the sea, now placated and sedate, carry joyfully and gently those who, like ourselves, are servants and ministers.

* * *

THE MOTHER OF GOD

Hail Mary, Mother of God, most venerated treasure on all earth, inextinguishable light, crown of virginity, sceptre of true doctrine, indestructible temple, dwelling place of Him who cannot be contained, Virgin and Mother, through whom we have been given Him who is call blessed *par excellence*, and who has come in the name of the Father.

Hail to You, who in your holy and virginal womb have enclosed the Immense and the Incomprehensible. Because of whom the Blessed Trinity is adored and glorified, and the precious Cross is venerated and feted throughout the earth. Because of whom Heaven exults, the angels and archangels rejoice, and the devils flee. Because of whom the Tempter was ejected from Heaven, and fallen creature was taken up to Paradise. Because of whom all men, fettered by the deceit of idols, come to the knowledge of truth. Because of whom holy baptism is given as a gift to believers, the oil of joy is obtained, the Church is rooted all over the world, and people are moved to penance.

And what more can I say? Because of whom the Only Begotten Son of God, shone the Light on those who worked in darkness and in the shadow of death. Because of whom the Prophets prophesied future events. Because of whom the Apostles preached salvation to the gentiles. Because of whom the dead rose and kings reigned, through the Blessed Trinity.

Who among men is capable of uttering the praise which Mary merits, who is worthy of all praise? She is Virgin and Mother. What a marvellous thing. I am filled with awe at this miracle. Who has heard of a case where the builder of a temple is banned from attending it? Who could be blamed for ignominiously having taken his own Slave to be his Mother?

The whole world then is joyful ... We too have to

adore and respect the union of the Word with the flesh, to fear and to worship the Blessed Trinity, to celebrate with our hymns to Mary, ever Virgin, holy temple of God; and to her Son, Spouse of the Church, Jesus Christ Our Lord.

To him be glory, for ever and ever. Amen.

Econium in Mariam Deiparam, Homilia IV in Concilio Ephesino

Saint Cyril of Alexandria

FAITH IN GOD'S WORD

Then the Jews fell into disputing with one another: How can this man give us his flesh to eat (John 6:53).

It is written in the Book of Proverbs ... *all that my tongue speaks is clear to the wise, and just to those with knowledge* (Prov 8:9), but for the foolish their meaning is easily clouded.

In fact, the wise listener guards the most evident teachings in the treasury of his soul without admitting the slightest doubt as to their truth. If any of them seem difficult, he considers them diligently and never stops seeking their explanation. In his eagerness to arrive at the truth, he reminds me of swift hunting dogs. With their wonderful sense of smell they run back and forth around the hiding places of the game they are seeking. In the same way do not the words of the prophet invite the wise man to do the same when he says: ... *seek diligently and you will dwell at my side* (Is: 21:12)?

The seeker must seek diligently, that is, he must put his whole soul into the search without wasting time on useless thoughts. The greater the difficulty he encounters, the greater the effort and enthusiasm that he must put in to lay bare the hidden truth.

On the other hand, the stupid and lazy man coming across anything he cannot understand, immediately throws up his hands in disbelief and rejects as ridiculous whatever is above his intelligence, and through this impudent rashness he is led into the very extremes of pride.

If we look into the nature of these things we will discover that this is the trap that the Jews fell into, because they did not accept the words of Our Lord, even though his divine goodness and extraordinary power, shown by his miracles, filled them with admiration. They did not reflect on the difficult words they had heard, so as to make an effort to understand them. But, in their stupidity, they asked: *How can such things be?*, as if they did not know that such a reference to God's words was utter blasphemy.

God can do everything effortlessly, but these were irrational men, as Saint Paul describes them, and as such they did not recognise *the things that are of the Spirit of God* (1 Cor 2:14), but considered this holy mystery to be madness.

Let us take this as an example then and amend our lives in things that have made others fall. We will then have a faith free of curiosity in accepting the divine mysteries. And when we are taught something, let us not answer with that *How* of the Jews, for in using that word they brought about their downfall.

If we want to be prudent, paying heed to the fate of the Jews, and to seek only what is good for us, let us not use *How* in regard to the things of God. Let us rather force ourselves to admit that God knows perfectly well what he is doing.

True enough, no one knows God's nature. Nevertheless, we are justified in believing ... *that He exists and rewards those who ask him* (Heb 6:6). Even if we do not know the way in which God carries out things in particular, we can still put our faith in their result and admit that God, who is above every existing thing, can do everything. Thus, we will receive no small reward for correct thinking. Therefore, let us ask the Lord of all things to give us this right attitude of mind, saying with the prophet: ... *my thoughts are not your thoughts, nor my paths your paths, says the Lord. Rather, as distant as heaven is from earth are my paths from yours and my thoughts from your thoughts* (Is 55:8-9). For why shouldn't he who so greatly surpasses us in wisdom and power, do things so wonderful as to be beyond our understanding.

I would like to add here an example that I think is very appropriate. Those among us who are skilled in the mechanical arts often say they are going to do something marvellous, using a method that their listeners cannot understand until they see it done. In such a case, however, we are quite prepared to accept it on faith alone, even before the experiment is carried out. In fact, we would be ashamed to admit otherwise. How then can we excuse from serious crime those who dare to not believe God, the supreme creator of all things, and at the same time dare to ask how he does something, even though they know he is the source of all wisdom and have been taught in divine Scripture that he is all powerful?

And to those Jews who persisted in their *How* I, in my turn, will imitate their folly and ask them: How did you escape from Egypt? How was the staff of Moses changed into a serpent? How did a hand become covered with leprosy and then return to its former state, as it is written? How was water turned into blood? How did you pass through the Red Sea as if on dry land? How did water spring from the rock so as to quench your thirst? How did manna fall from heaven to feed you? How was the river Jordan held back? How did your clamour cause the walls of Jericho to fall?

And after all that do you still go on asking *How*? Are you not amazed by all the miracles in which, if you ask *How*, you will destroy faith in divine scripture, in the writings of the holy prophets, and, above all, in the very books of Moses himself.

In conclusion, therefore, would it not be better to believe in Christ and identify ourselves with his words, making an effort to learn the manner of the Eucharist, without rashly asking: *How can this man give us his flesh to eat* (John 6:52)?

In Ioannem commentarium, IV, 2

SALVIANUS THE PRESBYTER

Salvianus was born in Cologne of Christian parents in the early years of the fifth century. He married a pagan woman called Palladia, who was converted together with her parents. Husband and wife resolved from then to live in continence. It is not known when he moved to southern Gaul. In 426 he began to live in a monastic community on the isle of Lerins, facing the Marseilles coast. Three years later he became a priest. He died towards the end of the century.

His writings reveal that he was a wonderfully cultured man, and his legal studies merit special attention. Of his numerous homilies and literary output a number have been conserved for us: some *Letters*, the treatise *ad Ecclesiam*, and *De gubernatione Dei*, his most important work, comprising eight books, where he develops the theme of divine providence.

Addressing Christians, he asks them to strengthen themselves in the faith and in their confidence in God, in the midst of a situation in which Christians found themselves under barbarian domination. In addition to its apologetic goals, the work also attacks the moral disorders at that time, and encourages conversion.

De gubernatione Dei is an historic source of great value, both for the events it relates as for the news it gives.

SALVIANUS THE PRESBYTER

THE LORD'S PRECEPTS

Perhaps, someone says, we do not endure for Christ in this day and age what the Apostles endured in their day. It is true there are no longer pagan princes nor persecuting tyrants. The blood of the saints is not shed, nor is faith tried by torture. Our God is content that we serve him in peace, that we please him by the very purity of righteous deeds and the holiness of an unsullied life.

Our faith and devotion are all the more due to him because He demands less and gives more. Our princes are Christian; there are no persecutions and religion is not disturbed. Thus, we who are not forced to prove our faith by more severe trials should, at least, all the more seek to please God in lesser things. He by whom the smaller things are well done will, in case of necessity, prove himself a capable performer of greater things.

Let us omit, therefore, the sufferings of most blessed Paul. Let us even omit what we have read in religious books written later on about the sufferings of all the Christians who, mounting to the doors of their heavenly palaces by the steps of their tortures, fashioned the stairs, so to speak, from wooden racks and scaffolds. Let us see if we can try to fulfil the Lord's commandments in those practices of religious devotion, the lesser and more common of which we Christians can perform peacefully and at all times.

Christ has ordered us not to be litigious. Who obeys this command? He not only ordered that, but He went so

THE PRECEPTS OF THE LORD

far as to order us to relinquish those things which are in dispute, so long as we get out of the law suit. He has said: *If a man will contend with you in judgement and take away your coat, let go your cloak also unto him* (Matt 5:40).

I ask who there are who yield to spoliation at the hands of their enemies? I ask, furthermore, who there are who try not to rob their enemies? So far are we from leaving them other things in addition to our coats that, if we possibly can do it, we take away the coats and cloaks of our enemies at the same time. Indeed, so ardently do we obey the Lord's commandments that we are not satisfied with refusing the least part of our garments to our enemies, unless, if circumstances permit, we can rob them of everything to the best of our ability.

To this command there is another and similar command added, in which the Lord says: *If one strikes you on the right cheek, turn to him also the other* (Matt 5:39). How many, do you think, would calmly listen to this command, or if they seemed to listen, would agree to it in their hearts? And how many are there who, if they receive one blow, do not return many for that one? So far is he from turning his other cheek to him who strikes him that he thinks he is winning when he has overcome his adversary, not by beating, but by knocking him down.

The Saviour has said: *All things whatsoever you would that men should do to you, do you also to them* (Matt 7:12). There is a part of this thought we know so well that we never omit it. There is a part we omit as if we were wholly ignorant of it. We know quite well what we wish done for us by others, but we do not know what we ourselves should do for them. Would that we did not know! Our guilt would be less if we could claim ignorance, according to the saying: *He that knows not the will of his Lord shall be beaten with few stripes, but he that knows and does not do according to the will of his Lord, shall be beaten with many stripes* (Luke 12:47). With us, the offence is greater, because we like a part of the holy command since it is to the advantage of our affairs, but we omit a part of it to the injury of God.

The Apostle, Saint Paul, in his function of preaching also amplified this word of God: *Let no man seek his own, but that which is another's* (1 Cor 10:24). And again: *Each one not considering the things that are his own, but those that are other men's* (Phil 2:4). You see how faithfully Saint Paul executed the precept of Christ. He was, indeed, a good servant of a good Master and an outstanding imitator of a singular Teacher. He so walked in the footprints of his Master that, with his own feet, he somehow made those of his Master more distinct and prominent. Which of these precepts do we Christians fulfil, that of Christ or of Paul? I think we obey neither. We are so far from doing something for others that would work to our own disadvantage, that we all give first consideration to our own affairs, no matter what discomfort it entails for others.

De gubernatione Dei, 3, 5-6

JOHN MANDAKUNI

Among ancient Christian writers, the Armenian contribution of the fourth and fifth centuries is less well known. It is, however, very rich in spiritual content.

Documented sources refer to the third century for the preaching of Christianity in Armenia, as the work of Gregory the Illuminator. But before this date there were Christians in the middle of the country, at the same longitude as Syria, from where the first evangelisation was launched.

The central figure of Armenian literature is St Mesrob, to whom is attributed the invention of the Armenian alphabet. He died around 440. One of his successors to the see was John Mandakuni, who was born around 415. He was a *catholikos* of Armenia from 478 until his death in 490.

A model shepherd of souls, John Mandakuni is the author of homilies, letters and prayers, many of which were translated into German in the last century.

The fragment below forms part of an address *On devotion and respect when receiving the Blessed Sacrament*, in which he stresses the real presence of Christ in the Eucharist, and the interior disposition with which the faithful ought to receive Him.

JOHN MANDAKUNI

HOW TO APPROACH THE BLESSED SACRAMENT

My bones tremble with fear. My soul quivers and is astonished when I realise that I am going to approach this venerable and great Sacrament. My spirit oscillates ceaselessly between two feelings: with great joy I should like to approach this coveted Sacrament, but my unworthiness keeps me distant. But to separate myself from him and to live far from him is the death of my soul.

Really, there are many who either approach him in sin or keep a distance from him in a manner which is not right: both are children of the devil. Some of them don't know the power of this wonderful Sacrament. They approach it out of routine habit with an uneasy conscience, not as regards health, but in justice (cf 1 Cor 11:29); they receive not the forgiveness of sins, but an increase in sin. The others appreciate it little, as something which is not of much value. They keep away from it as they do not consider it a necessity, for they are not aware of its strength and its grace, or, they believe that it is a sign of their esteem for the Sacrament if they do not receive it frequently. But this is to show little esteem, and is a sign of stupidity and lukewarmness in remaining distant from Life, and wanting darkness and death. This is what the Lord himself says: *I am the bread of life... I am the living bread that came down from heaven. Whoever eats of this bread will live forever; and the bread that I will give for the life of the world is my flesh...* (John 6:48-51).

How to Approach the Blessed Sacrament

When not to receive Communion

Did you know that when the Blessed Sacrament comes onto the altar the heavens above are opened and Christ descends and arrives, that the angelic choirs fly from heaven to the earth and surround the altar where the Blessed Sacrament of the Lord is, and are filled with the Holy Spirit? So those who are tortured by remorse of conscience, are unworthy to partake of this Sacrament until they have been purified by penance... Examine yourselves, probe your hearts, so that no one with remorse of conscience, no one practising hypocrisy, or living a life of pretence, no one with doubts or disbelief, approaches the Sacrament...

The Real Presence

I do not look on it as simple bread, nor do I have or consider it to be wine; for this wonderful mystery is invisible. Its power is spiritual, for Christ no longer visible has given us something spiritual in the Eucharist and in Baptism. We see the chalice, but we believe the divine Word, who says: *This is my body ... this is my blood ... Unless you eat the flesh of the Son of Man and drink his blood, you have no life in you. Those who eat my flesh and drink my blood abide in me, and I in them. The one who eats this bread will live for ever* (Matt 26:26-28; John 6:54-58). With true faith we know that Christ dwells on the altars, that we approach him, that we gaze on him, that we touch him, that we kiss him, that we take him and receive him into our hearts, that we make ourselves one body, members and children of God (cf 1 Cor 10:17) ...

Son of man, take a look at your room and consider where you are, whom you are contemplating, whom you kiss, whom you are introducing into your heart. You will find yourself among heavenly powers. You will praise with the angels. You bless with the seraphims. You contemplate Christ, you kiss Christ, you receive and enjoy Christ, you are filled with the Holy Spirit and you are illuminated and continuously fortified by divine grace. Those of you who are priests are ministers and dispensers of this Blessed Sacrament: approach it with fear, guard it with anxiety, administer it in a holy way and serve him with warmth; you have a real treasure; take care of it, and guard it with great awe...

Keep your heart pure for the moment of Communion and do not neglect it from one day to the next. It is no effrontery to receive communion many times, with a pure heart, for with it you clean your soul and give it new zest more and more. But if you were unworthy and were to have something for which your conscience reproaches you, and were to receive communion just once, this would be the death of the soul...

Occasional reception of Communion

You might, perhaps, be inclined to say: 'In Lent I will sanctify myself and receive Communion.' What use is it for you to refrain from what purifies you once, if you are going to be stained anew? What use is it for someone to clean you if later you are going to get dirty again? What use is it to build something if later you come along and destroy it? You wish to be without suffering only on feast days, and then you wish to be overcome by sufferings again. Do you wish to cure yourself of your sins one day and to receive the very same wounds again the next; for one day you separate yourself from the devil and then return to be tormented by him forever?

This is what happens to those who receive the Blessed Sacrament once and then are ceaselessly consumed in sin. Of what use is it to find precious stones on a feast day and to lose them the following day? Consequently, it is useless to receive communion on a feast day if you are going to perish once again because of the unworthiness of a bad life...

Or you may say to me: 'With the Lenten fasts I have sanctified myself; I wish to receive the Blessed Sacrament then.' I think it entirely reasonable and I praise it. But why don't you always receive it? You reply: "It's that I can't always remain without falling into sin."

If what you are going to say is: I am going to receive Communion on a feast day, but after that I am going to keep away from Communion, then even on the feast day you are unworthy, for your way of thinking is that of the enemy. What use is it approaching Christ, if at the same time you are going to continue your relationship with the devil? What use is it taking expensive medicines if your pain is going to continue on the inside? What use is it to run to the doctor if you are not going to show him your injuries? In the same way, you are not going to benefit from going to Communion if you do not cast aside your sins...

Preparation

We therefore look after ourselves, attentively. May we sanctify our heart, may we make our eyes modest, may we guard our tongue against gossip. Let us do penance for our sins. Let us dispel doubts. Let us discard stupidity. Let us joyfully tread on our laziness. Let us fast. Let us persevere in prayer. Let us be quick to help, and to practise the virtues with deeds. Let us become children as regards doing evil, and as regards faith, the opposite – perfect.

With all these virtues, then, we will make ourselves worth of this august and great mystery. With great desires and a consummate purity we will enjoy the most holy and life enhancing Body and Blood of Our Lord Jesus Christ. To Him will be the power and the glory for ever and ever. Amen.

Devotion and respect when receiving the Blessed Sacrament

JAMES OF SARUGH

James of Sarugh is one of the great fathers of the Syrian Church, coming to be called 'the flute of the Holy Spirit and the harp of the believing Church'. He was born in 451 at Kurtam, in the district of Sarugh, on the banks of the River Euphrates. His father was a priest. According to tradition he completed his ecclesiastical studies in Edessa, where he received a thorough knowledge of philosophy, theology and linguistics. At the age of 22 he became a monk and a hermit.

We do not have many details of his life. In 502 he was nominated a *chorepiscopus* – a kind of assistant bishop, an ecclesiastical office which he exercised with delegated jurisdiction from his bishop. During this period he paid visits to many monasteries, winning the esteem of monks and hermits. In 519 he was consecrated bishop. From then on he carried out extensive pastoral work until his death two years later.

Such was his fame for holiness that he is included in the liturgy and in the calendar of saints. In the Latin-rite Church his feast is on 29 October.

James of Sarugh has left many varied works. Those in verse are outstanding. According to some studies he preached some 750 homilies, although only about half have been preserved and many have not been published.

The following paragraphs, taken from his homilies on Our Lady, highlight the affection with which James spoke about the human and supernatural beauty of our Mother in heaven.

JAMES OF SARUGH

SEAT OF ALL GRACES

Such is my love that I feel impelled to speak of the One I love, for she is so beautiful; but the content is so much beyond my capability that I don't think I can easily explain it.

What, then, should I do? I shall shout to the four winds that I am not suited to it; and, with love, I will venture to proclaim the mystery of that noble creature. It is only love which errs when it does not speak; for love has perfection as its object, and fills with gifts the one who follows its suggestions. I tremble with emotion when I speak of Mary. I marvel, because the daughter of men reached the highest measure of greatness. What happened, by chance? Did the Son pour grace itself over Her? Or was she so pleasing to him that she was converted into the Mother of the Son of God? That he came down on earth as his own gift, is clear. And as Mary was all pure, he got hold of her.

Humility

He saw her humility, her meekness and her purity; and he dwelt in Her, because God finds it easy to rest in those who are humble. At whom, by virtue of his own grace, did he look at always, but at the meek and the humble? He had his eyes on Her, and lived in Her, for she was counted among those of humble stature. She herself has said: *He has looked on lowliness* (cf Luke 1:48), and lived in her. This is why she was praised, because she was pleasing.

The highest perfection has to be humility, when God looks at the man who humbles himself. Moses was humble, and famous among men; the Lord revealed himself to him on the mountain. Abraham also showed himself to be humble; being a just man, he called himself dust and earth (cf Gen 18:27). John, in his humility said he was unfit to untie even the straps of the sandals of the Spouse, his Lord. Illustrious men have pleased through humility, in all generations; because this is the principal way by which man gets closer to God.

A noble and pure soul

But no one in the world has humbled herself as Mary has; so we may deduce that no one has been exalted as she has. It is in the measure of humility that God grants glory: He made her his Mother, and who is going to compare our humility with hers?... Our Lord, seeking to descend on earth, searched among all women, and selected only one: one who was beauty beyond all others. He examined her in depth; all he found was humility and sincerity, good thoughts and a soul in love with the divinity; a pure heart with desires of perfection. That is why God chose that pure soul and filled her with beauty. He descended from his seat and dwelt in blessedness among women; for there was no one on earth who could be compared with her. There was just one maiden, who was humble, pure, beautiful and immaculate, who was worthy to be his Mother.

He saw a noble condition in her – she was unstained by sin, and passion which might incline her to concupiscence did not figure, or any thoughts which might lead to weakness, or worldly conversations which could lead to irreparable evil. There was no disorder caused by the vanities of this world, nor the childish behaviour of a little girl!

He saw that there was no equal to her in this world, and he took her to be his Mother, who would breast-feed him with pure milk.

She was prudent and filled with the Love of God; for Our Lord does not dwell where love does not reign. Scarcely had the Great King decided to descend to our earth, because he wanted to do so, than he found accommodation in the world's purest temple, in a pure womb, adorned by virginity and worthy thoughts of sanctity.

She was most strikingly beautiful in her nature and in her will, because she was not polluted by illegitimate thoughts. Since childhood no stain deformed her integrity; without stain, she journeyed all along the way without sins. Her nature was guarded by a free will fixed on the noblest things; she carried in her body the signs of virginity and those of holiness in her soul.

He who was made manifest in her has given me the strength to say all these things about her indescribable beauty. I have seen and I believe that She alone, among all women, having come to be the Mother of the Son of God, is pure in this world. From the time when she learned to discern good from evil, she has maintained purity of heart and upright thoughts. She has never departed from the justice of the law, nor have the passions of the flesh disturbed her. Since childhood she has held holy sentiments, and she has diligently pondered them in her meditation. The Lord was always before her eyes, and she gazed at Him so as only to shine in Him and to take delight in Him. And when God saw how pure and beautiful her soul was, he wanted to stay in Mary, who was immune from sin. A woman equal to her had never been seen; and the most admirable of works have been fulfilled in her.

Her beauty, restrained only by the limits within which nature can work, was not of her own doing. She achieved a human excellence to such a degree, that it is only God who could have granted what she did not already have. The just are capable of reaching to within a short distance of God; the fullness of grace filled her soul most excellently to this point. For God to be born in Her body is a grace of the Lord, and for this he has to be glorified: how merciful he is!

Mary's beauty achieved such excellence that nothing better than Her has ever emerged in the whole world. We will give thanks, now and for ever, to the Lord, who scattered his grace over all creatures without any measure.

Homily on the Blessed Virgin Mary, Mother of God

Saint Fulgentius of Ruspe

Fabius Fulgentius was born in 468 at Telepte in the province of Carthage. His grandfather had been a senator at Carthage, but his possessions had been taken away and he was banished to Italy, his two sons returning after his death.

Fulgentius' father died young and he was brought up by his mother. He studied Greek before Latin, although, his biographer tells us, that for a Latin the Greek aspirates were hard to pronounce.

As he grew up he was given more civic duties. But a desire for the religious life came over him. He practised austerities in private for some time until he was moved by one of Augustine's sermons to relocate to a monastery. His mother beseeched with tears at the door of the monastery to see her son; but he did not allow himself and her this consolation.

Fulgentius was later made co-abbot. Moorish raids led him to seek safer havens. After a pilgrimage to Rome he returned to north Africa. While the Arian king Thrasimund lived he tried, unsuccessfully, to avoid being made a bishop. He came out of hiding only when he thought all the vacant sees had been filled. But the port of Ruspe was still vacant and a reluctant Fulgentius was elected to it in 502. During his stay in that city he gave constant instruction in the faith, on the Blessed Trinity, and reconciled many who had been re-baptised by the Arians.

He gave himself to the care of the diocese; he was careful that his clergy did not wear fine clothes, nor devote themselves to secular occupations. He ordered fasting on Wednesdays and Fridays for all clergy and widows, and for those of the laity who were able.

He died on 1 January 527, in the 25th year of his episcopate.

He wrote a number of works against the heretics which he presented to the king. But he was exiled to Sardinia and was only able to return to Ruspe in 523 on Thrasimund's death. We still possess some fine treatises, sermons and letters. The best known is *De Fide*, a description of the true faith, written to a Peter, who was going on a pilgrimage to the schismatic East.

Saint Fulgentius of Ruspe

THE SACRIFICE OF CHRIST

The offering of carnal victims in sacrifice was imposed on our fathers by the holy Trinity itself, the one God of the new and old testament. These sacrifices were a sign of that most pleasing gift, the sacrifice by which the only God the Son was to offer himself according to the flesh for us in his mercy.

For *he gave himself up for us as a fragrant offering and a sacrifice to God* (Eph 5:2), according to the teaching of the Apostle. He is true God and true priest, who entered once into the holy of holies for us, taking not the blood of bulls and goats but his own blood. This was foreshadowed in the past by the high priest, who entered the holy of holies with blood.

He it is then who showed forth in himself alone all that he knew to be necessary to achieve our redemption – he who at the same time is priest and sacrifice, God and temple: the priest through whom we are reconciled, the sacrifice by which we are reconciled, the temple in which we are reconciled, the God to whom we are reconciled. He alone is priest, sacrifice and temple, because he is all these as God according to the form of a servant; yet he is not God alone, because he is so along with the Father and the Holy Spirit according to the form of God.

You must hold firmly, then, without any shadow of doubt that the only-begotten God, the Word, took flesh and offered himself for us as a fragrant offering and a sacrifice to God. Patriarchs, prophets and priests under the old testament offered animals in sacrifice to him with the Father and the Holy Spirit. To him now, under the new testament, under the Father and the Holy Spirit, with whom he is one only God, the holy Catholic Church continually offers the sacrifice of bread and wine in faith and charity throughout the whole world.

For in those carnal victims the flesh and blood of Christ were pre-figured, the flesh which he who was without sin was to offer for our sins, the blood which he was to pour out for the forgiveness of our sins. In this sacrifice, however, there is thanksgiving for and commemoration of the flesh of Christ which he has offered for us and of the blood which the same God has poured out for us. Blessed Paul speaks of this in the Acts of the Apostles: *Take heed to yourselves and to the whole flock, in which the Holy Spirit has placed you as guardians, to rule the Church of God, which he has won by his blood* (Acts 20:28).

So in the former sacrifices what was to be given to us was intimated in a sign: in this sacrifice, however, what has already been given to us is clearly shown forth.

In those sacrifices the Son of God was foretold, to be put to death for the ungodly; in this sacrifice he is proclaimed now slain for the ungodly. As the Apostle testifies: *While we were yet helpless, at the right time Christ died for the ungodly* (Rom 5:6), and again *While we were enemies, we were reconciled to God by the death of his Son* (Rom 5:10).

Believe firmly and do not doubt in any way that the Word made flesh retains that true human flesh in which he was born of the Virgin Mary, in which he was crucified, in which he died and rose, in which he ascended to heaven and is seated at the right hand of God, in which he will also come to judge the living and the dead. This is why the Apostles heard the angels saying: *he will come in the same way as you saw him go into heaven* (Acts 1:11). And St John says: *he is coming with the clouds, and every eye will see him, every one who pierced him; and all the tribes of the earth will wail on account of him* (Rev 1:7).

De fide ad Petrum 22-23, 61-63

Saint Caesarius of Arles

Caesarius was born at Chalons-sur-Saone in Burgundy around 470. He died at Arles in 543 on 27 August on the eve of the feast of his great master, St Augustine.

When quite young he entered the monastery at Lerins, where Julian Pomerius was master of rhetoric. But his health gave way, and the abbot sent him to Arles to recuperate. There, in 500, he was ordained deacon and priest. He was chosen to be bishop in 503, following the death of Bishop Eonius. He ruled the see of Arles for 40 years, with apostolic courage and prudence, and stands out as a foremost bishop of Gaul in that period. He took part in the Second Council of Orange (529) which condemned semi-pelagianism.

In the history of monastic life and reforms in Gaul, Caesarius occupies an honourable place between St Martin of Tours and St Honoratus of Lerins, and St Colombanus. Not a few of his disciples became bishops and abbots, and as such naturally introduced the idea of the kind of religious life created by their master.

Caesarius was best known in his own day as a popular preacher. In first place among his works are 238 sermons. Some forty of these deal with Old Testament subjects. They are quite brief (he set himself a 15 minute limit), clear and simple in language, abounding in images and allusions drawn from the daily life of a townsman or a peasant, the sea, the market, the vineyard, the soil, and reflecting in many ways the still vigorous life of southern Gaul, where Greek was still the spoken language and Asian merchants(!) occupied the Rhone delta.

He also wrote two treatises against semi-pelagianism and a third entitled *De mysterio Sanctae Trinitatis*. Three pastoral letters, and writings on monastic rules are also preserved.

Saint Caesarius of Arles

TEMPLES OF GOD

Dearly beloved, through the goodness of Christ, we are today celebrating with joy and exultation the feast day of this temple. But it is we who ought to be the true, living temple of God. Deservedly, Christian people devoutly celebrate the sacred feast of their mother, the Church, through whom they realise that they have been spiritually reborn. For we, who were *vessels fit for the wrath* of God through our first birth, have merited to become *vessels for mercy* (Rom 9:22-23) through the second one. The first birth brought us forth to death, but the second one recalled us to life.

All of us, beloved, were temples of the devil before baptism; after baptism we have merited to be the temples of Christ. If we reflect somewhat carefully on the salvation of our soul, we recognise that we are the true and living temple of God. God not only *dwells in buildings made by human hands* (Acts 7:48), or in those constructed of wood and stone, but above all in the soul which has been made according to the image of God and was formed by the hand of the Creator Himself. Thus the blessed Apostle Paul said: *The temple of God is holy, and you are that temple* (1 Cor 3:17).

Unity

These temples are made of wood and stone in order that the living temples of God may gather there and come together into one temple of God. A single Christian is one temple of God, and many Christians are many temples of God. Also notice, brethren, how beautiful is the temple which is constructed from temples; just as many members form one body, so many temples form one temple. Now these temples of Christ, that is, devout Christian souls, are scattered throughout the world, but when judgement day comes they will all be gathered together and will form one temple in eternal life. Just as the many members of Christ form one body and have one head, Christ, so also those temples have Christ Himself as their inhabitant, because we are members of Him who is our head. Thus the Apostle says: *May Christ inwardly dwell in your hearts through faith* (Eph 3:16-17). Let us rejoice because we have merited to be the temple of God, but let us be afraid that we may violate the temple of God by evil deeds. Let us fear what the Apostle says: *If anyone destroys God's temple, God will destroy him* (1 Cor 3:17).

God, who could without any difficulty form heaven and earth by the power of His word, deigns to dwell in you, and for this reason you ought to act in such a way that you cannot offend such an inhabitant. Therefore let God find in you, that is, in His temple, nothing filthy or dark or haughty. If He suffers an injury there, He quickly withdraws, and if the Redeemer departs, the devil immediately draws near.

Purity of heart

What will be the condition of that unhappy soul, when it is deserted by God and possessed by the devil? Such a soul is deprived of light and filled with darkness. It is drained of all sweetness and saturated with bitterness. It destroys life and finds death. It acquires punishment and loses paradise. Now since God has willed to make out of us a temple for Himself and deigns to dwell in us continually, with His help let us strive as much as we can to lay aside what is superfluous and to gather what is useful. Let us reject dissipation, preserve chastity, despise avarice, seek compassion, scorn hatred, and love charity. If we do this with God's help, brethren, we continually invite God into the temple of our heart and body.

For this reason, beloved, if we want to celebrate a feast of the Church with joy, we should not destroy the living temples of God within us by evil deeds. I will tell you what everyone can understand. As often as we come to church, we ought to prepare our souls to be such as we want to find the church. You want to find the church shining; do not defile your soul with the filth of sin. If you want a church to be full of light, God also wants your soul not to be in darkness. What our Lord says, should happen, that the light of good works shine forth in us in order that He who is in heaven may be glorified. Just as you enter this church, so God wants to enter your soul, as He promised: *I will dwell with them and walk among them* (2 Cor 6:16). Just as we do not want to find pigs or dogs in church, for they cause us to shudder, so God should not find in His temple, that is, in our souls, any sin which might offend the eyes of His majesty.

Receiving Holy Communion

As often as you desire to celebrate the feast of a temple, you ought to come to church temperately and peaceably. If we come to the feast of a church and the solemn festival of the saints in such a spirit, we will merit to obtain in its entirety whatever we have justly willed to ask of God. Above all it is necessary for you to come to church with pure hearts, just as you come with bright garments, for it does you no good to appear glittering in the eyes of men, if you are filthy in the sight of the angels.

To be sure, brethren, when we want to enter church and communicate we first wash our hands. A sheen on our body is not at all profitable for us, if purity is not preserved in our heart. If it is wicked and disgraceful to approach the altar with dirty hands, how much worse is it to receive the Body and Blood of Christ into a soiled soul? If you are unwilling to put your clothing into a chest full of mud, how have you dared to take Christ's sacrament into a soul that is full of sin?

When women come to the altar, they all wear glittering clothing in which they receive the sacrament of Christ. This they do justly and properly, but they should pay attention and reflect that, just as they wear bright clothes, so they should show that their souls are bright. If they do otherwise, Christ's sacrament will suffer injury in them.

True Christians

In order that we may deserve to receive our Lord's Body and Blood as a remedy and not to our judgement, with His help let us labour as much as we can that they may not suffer injury in us because of our evil deeds. Therefore if you do not spare yourself on your own account, at least do so for the sake of God who has deigned to make you His temple. All men who are drunkards, adulterers, envious or proud, injure Christ: All thieves and perjurers, all men who fulfil vows to trees or fountains, everyone who consults magicians' horoscopes and soothsayers or sorcerers on their own account or for the sake of their household – all who are men of this kind eject Christ from their hearts and bring in the devil. All Christians of this kind, as I said, even though they come to church, communicate at the altar, and are seen to sign themselves with the cross quite frequently, are proved to serve, not Christ, but the devil, unless they have amended their lives through repentance.

On the other hand Christians who are chaste, humble, temperate and kind, who come to church rather often, practise almsgiving, observe peace and charity, and do not bear false testimony – in such men the temple of Christ is kept intact, and Christ is known to dwell in them.

On being chaste

For this reason, brethren, with God's help let us avoid serious sins. As for the small sins of which we cannot be free, let us resist them by daily almsgiving and redeem them by continuous prayer, so that, as I said, Christ who desires to dwell within us may not suffer any injury. There are two who want to dwell within us: Christ our Lord and the devil our adversary. Both of them knock at the door of our heart.

Do not reject Christ, if you want to be unafraid of the enemy. Cling to the lawful king, and you will not fear the cruel tyrant. Hold fast to the light, and darkness will not dare to approach you. Love life, in order that you may be able to avoid death. Therefore let us fill our soul with the sweet perfume of chastity, and adorn it with the flowers of various virtues, in order that we may invite Christ our Lord in faith, feed Him with hope, and give Him to drink with charity. As often as there are solemn feasts, let us come to church, not only with a chaste body but also with a pure heart.

The sacrament of baptism can be denied to no man, dearest brethren, especially if bodily sickness seems to demand it. However, it is good and proper for those who are in good health to be kept for the Paschal feast. Know that you yourselves are a surety before God, dearest brethren, for the infants whom you have received in baptism. For this reason, then, endeavour to advise and rebuke them always, so that they may live chastely and justly and temperately.

Above all show them the Creed and the Lord's Prayer, and encourage them to good works, not only by words but also by examples. While men who live chastely and justly and temperately give the example of a good life to others, they will receive a reward both for themselves and for the others. Let us trust in the mercy of God, that He will inspire us to live in such a way that we may not be able to incur punishment because of our evil deeds, but rather to reach eternal rewards on account of our good deeds.

Sermon 229

Saint Caesarius of Arles

ON MERCY

Blessed are the merciful, for they shall obtain mercy (Matt 5:7). Sweet is the word mercy, dearly beloved; and if the mere name, how much more so the reality? Although all men desire to possess it, what is worse, not all live in such a way as to deserve it, for all want to receive it but few are willing to grant it. O man, with what feelings do you want to find what you neglect to give? If a man desires to obtain mercy in heaven, he should bestow it in this world. Therefore, since all want mercy, dearly beloved, let us make her our patron in this life so that she may free us in the life to come. Mercy abides in heaven, but it is reached by the exercise of it on earth. Thus the Scriptures tell us: *O Lord, your mercy is in heaven* (Ps 35:6).

Human and divine mercy

There is then, both an earthly and a heavenly mercy, the one human and the other divine. What is human mercy? It is to care for the miseries of the poor. And what is divine mercy? Doubtless, it is that which grants forgiveness of sins. Whatever human mercy gives on the way, divine mercy repays in the heavenly country.

In this world God is cold and hungry in the person of all his poor, for He said: *As long as you did it for one of these the least of my brethren, you did it for me* (Matt 25:40, 42). Therefore, God who deigns to give from heaven wants to receive on earth. What kind of creatures are we if we want to take when God gives but are unwilling to give when He asks it? If a poor man hungers, Christ is in need, as He Himself said: *I was hungry, and you did not give me to eat.*

Do not, then, despise the miseries of the poor, if you want to hope for the forgiveness of your sins without anxiety. Christ hungers now, brethren, for in the person of all the poor He Himself deigns to hunger and thirst; moreover, He repays in heaven whatever He receives on earth. I ask you, brethren, what do you desire or seek when you come to church? What, except mercy?

Therefore, grant earthly mercy and you will receive the heavenly. The poor man asks something of you, and you ask of God; he seeks a mouthful, you want eternal life. Give to the poor, in order that you may merit to receive from Christ; listen to Him say: *Give, and it shall be given to you* (Luke 6:38).

Charitable giving

I do not know with what feelings you want to receive what you are unwilling to give. Therefore, when you come to church offer alms of some kind to the poor in proportion to your means. One who can, should bring silver; if he cannot, let him give wine. If a man does not even possess this, he might give a mouthful to the hungry; if he has not the whole, some little portion. Thus may be fulfilled the Lord's admonition through the Prophet: *Deal your bread to the hungry* (Is 58:7). He did not say: Give all, lest perhaps you might become poor and have nothing more to give.

If we carefully heed the fact that Christ hungers in the person of the poor, brethren, it will be profitable for us. God allowed poor people to be in the world in order that every man might have the means of redeeming his sins. If there were no poor, no one would give alms and no

ON MERCY

one would receive pardon.

God could have made all men rich, but He wanted to assist us through the misery of the poor. Listen and see: a coin and a kingdom. What comparison is there, brother? You give the poor a coin and receive a kingdom from Christ. You bestow a mouthful and are given eternal life. You offer clothes and Christ grants you the forgiveness of your sins. Therefore, let us not despise the poor, brethren, but let us desire them all the more and of our own accord hasten to lavish ourselves upon them.

The misery of the poor is the remedy of the rich, as the Lord said: *Nevertheless, give alms; and behold, all things are clean to you.* And later: *sell what you have and give alms* (Luke 11:41; 12:33). Moreover, the Holy Spirit exclaims through the Prophet: *As water quenches a fire, so alms destroy sins*; and again: *shut up alms in the heart of the poor, and it shall obtain help for you against all evil* (Sir 3:33; 29:15). Therefore, let us exercise mercy, brethren, and with Christ's help keep the bond of His care.

Two kinds of alms

As I have frequently mentioned, there are two kinds of alms: the one good, but the other better; the one that you extend a mouthful to the poor; the other that you immediately forgive a brother who has offended you. With the Lord's help let us hasten to fulfil both types, in order that we may be able to obtain eternal forgiveness and the true mercy of Christ. He Himself has told us: *If you forgive, your heavenly Father will also forgive you your offences; but if you do not forgive, neither will your Father forgive you your offences* (Matt 6:14-15). At another time the Holy Spirit exclaims: *Man to man reserves anger, and does he seek remedy of God? He has no mercy on a man like himself, and does he ask mercy of God?* (cf Sir 28:3).

Likewise, blessed John says: *He who hates his brother is a murderer*. And again, *he who hates his brother is in the darkness, and walks in the darkness, and he does not know where he goes; because the darkness has blinded his eyes* (1 John 3:15; 2:11). Therefore, dearly beloved, in order that we may be able to avoid eternal evils and obtain perpetual good things, let us hasten as much as we can and as long as we live, both to possess ourselves and to impart to others the two kinds of alms which I mentioned above.

Then we may be able to say with assurance on judgement day: Give, O Lord, because we have given; we have done what You commanded, do You fulfil what You promised. May He design to grant this, who, together with the Father and the Holy Spirit, lives and reigns world without end. Amen.

Sermon 25

Roman the Cantor

The few biographical notes we have on Roman the Cantor come from the lesser documents which are liturgical in origin: the *Sissanarius* and the *Meneus*. According to these two texts, Roman was born in Syria, in the city of Emesa, around 490. Ordained a deacon in Beritus during the reign of Emperor Anastasius, he moved to Constantinople where he lived at the Church of the Most Blessed Mother of God. He dedicated himself to a life of prayer and mortification, characterised by his devotion to Mary.

At the shrine of Our Lady he received a charism for poetry. Tradition recounts that one night over Christmas Our Lady appeared to him and gave him a parchment to chew and swallow. He had barely done this when he rose to the lectern and composed a hymn in praise of the Birth of Our Lord. The poetic streak, miraculously outstanding in him, inspired new and numerous *kondaika*, hymns for the principal liturgical feasts of the year, especially those of Jesus Christ and Our Lady. In total he composed over a thousand. Many of them, in his own handwriting, are still preserved today at the Shrine.

He died between 555 and 562, and was buried in the church of Chus, where his feast is celebrated on 1 October.

Although the themes of his composition are very varied, the Marian ones are outstanding. The figure of Our Lady is reflected on in the light of the life and redeeming work of her Son. Thus, the most important prerogatives highlighted in the poems refer to the divine Motherhood of Mary and to her perpetual virginity.

ROMAN THE CANTOR

THE WEDDING AT CANA

We now want to narrate the first miracle worked in Cana by Him who had already demonstrated the power of his abilities to the Egyptians and Hebrews. In that case the nature of the water was changed miraculously into blood. He had punished the Egyptians with the curse of the ten plagues. He had turned back the sea for the Hebrews to such an extent that they crossed it as if on firm ground. In the desert, He had provided them with water flowing copiously from the rock. Today, during the marriage feast, He, who has accomplished everything with wisdom, carries out a new transformation of nature.

While Christ took part in the wedding and the whole multitude of those invited were feasting, the wine began to run short and it seemed that joy would turn to melancholy. The bridegroom was embarrassed, the servants muttered and the discomfort at such poverty began to spread everywhere, the tumult reaching the main hall. Faced with this situation, Mary, most pure, went to inform her Son: *They have no wine* (John 2:3). 'My child, I ask you, show your absolute power. You, who have done everything in wisdom ...'

Christ, responded to his Mother who had said, 'Grant me this grace': *O woman, what have you to do with me. My hour has not yet come* (John 2:4).

Some have wished to read into these words a significance which would justify their impiety. They are those who maintain that Christ was subject to natural laws, or they consider him, too, to be tied down by time. But this is because they do not understand the meaning of his words. The lips of the impious, who reflect on evil, are obliged to silence by the immediate miracle worked by him who fulfilled everything with wisdom.

'My son, reply now', says the all Pure Mother of Jesus. 'You who puts on time the brake of measure, how can you await the right time, my Son and my Lord? How can you await the time, if it is you yourself who has established the intervals of time, O Creator of the visible and invisible world, You who day and night direct with total sovereignty, and at your discretion, the unchangeable transformations. It is You who has fixed the passage of the years with perfectly regulated cycles. How can you wait for the right time for the marvel which I ask of you, You who have fulfilled all with wisdom?'

'Even before You noticed it, venerable Virgin, I knew that the wine was needed,' replied the Ineffable, the Merciful, to the most venerable Mother. 'I know all the thoughts in your heart. You felt within you: "The need will encourage my Son to do the miracle, but with the excuse of the right time, he is delaying it." O pure Mother, learn now the reason for this delay, and when you have understood it, I will certainly grant you this favour, I who have done all things with wisdom.

Lift up your spirit to the heights of my words and understand, O Incorrupt, what I am about to say. At the very moment at which I created from nothing heaven and earth and the whole of the universe, I could instantaneously introduce order into everything being formed. Nonetheless, I have established a certain order, properly subdivided. Creation occurred in six days. And certainly not because I lacked the power to do it; rather it was so that the chorus of angels, on seeing that all things were done at the right time, could recognise the divinity in me, celebrating it with the following verse: "Glory to you, powerful King, who has done everything in wisdom."

Listen well to this, O Saint: I could have rescued the fallen in another way, without assuming the condition of a poor person and a slave. I have, nevertheless, accepted my conception, my birth as man, milk from your breast, O Virgin, and so everything has developed in me in an orderly way, because nothing exists in me which does not have this characteristic. With that same order I now wish to work this miracle, to which I have consented for the salvation of men. I have done everything in wisdom.

If I had only shown this in those surprising marvels, they would have understood that I am God from before time, although I might have become man. But now, contrary to good order, and even before the preaching, You are asking miracles of me. Here then is the reason for my delay. I asked you to wait for the hour for working miracles, for this one reason. But as parents ought to be honoured by their children, I will consider this favour for you, O Mother, since I can do everything, I who have done everything in wisdom.

Tell, then, those who live in the house, to place themselves at my service, following my commands: they will soon be, for themselves and for others, witnesses to a marvel. I don't want it to be Peter who serves me, not John, not Andrew or any of my apostles, for fear that later, because of this, men may suspect being cheated. I want the servants themselves to serve me, so that they themselves become witnesses of what is possible for me to do, for me who does everything in wisdom.'

Docile to these words, the Mother of Christ hastened to tell the servants of the wedding feast: *Do whatever he tells you* (John 2:5). There were six stone jars in the house, as Scripture tells us. Christ ordered the servants:

Fill the jars with water (John 2:8). And immediately it was done. They filled the jars with fresh water and remained there, hoping to see what he intended to do, He who has done everything in wisdom.

I now want to speak about the jars and to describe how they were filled to the brim with that wine, which came from water. As has been written, the Master said to the servants in a loud voice: 'Take this wine which does not come from the vintage casks, offer it to the guests, fill the dry cups, so that everybody including the bridegroom may enjoy it; since I have given joy to everyone in an unforeseen way, I who have done everything in wisdom.'

When Christ clearly changed the water into wine through his own power, the whole world was filled with cheer, finding the taste of that wine most agreeable. Today, we can sit at the banquet of the Church, because the wine has changed into the blood of Christ, and we drink it in holy joy, glorifying the Great Spouse. Because the true spouse is the Son of Mary, the Word who exists from eternity, who has taken on the condition of a slave and has fulfilled everything in wisdom.

O Highest, Saint, Saviour of all, keep the wine in each of us unaltered, You who govern all things. Take away from here those who think badly, and in their perversity, adulterate your most holy wine with water; because always diluting your dogma with water, they condemn themselves to eternal fire. But preserve us, O Immaculate One, from the laments which will follow your judgement, You who are merciful, through the prayers of the Holy, Virgin Mother of God, You who have done all things in wisdom.

Hymn on the wedding at Cana

Saint Gregory the Great

St Gregory was born of an illustrious Roman patrician family around 540. In 572 he was appointed *praefectus urbis*. Two years later he gave up a career in politics to become a religious. He was ordained a deacon in 579 by Pope Pelagius II, and sent to Constantinople as nuncio. On his return to Rome he acted as adviser and secretary to the Roman Pontiff.

In 590 the Eternal City suffered the scourge of the plague. One of its first victims was Pope Pelagius II. The clergy, senate and people in a meeting unanimously elected the former prefect to occupy the chair of Peter.

St Gregory is considered one of the great masters of western classical spirituality. A man gifted with intelligence and a broad culture, he has left his mark as a Pope and as a Father of the Church.

His apostolic zeal had a wide influence in the evangelisation carried out during his pontificate. With his activity he contributed to restating the unity of the Church and to the primacy of the Roman Pontiff.

The literary heritage of St Gregory includes an abundant and varied collection of letters and commentaries on biblical texts, which contributed to transmitting an ancient culture to a world beginning to organise itself after the barbarian invasion.

Forty homilies on the Gospels are preserved. The first twenty were read to the people by a notary of the Roman church in the presence of St Gregory, who could not preach because of an illness. Not without an effort he himself preached the other twenty to the Romans during the liturgical festivities of 591.

In all of them St Gregory shows himself to be a great preacher. He speaks to the people in a simple and paternal form, explaining the biblical passages he has chosen, with clarity; and with happy intuition he applies them to practical cases in life.

One of the texts reproduced here is a fragment of his *Homiliae in Evangelia*. The other is taken from a lesson on St John's gospel; it praises the figure of the precursor as a model Christian for fortitude and humility.

Saint Gregory the Great

THE HOLY ANGELS

There are nine choirs of angels. Scripture tells us, for certain, that there are angels, archangels, virtues, powers, principalities, dominions, thrones, cherubims and seraphims.

The existence of angels and archangels is confirmed on almost every page of sacred scripture. The books of the Prophets make frequent reference to cherubims and seraphims. St Paul, writing to the Ephesians, mentions four other choirs when he says, *above all principalities, and powers, and virtues and dominions* (Eph 1:21). Writing to the Colossians he again states: *be they thrones or dominions or principalities or powers* (Col 1:16). Thus the thrones together with the four choirs about which he spoke to the Ephesians – principalities, powers, virtues, and dominions – make five choirs, specifically referred to by the Apostle. If to these are added the angels and archangels, cherubims and seraphims, we see that there are nine choirs of angels...

Angels and archangels

The name *angel* refers to a function and not to a nature. Thus, although the holy spirits of the heavenly homeland are all spiritual, not all of them can be called angels. Only those who have made announcements or pronouncements may be called angels (which means messenger). So the Psalmist says, *he makes the spirits into his angels* (Ps 103:4), as if clearly stating that God, when he so wishes, makes angels (messengers) of those celestial spirits which are always with him.

Those who make announcements of lesser importance are simply called angels. Those who have more important messages are called archangels. Mary is not sent just any ordinary angel, but the archangel, Gabriel. It was fitting that for this ministry, which was to announce the very best of news, one of the more exalted angels should be sent. It is for this reason that the archangels have individual names. Through their contact with men, then, their great power is made known to us...

Michael means *who is like God*; Gabriel, *the strength of God*; Raphael, *the medicine of God*. Whenever something needs to be done which requires a particularly awesome power, St Michael is sent. Thus it can be seen, in deed and in name, that no one can do what God can. For example, the old enemy in his pride aspired to be like God, saying, *I will ascend to heaven above the stars of God, I will set my throne on high; I will sit on the mount of assembly in the far north; I will ascend above the heights of the clouds, I will make myself like the Most High* (Is 14:13-14). At the end of the world he will be left to act with his own powers, so that he may suffer definitive torture. He will have to fight against St Michael the Archangel, as St John relates: *Michael and his angels fought against the dragon* (Rev 12:7). Thus he, who set himself up was proud and tried to be like God, would learn from his defeat by St Michael, that no one can haughtily elevate himself, attempting to be like God.

Gabriel is sent to Mary. He is called *the strength of God*, because he is to announce Him who deigned to appear humble so as to fight the infernal powers. Of Him the Psalmist says: *Lift up your heads, O princes! And be lifted up, O gates to eternity! that the King of glory may*

THE HOLY ANGELS

come in (Ps 24:7). And also, *Who is the King of glory? The Lord of hosts, he is the King of glory!* (Ps 24:10). Thus the Lord of armies, strong in battle, who came to wage war against the spiritual powers, ought in turn to be announced as *the strength of God*.

Rafael, as we have already said, signifies *the medicine of God*. When acting as a doctor, he touched Tobias' eyes and lifted the darkness from them. So it is fitting that he be called the *medicine of God*.

The angelic choirs

Now that we have amused ourselves interpreting the names of the angels, it remains for us to review briefly the significance of the angelic ministries.

Virtues are those spirits through whom miracles and prodigies are most often worked. *Powers* are those who, within their own order, have received a greater power to be able to subdue the enemy's powers, so that these are contained and do not tempt as much as they could. The *principalities* are those who direct the other good spirits, ordering them to do what they ought. They are the ones who preside over the others and are responsible for fulfilling the divine commands.

Dominions are those who are above even the principalities, because presiding implies being at the front or at the head, but dominating means having the others as subjects. Thus the angelic militia, who are outstanding because of their extraordinary power, insofar as they have others subject to their obedience, are called dominions.

Thrones are those over whom the all-powerful God presides regarding the fulfilment of his desires. In our language, a throne is a kind of seat. Those who have received the name *throne* are those so filled with divine grace that God is seated in them, and through them decrees his desires.

The *cherubims* are also called *fullness of knowledge*. These lofty armies of angels are called cherubims because the closer they contemplate the clarity of God, the greater they are replete with the most perfect knowledge. Thus, in so far as it is possible for created beings, they know everything proportional to the clarity with which they see the Creator, in keeping with their dignity.

Finally, *seraphims* are those armies of angels who by their particular closeness to the creator burn with an incomparable love. Seraphims are ardent and aflame. They are so close to God that between them and God there is no other spirit. They glow stronger the closer they are to seeing him. Their love is certainly a flame, for the more subtly they see the clarity of God, the more are they inflamed with his love.

Homiliae in Evangelia 34, 7-10

Saint Gregory the Great

TRUE AND FALSE JUSTICE

When proposing some considerations on the repentance of Mary Magdalene, before saying anything I should rather cry. For which heart, even if it were made of stone, would not be moved by the tears of this sinner to imitate her repentance? She had considered what she had done, and did not wish to place any barriers to what had to be done. She turned up amidst the guests, arriving without any invitation and offered her tears among the festivities taking place. You can deduce how much she was burning with love if she was not embarrassed to weep during a banquet.

But this woman, whom St Luke calls a sinner, the Apostle St John calls Mary. We believe that she is the Mary whom St Mark says had seven demons exorcised from her. And what do the seven demons represent if not all the vices? For just as the whole of time is understood to be seven days, so too all things are denoted by the figure seven. So Mary, who had all the vices, had seven devils.

But then she began to look at the stains of her twisted life and rushed, to be cleaned, to the fount of mercy; she was not ashamed of the invited guests, because she was so seriously embarrassed about herself interiorly, that she did not think there was anything to be ashamed of on the outside.

My dearest brothers and sisters, what should we admire more – that Mary goes or that the Lord receives her? That he receives her or that he attracts her. I would rather say that he attracts her and that he receives her. For he would undoubtedly receive her externally with his kindness, and with his mercy attract her internally...

But seeing this, the Pharisee began to despise him. He not only reprimands the sinful woman who came, but also the Lord, who receives her, saying to himself: *'If this man were a prophet he would have known who and what kind of woman this is who is touching him'* (Luke 7:39).

Here is a Pharisee really proud on the inside and falsely just. He criticises the sick person for the sickness and the doctor for welcoming her, although he himself suffers from the wound of pride and ignores the doctor.

In this way, the divine Doctor finds himself between two sick people: one in the midst of her fever keeps her balance; and the other who, because of his fever, has lost his head. She wept for what she had done; but the Pharisee, dripping with pride and a false sense of justice, increased the malice of his illness and lost his senses, for in fact he ignored the symptoms that he was far from being healthy.

If that woman had gone close to the feet of the Pharisee, he would doubtlessly have pulled his feet back, and kicked her out, considering himself stained by the sin of another. But not being in possession of true justice, he in fact caught the sickness of the other sick person.

Whenever we see any sick person, then, we should think about ourselves as the ones who have had the misfortune, for we ourselves perhaps have fallen or could fall in similar matters. And while it is true that the reproach of the teacher ought always to pursue vices with discipline, it is nonetheless advisable to distinguish carefully between the vices which ought to be dealt with severely and the person who should be treated compassionately. For if we have to punish the sinner, we then have to support him as

TRUE AND FALSE JUSTICE

a neighbour. And when he himself repents of what he has done, our neighbour is no longer a sinner, for as he has applied God's justice to himself, he has punished in himself what divine justice condemns.

Let us listen now to the words as a result which this proud and arrogant man became a blameworthy offender. The example of two debtors was given to him: one of them owed more than the other. After each had been forgiven, which of the two loved the person who forgave them more? He replied immediately: *The one for whom he cancelled the greater debt* (Luke 7:43).

It is worth noting that the Pharisee was condemned as an offender by his own lips, falling into the trap which he himself had set.

The Lord lists the good which the sinful woman has done and the evil which the falsely just Pharisee had done, saying: *I entered your house, you gave me no water for my feet, but she has bathed my feet with her tears, and dried them with her hair. You gave me no kiss but from the time I came in she has not stopped kissing my feet. You did not anoint my head with oil, but she has anointed my feet with ointment* (Luke 7:44-46).

What are we to think, my brothers and sisters, but that love is fire and guilt but soot. So it is said: *many sins have been forgiven her because she has loved much*. It is as if to say: the soot of her sins has been burnt, because it has been consumed in the fire of love. The more the sinner's soot is spent, the more the heart of the sinner is consumed in the fire of charity.

There you have it: she who had come to the doctor ill, is cured; but others have become ill because of her health. Those who sat at table began to whisper among themselves: *Who is this who even forgives sins?* (Luke 7:49).

The heavenly Doctor does not neglect the sick whom

he sees get worse with the medicine, but he assures the woman who had been cured, by uttering this sentence: *Your faith has saved you; go in peace* (Luke 7:50).

Her faith saved her, because she did not doubt that she would obtain what she was asking for; although she had already received the certainty of hope through the grace of Him from whom she had trustingly sought health. And he commands her to go in peace so that from the way of truth she does not return again to the path of scandal. For this reason it has also been said, through Zechariah, *to guide our feet into the way of peace* (Luke 1:79).

We will straighten up our steps, then, along this way when our actions follow the path which matches up with the grace of our Creator.

Homiliae in Evangelia, XIII, 1-4

Saint Gregory the Great

IN PRAISE OF JOHN THE BAPTIST

Let us listen to Jesus' comments about John the Baptist after his disciples had left him: *What did you go out into the wilderness to look at? A reed shaken by the wind?* (Matt 11:7). Speaking in this manner, Christ did not mean to confirm but rather to deny. A reed tends to bend over to one side in the slightest breeze. What does the reed signify but a carnal spirit, which when barely touched by praise or an insult, doubles over towards one side or another? If from the lips of men blows the wind of praise, it rejoices, it is filled with pride and melts completely into a puddle. But if instead of the wind of praise comes detraction, it immediately reacts the other way, and bursts into anger.

Fortitude

But John was not a reed shaken by the wind. He did not allow himself to be softened up by praise or to be irritated by insults. Prosperity would not make him vain, nor would adversity depress him.

John was not a reed shaken by the wind. From the beginning no human vicissitude would manage to take away his firmness. Let us learn from this, my dearest brothers, not to be like a reed shaken by the wind: let us strengthen our spirit, which is exposed to the gale of tongues, and let us remain inflexible in strength of soul. May no insult move us to anger, no favour incline us to sterile weakness. May no prosperity make us conceited, nor adversity disturb us. Rooted in a solid faith, we will not let ourselves be cast about by the changeability of transitory things.

Modesty in dress

Referring to John, Jesus continues: *Someone dressed in fine robes? Look, those dressed in fine robes are in royal palaces* (Matt 11:8). For John is described as wearing woven camel hair. And what does *'those dressed in fine robes are in royal palaces'* mean other than an open declaration that those who avoid suffering difficult experiences for the love of God and are dedicated only to external things, are fighting not for the kingdom of heaven but for the kingdom on earth? Let no one believe, then, that sin does not exist in luxury and in the preoccupation about dress, for if there were nothing blameworthy, Our Lord would not have praised John for the harshness of his dress.

What was said of John – that he did not dress luxuriously or effeminately – can also be understood in another sense. He never dressed luxuriously because he did not encourage the life of sinners with flattering remarks: he condemned it with the strength of a severe reprimand. *You brood of vipers! Who warned you to flee from the wrath to come?* (Luke 3:7). Solomon had already spoken: *The sayings of the wise are like goads, and like nails firmly fixed* (Eccl 12:11). The words of the wise are compared to nails and stings because they do not hide the faults of sinners but rather censure them.

What then did you go out to see? A prophet? Yes, I tell you, and more than a prophet (Matt 11:9). The task of a prophet is to foretell future events, not to point them out. John is more than a prophet, because in his position as a precursor, he was indicating, pointing, to Him whom he had prophesied about. But as he is neither a reed shaking in the wind, nor dressed in fine clothes, and as the name 'prophet' is not enough to designate his title, let us listen to the way he should worthily be called: *The Lord God says this: Look, I am going to send my messenger to prepare a way before me* (Mal 3:1). What in Greek is expressed by the word *angel*, when translated means 'messenger'. It is justifiable, then, to call the one who has been sent to announce the Supreme Judge, an angel. For the name reflects the dignity of the action to be done. The name is certainly high ranking, but his life was no less inferior.

Homiliae in Evangelia VI, 2-5

Saint Sophronius

Sophronius was born of noble parentage at Damascus about 560. He travelled extensively throughout the East; he became a monk in 580. Sophronius spent 20 years under the guidance of St John Mosco. Together they visited monasteries in Egypt, and later went to Rome. In 619 John Mosco died in Rome, and St Sophronius decided to return to Palestine.

From 633 he was the principal opponent of monotheletism. Conspicuous for his learning and piety, he became Patriarch of Jerusalem in 634. He died in 638, the year in which he saw with great sorrow the Holy City fall into the hands of the Muslims.

His own biography could be centred on two points of interest: his desire for holiness and his doctrinal orthodoxy (which caused him much suffering when defending the faith).

He was the author of biographies, homilies and hymns. Ten homilies which have been preserved deal mainly with ecclesiastical festivals, and are remarkable for their dogmatic and oratorical style. Numerous odes entitle him to a place among Greek ecclesiastical poets.

Saint Sophronius

HAIL MARY

In the sixth month the angel Gabriel was sent by God to a town in Galilee called Nazareth, to a virgin engaged to a man whose name was Joseph, of the house of David. The virgin's name was Mary. And he came to her and said, 'Hail, full of grace! The Lord is with you' (Luke 1:26-28).

O Virgin Mother, could there possibly be a happiness higher than this? What could be greater in excellence than this grace, which by divine will has come only to you? Is it possible to imagine anything more joyful or more splendid? All other gifts defer to the miracle which shines in you. All prostrate themselves below your grace. All, even the most tested ones, are secondary and have a splendour which is inferior.

The Lord is with you. Who, then, would venture to fight against you? God is on your side: Is there anyone who does not surrender immediately to you, and does not joyfully consent to grant you primacy and excellence? On considering your eminent privileges, way above all creatures, with the highest praise do I acclaim you: *Hail, full of grace! The Lord is with you.* Through you, this joy does not only spread to men but also to the heavenly powers.

You are truly *blessed among all women*, because you transformed Eve's curse into a blessing; because you managed to get Adam to become blessed, he who earlier had been humbled by the curse of sin.

Blessed are you among all women, because through

you the blessing of the Father shone before all men and he freed them from the old curse.

Blessed are you among all women, because through you your ancestors have found salvation; for you are going to give birth to the saviour who will obtain divine health for them.

Blessed are you among all women, because without a seed you offered the fruit which will bless the whole earth, and will redeem it of the thorns of the curse.

Blessed are you among all women, because being a woman by nature, you will be the Mother of God. For, as he who will be born is the incarnate God, you will be called the Mother of God, in your own right and out of merit, for it is God you are going to give birth to.

You carry God Himself enclosed within your womb. He abides in you according to the flesh, and through you he presents himself as he had promised. He will obtain joy for all and he will transmit the divine light to the whole universe.

In you, O Virgin Mother, as in a pure and resplendent heaven, God *placed his tabernacle; and he will come out of thee as the spouse from the bridal chamber* (Ps 59:5-6). Imitating the career of a giant she will be on the move all her life, filling all living beings with future salvation. And she will fill with divine warmth and life-giving splendour all those who journey towards her.

Oratio 2 in sanctissimae Deiparae Annuntiatione

Saint Sophronius

THE FESTIVAL OF LIGHT

Let us all run to meet him, we who honour and venerate the mystery of the Lord with pious devotion. Let us all go to meet him with pure minds. Let there be no one who does not share in this meeting, let no one refuse to carry a light.

We add to this bright shining candles. In this way we show the divine splendour of the coming of him who makes all things bright. In the abundance of eternal light all things are bathed in light when the evil shadows have been driven away. In this way we show the brightness of soul with which we must go to meet Christ.

The most chaste virgin Mother of God bore in her arms the true light and came to the help of those who were lying in darkness. In the same way we must hurry out to meet him who is truly light, enlightened by the beams of his brightness and bearing in our hands the light which shines for all men.

Indeed this is the mystery which we celebrate, that the light has come into the world and has given it light when it was shrouded in darkness, and that the day-spring has visited us from on high and given light to those who were sitting in darkness. That is why we go in procession with lamps in our hands and hasten bearing lights showing both that the light has shone upon us, and signifying the glory which is to come through him. Therefore let us all run together to meet God.

The true light which enlightens every man coming

The Festival of Light

into this world, has come. Brethren, let us all be enlightened, let us all be filled with light.

Let none of us remain a stranger to this brightness. Let no one who is filled with it continue in the darkness. But let us all go forth shining with light, let us all go together bright with that light, to welcome with old Simeon that everlasting shining light. Rejoicing with him in our souls, let us sing a hymn of thanks to the Begetter and Father of the light, who has sent the true light and driven away the darkness and made us all shine with light.

For we too have seen through him the salvation of God which he has prepared before the face of all peoples, and has shown forth for the glory of us who are the new Israel; and we have been freed at once from that mysterious and ancient sin just as Simeon was released from the bonds of this present life when he had seen Christ.

We have embraced Christ in faith as he has come to us from Bethlehem, and have been made the people of God instead of Gentiles, for he is the salvation given us by our God and Father. We have seen God made flesh with our very eyes and we are called the new Israel now that we have seen the visible presence of God and cradled him in our minds. That presence we celebrate with a yearly festival: we shall never forget it.

Orat 3:6-7

Saint Maximus the Confessor

St Maximus was born in Constantinople around 580. After receiving a good education, including religious instruction, he received a high-ranking state appointment. But in 630 he resigned to become a monk in a monastery at Chrysopolis, opposite Constantinople.

First he fought against the monophysites. Later he made every effort to fight monotheletism. He took part in several African synods and was also active in the Lateran Council of 649. This Council condemned both monotheletism and those patriarchs in favour of it. On his return to Constantinople he was arrested on the orders of Emperor Constans II, tortured and banished. He died in exile on 13 August 662, for orthodoxy and obedience to Rome.

St Maximus wrote a good number of ethical, exegetical and theological works. Also attributed to him is *A Life Of Mary*, a work recently discovered in a Georgian translation of the eleventh century. It would have been written before 626, and makes it the oldest *Life* of Our Lady extant. In addition to fundamental points on Marian doctrine, the author also highlights the very deep union of Mary with her Son and God at every moment of her life – even after the Ascension of Our Lord into heaven.

The paragraphs we have here are a sign of the attention paid by the Virgin Mary to the Apostles and disciples, in those early years of the Church. They are also an impressive testimony to the deep devotion which Christians have always had for the Mother of God and our Mother.

SAINT MAXIMUS THE CONFESSOR

CONSOLER OF THE CHURCH

The birth and adolescence of Her who conceived and gave birth to the Son of God, were more marvellous occurrences that had ever been seen in nature. Now, this Birth of the Truth, King and God of the Universe, was an unthinkable, incomprehensible and ineffable event... Later, along the journey of her fatiguing work, she suffered and bore many tribulations, trials, afflictions and laments during the Crucifixion of the Lord. She achieved such complete a victory, winning the crown of triumph, that she became the Queen of all creatures.

Her Son was the Word of God, true God and King of all creation. She had seen him rise from the tomb, an event greater than any other, and ascend into Heaven, with that human nature taken from Her. Despite all this glory she was not spared a life of trials and difficulties, she was not deprived of anxieties and worries. It was as if she was then to begin public life and to keep watch: *I will not give sleep to my eyes or slumber to my eyelids, until I find a place for the Lord, a dwelling place for the Mighty One* (Ps 132:4).

And when the Apostles dispersed throughout the world, the Blessed Mother of Christ, as Queen of all, lived in the centre of the world, in Jerusalem, in Zion, with the beloved disciple, who had been given to her as a son, by Our Lord Jesus Christ.

Our Lady not only encouraged and taught the Holy Apostles and the other members of the faithful to be patient and to bear trials, but she was party to them in their labours. She supported them in their preaching, she

CONSOLER OF THE CHURCH

was in spiritual union with the disciples of the Lord in their privations and petitions, and while they were in prison. Just as she had taken part in the passion of Christ, with her heart pierced through, now she suffered with them. She consoled these worthy disciples with her actions, she comforted them with her words, placing before them the model of the Passion of her Son the King. She reminded them about the reward and the crown of the Kingdom of Heaven, of eternal life and its delights for ever and ever.

When Herod captured Peter, the leader of the Apostles, having him in chains until dawn, She was also spiritually a prisoner with him: the holy and blessed Mother of Christ took part and shared his chains, prayed for him and asked the Church to do so too. And earlier, when the Jews stoned Stephen, when Herod aimed to execute James, the brother of John, all the persecutions, the sufferings and the petitions pierced the heart of the holy Mother of God: with sorrow in her heart, with tears in her eyes, she was martyred with them...

After the departure of John the evangelist, James, the son of Joseph, also called 'the brother of the Lord', took the blessed Mother of Christ in his care... In this way, too, the return of the holy Mother of God to Jerusalem, was a benefit: it was She who was the certainty, the harbour and the support for the believers who lived there. Whatever concern or difficulty that arose for the Christians, for they lived in the midst of the rebellious Jewish people, was entrusted to the Immaculate Mother. Before holy battles and before death, believers from all parts went to see her. She consoled them and gave them strength.

She was the blessed Hope of the Christians of that period and of those who were to come afterwards: she will be the mediatrix and strength of believers until the end of the world. But, in those times, her concern and effort was more intense, to correct and to consolidate the new law of Christianity, so that the name of Christ be glorified. The persecutions which befell the Church, the attacks on the homes of the faithful, the capital punishment of numerous Christians, the prisons and tribulations of every kind, and the persecutions, the labours and the oppression of the Apostles as they were expelled from one place to another: all this redounded on Mary. She suffered for every one and in word and in deed took care of each one. She was the model for doing good and the best teacher taking the place of the Lord, her Son. And in his sight, She was the intercessor and the advocate of all believers. She begged her Son to shower his mercy and offer his help to all.

The Apostles had chosen her as a guide and teacher. They informed her about every problem which arose. She gave them advice and made suggestions as to what they should do. Those of them who were passing through Jerusalem went to see her.

Those who had had to go to distant places, tried to return to Jerusalem at Easter each year, to celebrate the feast of the Resurrection of Christ with the Holy Mother of God. Each one described to her his preaching to the gentiles and the persecutions he had met from the Jews and from the pagans. Then, comforted by her prayer and her doctrine, they returned to their apostolate. This is what happened year after year, unless something serious prevented them. The one exception was Thomas. He could not make it because of the long distance and the difficulty of getting there from India! All the others went to visit the Queen every year; then fortified with her prayer they returned to announce the good news.

The Life of Mary

Saint Ildephonsus of Toledo

Ildephonsus was born in 607 of a distinguished family. Despite his father's opposition, at an early age he embraced the monastic life in a monastery near Toledo, in Spain. He was ordained deacon around 630 and was later elected Archbishop of Toledo (657). He died on 23 January 667.

It is related that Our Lady appeared in person to Ildephonsus and presented him with a priestly vestment to reward him for his zeal in honouring her.

His literary work is better known than the details of his life. It is rooted in patristic tradition. His principal effort was directed towards giving people 'the doctrine of the ancients' in an accessible form.

He himself divided his works into four parts. Within the first is a treatise, against the infidels, on the virginity of Our Lady. It displays a spirit of ardent piety and assures Ildephonsus of a place of honour among the devoted servants of the Blessed Virgin. It consists of a prayer and twelve chapters. The work ends in petition, where St Ildephonsus demonstrates how veneration of the Mother of God, far from taking away glory from Christ, in fact honours him and is very pleasing to him.

The second part contains his correspondence; the third comprises Masses, hymns and sermons. And the fourth contains works in verse and prose, especially through epitaphs.

Saint Ildephonsus of Toledo

TO HONOUR MARY

Service to the Virgin Mary

In my poverty and misery, and as reparation, I should like to come to be the servant of the Mother of my Lord. Separated from communion with the angels because of the fall of our first parents, I should like to be the servant of Her who is Handmaid and Mother of my Creator. As a docile instrument in the hands of the immense God, this is how I should like to be subject to the Virgin Mother: totally dedicated to her service.

Grant it to me, Jesus, God and Son of man. Grant it to me, Lord of all things and son of your Handmaid. Grant me this grace, O God humbled in man. Allow me, a man raised up to God, to believe in the childbirth of the Virgin and to be filled with faith in your Incarnation. When I speak of virginal maternity, allow me to have words gushing in your praise. And while loving your Mother, let me be full of your very love for her.

Make me serve your Mother in such a way that You recognise me as your servant. Let her be my Sovereign Mistress on earth, so that you may be my Lord for eternity. See with what impatience I long to be a vassal of this Queen, and with what faithfulness I dedicate myself to the joy of serving her. How much I wish to make myself servile to her will; with what ardour I wish never to back away from her commands. How I wish never to be taken away from her service… Make her admit me to the ranks of her subjects, and while serving her, allow me to merit receiving her favours, to live always under her mandate, and to love her for all eternity.

An appeal

Those who love God know my desire. Those who are faithful to him, see it. Those who are united with God understand it, and those whom God knows know it. Listen, those of you who are disciples. You, infidels, pay attention. Those of you who are thinking only about disunity, get to know it. You, sages of this world who appear silly in the eyes of divine wisdom, get to understand what makes you seem wise in the eyes of your foolishness... You, who do not accept that Mary was always a virgin, who do not want to recognise my Creator as her Son, and her as the Mother of the Lord; who refuse to believe that only she could have the Lord of creatures as her son; who do not give glory to this God as her Son; who do not proclaim as Blessed she whom the Holy Spirit has commanded all the nations to call so; who obscure her glory, deny the incorruptibility of her flesh; who do not render honour to the Mother of the Lord on the pretext of honouring God the Son; who do not glorify as God He whom you have seen become Man and be born of her; who confuse the two natures of her Son and shatter the unity of his Person; who deny the divinity of her Son; who refuse to believe in the true flesh and in the true Person of her Son; who do not believe that he suffered death as a man and rose from the dead as God...

Serving the King through the Queen

My greatest desire is to serve this Son and to have his Mother as Sovereign. I wish to serve Her, to be under the command of the Son. I long for the Mother to reign over me and be a witness, so as to be admitted to the service of

God. I aspire to come to be the servant of the Mother, so as to be in the devout service of her Son. For to serve the Handmaid is also to serve the Lord. What is given to the Mother, reflects on the Son, going from the Mother to Him whom she has fed. The honour which the servant renders the Queen reflects upon the King.

Blessing with the angels, singing my joy accompanying the celestial voices, enjoining my happiness with the angelic choirs: I bless my Sovereign Lady, and sing my joy to her who is the Mother of my Lord and the Handmaid of her Son. I rejoice with Her who has come to be the Mother of my Creator; with Her in whom the Word was made flesh. For with her I have believed what she herself knows, because I have known that she is the Virgin Mother, the Virgin who gave birth; because I know that her conception did not make her lose her virginity, and that one, unchanging virginity preceded childbirth, and that her Son has perpetually conserved the glory of her virginity.

All this fills me with love, because I know that it has all been done for me. I do not forget that, thanks to the Virgin Mary, the nature of my God has been united to my human nature, my human nature thus being assumed by my God; and there is but one Christ, Word and Flesh, God and Man, Creator and creature.

Liber de virginitate perpetua, Sanctae Mariae, XII

St Anastasius Sinaita

St Anastasius is a Greek ecclesiastical writer who was born in Alexandria in the first half of the seventh century. He died shortly after 700. This makes him one of the last Eastern writers who is recognised as a Father of the Church.

He was a priest and a monk, and abbot of the monastery of Mount Sinai. He was so active an opponent of the Monophysites, Monothelites (who denied the existence of a human will in Christ), and Jews that he was known as 'the new Moses'.

His principal work, *Hodegos*, Guide, is written in defence of the Catholic faith against these heretics. These polemics only came to an end in 681 with the Third Council of Constantinople.

Anastasius also wrote a short history of heresies and of the ecclesiastical synods, a commentary on the biblical narrative of the Creation, various homilies and a volume on predominantly moral questions.

Among his homilies is the *Sermon on the Holy Synaxis*, which is a summary of the doctrine on the Eucharist and exhorts Christians to receive Communion in a dignified way.

Saint Andrew of Crete

MOTHER MOST PURE

All of creation exults today. All nature is full of joy. The highest heaven rejoices, and the clouds scatter justice. The mountains drop sweet drops of honey and the hills are in jubilation. For the Lord has been merciful to his people and has raised up a powerful saviour in the house of David his servant, that is to say, in this most immaculate and pure Virgin, through whom will arrive salvation and the hopes of the people.

May good and grateful souls intone a canticle of joy. May nature convoke all creatures to announce to them the good news of its renewal and the beginnings of its change. May mothers jump for joy, for She who did not have descendants has now given birth to a Virgin and immaculate Mother. Virgins, rejoice! For a garden not sown by men will bring forth as fruit he who proceeds from the Father without separation, in a more admirable way than can be expressed. The women applaud, for if at another time it was a woman who was the imprudent occasion of sin, now too it is a woman who brings in the first fruits of salvation. And, if earlier one woman had been convicted, another is now magnificently approved by divine judgement: a Mother who knew no man, elected by the Creator, restorer of human kind.

May all created things sing and dance with joy, and contribute appropriately to this happy day. May today be a single common celebration for heaven and earth, and may as many as there are in this world and in the other feast in common accord. For today a most pure sanctuary for the Creator of all things has been created and established; and a creature has prepared for its Author new and appropriate hospitality. Today nature, previously banished from paradise, receives the divinity and runs with joyful gait towards the supreme pinnacle of glory.

Today, Adam offers Mary to God in our name, as the first fruits of our nature; and these first fruits have not been placed with the rest of the mass; they have been transformed into bread for the reparation of the human race.

Today humanity, in all the radiance of its immense nobility, receives the gift of its first formation through divine hands and discovers its ancient beauty once more. The shame of sin had hidden the splendour and delights of human nature. But the Mother of the most Beautiful *par excellence*, is born and this nature recovers in her its most ancient privileges and is shaped according to a model which is perfect and truly worthy of God. All this formation is perfect restoration. And this restoration is divinization. And this is an assimilation into our former state.

Today, the brilliance of the divine raiment has shone, and miserable human nature has been fitted out with royal dignity.

Today, following the prophecy, the cedar of David has flowered, the evergreen shoot of Aaron, producing for us Christ the strongest branch.

Today, a young virgin has come from Judah and David, carrying the herald of the kingdom and the priesthood of Him, who according to the order of Melchisidech, received the priesthood of Aaron.

Today, grace, purifying the mystery of the divine priesthood, has woven in a symbolic way the dress of the levitic seed, and God has tinged David's blood with royal colours.

To put it in a phrase: today the reformation of our nature begins, and the old world subjected to a totally divine transformation, receives the first fruits of the second creation.

> Homilia I in nativitaem sanctissimae Deiparae

Saint Germanus of Constantinople

St Germanus was born about 654 in Constantinople or its surroundings towards the end of the reign of the Emperor Heraclius (610-614). The son of Justinianus, a patrician, Germanus dedicated himself to the service of the Church and became a cleric of the metropolitan cathedral. He took part in the Third Council of Constantinople (681) which tackled the monothelistic heresy which denied the human will of Christ. Around 705 he was appointed bishop of Cyzicus, a metropolis of the ecclesiastical province of Helesport. In 715, having received the patriarchal dignity, he convoked a synod of bishops at which monotelitism was condemned.

During the iconoclast crisis he resisted the policy of Leo III the Isaurian who opposed the veneration of images. The emperor was keen to oblige Germanus to sign the decree against the use of images. But the patriarch, repeating both the reasons he had given earlier and his profession of faith, refused to obey the imperial orders and successfully appealed for the support of Pope Gregory II (729).

Then, putting aside the insignias of his patriarch's office, uttered a phrase which was destined to enjoy unending fame in eastern tradition. "If I am Jonah, throw me into the sea; but without an ecumenical council, my sovereign, it is not possible for me to establish this new doctrine." Under strong pressure from the emperor, he resigned the see and took refuge in Platanion, where he spent the last days of his life. He died in 733.

Current knowledge of the literary works of St Germanus indicate that they covered almost all fields of religious literature: theology, history, liturgy, homilies and letters. Among his homilies the seven which he preached on the occasion of the principal feasts of Our Lady are particularly outstanding. They are in the rhetorical style of the later Byzantines.

The sermons underline the sublimity and grandeur of the divine world. In spite of its perfection and total superiority, heaven does not distance itself from the earth: God, through Mary, lowers himself by becoming a man to attract us to himself. So one easily understands that the central point of St Germanus' Marian theology is the divine maternity of the Most Blessed Virgin Mary. Closely related with it are the other divine prerogatives, the most important ones being the immunity of Mary from original sin, her Assumption into heaven and her mission as mediatrix of grace.

Saint Germanus of Constantinople

MOTHER OF GRACE

O completely chaste, totally good and merciful Lady, consolatrix of Christians, most sure refuge of sinners, most ardent relief for the afflicted: Please do not leave us as orphans, without your help. If we are abandoned at a distance from you, with whom shall we shelter? What will become of us, O holy Mother of God, Who is to be the source of courage and spirit for a Christian? Just as breathing is a certain sign that our body is alive, so your most holy name, which is incessantly on the lips of your servants, always and everywhere, is not only a sign but is also for us the cause of life, of joy, and of help.

Protect us under the wings of your goodness; help us with your intercession; attain eternal life for us, you who are the Hope of Christians, a hope which is never misplaced. When it comes to deeds and divine ways of acting, we are poor. But contemplating the rich kindness you have shown us, we can say: *the mercy of the Lord fills all the earth* (Ps 32:5).

We are separated from God by the multitude of our sins; but we have sought him only through You. And on finding him, we have been saved. Your help is powerful to attain salvation, O Holy Mother of God. So great it is that there is no need for any other intercessor close to the Lord. Your people, your inheritance, your flock which is honoured by the name of Christian, now turns to you. We know from experience that when we resort to you insistently while in danger, we receive replies to our petitions in abundance. Your munificence has no limits. Your help has no limits. Your gifts are numerous.

No one is saved, O Blessed Virgin, if it is not through you. No one is freed from evil but through You, O Immaculate Mother. No one receives divine gifts, O Most Pure, but through your mediation. No one is granted the gift of mercy and of grace, but through you, O Sovereign Lady. Who, then, will not call you Blessed? Who will not extol your praises? Who will not add to your magnificence with all his might, although this will never achieve what you truly deserve? All generations shall praise you, because you are glorious and blessed, because you have received countless and stunning marvels from your divine Son.

Who, after your Son, is as interested in humanity as You are? Who unceasingly protects us in our tribulations? Who frees us so promptly from the temptations which assail us? Who makes as much effort as you do in pleading for sinners? Who takes the side of hopeless cases, pleading their defence?

In virtue of the closeness and the power which your maternity has obtained from your Son, although we are condemned by our crimes and do not venture to look towards the heavens, You save us with your petition and intercession from eternal torture. It is for this reason that when under pressure we seek refuge in You; that one who has suffered an injustice turns to you, and he who is full of faults invokes your help. Everything about you, O Mother of God, is marvellous. Everything is grander, everything exceeds our reason and our faculties.

Your protection surpasses all understanding. With your giving birth you have reconciled those who have been rejected. You have turned into children and heirs those who had been put to flight and were considered as enemies. By extending your helping hand, you pick up daily from the waves those who have fallen into the abyss with their sins. Just the invocation of your name banishes the wicked enemy of your servants, guards them and keeps them safe and unharmed. You free those who invoke you from all needs and temptation. You prepare these servants in good time against those temptations.

And so we diligently turn towards your temple. When we are within it, it seems as though we find ourselves in Heaven itself. When we praise you it is as though we are singing in the same choir as the angels. What human lineage, aside from Christians, has achieved such glory, such strength, such patronage? Who is there who, after trustingly raising his eyes to venerate your sacred cincture, is not immediately filled with joy? Who has gone away empty-handed, without obtaining what he asked for while fervently kneeling before you? Who, on contemplating your image, has not immediately forgotten about his difficulties? It is difficult to express with words the joy and happiness of those who meet in your temple, where you have wanted us to venerate the girdle of your Son and our God, who has come to this church today amidst our celebration.

O vessel from which we drink the cool manna after we have felt the ardour of evil! O table of food which fills with the bread of life those in us who were about to perish through hunger! O candlestick, which, with its brightness, illuminates with its intense light those of us who are in darkness. God has showered you with flowing honours worthy of you, and yet you do not reject our praises, undignified and of poor quality as they are, but offered with our deepest fervour and warmest affection.

Do not reject, O most praised, the hymn of praise which pours forth from stained lips, but which are offered with good will. Do not despise petitions which have been uttered by an unworthy mouth. On the contrary, O Lady glorified by God, considering the Love with which we say these things to you, grant us forgiveness of sins, the joy of eternal life and freedom from all faults.

Homilia in sancta Mariae zonam

Saint Germanus of Constantinople

WORTHY OF VENERATION TWICE OVER

What should I say first, and what will I leave for later? Will I sing aloud the praises of the sharing of your life with men, or will I applaud the glory of your Assumption according to the spirit? Both are marvels for special veneration...

When you left this earth, you undoubtedly ascended into Heaven; but before your departure you were already participating in the heavenly goods, and after your departure you continued to take part in earthly matters...

O Most Blessed Mother of God: as Heaven and, even more so, the earth, were adorned by you, is it possible that with your departure you have left men orphaned, without your care? We have never thought like that! Just as when you were living in this world you were no stranger to celestial customs, so too, after you changed your dwelling place, you have not departed in spirit from communion with men. On the one hand, through your womb opened by His weight, you have revealed yourself as a Heaven which divinely contains the Most High God. On the other hand, through the obvious use of your flesh, you have been a spiritual world for Him. So it is possible to believe that when you lived in this world, You were totally united to God; and that, afterwards, when you left, you did not abandon those who remained in this world.

Nonetheless, we who are used to venerating you faithfully, do ask ourselves unreasonably: 'Why have we not been considered worthy to have you physically present too?' For we consider those who have been joyful witnesses of your presence, as three times blessed, since they had you, Mother of Life, as a companion in their lives. In any case, although we would have liked to have you bodily with us, each day the eyes of our soul are impelled to look towards You...

You do not reject those you have saved; you do not abandon those you have reunited. For your spirit lives for ever and your flesh does not await corruption in a tomb. You take care of everyone. Your protective look stands guard over each one, in such a way that although our eyes are forced not to see you, Most Holy Virgin, You joyfully place yourself in our midst; You show yourself in various ways to those who are worthy.

Truly, the flesh is not an obstacle for the power and the capacity of your spirit. For your spirit breathes where it will, being a pure non-material spirit, incorruptible and immaculate, a spirit which lives with the Holy Spirit, a spirit highly favoured by the divinity of the Only-begotten. According to what has been written, You *are beautiful* (Song 2:13), and your virginal body is completely holy, completely chaste, a complete resting-place for God. So much so, that it is even 'unnatural' for the body to disintegrate into dust.

As regards your human body, it has been transformed for the supreme life of immortality; and it remains integral and glorious, vitally perfect and not subjected to sleep. It was not possible that the Vessel which contains God, and the living Temple of the Most Holy divinity of the Only-begotten, be laid down in a grave, a companion to death. O Mother of God, we therefore believe that you always journey beside us.

I will truly say with complete thanksgiving: Although

you went away, you have not separated yourself from Christians. You, the life of incorruptible purity, did not distance yourself from this corruptible world. You have remained close to those who invoke you. You are to be found by those who faithfully seek you. These are all certain signs of life, of the strength of an always active spirit, of a body not subject to decomposition. Really, how could the disintegration of the body reduce you to dust and ashes when you, through the Incarnation of your Son, have freed man from the ruin of death? You have gone away from earthly things so that the mystery of the inspiring Incarnation can be observed to have been really strengthened. All will now believe that You have conquered the chasm between things subject to time. So too the God born from you was also a complete Man, Son of a true Mother, who was also subject to the laws of physical necessities by divine decision and by the prescription of time. As You partake of our bodiliness, you have not been able to avoid the encounter with death, common to all men, following the way in which your Son too, and God of all, *suffered death* (Heb 2:9). He undoubtedly converted the sepulchral repose of your Dormition into a marvellous place, just as his own living sepulchre, thus making you a receptacle of life. In this way the two (sepulchres) received your bodies, but did not damage them in the least by corruption.

It was not admissible either, for You, Vessel which contained God, to be dissolved by the dust of corruption which destroys all bodies. As He who in you *emptied himself* (Phil 2:7), and he was God from the beginning, and Life older than all the centuries, it was necessary for the Mother of Life to cohabit with Life and to receive death as a dream. And, as Mother of Life, to be translated as if awakened. Just as a son seeks out and wishes to be with his own mother, and the mother anxiously wishes to be with her son, it was also fitting that You who loved your Son of God with a maternal heart, should return to Him. And it was also proper for God who loved you as his Mother, to make you a participant of the communion of life with Himself. In this way, You, O Mother of God, having suffered the loss of life, proper of decrepit things, have emigrated to the dwelling places which last for ever, where God rests and beside whom You live, without separating yourself from his company. Truly, You, Mother of God, have been the bodily home for his rest, and at the same time He is changed into a resting place in the definitive Fatherland. *This* – he says – *is my resting place forever* (Ps 132:14). The flesh which proceeds from you, O Mother of God, was assumed by Him. And not only do we believe that Christ showed himself like this, but also that at the end of time when he comes to judge the living and the dead, we will see him again in your flesh.

As you are already an eternal rest for your Son, He carried to his side you who were not injured by corruption. For he wished to possess you – to express it like that – and to remain in conversation with you, close to your heart. So, whatever you ask of him, He will grant you, who suffer for his children; and, with divine power, he provides so many things you request of Him, who is blessed for ever. Amen.

Homilia I in Dormitionem B. V. Mariae

Saint Andrew of Crete

St Andrew of Crete (sometimes called Andreas in English bibliography) was born in Damascus about the middle of the seventh century. At the age of fifteen he went to Jerusalem, entered a monastery and was enrolled as a cleric. Some time later he was sent as a legate by the Patriarch of the Holy City to the Third Council of Constantinople, which condemned monothelism. He stayed in Constantinople and was made a deacon. Later he was made bishop of Crete. He defended the legitimacy of the veneration of images. St Andrew died in 720, on 4 July, the date when his feast is celebrated in the Greek Church.

St Andrew was an excellent composer of hymns; the Eastern Church has included some of them in its liturgy. He is also known as a homilist, and some twenty homilies have come down to us. Those which refer to the Virgin Mary enjoy particular importance for they are an eloquent witness to the faith in the Immaculate Conception and the bodily Assumption of Mary into heaven.

In keeping with the Church's Tradition, St Andrew states that the Conception of Our Lady is the beginning of the renewal of human nature, injured by original sin. Mary, preserved by God from all sin, brings to the world 'the first fruits of the new creation'. As the liturgy sings, she is the iris which flowers among the thorns and the spiritual paradise where Jesus Christ, the new Adam, establishes his resting place.

St Anastasius Sinaita

RECEIVING HOLY COMMUNION WITH DIGNITY

Great are our miseries, my dearest ones. For we ought to have a burning spirit, to be attentive in prayer and supplication, principally at the celebration of the eucharistic mystery, and to be full of fear and trembling in the presence of the Lord as Mass is said. But not only do we not offer the Sacrifice with a clear conscience, with a contrite and humble heart, but during the Holy Synaxis we continue with our public business and the administration of many vain transactions.

There are some who are unconcerned about the sorrow for sins and purity they ought to have when approaching the Sacred Table; rather they wonder what clothes they are going to wear. Some come, but don't deign to remain to the end of Mass; they ask the others at what point the Mass is and if communion time has arrived. Then rapidly, like dogs, they scamper, grabbing the mystical bread and leave. Others, present in God's temple, cannot keep quiet, even for a moment, and concentrate more on gossip than on prayer. Yet others are not at all concerned about their conscience, or with cleaning off the stains of their sins through penance; they carry on accumulating sin after sin.

Tell me, then: with what kind of conscience, with what state of soul, with what thoughts, do you approach these mysteries, if in your heart your own conscience accuses you? Answer me: If your hands were stained with dung, would you dare to handle the king's garments with them? You would not touch your own clothes before washing your hands and carefully drying them; only then would you touch them. Well, why do you not give God the same honour which you give your vile clothes?

To enter a church and honour sacred images and venerated crucifixes is not enough to please God, any more than washing one's hands is sufficient to become clean all over. What is truly pleasing to God is that man flees sin and clears the stains through confession and penance, that he breaks the chains of his faults with humility of heart, and thus comes close to the immaculate mysteries.

Perhaps someone will say: I don't feel like crying and being sorry. Why is this? Because you do not meditate, because you do not think, because you do not reflect on the terrible day of judgement. With all this, if you cannot cry, at least maintain a grave and respectful look. Cast pride far away from you. Place yourself in God's presence, with eyes turned to the ground and with contrite spirit; recognise yourself to be a sinner. Do you not see that those who are in the presence of an earthly king, who often is impious, behave with reverence towards him?

Ask for mercy, ask for pardon, ask for remission of your past faults and see yourself free from future ones, so that you can approach such great mysteries with dignity, with pure conscience to participate in the body and blood of Christ, so that they serve to purify you and not to condemn you.

Listen to the words of St Paul: *Let a man examine himself, and so eat the bread and drink of the cup. For anyone who eats and drinks without discerning the body, eats and drinks judgement upon himself. That is why many of you are week and ill, and some have died* (1 Cor 11:28-31). Do you now understand how illness and death often come about, on approaching the divine mysteries unworthily.

You may be inclined to say, 'But who is worthy?' I too am aware of this difficulty. And, nevertheless, it will be a worthiness you desire. Recognise yourself to be a sinner; distance yourself from sin, flee from evil and anger. Practise works of penance. Review the way you practise temperance, meekness and longanimity. From the fruits of justice draw compassion and heartfelt mercy for the needy, and then you will have made yourself worthy.

Sermon on the Holy Synaxis

Saint Bede the Venerable

St Bede was born around 673. He was a Benedictine, and has left brief autobiographical details in his *Historia ecclesiastica gentes Anglorum*. As this is our only source of information about him, we will quote it here.

'All this concerning the ecclesiastical history of the Britons, and especially that of the English, I, Bede, servant of Christ and priest of the monastery of the holy Apostles Peter and Paul of Wearmouth and Jarrow... I was born in the territory of the aforementioned monastery, and at the age of seven I was sent to Abbot Benedict and then to Abbot Celfried to be educated. I dedicated my life to the meditation of the divine word. At the age of nineteen I was raised to the diaconate, and when I was thirty I became a priest. Since my ordination until now, when I am fifty-nine years of age, I have been collecting the texts of the Fathers and interpreting their meaning, writing several biblical commentaries, for my use and for those of my brothers...'

St Bede died in 735.

His theological doctrine follows that of the Western Fathers – Jerome, Ambrose, Augustine... His principal work was a history of the English speaking people. He wrote several poems including *In natali sanctae Mariae*, which is a testimony of his great devotion to Our Lady. His deep knowledge of the Fathers led him to publish a number of works of an exegetic and homiletic nature. He also composed the *Homiliarum Evangelii libri duo*, which are homilies for Sundays and the important feasts of the year.

Saint Bede the Venerable

MARY'S MAGNIFICAT

My soul magnifies the Lord, and my spirit rejoices in God my Saviour.

When she says this, Mary is, in the first place, acknowledging the special gifts she has been given and then she is speaking of the general blessings with which God never ceases from all eternity to come to men's aid. The soul that magnifies the Lord is the soul of the person who devotes all his spiritual energies to the praise and service of God and by keeping the commandments shows that he keeps steadily before his mind the divine power and majesty. A person can say that his spirit rejoices in God his Saviour if he makes it his sole delight to think of his Creator, from whom he hopes to receive eternal salvation.

All who have achieved perfection would be justified in using these words. But it was especially fitting that they should be spoken by the blessed Mother of God, for the privileges accorded to her special merits filled her with a great spiritual love for the One she was so happy to conceive. She had every right to rejoice in Jesus, that is, in her Saviour, with greater joy than other saints, because she knew that she was going to give birth in the course of time to the One whom she recognised as the eternal Author of salvation. For He would truly be her Son and her Lord, in one and the same Person.

For He who is mighty has done great things for me, and

Mary's Magnificat

holy is His name. We see that she attributes nothing to her own merits but speaks of all her greatness as the gift of the One who is power and greatness itself, the One who is constantly making His poor weak followers into characters of great strength. But she is right to add, *and holy is His name*, in order to remind her hearers, and in fact to teach all those whom her words would one day reach, that they must believe in His name and call on it and take refuge in it. For they too can achieve a share in eternal sanctity and true salvation, as the prophecy says: *All who call on the name of the Lord will be saved.* This is the name of which she said earlier: *My spirit rejoices in God my Saviour.*

So it has become an excellent and salutary practice in the Church for everyone to sing this hymn daily in the office of evening prayer. In this way the faithful, being reminded more often of the Incarnation of the Lord, are moved to devotion, and also strengthened in virtue by the regular thought of His Mother's example.

It is fitting that this should take place at evening prayer, for at the end of the day our minds are tired and a prey to distractions, and it is very useful to have this moment of quiet to recollect ourselves and gather our thoughts.

Homilies

Saint John Damascene

John was born in Damascus about 675, into a noble Arab family. He was ordained to the priesthood by John, Patriarch of Jerusalem (705-735). At the age of 50 he moved to the monastery of St Sabas, near Jerusalem, and died in the year 749. He is considered the last of the Fathers of the Eastern Church. In 1890 he was named as a Doctor of the Church.

When the future apologist reached the age of 23, his father began to look for a Christian tutor capable of giving his sons the best education. Among the captives in the market-place he came across a Sicilian monk, Cosmas, who helped John to make rapid progress.

At his father's death John Damascene was made *protosymbulus*, chief councillor, of Damascus. From this position John fought Leo the Isaurian who was against the veneration of images and had by edict forbidden this, and even their exhibition in public places.

Among his works the most important and best known is the *Fountain of Wisdom*, a title given by the author himself. It is divided into three parts. In the first, *Philosophical Chapters*, commonly called *Dialectic*, he deals almost exclusively with logic. It seems that John Damascene's purpose is to give readers such philosophical knowledge as was needed for an understanding of dogma. The second, *Concerning heresy*, compiles and then refutes all the heresies which had arisen in the Church's history until his time. The most important part is the third, *De fide orthodoxa* – *An exact exposition of the orthodox Faith*. Throughout its 100 chapters, St John Damascene following the teachings of Greek patrology, collects the doctrine of the Church: the existence and nature of God, creation, the redeeming incarnation, faith and the sacraments, the veneration of images, the eternal truths etc. It forms an extensive commentary on the Nicene Creed.

For many centuries *De fide orthodoxa* was considered as a classic manual on the dogmatic theology of the Greek Church. It also had a great influence on the Latin Church: Along with John Chrysostom, St John Damascene is the most quoted Eastern Father in the works of the leading scholastic teachers.

His exegetical works include a commentary on the Pauline letters, and homilies of the birth and passage to heaven of Our Lady, the Transfiguration ...

In the following pages we publish some paragraphs from one of his homilies on the Dormition of the Blessed Virgin. St John Damascene accepted that Mary died prior to her Assumption into heaven. It is a theological opinion which the Church has not wished to settle with her solemn Magisterium. The dogma of the Assumption promulgated in 1950 states that Mary, once she had finished her life on earth, rose in body and soul into heaven. It leaves theologians free to discuss whether Mary died and then immediately was assumed into heaven, or whether she was glorified without passing through the moment of death.

Saint John Damascene

MOTHER OF GLORY

To-day the holy Virgin of Virgins is presented in the heavenly temple. Virginity in her was so strong as to be a consuming fire. It is forfeited in every case by child-birth. But she is ever a virgin, before the event, in the birth itself, and afterwards.

To-day the sacred and living ark of the living God, who conceived her Creator Himself, takes up her abode in the temple of God, not made by hands. David, her forefather, rejoices. Angels and Archangels are in jubilation, Powers exult, Principalities and Dominions, Virtues and Thrones are in gladness: Cherubims and Seraphims magnify God. Not the least of their praise is it to refer praise to the Mother of glory.

To-day the holy dove, the pure and guileless soul, sanctified by the Holy Spirit, putting off the ark of her body, the life-giving receptacle of Our Lord, found rest to the soles of her feet, taking her flight to the spiritual world, and dwelling securely in the sinless country above.

To-day the Eden of the new Adam receives the true paradise, in which sin is remitted and the tree of life grows, and our nakedness is covered. For we are no longer naked and uncovered, and unable to bear the splendour of the divine likeness. Strengthened with the abundant grace of the Spirit, we shall no longer betray our nakedness in the words: *I have put off my garment, how shall I put it on?* (Cant 5:3). The serpent, by whose deceitful promise we were likened to brute beasts (Ps 48:13), did not enter into this paradise. He, the only begotten Son of God, God himself, of the same substance as the Father, took His human nature of the pure Virgin. Being constituted a man, He made mortality immortal, and was clothed as a man. Putting aside corruption, He was imbued with the incorruptibility of the Godhead.

To-day the spotless Virgin, untouched by earthly affections, and all heavenly in her thoughts, was not dissolved in earth, but truly entering heaven, dwells in the heavenly tabernacles. Who would be wrong to call her heaven, unless indeed he truly said that she is greater than heaven in surpassing dignity? The Lord and Creator of heaven, the Architect of all things beneath the earth and above, of creation, visible and invisible, Who is not circumvented by place (if that which surrounds things is rightly termed place), created Himself, without human co-operation, an Infant in her. He made her a rich treasure-house of His all-pervading and alone uncircumscribed Godhead, subsisting entirely in her without passion, remaining entire in His universality and Himself uncircumscribed.

To-day the Virgin, the life-giving treasury and abyss of charity (I know not how to trust my lips to speak of it) is hidden in immortal death. She meets it without fear, who conceived death's destroyer, if indeed we may call her holy and vivifying departure by the name of death. For how could she, who brought life to all, be under the dominion of death? But she obeys the law of her own Son, and inherits this chastisement as a daughter of the first Adam, since her Son, who is the life, did not refuse it. As the Mother of the living God, she goes through death to Him. For if God said: *He* (the first man) *might reach out his hand, and take also from the tree of life, and eat, and live forever* (Gen 3:22), how shall she, who received Life

Himself, without beginning or end, or finite vicissitudes, not live for ever...

When I had reached this point of my discourse, I was obliged to give vent to my own feelings, and burning with loving desire, to shed reverent yet joyful tears, embracing, as it were, the bed so happy and blessed and wondrous, which received the life-giving tabernacle and rejoiced in the contact of holiness. I seemed to take into my arms that holy and sacred body itself, worthy of God, and pressing my eyes, lips, and forehead, head, and cheeks to hers. I felt as if she was really there, though I was unable to see with my eyes what I desired. How, then, was she assumed to the heavenly courts? In this way.

The apostles and all the assembly of the Church may well have addressed some words to the blessed Virgin. When they saw the Mother of God near her end and longing for it, they were moved by divine grace to sing farewell hymns, and wrapt out of the flesh, they sighed to accompany the dying Mother of God, and anticipated death through intensity of will. When they had all satisfied their duty of loving reverence and had woven her a rich crown of hymns, they spoke a parting blessing over her, as a God-given treasure, and the last words.

What happens next? Nature, I conjecture, is stirred to its depths, strange sounds and voices are heard, and the swelling hymns of angels who precede, accompany, and follow her. Some constitute the guard of honour to that undefiled and immaculate soul on its way to heaven until the queen reaches the divine throne. Others surrounding the sacred and divine body proclaim God's Mother in angelic harmony. What of those who watched by the most holy and immaculate body?

In loving reverence and with tears of joy they gathered round the blessed and divine tabernacle, embracing every member, and were filled with holiness and thanksgiving. Then illnesses were cured, and demons were put to flight and banished to the regions of darkness. The air and atmosphere and heavens were sanctified by her passage through them, the earth by the burial of her body. Nor was water deprived of a blessing. She was washed in pure water. It did not cleanse her, but was rather itself sanctified. Then, hearing was given to the deaf, the lame recovered their feet, and the blind their sight. Sinners who approached with faith blotted out the hand-writing against them.

The holy body is wrapped in a snow-white winding-sheet, and the queen is again laid upon her bed. Then follow lights and incense and hymns, and angels singing as befits the solemnity; apostles and patriarchs acclaiming her in inspired song.

Her body is borne by the Apostles' hands, the King of Kings covering her with the splendour of His invisible Godhead, the whole assembly of the saints preceding her, with sacred song and sacrifice of praise until through the tomb it was placed in the delights of Eden, the heavenly tabernacles.

Just as the all-holy body of God's Son, which was taken from her, rose from the dead on the third day, it followed that she should be snatched from the tomb, that the mother should be united to her Son; and as He had come down to her, so she should be raised up to Him, into the more perfect dwelling-place, heaven itself.

It was meet that she, who had sheltered God the Word in her own womb, should inhabit the tabernacles of her Son. And as our Lord said it behoved Him to be concerned with His Father's business, so it behoved His mother that she should dwell in the courts of her Son, in the house of the Lord, and in the courts of the house of

Mother of Glory

our God. If all those who rejoice dwell in Him, where must the cause itself of joy abide?

It was fitting that the body of her, who preserved her virginity unsullied in her motherhood, should be kept from corruption even after death.

She who nursed her Creator as an infant at her breast, had a right to be in the divine tabernacles. The place of the bride whom the Father had espoused, was in the heavenly courts.

It was fitting that she who saw her Son die on the cross, and received in her heart the sword of pain which she had not felt in childbirth, should gaze upon Him seated next to the Father.

The Mother of God had a right to the possession of her Son, and as handmaid and Mother of God to the worship of all creation.

Homilia II in Dormitionem B.V.M., 2-14

Saint John Damascene

THE POWER OF THE CROSS

Every action of Christ and all His working of miracles were truly very great and divine and wonderful. But of all things the most wonderful is His honourable cross. For by nothing else except the cross of our Lord Jesus Christ has death been brought low, the sin of our first parents destroyed, hell plundered, resurrection bestowed, the power given us to despise the things of this world and even death itself, the road back to the former blessedness made smooth, the gates of paradise opened, our nature seated at the right hand of God, and we made children and heirs of God. By the cross all things have been set aright. *For all we who are baptised in Christ,* says the Apostle, *are baptised in his death* (Rom 6:3), and *as many of us as have been baptised in Christ have put on Christ* (Gal 3:27); moreover, *Christ is the power and wisdom of God* (1 Cor 1:24).

See how the death of Christ, the cross, that is to say, has clothed us with the subsistent wisdom and power of God! And the word of the Cross is the power of God, whether because by it God's might, His victory over death, that is, was manifested to us, or because, just as the four arms of the cross are made solid and bound together by their central part, so are the height and the depth, the length and the breadth, that is to say, all creation both visible and invisible, held together by the power of God.

This we have been given as a sign on our forehead, just as Israel was given the circumcision, for by it we faithful are set apart from the infidels and recognised. It is a shield and armour and a trophy against the Devil. It is a seal that the Destroyer may not strike us, as Scripture says (cf Exod 12:27). It is a raising up for those who lie fallen, a support for those who stand, a staff for the infirm, a crook for the shepherded, a guide for the wandering, a perfecting of the advanced, salvation for soul and body, an averter of all evils, a cause of all good things, a destruction of sin, a plant of resurrection, and a tree of eternal life.

That honourable and most truly venerable tree upon which Christ offered Himself as a sacrifice for us is itself to be adored, because it has been sanctified by contact with the sacred body and blood. So also are the nails, the lance, the garments, and such sacred resting places of His as the manger, the cave, saving Golgotha, the life-giving tomb, Sion the citadel of the churches, and others. Thus, David the forefather of God says: *We will go into his tabernacle: we will adore in the place where his feet stood,* and that he means the cross is evident from what follows: *Arise, O Lord, into your resting place* — for the resurrection follows after the cross. Now, if the house, the bed, and the clothing of our loved ones are dear to us, then how much more the things of our God and Saviour by which we also have been saved!

And we also adore the likeness of the honourable and life-giving cross, even though it be made of another material, not that we honour the material — God forbid! — but the likeness as a symbol of Christ. Thus, when He explained to His disciples saying: *Then shall appear the sign of the Son of man in heaven,* He meant the cross. For this reason, also, the angel of the resurrection said to the women: *You seek Jesus of Nazareth, who was crucified* (Mark 16:6). Likewise, the Apostle: *But we preach Christ crucified* (1 Cor 1:23). Now, there are many Christs and Jesus's, but only one Crucified, and he did not say *pierced by a lance* but *crucified.*

Therefore, the sign of Christ is to be adored, for, wherever the sign may be, there He, too, will be. If, however, the form should happen to be destroyed, the material of which the likeness of the cross was composed is not to be adored, even though it be gold or precious stones. Thus, we adore everything that has reference to God, although it is to Him that we direct the worship.

The tree of life which was planted by God in paradise prefigured this honourable Cross, for, since death came by a tree (Gen 2:3), it was necessary for life and the resurrection to be bestowed by a tree. It was Jacob who first prefigured the cross, when he adored the top of the rod of Joseph (cf Heb 11:21; Gen 47:31). And when he blessed Joseph's sons with his hands crossed (cf Gen 48:13-15), he most clearly described the sign of the cross.

Then there were the rod of Moses which smote the sea with the form of a cross and saved Israel while causing Pharaoh to be swallowed up; his hands stretched out in the form of a cross and putting Amalec to flight; the bitter water being made sweet by a tree, and the rock being struck and gushing forth streams of water (cf Exod 14:16ff, 17:11ff, 15:25, 17:6); the rod of Aaron miraculously confirming the dignity of the priesthood; a serpent raised in triumph upon a tree, as if dead, with the tree preserving those who with faith beheld the dead enemy (cf Num 17:8, 21:9), even as Christ was nailed up in flesh of sin but which had not known sin; great Moses calling out: *You will see your life hanging before your eyes on a tree* (Deut 28:66); and Isaiah: *I have spread forth my hands all day to an unbelieving and contradictory people* (Is 65:2).

May we who adore this attain to the portion of Christ the crucified. Amen.

De Fide Orthodoxa, 4,11

Saint John Damascene

MARY'S ASSUMPTION

What shall we say, O Queen? What words shall we use? What praise shall we pour upon your sacred and glorified head, giver of good gifts and of riches, the pride of the human race, the glory of all creation, through whom it is truly blessed. He who was not contained by nature in the beginning, was born of you.

O how does the source of life pass through death to life? O how can she obey the law of nature, who, in conceiving, surpasses (1 Cor 15:53) the boundaries of nature? How is her spotless body made subject to death? In order to be clothed with immortality she must first put off mortality, since the Lord of nature did not reject the penalty of death. She dies according to the flesh, destroys death by death, and through corruption gains incorruption and makes her death the source of resurrection.

O how does Almighty God receive with his own hands the holy disembodied soul of our Lord's Mother! He honours her truly, who being his servant by nature, He made his Mother, in his inscrutable abyss of mercy, when He became incarnate in very truth. We may well believe that the angelic choirs waited to receive your departing soul. O what a blessed departure was this going of yours to God. If God vouchsafes it to all his servants – and we know that He does – what an immense difference there is between his servants and his Mother.

What, then, shall we call this mystery of yours? Death? Your blessed soul is naturally parted from your blissful and undefiled body, and the body is delivered to the grave, yet it does not endure in death, nor is it the prey of corruption. The body of her, whose virginity remained unspotted in child-birth, was preserved in its incorruption, and was taken to a better, diviner place, where death is not, but eternal life.

Just as the glorious sun may be hidden momentarily by the opaque moon, it shows still though covered, and its rays illumine the darkness since light belongs to its essence. It has in itself a perpetual source of light, or rather it is the source of light as God created it. So are you the perennial source of true light, the treasury of life itself, the richness of grace, the cause and medium of all our goods. And if for a time you are hidden by the death of the body, without speaking, you are our light, life-giving ambrosia, true happiness, a sea of grace, a fountain of healing and of perpetual blessing. You are as a fruitful tree in the forest, and your fruit is sweet in the mouth of the faithful (cf Cant 2:3). Therefore, I will not call your sacred transformation death, but rest or going home, and it is more truly a going home. Putting off corporeal things, you dwell in a happier state.

Angels with archangels bear you up. Impure spirits trembled at your departure. The air raises a hymn of praise at your passage, and the atmosphere is purified. Heaven receives your soul with joy. The heavenly powers greet you with sacred canticles and with joyous praise, saying: *Who is this most pure creature ascending, shining as the dawn, beautiful as the moon, conspicuous as the sun?* (Cant 6:9). How sweet and lovely are you, *the lily of the field, the rose among thorns* (Cant 2:1), therefore the young maidens loved you (cf Cant 1:2). We are drawn after the fragrance of your ointments. The King introduced you into his chamber. There Powers protect you,

The Assumption of Mary

Principalities praise you, Thrones proclaim you, Cherubim are hushed in joy, and Seraphim magnify the true Mother by nature and by grace of their very Lord.

You were not taken into heaven as Elias was, nor did you penetrate to the third heaven with Paul (cf 2 Cor 12:2), but you did reach the royal throne itself of your Son, seeing it with your own eyes, standing by it in joy and unspeakable familiarity. O gladness of angels and of all heavenly powers, sweetness of patriarchs and of the just, perpetual exultation of prophets, rejoicing the world and sanctifying all things, refreshment of the weary, comfort of the sorrowful, remission of sins, health of the sick, harbour of the storm-tossed, lasting strength of mourners, and perpetual succour of all who invoke you.

Your soul did not descend to Limbo, neither did your flesh see corruption. Your pure and spotless body was not left in the earth, but the abode of the Queen, of God's true Mother, was fixed in the heavenly kingdom alone. O how did heaven receive her who is greater than heaven (cf Ps 15:10).

We, too, approach you to-day, O Queen; and again I say, O Queen, O Virgin Mother of God, staying our souls with our trust in you, as with a strong anchor. Lifting up mind, soul and body, and all ourselves to you, rejoicing in psalms and hymns and spiritual canticles, we reach through you to the One who is beyond our reach on account of his Majesty.

Homilia 1 in Dormitionem B. V. M.

Saint Theodorus the Estudite

Theodorus was born in Constantinople in 759 into a high-ranking family, working in the imperial court. He was given a good education and came to form part of the civil service of the Empire. Encouraged by his uncle, the abbot of Bythinia, at the age of twenty-one Theodorus retired to a monastic life with his father and brothers. He was ordained to the priesthood. Known for his ability and for a life of piety, he succeeded his uncle as abbot, and looked after the running of the monastery.

As a consequence of making public his opposition to the moral behaviour of the emperor, he was sent to prison. Later, Empress Irene gave him his freedom, and he was installed in the monastery of Estudion, which had been founded in Constantine times by Studius, a Roman, but which had fallen into disrepair because of the iconoclast persecution.

Theodorus was known as a defender of the faith. Under his guidance the Estudion monastery became one of the most important monastic centres of the capital, housing some 700 monks who observed a rigorous discipline.

Theodorus faced numerous difficulties, with further detention and imprisonment, when he defended the Church against undue imperial interference in ecclesiastical matters. He suffered particularly badly during the iconoclast persecution conducted by Leo of Armenia from 815.

Theodorus was known for his zeal in defending the dignity and freedom of the Church, for his love and union with the Holy See. With the help of his brother Joseph, Archbishop of Thessalonica, he defended the veneration of images, following the decrees of the Second Council of Nicaea (787).

His works cover a number of fields and demonstrate his burning piety. In addition to exegetical and canonical works, meant for the formation and governance of the monks, he produces numerous polemical works related to the controversies raging in the East at that time.

Several times a week, especially during the liturgical festivities, he directed his teachings to the monks. The following passage is a selection from his prayer on the Cross, on the occasion of the solemn rite of adoration over which he presided on Good Friday.

Saint Theodorus the Estudite

THE SAVING CROSS

Today is a day of exultation and joy, because a sign of grace has been exposed to our view. We break forth into a chorus of praise, on contemplating this most holy wood.

O gift of incalculable price! Glory to the splendour of your presence! Unlike the tree of Paradise, it does not produce fruit for good or evil, but in it is harmony and beauty both to sight and to taste. It is the tree which engenders life, not death; which lights up, without creating shadows; which introduces us into Paradise without expelling us from it; it is that tree which, like the king in his chariot, Christ mounted to thwart the devil who reigned over death, and to liberate human kind from his tyrannical servitude. It is that wood on which the Lord, like an excellent warrior unconcerned that in battle his own hands, his feet and his divine breast might be wounded, cured our wounds, that is to say, our nature hurt by the pernicious dragon. To use the words of a song, that wood on which the blood of the Lord was shed, pours over us insuperable power to exterminate the demons and to illuminate the world...

Adoration

Today the most holy Cross is adored, and the resurrection of Christ is announced. Today the tree which gives life is adored and the entire world awakens to extol praise for it. Today we adore the three arms of the Cross, and the four cardinal points glow, celebrating in deepest joy. *How beautiful upon the mountains are the feet of the messenger who announces peace, who brings good news!* (Rom 10:15; Is 52:7; Nah 1:15). It will also proclaim as blessed those eyes which contemplate this trophy of universal peace and the lips which kiss this sovereign sign. Copious grace is offered to all. Perennial spring, from where holiness gushes, who rejects no one from such teeming riches; but rather purifies even more the one who is already pure, and takes away the stain of sin; cuts the proud and conceited down to size, awakens the lukewarm and the lazy, subjects the loose-living to the yoke of the law, softens the hard and inflexible. Whoever has already made resolutions to change, may approach these divine gifts without arrogance or boldness, for the Cross loves the humble and the modest, while it distances itself from those who behave to the contrary.

The tree of life

This tree of life, applied to the eyes, works like a medicine against that longing gaze which the tree of Paradise seduced, by its attractive appearance. When we place our lips and our eyes to this tree, we are freed from contact with a liking for the death-delivering tree. Great indeed is the gift shown to us! Happiness three times blessed! Death in olden times because of a tree; now, through another tree, we find life. Deceived earlier beside a tree; beside this one we crush the sly serpent. See a new and singular opportunity: life is given to us instead of death; incorruption in place of corruption, glory instead of dishonour. Did the Apostle not cry out: *May I never boast about anything except the Cross of our Lord Jesus Christ, by which the world has been crucified to me, and I to the world* (Gal 6:14). For the highest wisdom which flowered from the Cross, rejected the arrogance and foolishness of

THE SAVING CROSS

worldly wisdom. Good of all kinds came to fruition from the Cross, getting rid of the shoots of malice and perversity.

Let us turn to the Cross anew, stopping, not without pleasure, to sing its praises. The Cross, worth more than all riches. The Cross, most certain refuge for Christians. The Cross, a light burden on the shoulders of the disciples of Christ. The Cross, consoler of great sweetness, for those suffering afflictions. The Cross, a pathfinder for the way to heaven, which no obstacle can block. The height and the width of the Cross, the widest precinct to shelter the assembly of saints. The figure and power of the Cross, a victory over all enemy power. The beautiful figure of the Cross, more admirable than any marvel. The brilliance and splendour of the Cross, more luminous than the sun and its rays. The grace and glory of the Cross, more gracious gift than all grace. The Cross, pacifier and reconciliator of heaven and earth. The name of the Cross, a proclamation of holiness when uttered by the lips and welcomed in the senses.

Fruits of the Cross

Through the Cross, death died and Adam came back to life. Through the Cross, each Apostle attained glory, each martyr obtained a crown, each saint achieved sanctity. Through the Cross, we are clothed with Christ, discarding the old man. Through the Cross, we sheep of Christ are reunited in the same flock and destined for the heavenly feast. With the Cross we are freed from the restraint of the enemy and we clutch on to the strength of salvation. With the Cross we cast away disquiet and we acquire supernatural life. Whoever carries the Cross on his shoulders imitates Christ and with Christ will receive obvious glory. The Cross draws out praise from the angels and confuses demons. On meeting the Cross the good thief entered Paradise, winning the kingdom instead of being condemned. Whoever turns to the Cross scatters away fears and recovers peace. Whoever takes the Cross as protection will not fall into the hands of bandits but will arrive unharmed at his destination. Whoever loves the Cross hates the world and falls in love with Christ.

The Cross of Christ, a glorious celebrity of Christians. The Cross of Christ, centre of apostolic preaching. The Cross of Christ, royal crown of the martyrs. The Cross of Christ, precious insignia of the prophets. The Cross of Christ, most luminous distinction of nations.

And addressing her as something alive: Cross of Christ, protect those who with burning hearts sing to you; protect those who with faithful spirit kiss and embrace you; govern your subjects in peace and true faith; bring to all the glorious day of the resurrection of Christ; guard the Pope, the bishops, emperors, monks and every kind of person; and reunite everyone around our Lord Jesus Christ.

To him be the glory and the power, with the Father and the Holy Spirit, now and for ever. Amen.

Oratio 2 in adorationem Crucis

Subject Index

Almsgiving, 424, 469
Angels, 45, 71, 81, 479
Anger, 320, 403
Apostolic spirit, 12, 148, 214, 223, 257, 281, 346
Ascetical struggle, 9, 25, 127, 161, 194, 210, 245, 257, 261, 269, 341, 371, 407

Baptism, 11, 131, 173, 224, 465
Beatitudes, 214
Bishops, 10, 232, 237, 293

Charity, 4, 125, 153, 323, 338
  and patience, 97
  fruits of, 340
Chastity, 10, 11, 137, 141, 167, 205, 230, 329, 465
Children, 277
Chrism, 131
Christian vocation, 30
  another Christ, 181
  love for the world, 31, 344, 348
  naturalness, 31, 195
  soul of the world, 31, 257
Church, 350, 360
  and Holy Spirit, 54
  and Our Lady, 498
  doctrine, 5, 382
  unity, 52, 93
Communion, reception of, 188, 331, 442, 463, 520

Compassion, 205, 217
Confession, 72, 115, 521
  and joy, 74
  delaying it, 74
Creation, 32, 119, 177, 297, 473
Cross, 534, 543

Death, 160, 171, 335
Detachment
  and apostolate, 149
  and riches, 63, 155, 215, 280, 314
Devil, 364, 389, 409, 415
Difficulties, 241
Divine filiation, 171, 173
Divine mercy, 120, 197, 205, 368, 467
Doctrine, 203, 231, 381, 387

Ecumenism, 323
Eucharist, 185, 251, 263, 328, 436, 443, 456, 464, 476
Examination of conscience, 403

Faith, 11, 122, 143, 153, 245, 325, 357, 376, 387, 397, 433
  and friendship, 191
  and good works, 4, 238, 404
  and prayer, 71, 211
  and sacrifice, 87
  in deeds, 87, 286
Family, 233
Fishing, 223, 224, 346

Flattery, 192
Fortitude, 10, 127, 167, 305
Freedom, 136
Friendship, 189, 209, 275

Giving fruit, 234
God's gifts, 4, 5
Good Shepherd, traits of, 9
Guardian angel, 81

Heaven, 333
Heresy, 58, 387
Holy Innocents, 422
Holy Spirit, 56, 131, 139, 169, 208, 247
  fruits of, 140, 170
Hope, 122, 153, 375
Hospitality, 153
Humility, 11, 84, 115, 155

Ignatius, 242
Immortality, 136

Jacob's ladder, 45, 219
Jesus Christ
  and Our Lady, 107, 473
  as friend, 193
  birth of, 12, 411, 416
  Cana wedding, 473
  childhood, 421
  Eucharist, 185
  Judge, 32
  King, 32
  Our Father, 363
  Passion of, 44, 321, 373, 397, 534
  precepts, 438
  pre-figure of, 90, 185
  Saviour, 32
  true God, 157, 181, 412
  true Man, 157, 412, 420
Job
  a type of Christ, 127
  fortitude, 167
John the Baptist, 487
Justice, 218, 238, 288, 305, 483

Kindness, 154

Lent, 403, 424
Light, festival of, 494
Longanimity, 153
Love
  for God, 423
  fraternal, 153
Lukewarmness, 343

Man, dignity of, 135, 177, 413
Manna, 57, 188, 513
Marriage, 10, 138, 300, 330
Martyrdom, 16, 194, 242
Mass, 455
Meekness, 154, 167
Moderation, 205
Modesty in dress, 488
Monastic life, 165
Mortification, corporal, 154

Natural Law, 37, 238, 252

Obedience, 232, 475
Original sin, 46, 119, 415
Our Father, 363
Our Lady
  and the Church, 498
  Annunciation, 492
  Assumption, 532, 537
  glory to, 104, 110, 118, 301, 502, 515, 529
  Most pure, 506
  motherhood, 273, 301, 415, 429
  Seat of grace, 448, 511
  virginity of, 13, 515, 530
  Visitation, 83, 207, 524

Parables
  lost drachma, 199
  lost sheep, 198
  prodigal son, 199
Parents, 267, 277
Patience, 11, 96,
  fruits of, 99
Perseverance, 96

Subject Index

Pope, 93
Prayer, 69, 424
  before God, 80
  fruits of, 70, 79, 114, 168
  how to, 116
  obstacles to, 113
  Our Father, 363
  without ceasing, 82, 112, 209, 311
Presence of God, 166, 394, 461
Priesthood, 86, 229, 265
Prudence, 305
Psalms, 201

Redemption, 44, 321, 455
Repentance, 270
Riches
  an instrument, 64
  of psalms, 201
  value of, 62

Sacrifice, 88, 190, 368
Saint Joseph, 288
Saints, 241
Sanctity, 3
Serenity, 165
Sin, 172
Soul, 298
Spiritual childhood, 419
Spiritual reading
  bible, 167

Temperance, 154, 283, 305
Temptations, 326
Thanksgiving, 393
Thieves, two on Calvary, 46
Time, 161
Truth, 127, 423

Unity, 94, 461
Unity of life, 81

Virginity, 137, 154
Virtues, 153, 202, 211, 305
Vocation
  giving fruit, 234
  response to, 222, 350
  salt and light, 257
  selection, 221, 350

Wisdom, 37
World, separation from, 165

Youth, 283